Y0-CCZ-594

Internationalizing Library and Information Science Education

A Handbook of Policies and Procedures in Administration and Curriculum

Edited by John F. Harvey and Frances Laverne Carroll

Greenwood Press
New York • Westport, Connecticut • London

Library of Congress Cataloging in Publication Data

Internationalizing library and information science
    education.

   Bibliography: p.
   Includes index.
   1. Library education.   2. Information science—
Study and teaching.   3. International librarianship.
4. Libraries and state.   5. Information services and
state.   6. Library schools—Administration.   7. Library
schools—Curricula.   I. Harvey, John F. (John Frederick),
1921–   .   II. Carroll, Frances Laverne, 1925–   .
Z668.I6   1987   020'.7   86–9946
ISBN 0–313–23728–X (lib. bdg. : alk. paper)

Copyright © 1987 by John F. Harvey and Frances Laverne Carroll

All rights reserved. No portion of this book may be
reproduced, by any process or technique, without the
express written consent of the publisher.

Library of Congress Catalog Card Number: 86–9946
ISBN: 0–313–23728–X

First published in 1987

Greenwood Press, Inc.
88 Post Road West, Westport, Connecticut 06881

Printed in the United States of America

The paper used in this book complies with the
Permanent Paper Standard issued by the National
Information Standards Organization (Z39.48–1984).

10 9 8 7 6 5 4 3 2 1

Copyright Acknowledgments

We gratefully acknowledge permission to reprint material from the following
sources:

Lester Asheim, *Librarianship in Developing Countries*. Urbana: University of Illinois
Press, 1966.
Material developed by the Committee on International Affairs, George Peabody
College for Teachers of Vanderbilt University.

CONTENTS

INTRODUCTION

Frances Laverne Carroll and John F. Harvey

As far as librarianship is concerned, nationalism is dead and internationalism has replaced it.[1] Essentially, this statement means that we must keep abreast of change in a special area, the international affairs of librarianship.

While nationalism may not yet be completely dead, internationalism is vigorously alive, and in librarianship the relationship between the two is tenuous and complex. For that reason this book is important: it should be useful to every librarian in the world because it deals with the influences, issues, and problems of national library and information science schools which must now operate on an international basis, through which extensive borrowing of ideas, activities, and technology occurs from one nation to another.

The title of this book, with its recognition of a major world transition, may first attract internationalists and futurists. These groups are innately drawn to international affairs and find the broader intellectual and cultural milieu exhilarating. However, this book should have a much broader readership: it should be useful to anyone in librarianship, for it is based on the premise that an important change is occurring in the world and in librarianship, which was previously considered a nationally oriented field of study. This handbook will be especially helpful to the faculty and students of library and information science schools because it attempts to implement internationalism in their daily activities.

The book's target audience also includes university international program heads, international student advisors, and educational planners. In addition, some of its ideas may be interesting to administration and faculty members in other professional schools. Finally, the book is intended not just for a North American or an English-speaking audience but for people in all nations.

SUGGESTED DATA COLLECTION AND RESEARCH PROJECTS

There is a compelling need for regularly collected statistical data on world library school programs, covering every major aspect of school operation. A compilation of activities or projects carried out by library and information science schools, with a breakdown for those affecting students directly, is especially helpful in suggesting the degree of internationalization existing in the schools.

Such a study may show that several countries, like the Federal Republic of Germany and the United States, are relatively nationalistic and independent in teaching primarily ideas and practices developed nationally, whereas countries such as Indonesia and Kuwait are relatively international and dependent in teaching primarily ideas and practices borrowed and to some extent adapted from abroad. Does this suggest a contrast of earlier versus later historical development, or a contrast of the developed versus the developing country's library and information science capability?

Studies on the relationship of languages to internationalism can be suggested. Is there a positive personal correlation between foreign language interest, facility, and internationalism? Alumni working abroad may be asked what international course and curriculum changes are recommended.

Another way of approaching the curriculum problem is first to compile a comprehensive manual on internationalizing a specific library and then work out the library school instructional program required to prepare personnel competent to staff it properly. Still another way of checking instructional internationalization is to determine the percentage of nonnational course syllabus citations to which students are referred per school.

Additional studies can be made for specific courses and specific aspects of school administration. The student can begin by compiling a comprehensive bibliography of international material, foreign and national, which is potentially useful in a specific course. And finally, a survey of policies and material used in teaching a specific course in twenty-five other countries should reveal not only a variety of viewpoints, but also information helpful in local teaching.

As used here, the term *internationalization* means the process by which a nationalistic library school topic, an entire curriculum, or an entire school is changed into one with a significant and varied international thrust, the process by which it is permeated with international policies, viewpoints, ideas, and facts. This process requires use of a new perspective. It uses ideas from many nations and contrasts them with domestic or national ideas, thereby encouraging a more analytic and mature approach to study. In contrast, *national* refers to all library and information science schools teaching primarily the library policies and practices currently used in the country where the school is located.

ACKNOWLEDGMENTS

The principal theme of this handbook is change from a national to an international mode.[2] Each contributor to the work was asked to prepare a chapter that would discuss an aspect of internationalism (Part I), describe how to internationalize an area of library and information science school administration or service (Part II), or describe how to internationalize a specific course or cluster of related courses (Part III). These authors were urged to explain the many methods of internationalizing their subjects.

We owe a great debt to our distinguished authors, all twenty-eight of them, for their hard work and insights, but we take full responsibility for any errors or misconceptions that may appear herein. We would also like to thank Cynthia Harris, Mary Sive, and Marilyn Brownstein of Greenwood Press for their patience and their faith in our project. Finally, we thank our exemplary secretaries—Eleni Mavridou, Foulla Pavlidou, Memna Hadjiharou, Evridiki Mavrommatis, Anthea Sheppard, Georgia Agapiou, Karmah Farah, and Demetra Araouzou of Nicosia—for extensive typing and retyping of letters and manuscripts almost without end.

NOTES

1. Maro Chauveinc, "A Prospective View of IFLA's Future," in Willem R. H. Koops and Joachim Wieder, eds., *IFLA's First Fifty Years, Achievement and Challenge in International Librarianship* (Munich: Verlag Dokumentation, 1977), p. 139.
2. Carter V. Good, ed., *Dictionary of Education* (New York: McGraw-Hill, 1973).

BIBLIOGRAPHY

The ALA Glossary of Library and Information Science. Ed. by Heartsill Young. Chicago: American Library Association, 1983.
Harvey, John F., ed. *Comparative and International Library Science.* Metuchen, N.J.: Scarecrow Press, 1977.

PART I

THE CONTEXT OF INTERNATIONALIZATION

Internationalizing Library and Information Science Education

A Handbook of Policies and Procedures in Administration and Curriculum

Edited by John F. Harvey
and Frances Laverne Carroll

Greenwood Press
New York • Westport, Connecticut • London

1987

1

THE CASE FOR
INTERNATIONALIZATION

Frances Laverne Carroll

I

The library and information science schools of certain countries are twenty to fifty years out of date, unsynchronized with international events. Many students are therefore receiving an education that reflects provincial or colonial attitudes stemming from a strong sense of nationalism. As the differences in library policies and publication distribution systems in other countries become better known to librarians, the provincialism of the past, fostered by an inward-looking concern for one's national system only, will be increasingly apparent.

Neither a provincial nor a colonial attitude is a very effective method of influencing international activities. All groups dealing with international affairs are seeking more flexible methods and new forms of cooperation in order to reduce the inefficiency caused by narrow attitudes.

The cognitive knowledge of library and information science school students can be improved as descriptive publications about other countries' libraries grow in number and availability. In addition, international library organizations, the methods and degrees of cooperation employed by various agencies, and the key people should be more widely known.

International librarianship groups are growing in number, size, and influence. Also important to librarianship is the range of social influences stemming from an international world. Publications from other academic fields can assist in interpreting these effects; such knowledge is also needed as libraries are drawn increasingly into interactive national, regional, and world information systems. Business, law, and medicine have led other fields in the new internationalism. Multinational companies have developed as a new type of business structure; international law has added the law of the air and outer space to its first concerns, the sea and corporations; and medical research and health care improvements have great mobility among countries.

International governmental relations have been altered to accommodate the rapid proliferation of nations. The significance of these events is twofold: many common problems are seen as solvable only by nations working together, and human extinction is a real possibility unless new ways are found to increase cooperation and world orderliness. There is an increasing interest in international research and study, and much of it is directed to the effects of war and peace.

Librarianship is attempting to reach higher levels of cooperation. Most libraries have collections of international resources, but today national libraries are not the only ones carrying out international tasks. Many libraries exchange material, and librarians cross militarized zones, seemingly ignoring political conflicts between nations. More significantly, UNESCO has given librarianship an international role in its General Information Program which effectively links a small occupational field to a much larger communication concern. This step constitutes recognition of a shared philosophy: that information is a component of world understanding, essential to any negotiation process, basic to planning and directly influencing national development. This suggests that librarianship is moving toward internationalism and that many librarians may not understand the import of this trend.

As a result, a new field called international librarianship is developing, and certain aspects of comparative librarianship, once the term linked to international librarianship, have been encompassed in research methodology. The focus of international librarianship is international organizations and cooperation through which international data transmission networks are established. In establishing these networks, international cooperative library activities are leaping over cultural and geographic barriers.

The scope of international librarianship has to be large and reflect the geopolitical world which affects trans-border information flow. Giving impetus to this leap has been the realization of the need for a worldview and the assumption that such information transfers may occur without a deep understanding of the similarities and differences in national librarianship. Countries without sources of technological information, for example, welcome the tools that can help them locate needed information, even though its usefulness is marginal or its use requires adaptation.

Quite possibly, however, the deeper cultural understanding provided by comparative studies which can be limited to a few countries will be beneficial, perhaps even necessary, to continue the success of initial attempts at effecting large-scale international information exchange. This book attempts to address the need for further developing international librarianship as a body of knowledge unlike that which developed around comparative librarianship.

A major part of this handbook is devoted to the courses most often offered in library school curricula because the curriculum is the regular "offering" which may change student attitudes and competencies. As more librarians receive formal library and information science education, course content becomes increasingly influential on practice. A course in comparative and international librarianship is not included. A course in international librarianship may be instituted, but very few are known to exist and their content is often introduced in a beginning or a trends-and-issues type of course.

Librarians are unsure whether their field should emphasize evaluative work on information or information delivery or archival work. Library education must determine the future direction of the field and must fit its goals, objectives, and procedures within a larger perspective than that of a single nation. This may clarify the librarian's role.

Tertiary education deals with a universal body of knowledge and has gained greater recognition now that Eastern and Western cultures are treated more equitably. However, most library schools have not yet integrated this type of broadened geographical and cultural scope into the curriculum. Faculty and student mobility has been especially effective in creating change. Perhaps weaknesses can be modified if internationalization is clarified and strengthened. Following the study of these facets and the setting of priorities, curriculum planning and course changes should emerge.

Education for librarianship operates within a world setting, within tertiary education, and within a pool of "pressive professions" in the social sciences, attempting to keep pace with various aspects of internationalism. This handbook seeks to stimulate thinking about the concepts of internationalized library education and to provide a comprehensive guide to national implementation. Another purpose is to share the knowledge gained from internationalized fields with those persons interested in supporting library internationalism. Specifically, the objectives of this handbook are:

1. To explain or review the internationalization concept in library education, its goals and objectives, definitions, scope, rationale, and progress.

2. To help restructure the library and information science school curriculum and units of study.

3. To identify, define, or analyze relevant problems in internationalizing library schools and to provide responses applicable to them.

4. To contrast nationalized, regionalized, and internationalized library schools.

5. To provide a literature guide.

6. To assist schools in attaining a higher level of internationalism in all program
    and structural aspects.

ASSUMPTIONS

The most important assumption in this work is that internationalism
is a vital but unproven educational asset (with the exception of one of
its major activities, personal mobility). A second assumption is that most
library and information science schools will soon attain higher levels of
internationalism. Third, all nations are increasingly being influenced by
the activities of other nations, and international thought, study, and
research are increasing in most fields.

This book suggests that international aspects be integrated into the
management and courses of all schools. What is proposed for incopor-
ation into the curriculum is more than enrichment, that is, adding information about countries. The anticipated changes should be based on
the realization that information is important, is being shared by countries, and is producing gains for them. As a result of this important
factor, international activities have assumed a more important social role
and new terms and techniques have been introduced.

Although insecurity resulting from ignorance of library developments
in other countries is being overcome, many librarians do not have access
to sophisticated means to effect the change to an international scope.
The international aspects are assumed to be influential in all of librarianship (and, therefore, in all study units), but their usefulness is a matter
of scale, being greater in certain courses than in others.

The demands of internationalism fall primarily on the library school
faculty members who are most directly responsive to student needs. Each
faculty member must make a commitment to attempt to change student
attitudes as well as course content and methods. This commitment also
requires the support of administration.

Most library schools have made only limited progress toward internationalization and need assistance in determining directions. For instance, reducing national emphasis may come easily, but what is a logical
intermediate step? Certainly, one place to begin internationalization is
in curriculum planning. Of course, schools will internationalize at different rates and with different approaches, but greater international
emphasis in a school will increase its significance and contribution to the
field.

Internationalization will not only increase the librarian's competence,
but also contribute to the social foundations of librarianship. The ability
to sort out the culturally universal from the peculiar is becoming easier
because of the field's rapid incorporation of technology. Librarians seem
always to need change, but, according to an international survey, they

also "feel the need of the elaboration of the librarianship's theoretical fundamentals."[1] They apparently want a base for anticipated changes.

For a number of years an attempt has been made to delineate a structure for international librarianship and to redirect our understanding of the field. The ultimate goal is to formulate a philosophy of librarianship, a wish that is beyond the ever-apparent agonizing over paradoxes that seem to beset the field. Setting out some of the reasons here for recommending changes in a library school, particularly in its curriculum, is not the same as stating a philosophy or establishing goals for anticipated course changes.

If the dominant educational direction is indeed toward more internationalism, then national schools must move conscientiously and methodically to achieve that objective. They cannot wait for internationalism to "evolve" in its own good time. Short courses of study designed for people from different countries have been initiated, especially under UNESCO sponsorship. Longer periods of study have also been made available to groups with mixed nationalities. Consequently, these schools have already accomplished some degree of internationalization; identifying this step or any other as international should enhance a program.

In working toward internationalization, a required comparative and international librarianship course is often discussed as a primary means of achieving it. However, the peripheral manner of offering such a course has long condemned it to a minority status. Furthermore, Nasser Sharify has recommended an array of courses for those wishing to specialize in international librarianship. Attention has also been directed to an international library school (not to be confused with an internationalized national library school) as one method of internationalizing library education.

This point of view has led to confusion about how a national library school may be internationalized and has compelled reliance on the typical activities of the international education field (most of which were set out in the early twentieth century) without thoughtfully making the goals and objectives relevant to librarianship.

Internationalization has also been slowed down by the position that internationalism is needed only for those whose future involves work abroad or for those who utilize it in a specialization such as area studies librarianship. Librarians have had minimal preparation for many aspects of internationalism. The current effort to internationalize library schools is being made primarily to benefit the beginning student whose future will undoubtedly be influenced by the international aspects of librarianship no matter what type of work is chosen or where it is practiced.

It will not seriously compromise the interest of students to work locally. Since all schools educate the next generation, library education must show progress in its programs commensurate with the anticipated complexities of the years ahead. The role of library education is to translate the current knowledge of international librarianship into curricula. Expectation of change within the field requires a decreased status quo and increased progress toward new fluid processes based on the use and understanding of social change at the international level.

II

The topic of nationalism as opposed to internationalism has produced considerable polarization. While this polarization cannot be expected to be easily surmounted, it is desirable that the international aspect be clearly emphasized.

Definition

Although the definition of the term *international* is still changing, its meaning in this chapter is based on a previously reasoned statement.[2] When the term is used in the sense of two or more nations, it should be so employed to describe the present configuration of nations. This idea is often expressed as East-West and North-South.

A definition helps identify those relationships that may be valuable to many nations. Library education is international by definition: library schools do not want isolation but rather seek relationships with schools abroad. The definition supports also the process of internationalizing a nation's library schools. In any school, all classes should be presented from more than one national orientation.

Librarianship is usually international during times of crisis. For example, relief assistance has been extended to libraries after wars or such events as the 1966 flood in Florence.

The weak, piecemeal, uncoordinated international activities attempted in the past have done little to enhance library education, but the opportunity now exists to accept the implications of a world scope. The International Federation of Library Associations and Institutions (IFLA) has announced three new programs: advancement of librarianship in the Third World, conservation and preservation, and trans-border data flow. The implications of these programs for library education are straightforward. For example, successful trans-border data flow moves information across national boundaries to an ideal of an open communication system for all. The importance of global communication is a well publicized issue. While the issue deals with mass media, it foreshadows the role of libraries in free international flow.

This section traces the origins of international librarianship and attempts to sort out certain confusions surrounding internationalization of this field. Internationalism should be neither isolated nor compartmentalized in future librarianship; rather it should permeate the field. Other major influences on librarianship, such as automation have exhibited this same pattern. All library school personnel should have knowledge of those who have previously articulated a world viewpoint. Both a lack of understanding and an inability to handle an accelerated growth rate of international problems characterize the current unsatisfactory situation.

All library schools should provide an international outlook for all students so that the student can adapt to the complex and changing world in which national interests are strongly influenced by international relationships.

Problems

Internationalization requirements can be satisfied within normal library instruction planning, but the process is slower. Moreover, student attitudes toward other nations are formed before they enter library studies, and this too might constitute a detriment. In order to change attitudes, library schools must study the student's pre-entry international experience and viewpoints.

Many works have urged library school preparation for national service. Even now the primary cause of lack of internationalization in the field is a highly localized job market. Of course, local placement is apt to continue for some time. John Balnaves of Canberra has said that a library need not stand alone, that each library should see itself as part of a system (informal cooperation).[3]

Many libraries today have achieved internationalization: in the exchange of ideas on the design and use of buildings, international collections, staff, and users. Systems, informal and formal (organized data bases for sale), are now international, and more trans-border information flow is anticipated. The field must consider the type of personnel needed to support these undertakings.

Some international information systems have proposed establishing their own training programs, bypassing library schools. But this could isolate library automation and cause the underutilization of existing international collection development and organization procedures. Recent library school establishment in many countries and the natural mobility of people has reduced the influence of local learning situations and started a trend toward internationalism. An unofficial *esprit de corps* and a slap-dash messianic drive are not enough; a grass-roots constituency must share the international concept.

Each library school is part of a school education network with international aspects. Ronald Benge supports indigenous library schools and encourages already qualified librarians to study abroad.[4] Others support study courses with more theoretical content for multi-country personnel and enlarging the number of short courses.

Certain schools have been influenced by student and faculty mobility and by library education content transfer from one country to another, but some critics have questioned the appropriateness of such transfer. Aside from the infusion of international aspects of practice into the curriculum, there is an obligation to alert students to foreign educational programs.

Mobility promotes internationalization and increases the need for worldwide cooperation. At the moment, such cooperation is between specific schools. The concept of a world library school network is based on both course and school articulation. Evaluation and equivalency of credentials are not being set aside; rather, they provide students with more information, for better decision-making is being advocated. A first step nationally is to make public statements about assistance to foreign students who will be prepared for an increasingly international career.

Goals

In order to sort out confusions, it is essential that statements of goals, objectives, and activities in internationalizing library education be made and aligned with international tertiary education goals. The Swedish Committee for Internationalizing University Education gives primary emphasis to the general internationalization motive, with the labor market motive a secondary one. The goals most often attributed to international education are international understanding (communication to advance human welfare and self-knowledge) and advancing knowledge (a fundamental education goal).[5] The first goal has been weak, but the second has gained support.

For librarianship, improvement of human welfare may be the primary goal if it is related to the field's international goal, information transfer worldwide. This is often termed the peace goal. As Bowden asks, can global peace and harmony be achieved without library and information service? He feels that our humility may be detrimental to the field's standing.[6]

With an international background, a student should also be able to advance classroom discussion through insight into national needs. Worthy goals exemplify the magnitude of librarianship's potential world contribution. Lack of success in a sufficient number of library schools has adversely influenced the success of internationalization in general. This failure is more a reflection of a lack of specific objectives than of a lack of goals. International library education has given greater attention to activities than to objectives. When changing to a new program, it is natural to stress the practical aspects without thoroughly discussing the rationale of the new program. Evaluation of education's international component may be poorly done. If internationalization is to have a permanent impact, international objectives need more careful statement and evaluations.

Under the headings of personnel, publicity, finance, curriculum, and awards, the international objective should be identifiable and a library school's internationalism should be evident. Annual reports should detail international activities in each category in relation to the objective attempted. Other evaluation methods have been suggested: biographies of mobile instructors in recognition of successful international career goals; historical or case studies of international library school programs; and comparative studies of textual material to show terminology, description, and philosophy changes.

Some will find the evaluation of textual material to be sufficient while others will want to examine changes in student attitudes. There is merit in evaluating the effect of international library education on the student beyond the completion of normal course criteria.

Activities

International library education has borrowed many ideas from international education. In 1900 the advancement of international education was achieved through (1) publication of purely descriptive reports, (2) international conferences, (3) international agreements on organization and structure, (4) international statements on the rights of the individual, (5) textbook revision to eliminate hatred and emphasize mutual trust, and (6) efforts to eradicate racial prejudice.[7] The following list presents a brief status report on library activities in these areas:

1. Publications describing most of the nations' library systems and their library education now exist; however, many need updating and extending.
2. International meetings are numerous. International role statements are expressed through IFLA General Council meetings.
3. Internationally standardized terminology, procedures, and statistics agreements relate to structure and organization, and are proceeding rapidly.
4. Few international documents on people's rights to information are available, but the United States' *Public Library Manifesto, Charter of the Book*, and *Guidelines for the Planning and Organization of School Library Media Centers* are examples.
5. Certain textbooks are being written with an international scope.
6. Librarians' humanitarian concerns are being expressed in certain libraries and formalized in certain library schools and associations through the term *social responsibilities*.

The area most easily advanced by library school internationalization is publications that will correlate with teaching methodologies comparing theories, data, and methods in various countries. In the same study in which goals were determined, forty-eight specific activities were identified and grouped in communication, mobility, research, and curriculum. These groups are applicable to any library school.[8]

Although this book deals primarily with curriculum internationalization, some attention is also given to student mobility. We have yet to achieve an equal student exchange. That is, large numbers of students from developing countries go to library schools in developed nations, but few students from developed countries go to schools in developing countries. Mobile students are apt to stay in international relations, and their influence will also be felt in international associations. The proliferation of international activities provides only a quantitative measure; a school should be practical and increase its activity component with reason and commitment.

Curriculum

The curriculum may be seen as a tool in evaluating internationalization, and the following activities can be recommended:

- Introducing the concept of induced social change.
- Reorganizing the core program around the field as a responding unit within the international system.
- Requiring an undergraduate liberal education (including non-Western culture).
- Infusing traditional courses with new material on the contemporary world.
- Providing electives to prepare international librarians.
- Securing internships abroad for area studies students.
- Developing the interdisciplinary area studies programs of librarians.
- Experimenting with multicultural teaching approaches.
- Emphasizing regional needs.
- Using the comparative method in problem-oriented courses.
- Evaluating descriptions of foreign library activities.

Each library school should have a broad international outlook, viewing the library as a social communication agency, and should include curricular information worldwide.

The curriculum should solve each student's professional needs for advancement, influence, and enhanced ability in any society. Deciding what kind of world knowledge will make the student intelligently informed and determining what are desirable world attitudes depend on one's definition of international understanding. Ralph Hunkins has contributed three identification levels: knowledge of other countries to encourage friendliness and cooperation; knowledge to assist people in need of information for activities such as business; and strategic knowledge for understanding others' intentions and for decision-making.[9]

The curriculum should include information on librarianship in other countries, making use of the East/West, North/South formulation, particularly for quality, as well as Hunkins' three identification levels. Instructors may also use these guidelines for a course-by-course attempt to internationalize. Ronald Benge discusses the selection and management courses as specifically appropriate for indigenous conditions.[10] New international programs generally include area studies and foreign consultants. Perhaps core areas should be internationalized only half as much as other areas.

Library educators have described the integration of internationalization as a process of harmonization, cooperation, or eclecticism. It is best approached on a course-by-course basis, but ultimately the whole curriculum should feel its influence. The "infusion" of information is recommended rather than "adding it on" because infusion provides more permanency. Course content should include the process of induced social change and cross-cultural communication techniques.

Large-scale systems may require a better understanding of cross-cultural communication. A recognition of appropriateness and interdependence should later converge through standardization. Many terms and examples in an internationalized curriculum come from sociology, psychology, anthropology, law, economics, and political science. A curriculum plan is apt to be more sophisticated than previously if penetration from other disciplines is being experienced.

Change may be based on internationalization alone, and exposure to this concept should not require specialization. The curriculum should also contain the course that specializes in international librarianship. As early as 1968, Nasser Sharify proposed that all students study the international aspects of librarianship in an introductory course and that other courses include specific information.[11]

Herbert Coblans believes that two influences are closely associated: the international approach implies standardization, which requires an attitude of positive neutrality between national systems. This outlook is very new; perhaps it is the most immediate influence of the computer in documentation.[12]

Because the advancement of knowledge and the fostering of international understanding are often present outside the curriculum, the total library school program should be examined and cooperation should be sought with every other library system agency. To continue to see librarianship as national is to seriously compromise faculty and students and to offer an unreal perspective. In the past, library science has not taken a strong stand in favor of a new idea even when information about it has been extensive and resources have been available. Other international education programs have broken down repeatedly from lack of communication.

Alternatives

Faculty have commitments to course content and must make needed changes in curriculum. Certain faculty members need assistance in internationalizing courses, whereas others need international experience. Tenured faculty are often the ones who are most willing to experiment. World library school faculties are an unorganized group; however, a proposal for an International Association of Library Schools remains quite valid. It is hopeless to propose changes without the consistent contribution of many creative individuals within the field.

Some schools have become international through circumstances beyond their control. The Australian library schools, for example, were strongly influenced by American and British library education and in turn influence Eastern cultures. On the other hand, American schools are only slightly international; they are unable to see beyond their own problems.

In the years since library schools articulated the two major international goals of library education, new views have strengthened the efforts to achieve them. International understanding is becoming stronger as people's rights have become an issue for many. The first goal, the humanitarian librarianship goal, consists of granting all people access to a wide variety of information. The second goal, the advancement of knowledge, has also been reinterpreted. According to Budd Hall, "We have come dangerously close to creating a situation in the social sciences that denies the knowledge-creating abilities in most people."[13] This is a severe criticism of the academic world. Major library education problems surface in the international level, perhaps pointing to a need to consider them from new directions.

Internationalism, with its union of traditional and new, should lessen polarization. A restructured view is one in which an international library school system supported by an international library system supports the international goals of the national schools in educating for the future.

NOTES

1. J. Boldis, "Draft Program of the Committee on Library Theory and Research Activities for the Years 1971–73" (Moscow: International Federation of Library Associations, 1970), p. 5 (mimeographed).

2. Frances Laverne Carroll, "World Librarianship," in *Encyclopedia of Library and Information Science* (New York: Marcel Dekker, 1982), Vol. 33, pp. 249–254.

3. Address to the Western Australian Secondary Teachers College, Department of Library Studies, 1978.

4. Ronald Charles Benge, *Cultural Crisis and Libraries in the Third World* (London: Clive Bingley, 1979), p. 211.

5. Frances Laverne Carroll, "The Development of an Instrument for the Evaluation of Internationalism in Education for Librarianship" (Ph.D. Dissertation, University of Oklahoma, 1970), p. 53.

6. Russell Bowden, "A Small Part to Play for Peace," in *The Nationwide Provision and Use of Information* (London: Library Association, 1981), p. 374.

7. Francis Kemeny, *Entwurf einer internationalen Gesamt-Academie: Weltacademie* (Budapest: R. Lampel, 1901), in David G. Scanlon, ed., *International Education, A Documentary History* (New York: Teachers College, Columbia University, 1960), p. 11.

8. Carroll, "The Development of an Instrument."

9. Ralph Hanel Hunkins, "Education for International Understanding: A Critical Appraisal of the Literature" (Ed.D. Dissertation, University of Indiana, 1968).

10. Benge, pp. 214–15.

11. Nasser Sharify, "Proposal for the Establishment of a Center for International Librarianship Studies." Pratt Institute Graduate School of Library and Information Science, December 3, 1968 (Mimeographed.)

12. Herbert Coblans, *Librarianship and Documentation: An International Perspective* (London: Andre Deutsch, 1974).

13. Budd L. Hall, "Knowledge As a Commodity," in Irving J. Spitzberg, Jr., ed., *Universities and the International Distribution of Knowledge* (New York: Praeger, 1980), p. 31.

BIBLIOGRAPHY

Bramley, Gerald. *World Trends in Library Education*. London: Clive Bingley, 1975.

Harvey, John F., ed., *Comparative and International Library Science*. Metuchen, N.J.: Scarecrow Press, 1977.

Price, Paxton, P., ed., *International Book and Library Activities*. Metuchen, N.J.: Scarecrow Press, 1982.

Thompson, James. *A History of the Principles of Librarianship*. London: Clive Bingley, 1977.

2

THE HISTORY OF LIBRARY SCHOOL INTERNATIONALIZATION

Donald G. Davis, Jr.

Although the movement toward internationalizing library education may be viewed primarily as a phenomenon with present and future dimensions, one should examine the historical context out of which present interests have arisen. The primary objective here is to present a historical survey and assessment of attempts to develop a global perspective within library education.[1] Focus will be on how library schools go beyond instruction for national practice, emphasize topics with international dimensions, and promote a sense of a globally linked field. In cooperation with educational institutions, national and international organizations have also contributed to the movement.

HISTORY

Pre-World War I. Modern library education began in the nineteenth century in response to the efforts of European and American librarians to meet their institutions' demands. At least three library education aspects manifested themselves in that period: conferences, associations, and certification programs.

The École des Chartes in Paris, established in 1821, for example, responded to the need for educated archive administration personnel. Karl Dziatzko of Göttingen, Germany, and Melvil Dewey at Columbia University launched library instructional programs in 1887. Europeans favored an examination and certification process, whereas Americans preferred formal education as a means to the same end—an adequate number of qualified personnel.[2] British external examinations also assisted students who could not attend school.

The American Library Association (ALA) was organized in Philadelphia in 1876 and the Library Association in England in 1877.[3] Among

early instances of international awareness were the international conferences of 1877 in London, 1893 in Chicago, and 1896 again in London.
The educational benefits of these meetings are evident inasmuch as their
papers included historical and theoretical topics, practical problems and
procedures, and reports of structured education and certification
programs.

In an era when apprenticeship and certification were the usual entry
portals, travel and library tours were important educational experiences.
The "grand tour" of libraries to share practices and experiences may
thus be seen as an early but effective tool for internationalizing library
education. A study of early library educators would reveal the impact
of travel experience.

Soon after the first American library schools were founded, beginning
with Columbia (later, New York State in Albany) in 1886, foreign students enrolled, and many eventually returned to work in their home-
lands. By 1916 the Albany school had attracted more than a dozen
foreign students, for example. Conferences, held in conjunction with
international exhibitions in Paris (1900), San Francisco (1904), and Brussels (1910), may have stimulated global vision and in America, at least,
drew visitors to ALA conferences.

As schools of librarianship developed in the United States and Europe
and summer schools began in Great Britain in the 1890s to help candidates prepare for Library Association examinations, the first International Library School proposal was made by Guido Biagi, an Italian.[4]
Although this effort was premature, early European enthusiasm for
bibliographic standardization, cooperation, and scholarly publishing was
not lost on foreign counterparts.

World War I contributed to international awareness. Library educators, present and potential, participated in the ALA-sponsored Library
War Service in France, Belgium, Germany, and elsewhere. Many acknowledged the role of that experience in shaping national programs.

Between the World Wars. The end of European hostilities stimulated
interest in international cooperation. Library education moved forward
when the first permanent British library school was launched in 1919 at
the University of London. The revival of Library Association summer
schools at Aberystwyth and then at Birmingham attracted overseas students as did the American schools. The ALA-sponsored American Library in Paris and its library school (1924–1929) provided a European
demonstration of American methods.[5]

Arne Kildal has suggested that considerable American influence on
European librarianship in recent decades came through publications,
lectures, addresses, exchange of visitors, international conferences, prolonged foreign librarians' service in American libraries, and study in
American library schools. During the first fifty years of American library

education, over 150 students from other countries studied in the United States.

A concomitant development of the growing international consciousness of library educators was an initial impetus to study systematically the "relationship between libraries (and books) and contemporary social (or economic or political) conditions . . . with respect to different countries, states, and periods."[6] That this aspiration came from the University of Chicago Graduate Library School signified a serious research commitment. During this period a number of American library educators served as consultants abroad.[7]

One of the most promising events to shape a global concept of librarianship was the establishment of the International Federation of Library Associations and Institutions (IFLA) in 1927.[8] A committee soon began work to regularize formal education as an employment requirement. During W. W. Bishop's 1931–1936 presidency, discussion began about the reciprocity of qualifications and the international exchange of librarians. World support for an organization that was primarily Western European in tradition and influence marked an advance in internationalizing library education. The cooperative spirit of the 1930s prepared the way for later growth.

U.S. government entry into the Latin American cultural scene in the late 1930s signaled an advance in American librarianship's relationship with other nation. The ALA Committee on International Relations (established in 1900) and Committee on Library Cooperation with Latin America (established in 1921) were active, and in 1942 the two organizations were united in the International Relations Board (IRB) which focused on Europe and Latin America. The Board's executive arm was the International Relations Office (IRO), established in Washington, D.C., in 1943 by a Rockefeller Foundation grant. Several wartime projects supported library education programs in Latin America.

During World War II library educators worked with programs dealing with library material in war zones, served with troops directly, staffed information and cultural centers, and procured foreign material for allied libraries.

Postwar Period to 1960. Just as World War I set the stage for international library outreach, so did World War II. The coming of peace, the creation of UNESCO, and American foundation and government efforts to assist other countries assured a new global interest period. Library educators participated fully in these developments. Although the financial impetus still lay largely with Americans, by the end of the period Western European Library schools were participating in outreach as well.

IRO, which contributed so much during the war, did not long outlive Ralph R. Shaw's searching 1947 evaluation. Although he favored expansion and more careful focus, lack of organizational support, enabling grant expiration, and preoccupation with national issues brought the office to an end by 1949. The IRO was reestablished in 1956 with Rockefeller Foundation assistance.

IRB continued to work with the U.S. Department of State to enable foreign library groups to visit the United States for short educational tours. The countries represented included seven Latin American nations, Sri Lanka, Egypt, Finland, Greece, Netherlands, India, Italy, and Japan. At about this time the group that would bcome the ALA's International Relations Round Table began to support the Association's international activities.[9] The group pushed for American librarians to receive education for foreign service and found support among library educators.

Begining with the 1948 International Summer School in Public Library Practice in Manchester (attended by fifty librarians from twenty-one countries), UNESCO sponsored many conferences.[10] This program emphasis came to an end with the 1959 Seminar on Library Development in Arabic-Speaking Countries.

The expanded role of travel was exploited by UNESCO's fellowship program for travel and study abroad, about 5 percent of which has been used by librarians. Until 1960 most awards went to Asian countries, and Western Europe was the most attractive area to visit. Under an enlarged program after 1960, more fellowships were awarded to African countries, as well as those in Asia and the Middle East. Throughout the program, the Scandinavian countries received the most visitors, especially the Royal School of Librarianship, Copenhagen.

Americans assisted in establishing new library schools at Keio University (1950—U.S. Government and Rockefeller Foundation), University of Ankara (1954—Ford Foundation), and University of Antioquia, Medellin (1957—Rockefeller Foundation). In drawing experienced educators into these enterprises for periods up to several years, international links were formed and the programs served as prototypes for the next amibitious decade.

Since its inception in 1948, the Fulbright Lectureship program has made the foreign teaching experience possible for American library educators. By 1970 sixty-two lectureships had been granted in twenty-three countries. The British Council, established in 1934 to promote British books and culture, provided similar opportunities for United Kingdom educators, primarily in Commonwealth countries.

The International Youth Library, which opened in Munich in 1949, is a symbolic example of this period. Founded by Jella Lepman to acquaint her fellow citizens with the vast array of children's books from other cultures, the library began with Rockefeller Foundation support but soon shifted to German funding and has since become a unique vehicle for international understanding and education for children's librarianship.

If America's early postwar period efforts were directed at war recovery, the period through the early 1960s was directed to combatting the real or presumed communist infiltration threat. International funding seemed to parallel Cold War priorities. Fortunately, by this time other nations were beginning to enter the international library arena. In retrospect American retrenchment during 1955–1960 appears to have been a momentary lull before a storm of activity.[11]

1960 to 1970. The 1960s saw the period of greatest advance in making library education a global concept. The industrialized countries enjoyed a prosperous period and expressed altruism toward Third World neighbors. International organizations likewise engaged in extensive programs in developing nations with repercussions for library education. Generally, the decade represented a further loosening of the bonds that kept national interests tightly within country boundaries. The Peace Corps seemed to symbolize the new spirit for Americans. Some Peace Corps members were librarians who gained new awareness of the library's role in international understanding. A wave of library publishing reflected this emphasis.[12]

American funding of international library education programs provided immense help. Specific faculty assistance for U.S. government-sponsored library education projects in seven countries involved sixteen instructors, all but one underwritten by Fulbright lectureships. They brought Americans into contact with the needs of developing nations. The Rockefeller and Ford Foundations focused on higher education development, including both libraries and library education.

Although the IRO functioned primarily as an administrative contract agency for government and foundation projects, it brought a certain international involvement to American librarians. Unfortunately, while support continued to 1972, through U.S. Agency for International Development contracts, the rank and file of ALA membership was not touched and the Office closed.

The highwater mark of American involvement in overseas projects coincided with the unprecedented number of foreign students who went to the United States, Canada, and Great Britain for their education. During the decade an estimated 1,000 overseas librarians visited the United States each year. As the phenomenon continued into the next decade, American faculties were concerned about how to assimilate these students into existing programs and how to prepare them for productive careers in their own countries.[13]

IFLA continued surveying study and exchange possibilities, personnel recruitment and education, and frameworks for equivalency agreements—some jointly with the International Federation for Documentation (FID) through its Education and Training Committee. The search for acceptable standards and more unified international objectives culminated in the 1969 IFLA conference with the theme, "Library Education and Research in Librarianship." The resulting discussion led to a request that UNESCO fund "a worldwide statistical survey of library education in order to provide a data base for its improvement."[14]

This request seemed to be in line with UNESCO's shift in emphasis from the mid–1960s "public library development in furtherance of fundamental education to planning library services integrated into the overall planning for economic, social, and cultural development."[15] Library education was an issue in regional conferences held in Quito (1966), Colombo (1967), and Kampala (1970). UNESCO coordinated the efforts of the various international library organizations. Through support from other regional meetings, emphasis now focused on more sophisticated information handling that involved multinational cooperation.

The Organization of American States' Library Development Program, launched in 1961, included a broad range of library and information initiatives from the expansion of popular publishing to technical training assistance.[16] Carried on in conjunction with other economic and cultural development programs and with the support of the recently established library institutions, this program waned after 1968.

The Inter-American Library School at Medellin set a precedent for regional schools. The decade saw the beginning of the School of Librarians, Archivists, and Documentalists at Dakar (Senegal) and the East African School of Librarianship at Kampala (Uganda) in 1963. The West Indies School at Kingston (Jamaica) followed in 1971. All three schools involved cooperative funding from national and international sources and drew faculty members and students from several countries. Two proposals symbolized the highwater mark of library education internationalism: in 1963 Harold Lancour proposed an international association of library schools, and in 1969 Guy Marco proposed an international library school.[17]

Since 1970. In several ways, the crescendo of interest in international library education (and librarianship) was reduced in the early 1970s. By 1980 there was a return to nationalistic government policies in the Western world and difficult financial times for both industrialized and developing countries. Post-World War altruism had slowed down. Ironically, systematic comparative librarianship treatments had just begun to appear in Anglo-American library literature.[18]

With American activity reduced, in part because work was being carried on by nationals and in part because of limited financial resources, American educators now joined others in working through IFLA, FID, and other international organizations. ALA members worked through a committee, a round table, and a newsletter, *Leads.*

The Carl Milam International Lectureship was established in 1971 to bring an international figure to speak for one year on tour in American library schools. In contrast, the Library Association (UK) has maintained regular contact with its own considerable number of overseas members and Commonwealth librarians despite budget constraints.

By the 1970s IFLA's scope had changed, too. No longer primarly a consortium of Western European executives, with a few North Americans added, it was becoming more representative of the worldwide community. Sharing bibliographic knowledge among the technologically rich and poor nations manifested itself in a variety of projects. Library educators labored on standards that would improve education worldwide. UNESCO's *World Guide to Library Schools and Training Courses in Documentation* (1981) was a link in this movement, as was adoption and publication of library education standards in 1976.

Although there was interest in integrating the sophisticated North American and European bibliographic utility networks and in applying their standards worldwide, the international bodies also put a high priority on improving the bibliographic resources of developing countries. Thus, the general organizations aimed at broad scope while the specialized and private industrial agencies focused on the sophisticated networks.

An example of this cooperative effort was the 1980 UNESCO symposium of heads of Latin American schools of librarianship, information science, and archival studies which convened in Costa Rica, "to harmonize curricula and levels of study in Latin American professional training institutions. Short term courses for information specialists and managers of information systems were held in Sofia, New Delhi, and Peking. Participants came mainly from developing nations."[19]

At the same time, international exchange and library education received a boost through increased UNESCO fellowships to developing countries whose recipients elected to study primarily in Northern Europe and North America. Launching the International Graduate Summer School at the College of Librarianship, Wales, in 1973 was a landmark event, as was the first annual FID/UNESCO summer school at Sheffield in 1975.[20]

Yet, as the 1980s began, a decline in interest seemed apparent in the Western library schools. Funding was reduced, faculty and student exchange slowed, uncertainty in national and international affairs emerged, and Western students showed little interest in internationalism. These symptoms of disquiet suggested caution in forecasting internationalism's advance.

SPECIFIC INFLUENCES

Throughout this survey (and despite the surveyor's limited perspective), several trends have manifested themselves. The influence of certain national library education policies has been greater than others. Moreover, individual schools have been influential—some consistently and others sporadically—and certain individuals stand out.

The nations that have provided leadership in internationalizing library education have been those (a) with the earliest and best developed library field and education programs or (b) with a political and/or cultural hegemony over another nation or geographic/economic region. The United States, Canada, and Great Britain have tended toward the first condition, whereas France, the Soviet Union, and Egypt toward the second. Scandinavian countries are difficult to classify but were clearly involved in internationalization.

In the United States, the Columbia University School of Library Service has been internationally oriented. A number of faculty members served abroad or had international influence, among them Dorothy Collings, Jack Dalton, and Carl White. The school had a well-organized program for foreign students which was a model for other schools. Other American schools attracting large numbers of foreign students were Catholic, Michigan, Minnesota, Indiana, Peabody, and Simmons—each with internationally minded faculty members and traditions of outward perspective.[21]

Certain schools were also to take advantage of their environments. Texas under Nettie Lee Benson established a specialized Latin American library studies program in the 1960s. Hawaii, in cooperation with the University East-West Center, provided an educational exchange program in Asian librarianship; a special relationship with the University of Indonesia began in the early 1970s.

Maryland, Kent State, and Oklahoma had unique international involvements. Oklahoma has consistently emphasized the goals and objectives of international library education and sponsored a 1969 conference on Internationalism in the Curricula of Library Education. Drexel launched a popular summer study tour of Europe. Among Canadian schools, Dalhousie, Toronto, and Western Ontario were active with faculty assignments abroad and numbers of foreign students.

Of course, individuals at other schools also played leading parts. Lester Asheim and Boyd Rayward at Chicago, Nasser Sharify at Pratt, and Robert Downs at Illinois are only representative. Certainly David Kaser, Frances Laverne Carroll, Jean Lowrie, Josephine Fang, John Harvey, and others might be mentioned as well. Pittsburgh led in vision and formalized international projects. The faculty and their doctoral students were known for their varied nationalities and international experience.

The British international library education leader, the College of Librarianship, Wales, enrolls 400 students, 10 percent of whom represent twenty foreign countries. More than three-quarters of its faculty members have had significant overseas experience. The College library concentrates on collections of reports from a large variety of nations. Short courses designed for overseas students occur regularly, and faculty members engage in consulting assignments abroad.

The University of London's School of Library, Archive and Information Studies and other British schools have served international interests. Among the most prominent international library educators have been Bernard Palmer, D. J. Foskett, and Peter Havard-Williams.

In other European countries library education is more often concentrated in one school, in the national capital, and attached to a national university library. Notable examples are Paris (and Villeurbanne), Copenhagen, Cologne, Leningrad, and Moscow. Regional schools are located at Cairo for the Arab world and at Karachi for the Islamic tradition. Formal library education has been established in many progressive developing nations, notably in Iran and India. Internationally active library educators have included S. R. Ranganathan and Carlos Victor Penna.

Not surprisingly, British educators are active in Commonwealth countries and the Middle East, the French in Francophone Africa, Russians in Eastern Bloc countries, and Scandinavians in Africa. While Canadians have followed the British pattern, American educators have focused on Latin America, but with a number of continuing contact points in Asia, Africa, and the Middle East. Although most large-scale projects have ended, ties and influence remain.

One interesting aspect of the new melding of national influences is that some countries represent more than one foreign strain, each one also modified by the local culture. Nigeria experienced first British and later American library education contributions. China was first under Western influence, then Soviet, and most recently American, and Australia has experienced British influence on public libraries and American on school libraries.

RECENT TRENDS

First, an increasingly cooperative spirit is apparent at many levels. The bibliographically rich nations are developing technologies that enable poor nations to establish their own cultural identity as well as to link with the world's recorded knowledge store. This bodes well for continued cross-cultural and international interests. Although bibliographic equality does not prevail among nations, the seeds of the ideal have been planted.

Second, institutions are taking shape which can accomplish the internationalizing task. The renewed status of library education within IFLA and the participation of many library educators are promising. International and regional conferences held outside Europe and North America should spread global awareness. Bibliographic utilities, such as OCLC and EURONET, and the data base vendors, such as Lockheed and Systems Development Corporation, together with advanced telecommunication possibilities, will facilitate many changes. Third, an increasing amount of publication is accumulating on international librarianship, much of it prepared by educators.

Finally, the spirit of collegiality has increased. No longer is there the stereotyped, paternalistic assistance program, but rather a shared opportunity to broaden viewpoints and modify concepts. A result of international cooperation is a greater awareness of a common knowledge core. Consequently, faculty and student exchanges no longer result in trauma. The recent movement to regularize librarian exchange in English-speaking countries is encouraging.

Although some library internationalists may be enthusiastic about these trends, others are discouraged by the slowed progress in the internationalization of library education. An obvious cause (or result) of this decline is the drop in funding. Second, library school emolument and funding in industrialized countries have suffered in the past decade. Third, at least two circumstances have accompanied school funding decline. Many faculty members feel less secure in their positions; thus, without the former exchange and consultant appointments they are more reluctant to endure the risk of individually negotiated opportunities to work abroad. When both the sending nations and the receiving schools in the West cut aid programs, the stream of foreign faculty members and students declines. Even those who are self-supporting must satisfy increased tuition costs.

RESEARCH SUGGESTIONS

First, the impact of returning students on their home countries needs further study. Second, the ties that specific schools have had with certain foreign schools and international projects deserve study. What has, in fact, been the lasting contribution of Aberystwyth, Pittsburgh, or Texas? Third, there is ample subject matter for biographical study. What motivated the international library education pioneers? How were they received? What did they accomplish? What remains of their legacy? Bishop, Mary Elizabeth Woods, and Mary Parsons have been the subjects of numerous research projects. But what about William A. Boren (India), Asa Don Dickinson (India), Ralph Munn (Australia and New Zealand), Arthur Bostwick (China), Nettie Lee Benson (Latin America), Sara Fenwick (Australia), and others? Fourth, one could wish that various nations and international bodies would chronicle and analyze their overseas programs along the lines of Beverly J. Brewster's exemplary work. In short, this chapter's subject matter deserves more thorough investigation.

NOTES

1. For other treatments, see Gerald Bramley, *A History of Library Education* (London: Bingley, 1969); John F. Harvey, ed., *Comparative and International Library Science* (Metuchen, N.J.: Scarecrow Press, 1977); and Beverly J. Brewster, *American Overseas Library Technical Assistance, 1940–1970* (Metuchen, N.J.: Scarecrow Press, 1976).

2. Sidney L. Jackson, *Libraries and Librarianship in the West: A Brief History* (New York: McGraw-Hill, 1974).

3. George B. Utley, *The Librarians' Conference of 1853* (Chicago: American Library Association, 1951).

4. Gerald Bramley, *Apprentice to Graduate: A History of Library Education in the United Kingdom* (London: Bingley, 1981), pp. 39–53.

5. Arne Kildal, "American Influence on European Librarianship," *Library Quarterly* 7 (1937), pp. 199–200.

6. Leon Carnovsky, "Why Graduate Study in Librarianship?" *Library Quarterly* 7 (April 1937), p. 258; see also Wilhelm Munthe's *American Librarianship from a European Angle* (Chicago: American Library Association, 1939).

7. John D. Cowley, "The Development of Professional Training for Librarianship in Europe," *Library Quarterly* 7 (April 1937), pp. 169–195 and Flora B. Ludington, "The American Contribution to Foreign Library Establishment and Rehabilitation," *Library Quarterly* 24 (April 1954).

8. Willem R.H. Koops and Joachim Wieder, eds, *IFLA's First Fifty Years: Achievement and Challenge in International Librarianship* (Munich: Verlag Dokumentation, 1977), and Mathilde V. Rovelstad, "IFLA and Library Education," *Journal of Education for Librarianship* 16 (Fall 1975), p. 106.

9. See Leon Carnovsky, "Education for Librarianship Abroad," in Bernard Berelson, ed., *Education for Librarianship* (Chicago: American Library Association, 1949), pp. 66–89.

10. Michael Keresztesi, UNESCO's Work in the Field of Library Education and Training: An Overview and Assessment," *International Library Review* 14 (October 1982), pp. 349–361.

11. See Wilfred J. Plumbe, issue ed., "Current Trends in Newly Developing Countries," *Library Trends* 8 (October 1959), pp. 125–341.

12. See Harold Lancour and J. Clement Harrison, issue eds., "Education For Librarianship Abroad in Selected Countries," *Library Trends* 12 (October 1963), pp. 121–355; Louis Shores, "Comparative Library Education: Homework for a National Plan," *Journal of Education for Librarianship* 6 (Spring 1966), pp. 231–233, and George S. Bonn, ed., *Library Education and Training in Developing Countries* (Honolulu: East-West Center Press, 1966).

13. Leon Carnovsky, "The Foreign Student in the Accredited Library School," *Journal of Education for Librarianship* 1 (Fall 1960), pp. 94–107; Raynard D. Swank, "The Education of Foreign Librarians," *Journal of Education for Librarianship* 1

(Spring 1961), pp. 191–199; and Leon Carnovsky, *The Foreign Student in the American Library School* (Washington, D.C.: Office of Education, Bureau of Research, 1971).

14. Mathilde V. Rovelstad, "IFLA and Library Education," *Journal of Education for Librarianship* 16 (1975), p. 113. See also Rovelstad's "Half a Century of IFLA Concern for Library Education," *IFLA Journal* 3 (1978), pp. 327–331.

15. Keresztesi, pp. 349–361.

16. Jane Wilson and Marietta Daniels Sheperd, "Organization of American States," in Allen Kent, et al., eds., *Encyclopedia of Library and Information Science* (New York: Marcel Dekker, 1977), Vol. 11, pp. 16–35.

17. Harold Lancour, "Library Associations and Library Education," in Larry E. Bone, ed., *Library Education: An International Survey* (Urbana: University of Illinois Graduate School of Library Science, 1968), pp. 380–381; Guy Marco, "The Idea of an International Library School," *Library World* 72 (December 1970), pp. 191, 193; and Marco, "Advances in Library Education: Education for Librarianship," in George Chandler, ed., *International Librarianship* (London: Library Association, 1972), pp. 140–152.

18. Among notable examples are: M. Mackee, ed., *A Handbook of Comparative Librarianship* (London: Bingley, 1983), and J. Periam Danton, *The Dimensions of Comparative Librarianship* (Chicago: American Library Association, 1973).

19. Keresztesi, p. 355.

20. Michael Keresztesi, "Diffusion of Modern Library Thought and Practice by Means of Unesco Fellowships for Travel and Study Abroad," *Libri* 29 (October 1979), pp. 193–206; and Marco, "An International Structure for Library Education," *International Library Review* 13 (October 1981), pp. 357–363.

21. Information on library school programs is drawn from appropriate articles in the *Encyclopedia of Library and Information Science*, 33 vols. (New York: Marcel Dekker, 1968–1982). Biographical data appear in *Who's Who in Library and Information Services* (Chicago: American Library Association, 1982).

BIBLIOGRAPHY

Benge, Ronald C. *Cultural Crisis and Libraries in the Third World.* Hamden, Conn.: Linnet Books, 1979.

Benge, Ronald C. *Libraries and Cultural Change.* London: Bingley, 1970.

Coblans, Herbert. *Librarianship and Documentation: An International Perspective.* London: Andre Deutsch, 1974.

Danton, J. Periam. *United States Influence on Norwegian Librarianship, 1890–1940.* Berkeley: University of California Press, 1957.

Hewitt, Vivian D. "Services to Library Life Abroad." In Sidney L. Jackson, et al., eds. *A Century of Service: Librarianship in the United States and Canada.* Chicago: American Library Association, 1976, pp. 321–340.

Kraske, Gary E. *Missionaries of the Book: The American Library Profession and the Origins of the United States Cultural Diplomacy.* Westport, Conn.: Greenwood Press, 1985.

Rayward, W. Boyd. "Librarianship in the New World and the Old." *Library Trends* 25 (July 1976), pp. 209–226.

Rochester, Maxine K. *Foreign Students in American Library Education: Impact on Home Countries.* Westport, Conn.: Greenwood Press, 1986.

Whatley, Allan, ed. *Handbook: International and Comparative Librarianship Group, The Library Association.* London: Library Association, 1977.

White, Carl M. *A Historical Introduction to Library Education: Problems and Progress to 1951.* Metuchen, N.J.: Scarecrow Press, 1976.

3
INTERNATIONALISM AND HIGHER EDUCATION

Martha Boaz

This chapter is devoted mainly to what universities in general are doing in the international arena. It assumes that such activities support international library education and that information on them will be useful to library schools. The chapter will try to establish the university setting for international activities and discuss the reasons why they may be undertaken there.

The term *international education* is used to describe an institution with an educational philosophy and program that extend across national boundaries and involve planning services based on cross-national principles, needs, and outlook. The term is defined broadly here to include comparative, transnational, and world studies and activities. The phrase *international curriculum* is subject to interpretation in the humanities and social sciences but is more or less constant everywhere for the physical sciences and mathematics.

International studies has traditionally included the study of foreign countries and regions—commonly referred to as foreign area studies or area studies—and international relations. International relations focuses on the interactions among governments and other organizations, public and private, as well as individuals, and typically is taught in political science departments. In contrast, area studies tend to be interdisciplinary, involving such fields as political science, history, literature, sociology, and the languages of the region concerned.[1]

The establishment of the United Nations (UN) in 1945 marked a worldwide move from traditional nationalism toward a new set of international values. Since that time, a continuing effort has been made toward international education. We are told that only a sense of urgency will drive us to implement internationalism fully, however, and if humanity is to survive that we must think in terms of world citizenship.

In 1965 the UN Advisory Committee on the Application of Science and Technology to Development established eight high priority areas for international collaboration which included new educational techniques appropriate for developing countries. Much of the collaboration still exists on paper only, but in the decade following 1945 the UN set up UNESCO, an expanded teacher preparation program and an educational system design for the Third World countries.

THE ROLE OF THE UNIVERSITY AND THE NATIONAL GOVERNMENT IN INTERNATIONAL EDUCATION

What is the role of universities, and why should they be interested in international education? The term *university* implies a world of human experience and requires an organized group of people whose major purpose is the search for truth, the discovery, sharing, and extension of knowledge. This "reason for being" cannot be limited by national boundaries. Glen Taggert has said that a basic liberal education component must be an understanding of the changing world and that the universities must vastly increase the number of specialists trained for international service. Still another need is to develop a spirit of educational cooperation among world scholars, to build additional world problem-solving activities into the service areas of institutions, to assemble in our faculties scholars from every discipline and culture so that together we may explore the questions that humans find so troublesome.[2]

Taggert was optimistic about achieving certain objectives through a new national intermediary organization, the Association for International Cooperation in Higher Education. Sponsored by six American associations, this organization proposed to develop ways of tying together the institutional needs and interests of the United States with those of other countries. The academic world must realize the need for an international approach to education and for working with both foundations and government agencies to achieve objectives.

Educators have learned that outside initiatives and support must be combined with broadly based institutional commitments in matters of curriculum change. Indeed, unless staff members are willing to acknowledge the deficiencies in the international education of students, unless they can commit themselves to a new concept of education for world citizenship, no amount of support will be effective.[3]

The objective is to develop new methods of working on the international scene, to negotiate linkages to institutions in other countries. The reasons for improving international education can be summarized as follows:

1. The proper concern of education is the whole world, not just part of it.
2. Knowledge respects no national boundaries.

3. The ability of educated people to use what they know in the development of any human enterprise is greatly enlarged by the acquisition of knowledge and skills that enable them to function effectively in more than one country or culture.[4]

Clark Kerr deplored the erosive international education trends prevalent in the United States in the 1970s and declared that we should:

1. Give more attention to global perspectives and languages in the development of the curriculum.

2. Continue to encourage students to study abroad.

3. Prevent exploitation of foreign students by institutions that seek only to bolster their own enrollment.

4. Prevent foreign student exploitation of educational opportunities as a means simply of gaining entry to the country.

5. Devise better government mechanisms for the improvement and encouragement of international education.

6. Develop the expertise and library resources needed for international education programs without concern for their enrollment levels.

7. Recognize the importance of international scholarship, not only for serving the national interest, but also as a means of meeting long-term needs for intellectual competence in understanding cultures in the world around us.[5]

The international academic community has little political power, and its only influence derives from society's dependence on it for educated personnel, research, and service. In recent years, however, university systems have become more closely associated with political bodies through government grants. The U.S. government has made limited efforts to support international education. The National Defense Education Act provided funding for instructional resources in international studies, for language and area-study centers, and for international studies research. Through the Fulbright program, foreign nationals and Americans have been given opportunities to study, teach, and research abroad.

All countries need to give national government support to student and faculty exchange, the promotion of international scholarship and foreign language studies, foreign affairs research, and the cultivation of educational efforts among countries. Clearly, both the national government and higher education are responsible for international education leadership.

THE HIGHER EDUCATION FUNCTIONS OF
INTERNATIONAL ORGANIZATIONS

What is the purpose of international higher education organizations? They can deal with matters that concern the international *intergovernmental* community or with questions that are raised by members of international *nongovernmental* organizations. UNESCO is an international intergovernmental organization that has close and extensive contacts with the international nongovernmental community through the network of organizations associated with it. Another question that arises is, how can professional and technical problems be separated from political issues?

International cooperation cannot be conceived to be purely professional and technical because in the world of interdependence all aspects of social, political, economic, and educational life are closely linked. In particular, the role that higher education plays in economic, social, and political development is so important that no rational person can isolate educational developments from any set of social, economic, and political conditions.[6]

In 1950 the International Association of Universities was established, and in 1959 the Joint UNESCO-International Research Programme in Higher Education was created. The latter organization promotes innovative experiments, stresses regional and international cooperation, and encourages teacher, researcher, and student mobility. Among other topics, the 1981–1983 UNESCO program is focusing on higher education planning, democratic and interdisciplinary approaches to international needs, educational technology use, and education's responsibility for promoting international peace and respect for human rights.

UNESCO has become more interested recently in educating librarians, documentalists, and archivists. It has helped establish library schools in several nations. Other projects include:

a pilot project in Malaysia which led to the establishment of a co-operative automated cataloging system among university libraries. University library manpower requirements were assessed, development of a university library network was proposed and a reorganization plan of the library at North Sumatra University in Indonesia was prepared.[7]

A number of other groups are working on international education problems. Among governmental organizations are the Organization for Economic Cooperation and Development, the United Nations University, the Council for Mutual Economic Assistance, and the Council of Europe. An active nongovernmental organization is the International Association of Universities.

A clearinghouse for communications between American and foreign higher education institutions should also be established:

Such an organization would facilitate international contacts, attempt to meet the information needs of foreign agencies seeking to place students in U.S. universities and facilitate access by foreign institutions to the appropriate institutions for purposes of technical assistance, program development, collaborative research, and staff development.[8]

Efforts are being made in several countries to strengthen international undergraduate education. Sweden is trying to internationalize its whole educational system, and Great Britain and Japan are emphasizing the importance of international education. The United States established the International Communication Agency in 1978 to increase mutual understanding with other countries, and the National Endowment for the Humanities has given increasing support to international studies. Another positive action was to appoint a Commission on Foreign Language and International Studies which emphasized the strong need for upgrading international education.

UNIVERSITY ORGANIZATION AND INTERNATIONAL POLICIES

Universities should issue internationalization policy statements to guide the activities of staff members. The following partial inventory indicates what such a checklist might contain when the objective is to teach and research within a world context:

- The international concept should strongly influence all teaching, research, and service.
- The world viewpoint should be pushed strongly in all schools, departments, and offices, so that on and off campus courses reflect a strong sense of global awareness.
- On and off campus extracurricular activities should involve the culture of other nations.
- Active foreign recruitment should be carried out for well-qualified students.
- Foreign students should be given special admission, course, and personal counseling to assist in orientation and meeting visa responsibilities.
- Otherwise well-qualified faculty and staff members with experience in other cultures should be recruited actively.
- Classroom textbooks and other print and nonprint material should be chosen in part because of global awareness.
- Library material should be selected to reflect the university's strong international concern.

- Language teaching should represent all major cultural groups.
- National language instruction should be provided for foreign student applicants.
- Special teaching and research projects and institutes located abroad should be encouraged.
- Research projects should be encouraged which relate closely to foreign cultures.
- Alumni group and fund-raising activities in other countries should be encouraged.

Several campus international activity offices may exist, as follows: (1) The International Project Office establishes and manages international contractual projects to provide teaching, research, and other services located on the campus, elsewhere in the country, or abroad, such as semester programs abroad, study centers, and foreign visitors reception. It also administers government and foundation project funds. (2) the Foreign Student Admission Office administers the special requirements and routines for foreign students. (3) the Foreign Student Advisement Office, a branch of the university student counseling service, advises on personal and visa problems, and assists foreign student clubs, advisors, and hosts. (4) The National Language Institute teaches the national language to foreign student admission applicants.

FOREIGN STUDENTS

Planning for an internationalized library school can be facilitated by gathering information on the foreign students already enrolled in the country. In the United States, the total number of foreign students continues to grow; at the same time it represents only a small fraction of all students. For the past twenty-six years, foreign students have made up approximately 2.6 percent of all American higher education students.

According to a report published in 1980, the most popular study field was engineering, with 25.8 percent of the students reported. Business management was second with 17.4 percent, social sciences third with 7.8 percent, and natural and life sciences fourth with 7.4 percent. Library science had 610 or 0.2 percent of the foreign students. The primary sources of finance for foreign students were personal and family funds, their home governments, and their universities.[9]

International students are required to undergo special application and admission procedures. Most universities that accept foreign students maintain one or more special offices and sponsor orientation programs to serve their needs. In order to succeed, a student must be fluent in the language of the country. A health examination is usually required as well as a financial support affidavit. The prospective student must also apply through a consulate for a visa to enter the country.

THE FOREIGN STUDENT AND INSTITUTIONAL RESPONSIBILITIES

In the internationalization campaign, efforts are being made to attract students who are not only broadly representative of other countries but also have sufficient ability to complete their programs successfully. Otherwise, they may risk unpleasant experiences and failure. The host institution has certain additional responsibilities: it should have a staff to give special services in assisting foreign students to adjust to the new setting; it should check admissions requirements carefully and ensure that foreign students receive proper counseling; it should inform students about the differences between this institution and those of their home countries; and it should assist students in their early subject mastery by providing tutoring services.

Faculty and staff members can advise foreign students with regard to both their professional and personal interests and problems. Students can profit by participating in academic and recreational cross-cultural activities. Along with their opportunities to study and live in other cultures, the students have responsibilities to the country and the host institution. The National Association for Foreign Students has listed some of them, namely: the students must strive to understand and tolerate the host country's educational and cultural setting, including standards of conduct, law, respect for others, honesty, and integrity; respect others' rights of self-determination; observe the laws and respect the culture of the host country; participate as fully as possible in the life of the host university and country; seek to participate in joint and cooperative ventures of an educational, social, or cultural nature with citizens and students of the host country and with other international students and scholars; individually and in groups, act with respect for the rights of persons from other countries, cultures, and subcultures, without abridging those rights even in the pursuit of one's own rights; and in general, by actions and deeds, accept responsibility for the best interests of international educational interchange programs, so as to gain the largest amount of public support for them and the widest possible involvement in them.[10]

INTERNATIONAL PROGRAMS

Study abroad provides an enriching experience. Information about study-abroad program students sponsored by American universities appeared in the 1980–1981 *Open Doors* report. Europe was the primary study center with 19,620 or 65.8 percent of the total number of students, and the students were studying in twenty-one countries. The next largest number, 19.9 percent, was enrolled in programs that sent students to more than one world region. Social science programs led, with arts second. Many American universities offer courses in many foreign countries, on both full-year and summer-session-only schedules, and experienced faculty members work in these programs. Excursions supplement classroom lectures, and housing is arranged in university halls.

In addition to these study-abroad programs which are extensions of American universities, other progams originate from American institutions that are permanently based abroad. The American University of Beirut (AUB) is a private nonsectarian institution, founded in 1866 and administered by a Board of Trustees under a New York State charter. University income comes from tuition, endowment, and contributions from business, industry, and individuals in the United States and the Middle East. For many years a large share of the AUB's income has come from foundation and government grants, especially the U.S. Agency for International Development.

The American education program has five faculties: Arts and Sciences, Medicine, Health Sciences, Engineering and Architecture, Agricultural and Food Sciences. In addition, there is a Division of Education and Extension Programs. The language of instruction is English. In 1982 the 4,700 students came from fifty-four countries. Over 85 percent of them were from Arab countries of the Middle East and North Africa. Of the faculty, numbering 400, 80 percent were from the Middle East and 20 percent from the United States and other countries.

In its policy statement, AUB declares its purpose to be to share in the education of the youth of the Middle East, in the service of its people, and in the advancement of knowledge. Some persons have recently suggested that AUB should interpret Middle Eastern culture in America just as it has represented Western civilization in the Middle East.

The American University in Cairo (AUC), a private institution which opened in 1920, is devoted to teaching and research in the arts and sciences and to Egyptian community service. It is multinational, with more than sixty nations represented in the student body, although the majority are Egyptian with the second largest group being American. Professors come from the Middle East, Europe, Asia, and the Americas. The goals of the AUC are to offer an undergraduate program in liberal education relevant to students of the Middle East and a graduate program designed to prepare students for professional life. Overall, the University hopes to foster an understanding of the Arab world in the West. The AUC is incorporated in Washington, D.C., and is licensed to grant degrees by the District of Columbia Board of Higher Education.

The AUC initiates cooperative programs with other Egyptian universities and with government ministries. It works with a consortium of American universities that have Middle East study centers and educational programs. Similar projects involve AUB, Kuwait University, and King Abdul Aziz University in Saudi Arabia. The AUC has selective admissions policies and teaches in English. Research focuses on studies which will advance the arts and sciences and benefit the Arab world. Total enrollment for 1979–1980 was 9,593.

Support for the AUC comes primarily from individual Americans, government agencies, corporations, private foundations, and alumni. The U.S. Office of Education supports both the Center for Arabic Study Abroad, which brings American students to AUC for Arabic instruction, and the Egyptian Seminar for American Universities and State Offices of Education. Scholarships, fellowships, financial aid, and work opportunities are available to eligible students.

Additional examples of this type include Patrice Lumumba Friendship University, a state coeducational institution located in Moscow, USSR. It was founded in 1960 to serve primarily students from developing countries. The students receive free transportation to the University and return after graduation, as well as a monthly government stipend. No tuition is charged. The curriculum extends for six years, with the first year concentrating on orientation and Russian language instruction. In 1980 there were 7,500 students from eight-five countries.

The American Schools of Oriental Research, founded in 1900, is a consortium of 140 American, Canadian, European, and Australian universities, museums, libraries, and research institutes which sponsors research projects on the ancient Near East. It operates three permanent research institutes, located in Jerusalem, Amman, and Nicosia, publishes a variety of research and news publications, and maintains an extensive travel grant and scholarship program.

An example of a library education program which focuses on international matters is sponsored by the College of Librarianship Wales in Aberystwyth and the University of Pittsburgh School of Library and Information Science. The annual International Graduate Summer School in Librarianship and Information Science has developed from a growing interest among librarians in the field's international and comparative aspects. The School's purpose is to provide education and training in various professional subjects pertinent to modern librarianship and information work in its worldwide context. The faculty is assisted by visiting experts and internationally experienced teachers. Courses are offered to students wishing to enlarge their areas of knowledge or update their competence. The courses carry graduate credits which are accepted in major educational institutions throughout the world. All instruction is in English.

Experience shows that higher education planning should be closely related to the country's needs rather than to other countries' standards and norms. Historically, higher education programs in developing countries have followed European models. There have been counterbalancing problems, in expanding higher education in developing countries, owing largely to a mismatch between the number of graduates and of employment opportunities. Some areas have an undersupply of graduates and others an overabundance.

A very different type of university, the United Nations University sponsored by the UN and UNESCO, began operating in 1975–1976 in Japan. It is viewed as a worldwide network of advanced research and training institutions devoted to pressing global problems of human survival, development, and welfare. This university has no educational program leading to degrees, but concentrates on advanced research, training, and knowledge dissemination. It tries to bring together the best scholars and the most perceptive minds from around the world to pursue cooperative studies that will be of the greatest value on a worldwide basis.

The general purpose of the United Nations University is to give impetus, universality, and permanence to the search for practical knowledge needed to assure civilized survival. A major objective is to sponsor strong academic and scientific programs, especially in developing countries. This institution represents a growing awareness that the great problems confronting humanity are not those of single nations but of the entire world.

PROBLEMS

Higher education faces many problems, and international education will have to pass many hurdles before it advances to a better status. The general problems that must be considered include the curriculum, staff, teaching, research, and costs.

The growth of higher education and the increasing number of graduates who are unable to find employment present problems. Many students attend universities on a part-time basis only, and the number able to study abroad will undoubtedly decrease in the future. In certain nations, students are now concentrating more on vocational aims and job preparation than on a broad general education. Increasing emphasis on skill development and computer use will attract students for engineering, business, and law and decrease the number of students with a strong cultural focus and broad educational base. Evaluation on foreign course work may be a problem for certain students transferring credit.

Countries should encourage the study of other languages, for language is basic to understanding and communication with another country. The unfortunate decline of American foreign language study is well known. Along with the language, students should study foreign culture and an academic or occupational specialty. Foreign language study should begin as early as possible, and international cultural studies should be included in early undergraduate work. Living abroad can be an enriching experience for a student.

There are problems in international faculty exchange. Salary differentials discourage many faculty members from applying. Another factor is the concentration of visiting scholars in the better known, research-oriented universities. This leaves many good institutions with no visiting scholars. The major problem, however, is finance, and only the cooperative efforts of universities, government, and private agencies can solve it.

Certain issues that have attracted the educational community's attention are (1) unstable enrollment (in certain countries enrollments have declined); (2) limited resources (funds from many public sources are not growing, and many educational institutions face serious financial problems); (3) the teaching field (great expansion followed by little growth has created strains); and (4) public distrust of universities in certain countries (both the public and the government now distrust universities and criticize them for failing to solve key social problems). Of these the latter is particularly relevant to international education since many of the problems of society are international.

In university-society relations, universities have become more visible and have received more public funding than ever before. Some persons say that universities have become politicized and that this change has restricted academic independence. Without doubt public authority— government—is winning the "struggle" for accountability and universities are adjusting to demands for data and for participation in academic affairs. Government concern for international education has been minimal with the exception of sporadic emphasis on language study. The need for leadership from higher education is apparent.

More attention to international education could have been included in the recent higher education reform era. Having to play "catch up" is always unfortunate. Experiments are being tried to relieve problems in certain countries; the British Open University, for example, has initiated a program for nontraditional students and other people who did not attend universities. This program uses short-term seminars, television, and especially prepared outlines, manuals, and books for instruction. Britain has also experimented with courses that alternate with on-the-job experience. The two-year community college program has become popular in the United States.

A number of European countries, notably West Germany, have begun to restructure their post-secondary educational systems in order to give technological institutions and other schools university status, and to provide a range of programs in university-level institutions. In addition, traditional academic disciplines have been criticized as stumbling blocks to advancing knowledge. In an effort to force changes in the traditional disciplines and faculty organization, new interdisciplinary structures have been created in West Germany, France, and Sweden.

When universities face financial exigencies, one wonders about the practicality of planning for international scholar exchange, which is an expensive process. Of course, in certain cases, using Western Europe as an example, the funding required is comparatively modest. There are advantages to such exchanges. In any case, visiting faculty members should be involved not only in teaching but also in advising students on study opportunities abroad.

International faculty exchanges offer important benefits in enabling faculty . . . to learn something of higher education systems elsewhere and to see problems in an international perspective. . . . Visiting faculty should be made members of university committees concerned with future problems and directions.[11]

In spite of the problems, considerable progress has been made in higher education internationalization. Students may learn many languages, prepare to become area specialists, and learn about foreign societies. A substantial increase has also occurred in the number of persons in study-abroad programs.

RESEARCH

There is a growing interest in higher education research, both from the viewpoint of individual countries and from a cross-cultural perspective. This interest is probably due to the university's development into a major public institution. Research has been stimulated by crises such as student revolts, curriculum reform demands, student attrition, and financial and general accountability demands. Certainly, higher education economics and the academic environment's psychological aspects concern many people. Research study topics as well as methodologies are often governed by a funding agency rather than the researcher, the focus on topics reflecting the agency's interests rather than those needed for a comprehensive and scholarly study.

A number of national agencies have become interested in comparative education, including the Carnegie Commission on Higher Education in the United States and the Robbins Committee in Great Britain. It is also encouraging to know that interdependence is growing as reflected in the increasing number of joint international research studies.

Among the private American foundations which have funded higher education research is the International Council for Educational Development. The Ford and Rockefeller Foundations have funded research that has been of particular assistance to Third World countries. Other international agencies which have funded research include the UN and UNESCO, the World Bank, the Organization for Economic Cooperation and Development, and the International Association of Universities. International teams have made studies in various countries, although, in some cases, European and American models may have been overemphasized.

Research, which is highly valued in developed countries, receives comparatively little attention in Third World countries which need to study certain of their own problems. Third World universities have weaker academic traditions, little funding, and little research. Research should be done on ways to hold educational institutions accountable for the quality of courses offered abroad. Research is needed to show in which subject fields internationalism has made the most progress. We also need to learn more about the transferability of international programs to library education.

OBSERVATIONS AND SUGGESTIONS

An international experience is a vital part of cultural life. In addition, it may provide an element of professional competence in a society in which all progress has an international dimension. All fields need information about developments abroad and should establish communication channels with foreign counterparts. The value of study and living abroad is widely acknowledged. Several ideas have affected international educational development; one of them has been the democratization (accessibility and relevance) of education.

In certain educational surveys, students have indicated that international affairs are very important to their future. A renewed interest in a core curriculum with language study may stimulate interest in international education in the United States. Because of national differences in higher education, it is difficult to make plans that would apply across the world, but certain common elements may be pursued to advantage. Barbara Burn has suggested ways in which institutions can strengthen their international education programs:

1. Use foreign students as a teaching resource.
2. Involve faculty with experience in development assistance in international studies programs.
3. Use experts in international studies for the pre-departure orientation of faculty who are about to participate in development assistance programs.
4. Increase collaboration between international education programs and professional schools, with the goal of internationalizing curricula in the professional

school and encouraging area-studies majors to obtain professional as well as international education.

5. Incorporate overseas experience into academic counseling.

6. Use international studies faculty and graduate students to develop links with higher education institutions in appropriate regions.

AN INTERNATIONAL LIBRARY/INFORMATION SCHOOL

Library science could also render a service by establishing an international library school to develop an awareness of international perspectives. Students could be educated to give service in all subject categories and across all borders. Attention could be given to advanced study and international matters rather than to introductory course work. If there is only one international library school, the curriculum should be open only to advanced students.

The faculty should be outstanding with strong formal qualifications and impressive experience. A Master's degree in library/information science or its equivalent should be required for admission. Based on the objectives, adequate financial support should be ensured for a reasonable number of years. Faculty members with different specializations and experience should be recruited. The student-staff ratio should be small.

In addition to the above recommendations, the school should make a feasibility study to locate the best site; explore the possibility of having the school located at the United Nations University; seek joint UN and UNESCO sponsorship; draft a school charter; decide the appropriate type of organizational structure; determine the school's operational priorities; ask UNESCO, the International Association of Universities, and the Joint UNESCO-International Research Program in Higher Education to sponsor research and later a conference dealing with the need for an international library/information science school; seek guidance from the International Council for Educational Development; establish a Council for International Cooperation in Library and Information Science to serve as a clearinghouse for interinstitutional and international needs in library/information science education, its objective being to assist libraries and educational agencies to meet the information needs of organizations, agencies, and individuals; create an international center to collect data on specialists by discipline, country, and language; maintain a library field competency pool; and maintain liaison with government and private agencies, professional associations, and business to work for international study.

The idea of an international library school has been talked about for some time, but to date such a school does not exist. If such a school could be established, it would be a giant step forward for the library/ information world.

NEED FOR LIBRARY/INFORMATION EDUCATION STANDARDS

The curricula and standards in North American schools are more uniform than in other world regions mainly because of their need to meet ALA accreditation requirements. Standards are basic to any good library education program, and prior to planning the educational program, library service must be planned. Questions to consider are: (1) What are the overall information and library needs and desires of society, on local, national, and international levels? (2) What types of educational programs will prepare people to respond to these needs and to provide these services?

Both qualitative and quantitative standards are needed in any educational program, and they are crucial in an international program. A library school committee of the International Federation of Library Associations and Institutions (IFLA) has suggested that the international standards might be officially adopted by a country or region acting through professional associations or agencies.

Formulating global standards is not a simple matter, but educating people for library service in any region, nation, or internationally requires high standards. On an international level this issue bcomes complex, but persistence and hard work have solved problems in the past, and it still seems desirable to combine the realistic with the idealistic to shape a better world.

NOTES

1. Barbara B. Burn, *Expanding the International Dimension of Higher Education* (San Francisco: Jossey-Bass, 1980), p. 4.

2. Glen L. Taggert, "Association for International Cooperation in Higher Education and Research," in Stephen K. Bailey, ed., *Higher Education in the World Community* (Washington, D.C.: American Council on Education, 1977).

3. James M. Hester, "To Illuminate Tomorrow: Higher Education in an Independent World," in Bailey, ed., *Higher Education in the World Community*, pp. 8–9.

4. Clark Kerr, "Global Education Concerns of Higher Education for the 1980s and Beyond," in Burn, *Expanding the International Dimension*, p. xix.

5. Ibid., pp. xix-xxi.

6. Dragoljub Najman, "Functions for International Organizations in Higher Education," in Bailey, ed., *Higher Education in the World Community*, p. 53.

7. *World List of Universities*, 15th ed. (New York: De Gruyter, 1982), p. 490.

8. Burn, *Expanding the International Dimension*, p. 152.

9. Much information was gathered from Institute of International Education, *Open Doors: 1979/80*; *Report on International Educational Exchange* (New York: The Institute, 1980).

10. National Association for Foreign Student Affairs, *The Relevance of U.S. Graduate Programs to Foreign Students from Developing Countries* (Washington, D.C.: The Association, 1979), p. 21.

11. Barbara B. Burn, "New Exchange Opportunities," in *Higher Education in the World Community*, p. 96.

BIBLIOGRAPHY

Bluhm, Harry P. "The Role of State Departments of Education in Promoting International/Global Education." *International Education* 11 (Spring 1982), pp. 21–26.

Garrett, Larry N., and C. Joanne Garrett. "The International Student and Academic Advisement: The Bus Stops Here." *International Education* 10 (Spring 1981), pp. 20–24.

Lundu, M. C. "Library Education and Training: At Home or Abroad?" *International Library Review* 14 (October 1982), pp. 363–378.

Murphy, Peter James. "International Aid for Educational Development: A Cooperative Venture." *International Education* 12 (Fall 1982), pp. 34–40.

Tenkin, Humphrey. *The World in the Curriculum: Curricular Strategies for the 21st Century*. New Rochelle, N.Y.: Change Magazine Press, 1981.

4

AN INTERNATIONAL INTEREST LEVEL-RAISING PROGRAM

John F. Harvey

This chapter discusses methods of increasing awareness and interest in international education. Many library and information science faculty members have little interest in internationalization, no concern for their lack of interest, nor even an awareness that it might be thought desirable. To change internationalism awareness and interest levels requires a long-range education program.

What is meant by awareness level and interest level-raising programs? One can be distinguished from the other by saying that, first, the person must be made aware that an international concept exists and then be aroused to the point of interest in it. These are two phases of an interest continuum. To raise these levels means to make the target person increasingly alert to the internationalism existing around him or her and to the benefits derived from increasing emphasis on this concept.

With awareness sharpened, interest may be extended by exposing individuals to a new perception of information in one of their specialties. Sets of projects should be developed to do this within an information school. The campaign should seek eventually to make the intiate a strong internationalization advocate.

A program means a well-defined, carefully thought out, systematically organized, and consistently pursued activity with certain explicit concepts and well-understood goals. The early stages should be coordinated by an enthusiast or a small group of enthusiasts. They may meet as an ad hoc mission-oriented faculty group, and they should avoid gaining a reputation as complainers since they seek positive change by infusing the school with a new viewpoint. The internationalization goal is school evolution into an all-pervasive international educational mode.

RAISING INTERNATIONAL AWARENESS AND
INTEREST LEVELS

First, colleagues should be stimulated to recognize the need to raise awareness and interest levels. Before a blind spot can be addressed, however, it must be outlined and understood; then a plan can be developed for educating target persons. The plan must be customized for each person, school, and nation in the light of existing knowledge, sophistication levels, and nationalism strength.

Let us contemplate the consequences of nationalism in information education. In this context nationalism is the opposite of internationalism, its competing philosophy. Nationalists promote the information concepts that are used locally to the exclusion of the varied concepts used abroad. Internationalists try instead to enrich instruction by combining local and foreign concepts.

Nationalism circumscribes subfield views and suggests that national ideas are more likely to be useful than foreign ideas. Nationalism suggests that most concepts originated with local leaders, though for many nations the fuller picture shows that they were imported. Nationalism teaches information history primarily in its local phase, not in its original and development phases.

Nationalism influences instructors to prepare students primarily for work in the more traditional and provincial libraries. Preparation for work in cosmopolitan libraries would entail increasing emphasis on foreign and international sources and institutions, thereby diminishing national emphasis. Thus, national often equals provincial and excludes 99 percent of the world. A nationalistic school may focus class attention on the work of certain nationals and exclude influential foreign leaders. Nationalistic children's literature may reinforce local culture but also elevate mediocre authors to stardom.

Most schools need to support national government interests. Does teaching internationalism meet this expectation? If handled properly, it does. Each nation needs to learn more about its neighbors in all areas, and few national heads would disagree. Consequently, to encourage cross-cultural understanding should harmonize well with local goals and even make the information school a national educational asset.

Many schools still market their services in a conservative and nationalistic manner, extending them over little more than one or two provinces or a country. Schools should broaden both their conceptual and geographic service areas by adopting and publicizing a comprehensive international education program.

By broadening a nationalistic curriculum and adding international continuing education, the school can provide better quality service, reach a wider geographic area, and attract a larger number of future leaders.

Of course, language specialization may limit such broadening intitiatives to parts of nearby nations. Internationalism can be carried too far, however. If international and foreign concepts replace most currently used national concepts, then graduates may be incompletely educated for national library leadership.

Some students believe that the United States should serve as an international role model, but being resolutely nationalistic, most American information educators believe other nations can teach them little. The United Kingdom assumes an international leadership role in absorbing foreign ideas, especially certain library associations and schools. This role is strongest with nearby European countries. International interest levels are also high in Scandinavia. Both the British and Scandinavians consider themselves to be enriched by the ideas of other nations.

The Soviet Union uses the concepts of other nations to some degree, especially in informatics. Their basic thrust, like the American, is to fit concepts around their own political and social ideology. By heritage and location, Australia has been influenced by both the United States and the United Kingdom and in turn influences other Asian nations as well.

In every subject field and country, a few occupational schools stand above the rest and move into a more enlightened posture. Two schools can be singled out as internationalism leaders: the College of Librarianship, Wales, and the School of Library and Infomation Science, University of Pittsburgh, in the United States.

More important than looking to another nation or school for leadership is the idea that each one should proceed independently and thereby move toward a regional or global model. Pacesetting is possible for a school and for creative and ambitious faculty. Nor should the internationalist downgrade the single individual's contribution. If he or she becomes a persuasive advocate, what a strong gain has been made!

SAMPLE INTERNATIONALIZATION PROJECTS

An early project should be to inventory every element within existing school internationalism—students, administration, courses, publications, research, class material, services, laboratories, and alumni. Some international units and activities will be discovered so that activists will not start at absolute zero. Many schools are at least 5 percent to 10 percent internationalized. Success levels should be studied, as should the possibilities of improving them and extending influence to other spheres.

In a related project, each faculty member can be encouraged to determine the full international needs of each course. An inventory can be taken of what should be taught in specific course units, what information is available with which to do that, and what more is needed. Students' internationalism needs also vary. Those with strong international backgrounds through study and experience will need less extensive instruction than those with only national backgrounds.

Another early project can be a series of well-publicized discussion meetings in which the internationalism concept is discussed and clarified and audience support is attracted. A full explanation is needed before decisions can be made. These awareness and interest level-raising meetings should be led by an experienced internationalist and held alongside a series of individual talks, panel discussions, and films with international themes. They should have considerable audience appeal of their own.

A budgeted and staffed international information center can be established as an early project because its usefulness will take several years to develop. It can supplement the information school's information center by specializing in foreign and international library and information science pamphlets.

In addition, the school may develop close cooperative relationships with one or more foreign schools, libraries, or information leaders.[1] The closer that relationship is, the larger the group of persons who can be involved in it. Exchange of publications, catalogs, research, faculty members, students, and comparative studies of curriculum and organizational patterns between schools are obvious mutual activities. A single foreign weekend visitor can move the school very little, but the visitor who stays an entire semester can be a strong inspiration.[2] The personal experience of an exchange program can bring home the stimulation of foreign ideas.

An international publication program can also raise interest levels, as a result partly of printed material visibility. Publishable manuscripts can be solicited from foreign schools, associations, and government offices and issued in the school's book or journal program. In a related project, a teaching material exchange program can enable faculty members to obtain useful print and nonprint material from foreign schools—notably, syllabi, lectures, lecture notes, course outline and assignment lists, reprints, and reports.[3] The school will wish to use the FID *Newsletter* to announce its own special course work and to check other schools' activities.[4]

Special scholarships are needed. An existing scholarship can be restricted to foreign applicants. Perhaps the foreign student affairs office on campus can make additional full and partial scholarships available. National scholarships may be located through foreign or ethnic affairs associations. With alumni association aid, a scholarship fund solicitation program for students in developing countries can be started to raise additional funds.

THE COUNCIL AND THE PLAN

The ad hoc enthusiasts may establish a schoolwide Internationalization Advisory Council to plan and guide program development. With official appointment and status, this council can accomplish more in certain areas (and perhaps less in others!) than can a small and informal group. A council can persuade administrators to collect school data and request project budget allocations.

A full rationale, an extensive and staged implementation plan, and a calendar of events and dates should be developed and published for all constituencies to read. Objectives, assumptions, policies, and steps should be clarified. A project-by-project approach can be recommended, and after agreement, the plan should be implemented in one-year stages.

At this time, internationalization should be added to the school's formal objectives statement. A two- to three-year council appointment should allow time to complete medium-term projects, and a two- to three-year renewal should be sufficient to complete long-term projects. The council should work closely with other campus, community, and national internationalism groups.

When can the internationalization program be called successful? At what saturation level should the plan aim? Perhaps the objective should be to internationalize fully every aspect of school activities. Graduating nationalism-free persons fully sensitive to library and information science's international aspects is desirable but will be difficult to measure.

In this connection, a set of school internationalization standards with checklist and rating scale is needed.[5] For each major curriculum and management area, they should show several internationalization levels based on the ratio of international to national and provincial activity and on the usefulness of international information for full and practical understanding of each subject field. They should be based on specific accomplishments and enable any school to measure its current status. A good standard will require at least a 50 percent score for each category. A school scoring high will have implemented most of this book's ideas; the contents table should be checked for appropriate categories.

Once activists have seen the mission move forward, project success should be publicized so that the international information education community will look to the school for additional progress. Gaining a reputation as an international interest center is desirable. News releases are needed, with international distribution made to information bulletins, newspapers, and libraries. A school known to be friendly to international initiatives can thereby attract like-minded personnel and projects.

STRATEGY AND LOGISTICS

A few practical suggestions can be made for the ad hoc group and the council. An early step is to determine audience awareness level and receptivity, identifying supporters, enemies, and the uncommitted—in other words, counting noses. Receptivity can be judged by the degree of general openness as well as reactions to the new internationalism. The receptive can be cultivated and the extent of their knowledge and commitment calculated.

Colleagues found to be unreceptive should be isolated; they are probably mired in national or even provincial concerns. Failure to explain internationalism successfuly will make more difficult the creation of a sympathetic intellectual climate and innovation adoption. Certain "easy" or "soft" projects can be started with the expectation of early success, thereby enlarging the group's foothold and reinforcing its optimism. Then, after careful study, the "hard" or complex projects can be planned. Some of them can be subdivided by chronology, geography, or subject field and attacked one part at a time.

Program permanence should be stressed. Internationalism should not be adopted because it is fashionable today; an internationalized school has made a permanent contract. Advocates should not neglect the domino effect; convinced opinion leaders will bring along their followers.

A variety of general approaches is possible for each activist. Should he or she approach awareness and interest level-raising projects on an individual by individual basis, school by school, nation by nation, region by region, or else use a worldwide approach? Should the activist work at the task from the bottom (individual) up or the top (worldwide) down?

Simplest is a one-on-one approach with one's own school colleagues. Some will convert easily and others never. By converting several persons over a one- to two-year period, the advocacy group will grow. One-on-one persuasion is the basic activity mode in all contexts. The school-by-school approach—to internationalize national schools one by one—requires the cooperation of converts elsewhere. One or more of them must carry on the activity in each school.

A national approach requires working from the top down through national information associations to raise awareness and interest levels. The advocate must also work through government officials to change bureaucratic concepts. Improving the climate for international activities is a worthwhile interim objective in certain situations.

The regional approach is simply a broadened national approach. The potential gain is significantly larger, but so is the difficulty of extending ideological influence to the schools. Regional and national conference and committee work, correspondence, travel, and friends must be used to reach key individuals. Global coverage is a long-term project and can be implemented through international information associations. Journal papers and books can help to put the message across. This book illustrates one worldwide approach.

The proper person must be selected to exert pressure on administrators to achieve favorable decisions. It can be done directly by an advocate who has influence over that person or to whom the administrator is indebted. In other situations, pressure should be brought on an uncommitted committee member rather than on an admnistrator.

Changing other persons' minds requires understanding them and the influences on their thinking. Changing minds usually requires a slow process of wearing down resistance by accumulating evidence favorable to the cause. Activist patience and sensitivity are required to avoid overemphasis. An emotional appeal or strong student demand may be needed to bring about the most favorable conclusion.

NOTES

1. See Guy Marco, "Library Schools in North America and Elsewhere: Cooperative Agreements," *UNESCO Journal of Information Science, Librarianship and Archives Administration* 2 (July-September 1980), pp. 180–94.

2. See Hwa-Wei Lee, "International Library Internships," *International Library Review* 17 (January 1985), pp. 17–25.

3. Contact the Clearinghouse on Information Education and Training Material, International Federation for Documentation, The Hague.

4. *Newsletter on Education and Training Programmes for Information Personnel* (The Hague: International Federation for Documentation, quarterly), Vol. 1, 1979 to date.

5. See Frances Laverne Carroll, "Internationalism in Education for Librarianship," *International Library Review* 4 (April 1972), pp. 102–26.

BIBLIOGRAPHY

Bowden, Russell. "Improving Library Education in the Developing Countries." *UNESCO Bulletin for Libraries* 30 (September-October 1976), pp. 255–261.

Bowden, Russell, ed. *UNESCO Pre-IFLA Conference Seminar on Library Education Programmes in Developing Countries*. München: Saur, 1982.

Bramley, G. *World Trends in Library Education*. London: Bingley, 1975.

Brewster, Beverly. "International Library School Programs." *Journal of Education for Librarianship* 9 (Fall 1968), pp. 138–143.

Dean, John. *Planning Library Education Programs*. London: Andre Deutsch, 1972.

Marco, Guy A. "An International Structure for Library Education." *International Library Review* 13 (October 1981), pp. 357–363.

Marco, Guy A. "A Rationale for International Library Education." *International Library Review* 9 (October 1977), pp. 355–362.

PART II

ADMINISTRATIVE SERVICES

5
STUDENT RECRUITMENT AND SELECTION

Peter Havard-Williams

The internationalization of library and information science education through peoples' mobility is not new. For many years—certainly since World War II—library science students have moved from their own countries to study. Indeed, international students have existed since the European Middle Ages, but only since librarianship began to approach professional status have librarians sought qualifications abroad. Thus, developing countries in particular have looked toward the industrialized nations, especially the United States and the United Kingdom, to Germany, France, and the East European countries.

The countries to which they look depend on the language involved (especially French or English), their ideological affiliations (e.g., capitalist or socialist), and/or their religious affinities (e.g., Christian or Muslim). The foreign student market was for many years taken for granted as part of post-World War II reconstruction and colonial independence (as in Africa or Southeast Asia), or the spread of ideological influence (as in Eastern Europe).

A foreign student is one whose nationality differs from that of the country in which he or she is studying. Occasionally, restrictions are stated in terms of language (e.g., a candidate whose national language is not English, French, or other language of instruction). English is of particular significance in library science since 76 percent of its literature is in that language.[1]

Recruitment implies an active approach, seeking students from other countries, while selection is the next admissions process stage. In the 1950s and 1960s, most recruiting and pressure exerted for British places was done by external agencies, for example, UNESCO, the British Council, cultural attachés, and foreign governments.

Active student recruitment is seldom done by library schools, though certain exceptions have existed, notably, Drexel, Pittsburgh, Kentucky, Tehran, Louisiana State, and the College of Librarianship, Wales. However, a library school's parent university may recruit or place publicity in order to encourage foreign student applications. With students eager to study in the industrialized world and the diminishing class rolls of the 1970s and 1980s, foreign students have been encouraged to apply, particularly to institutions which, without their numbers, might have had to close down.

In the United Kingdom, in 1980 the government's introduction of full cost fees for overseas students and the real-term reduction of government grants to universities led to the pursuit of foreign students. Other governments, however, have sought to reduce the increase in foreign students because of the cost, and still others have introduced quotas to reduce the number. Indeed, the number of foreign students in any country depends on a mixture of government and institutional policies (except perhaps in East European countries where the national government determines policy) and on historical connections between countries and institutions. Even countries like New Zealand with a liberal foreign student policy have recently introduced differential fees because of pressure from students in developing countries.

Active foreign student recruitment does not appear to be a major library school concern. For instance, of 200 questionnaires which this author sent to library schools, only 54 (27 percent were returned), and the answers in those returned indicated a low level of concern. It may be fair to infer that the low response level reinforces that view. Of course, there may be a difference between schools that are part of another institution and those that are autonomous.

The École Nationale Supérieure de Bibliothecaires, for instance, is bound by national policy. Whereas French candidates are chosen by competition, foreign candidates are chosen on recommendation of a special commission of Ministry of Culture, Education and Foreign Affairs inspectors and civil servants. All candidates must speak French, and have a university degree and library experience. Academic assessment plays a major part in selection, and foreign candidates should constitute no more than 33 percent or less than 20 percent of the total. However, with recent fluctuations in the annual number of French candidates (sometimes down to single numbers), foreign candidates have permitted the school to remain viable.

Many schools are part of a tertiary education institution. The larger institution sets the standard and determines the recruitment pattern. Many tertiary education institutions have adopted sophisticated public relations techniques. The more they need to recruit, the more effort is expended and the more glossy the publication. But as Maureen Mackay points out,

Publicity is no newcomer to the colleges. In an 1869 inaugural address, Charles W. Eliot, President of Harvard, spoke of the need for the University to "influence public opinion toward learning." In 1900 he engaged the services of the Publicity Bureau, the nation's first public relations firm, to obtain national recognition for Harvard.[2]

However, with the development of new public relations methods and the shift in higher education in many industrialized countries from a seller's to a buyer's market, what was good enough for Harvard then may not be suitable today. A 1976 admissions colloquium suggested, among other things, how universities can duplicate marketing success: "The secret . . . is positioning: distinguishing a product clearly from its competitors in order to fix it in the buyer's mind."[3]

Hence, the only way to compete with Oxford or Harvard is to acknowledge its top rating and show how another institution relates to it. Of course, this is only one view. Other agencies give advice on what information students require and how to present it. Recruitment appears to be a major concern in the United States, but so far in the United Kingdom it is concerned primarily with foreign students.

Foreign student recruitment presents a number of problems, including outright deception—about subjects offered (and on what level), job prospects, even institutional location, recruiting agency integrity, immigration procedure entanglement, and the complexity of the foreign student's requirements.[4] U.S. admissions procedures, for instance, appear inordinately complex to a student accustomed to other systems.

Rhoda Garoogian has examined older admissions criteria and has concluded that many of the same factors operate today—mental ability, previous scholarship record, intellectual interests as revealed by reading habits, previous library work experience, and the personal character traits found most useful in librarianship. Age and modern languages are sometimes included also. "The most common selection practices are based on college undergraduate records, Graduate Record Examination (GRE) scores, references, personal estimates obtained through interviews, and work experience."[5]

Undergraduate records have always been important in gaining admission to library schools. In the U.S. schools generally the Grade Point Average (GPA) required for admission is between 2.5 and 3.2 (on a four-point scale). More than half of the accredited schools in the United States claim to require a 3.0 minimum. In the United Kingdom, most schools require an honors degree, many demand at least second class honors, and the best schools require at least an "upper" second (perhaps the nearest equivalent to the United States' 3.2 GPA). Several Commonwealth countries follow this practice.

In the United States, over half the schools require the GRE, with acceptable scores ranging from 750 to 1000 (though foreign and minority students may score as low as 650 and still be accepted). This examination is used because collegiate institutions and standards vary so widely. However, the GRE's credibility has been questioned in recent years. Hence, previous experience is given greater weight than the GRE.

Only the United States insists on a baccalaureate with a broad academic background. In other countries, particularly in Europe, a broad background is expected only at the secondary level, and a narrowly focused honors degree or its equivalent is usually regarded as the best evidence of intellectual attainment. The United States, too, is beginning to allow some exceptions. The danger is that the exceptions may grow if enrollment falls farther and admissions standards are then lowered to fill the lecture room.

Many library schools, especially those in North America, are facing a steady decline of student population. According to William R. Eshelman,

From 1979 to 1981 in Master's programs, full-time equivalent (FTE) enrollment dropped 10 percent. Although academic administrators rely on FTE figures and monitor them closely, some critics argue that the drop in *full-time* enrollment is more significant. It is down 11 percent. Of the 60 schools that reported to the Association of American Library Schools in both of these years, 34 showed a decline in full-time enrollment, 23 a gain, and three held steady. Six schools had from two to 15 full-time students enrolled in 1981/82, surely too few to achieve the "critical mass" that White of Indiana University, among others, believed necessary. When part-time students are included (thus making up FTE's), the picture is even bleaker: 38 schools declined, 20 gained, and one held steady.[6]

This decrease in population could be offset to some degree by recruiting overseas students; thus, the issue of recruiting and selecting overseas candidates is increasingly important. A more direct approach is needed to attract a larger number of overseas students.

According to the author's questionnaire replies, more data and research are needed in this area, particularly to determine the educational needs of students in developing countries and the comparative relevance of levels and course content in recruiting institutions. Such data will enable us to understand students' needs—as articulated by their domestic work situations—and the sophisticated library school programs in industrialized countries.

Among other data needed are information on the career paths of foreign students and the extent of their usefulness on return to their native countries. It would be interesting, for example, to learn the extent to which education for library or information science in a country is influenced by those who have completed the course overseas. More knowledge of equivalencies in educational and experiential background is needed.

Psychological, social and linguistic problems affect the ability of foreign students to gain full advantage from their courses; thus, more research on these issues is also desirable. For example, what proportion of overseas students return to their own countries permanently? The fluctuation in the number of overseas students is affected by the economic situation and government policies in both the sending and receiving countries. For example which countries are interested in supporting their citizens' desire to study abroad? The answer to the question would help determine recruitment target areas as well as learn about scholarship resources in receiving countries, information that is only partly available in UNESCO's *Study Abroad*.

It would also be valuable to learn specific government policies about sending students to developed countries (e.g., the effect of higher fees on choice and preferences for postgraduates as opposed to first-degree courses). On the other hand, the number of foreign students entering North American schools is apparently dwindling because of present immigration regulations affecting employment and because of rising tuition costs. It would also be useful to see comparable statistics for other countries.

With enrollments declining, the selection process has become more passive, and at the same time recruitment activities are increasing. Attention is being given to placing newspaper advertisements, direct mailing of brochures and course details, posters, visits to other universities, and conference exhibits. In some cases recruitment is even more direct. For example, British universities are now trying to attract foreign students by sending recruiting agents abroad, by using recruiting agencies, such as Gabbitas Thring, the educational consultants, and by using more sophisticated public relations material.

British institutions have British Council support in advising persons abroad who wish to study in the United Kingdom. British Council libraries also serve as British educational facility information centers. In the United States special efforts are being made to attract students with good science and mathematics qualifications, and ethnic and other minorities are being sought. On both sides of the Atlantic, too, the schools are providing better facilities for part-time students and practitioners. Garoogian points out that they have upgraded career-advising and placement activities for current students as well as for alumni. She states that this kind of activity represents an indirect approach to recruitment, the area in which she considers the schools to have been most creative.[7]

Job placement work is often conducted by university placement centers. In the United Kingdom, for instance, the Loughborough University Career Service collaborates with the Department of Library and Information Studies in a session-long program of application writing and "headhunter" interviews. The Service also monitors posts obtained by

graduating students. At the University of California, Berkeley, a placement brochure is circulated to potential employers. With the lack of
traditional opportunities, graduates have found posts as freelance researchers, consultants, and information scientists as well as in management, public relations, marketing, and computing firms.

Few library schools replying to my questionnaire have international
objectives; they simply want to select the most appropriate candidates.
As one school states: "We have done little to recruit overseas students
because . . . those recruited failed to measure up to (our) rigorous admission requirements." On the other hand, the University of Southern
California seeks to recruit the best possible students for twenty to twenty-
five of its 150 full-time equivalent student slots from other North and
South American countries and another twenty to twenty-five from other
parts of the world. The university "has an active world-wide recruitment
program and our school participates to advantage."

About 35 percent of the questionnaire respondents have a worldwide
policy, while 24 percent operate a restrictive policy. For example, they
are thinking primarily of students from developing countries. Austra-
lasian schools see themselves as limited to neighboring Asian, South
Pacific, and sometimes African applicants. Nearly half of the respondents
have no explicit policy but take what comes along.

Of the English schools, four or five have a large stake in overseas
students. The largest university school with approximately 400 students
at Loughborough has participated in the University policy to attract up
to 700 overseas students out of a 5,500 to 6,000 total. At the Loughborough Department of Library and Information Studies foreign university graduates normally compose a fifth to a third of the total.
Undergraduates are taken only from countries that have no undergraduate library science facilities. Candidates must be in good standing
in their own countries, and have appropriate library experience and a
mark of at least 7 in the British Council English test. Certain British
schools require a preliminary term for foreign students to allow for
culture shock.

Most American universities have foreign student admission offices
which are concerned with recruitment and selection. Admissions criteria
for foreign students are in general determined by institutional policy on
the Test of English as a Foreign Language (TOEFL) and GRE scores.
The foreign qualification assessment is usually an admissions office matter. However, close liaison is needed between the admissions office and
the school. Because a high proportion of admission decisions are based
on paper qualifications, the opportunity to make a professional assessment is rare. Moreover, references from abroad do not convey the same
nuances as references from one's own country, and so they can be
misleading.

Several countries have a language requirement not only for foreign students but also for national students. The United States, for instance, requires that immigrants communicate well in English. The School of Library and Information Science, Mara Institute of Technology, Malaysia, teaches in Malay. Moreover, candidates need to be of the Malay race and the Islamic religion, though some other Malay-speaking Muslim nationals have recently been admitted.

Few schools have special recruiting staff members other than the admissions staff. Indeed, much foreign student selection has to be "by guess and by God." That so much diplomatic selection is successful suggests that the developed countries receive the better local candidates.

Satisfied clients are the best advertisement. Hence, graduate representation in countries from which one wishes to recruit is a sound advertising method, particularly if they work there in the Peace Corps, Voluntary Service Overseas, or similar national services. A general university-wide policy will facilitate recruiting. Area studies and language students may be helpful. Schools with international subject specialists, for example, specialists in Latin American studies, can make beneficial contacts.

National recruiting networks exist informally, either through alumni use, cooperative arrangements with other schools, or known practitioners. Minimizing student travel expense is a problem for everybody, and so printed material and brochures for the university and the school are important. One of the most active British schools in the area of public relations is the College of Librarianship, Wales, which sends large quantities of well-produced public relations material all over the world.

With regard to the use of alumni associations in recruiting, they have had varying successes and are more in evidence in the United States than elsewhere. Many American schools have highly organized alumni groups activated by the university as well as by the school. These groups are more successful on the American scene than elsewhere because American tax laws favor gifts to public institutions. A number of institutions encourage alumni to recruit, but, except informally, foreign alumni are excluded from this effort.

International conferences are also useful in recruiting. Professors and alumni at the International Federation for Documentation, the International Federation of Library Associations and Institutions, and the International Council on Archives conferences may contact foreign students keen to study in their countries. Attendance at other conferences also offers an opportunity for recruitment and for on-the-spot candidate assessment to assist selection. This kind of recruitment is directed primarily toward doctoral students.

A number of U.S. schools offer student teaching, library work, and research assistantships and internships (on both the Master's and doctoral level) which usually cover fees and provide a modest salary. These funds frequently come from the university as a whole, though with cost being allocated on a "cost-center" basis, many scholarships and assistantships must be financed within the school budget or through alumni activities.

In British universities, most foreign student help comes from the British Council which offers scholarships (a full year's support) or bursaries that give part support, depending on the government's assessment of the country's (and the candidate's) means. The British Council administers funds available from the Overseas Development Agency which is determined to improve the government's image with developing countries. British policy has led many students to look to education in the United States, Australia, Canada, and New Zealand. The foreign student increase has been so large in Australia that the consequent displacement of Australians has provoked some concern.

My questionnaire returns suggest that few schools use trips and meetings explicitly for recruitment, though recruitment and perhaps selection may be a byproduct. Opinions differ about the value of interviews, but interviews between nationals of different countries definitely aid mutual understanding.

What does a school undertake when it accepts a foreign student? First, it aims to provide a library education within the context of its own culture, practice, history, and administration. Second, in certain cases, it also undertakes to help the student through the period of culture shock. Student difficulties are best solved by faculty members close to the problem; hence, the tutorial aspect of foreign student work is extremely important. Student learning is facilitated by leaving the student's problem to the school rather than to an international student agency.

Some schools cater to foreign students more than other schools. Among the schools that try to attract foreign students are the following: in the United States, the schools at Columbia University, Peabody College, and the University of Pittsburgh; in France, the École Nationale Supérieure des Bibliothecaires; and in Britain, Polytechnic of North London, College of Librarianship, Wales, and the Loughborough University of Technology.

North London and Wales require preliminary foreign student "acclimatization" processes. North London has an attachment program for library science instructors from other countries, whereas Loughborough has an advanced Master of Arts program for instructors (commonly known as MA/ALISE). Loughborough's program attracts eight to ten students a year and is a joint enterprise of the Departments of Library and Information Studies and of Education. Recently, Wales established a similar course.

In the United States, to facilitate foreign student entry certain schools operate a flexible system requiring extra courses before beginning the full Master's program. Whether or not courses are oriented toward overseas students, the students should be able to include classwork that will assist them in their own countries. Many foreign students become senior librarians there (particularly advanced students), and a year of study offers them the opportunity to consider their own country's problems in the context of a country with a more fully developed library system.

This year of study also allows the student to consider problems dispassionately and without practical responsibility for implementing solutions. If course work subjects, term essays, dissertations, or theses can be directed toward their own country's problems, a spin-off value should result. Reflection on a topic in tranquility and the process of writing may provide students with ammunition to use at home.

Even more important to the foreign student is the school's environment. Professional commitment is taken for granted in industrialized countries, but it may not yet exist in a developing country. The service environment, therefore, contributes to foreign student education so that he or she returns home not with an attitude of self-importance but with a commitment to do the job properly there. Postgraduate service to foreign students is also important, for when they return home, stagnation and bureaucratic difficulties may obstruct action.

Corrrespondingly, the school should make a commitment to its foreign students. If there are many such students, the school should promote the idea of community among them, encouraging them to discuss their problems with contemporaries who may be in similar situations. Foreign students may also broaden the perspectives of staff members and students. The education of foreign students represents a substantial contribution to world peace through mutual understanding and through creation of a more literate and tolerant world.

NOTES

1. This is the result of a private survey conducted for the Library Association in 1980.

2. Maureen Mackey, "The Selling of the Sheepskin," *Change* 12, No. 3 (1980), pp. 28–33.

3. College Entrance Examination Board, *A Role for Marketing in College Admissions* (New York: College Board, 1976).

4. Edward B.Fishe, "Ethical Issues in Recruiting Students," *New Directions for Higher Education* 9, No. 1 (1981), p. 43.

5. Rhoda Garoogian, "The Changing Role of Library Schools in Recruitment and Selection: Implications for the Profession," *Drexel Library Quarterly* 17, No. 3 (1981), pp. 75–93.

6. Wiliam R. Eshelman, "The Erosion of Library Education," *Library Journal* 108 (July 1983), pp. 1309–1312.

7. Garoogian.

6

ADVISEMENT AND PLACEMENT

Kieth C. Wright

When Richard Krzys and Gaston Litton considered the future of world librarianship, they saw that

Librarianship will have become a profession throughout the world, and its body of knowledge—library science—will by then be composed of the philosophy and theory adequate to the realization of the profession's problems and goals. Not only knowledge...but also freedom will be shown through the inner-directed mobility of the librarian of the future...no longer will a practitioner feel compelled to work in one city, rather, the global librarian will...be able to practice librarianship wherever in the world he or she might choose.[1]

This chapter discusses student advisement and placement service in the context of the total system of student program interactions. The advisement-placement process should be helpful in:

- Screening applicants for library education programs.
- Directing the dissatisfied toward other careers.
- Illustrating the range of library and information service career options.
- Guiding the student in acquiring the skills essential to specific career goals.
- Assisting the student/recent graduate in applying for and securing the first professional position.
- Evaluating library education program effectiveness from the perspective of graduates.
- Highlighting curricular changes necessitated by the field's changing job requirements and evaluating graduates' job success.

PROSPECTIVE STUDENT ADVISEMENT

The advisement process begins when an individual contacts the school to inquire about library education. Although most questions may focus on costs and required courses, others deal with the job market, state requirements, and compensation rates. In the United States salary information has been collected and organized by the American Library Association (ALA).[2] In England, the Library Association (LA) regularly surveys graduating students to determine their success in finding employment.

Questions may also be asked about the types of library education programs available. In many countries a variety of possibilities exist, depending on the type of career desired and the student's educational experience. American students have options at the undergraduate and graduate levels as well as between accredited and nonaccredited programs.[3] Credit hours can vary from twenty-eight to forty-eight for the same degree.[4]

A variety of joint degree programs such as history and library science, public administration and library science, or computer/information systems and library science are offered. They seem to be favored by large academic and research libraries. Enrollment options also vary. In certain programs students must be enrolled on a full-time basis for at least a portion of their studies, though most programs permit part-time study throughout the course of study. Within Commonwealth countries, postbaccalaureate programs are often full time, one year plus examination programs.

Recently, the LA provided a series of approved steps leading to registration as a chartered librarian. These steps showed a number of alternative combinations of work experiences, part-time study, full-time study, and licentiate work following study.

Prospective students need to learn about the job market both within and beyond the immediate geographic region. In most contexts, the individual with geographic mobility has the greatest chance of finding successful employment. Geographic areas vary in terms of library vacancies, and a thorough knowledge of the local and regional setting is essential to truthful student advisement. If used with care, job market and library education graduation surveys may also be helpful.[5]

In times of rapid social change, forecasting the job market for particular types of information personnel is difficult. Faculty members must not advise prospective students to go into specializations that will soon cease to exist or to take "deadend" positions from which advancement is impossible. The pace of change in technology and the world social order necessitates that students be prepared for information careers in areas that may not yet exist.

Prospective student advisement is complicated by the general attitude of the field toward library education programs. There has long been widespread dissatisfaction with the quality of library education, the lack of emphasis on specific skills training and/or theory (or both).[6] Much of the general public views the library from the perspective of clerical routines easily observed.

Librarians have been defined by what they do, and often library education has merely maintained the status quo. "One of the key features would appear to be reluctance amongst a majority of information professionals to acquire the skills necessary to establish and operate computer-based information systems."[7] The lag between what is actually happening in a field (social reality) and what librarians ought to be doing (intellectual ideals) has been illustrated by J. C. Colson. He has pointed out that computers were introduced into libraries (and library schools) in the late 1950s, yet graduation with no exposure to computers was still possible thirty years later.[8]

Krzys and Litton note that this resistance to change in practice has continued from the time of papyrus (to be preferred to typewritten cards) to the slow acceptance of audiovisuals. Individuals who are considering librarianship as a career should be assisted in overcoming the stereotypes about the librarian's roles. There is a concern that library education programs around the world should not only recruit but also select good quality students.

Library directors and supervisors frequently ask, "Why don't you send us a better qualified applicant?" To which the educator responds, "Why do your jobs require so little of our graduates beyond clerical activities?," or "Why is the pay so low for any interesting and challenging job?"

The advisement process also includes the interpretation of faculty (and university) admissions criteria and procedures. Historically, library education program criteria have been similar to those of other graduate and professional disciplines. Selection criteria can include: grade Point Averages (range 2.0–3.2 with A equals 4.0, as minimum); Graduate Record Examination scores (range: 650–1,000 as minimum)—the Miller Analogy Test is sometimes accepted; letters of recommendation (usually three); personal interviews (often optional); and previous library experience.

Exceptions to the usual selection criteria are based on academic records (often stressing the last two years of study); an increased number of references; library or professional work history; personal interviews (often required); unique or disadvantaged background; additional examinations; and taking courses as "special students" and submitting grades. Provisional admission with some performance provision ("B or better in the first 12 semester hours") is often granted to students who do not meet the stated selection criteria.

Selection criteria have long been suspect, especially the relationship between library school grades and such variables as pre-professional scholastic preparation, occupational experience, age, size of home community, and father's occupation. The selection process has two purposes: to choose potentially successful librarians and to choose potentially successful graduate students. Presently used selection criteria (including references, course work, grades, and standardized tests) have been found to be of little value in predicting which library student will achieve success in school.

The recent explosion of criticism of U.S. public education has stimulated a response from the library community which includes recommendations relating to library personnel recruitment, screening, preparation, compensation, and continuing education. A major problem in student recruitment and selection is that library education programs have no control over the compensation of librarians and information specialists.

An examination of job announcements from any type of library will show clearly that the skills expected of the "professional" are not adequately compensated by the employing institution. Even large national libraries publish job descriptions requiring experience, varied linguistic skills, and computer (or systems) experience combined with low starting salaries. It shuld be made abundantly clear to both prospective and enrolled students that job responsibilities and requisite skills will exceed the pay rate received. Library education schools "publicize" their programs in a variety of ways, but students recruit themselves.

MATRICULATED STUDENT ADVISEMENT

As the prospective student matriculates, the advisor must assume the role of university and program interpreter. Most library education programs exist within the context of a larger set of regulations and policies imposed by the higher education institution and by government commissions and agencies involved in public education regulation.

In addition to these larger policies and regulations, the library education program has a series of internal faculty regulations concerning courses of study, course sequencing, prerequisites for advanced courses, full-time student residency, and, often, a required core of courses. Although many of these requirements are spelled out in official university catalogs and unofficial program guides and brochures, faculty advisors cannot assume that students understand any of them. The catalogs and other material sent to prospective students by ALA-accredited library schools have been found to contain less than half of the information needed.

A large part of the advisement process is involved in clarifying requirements and in denying misinformation gathered from gossip sources. Nearly every library education program seems to acquire students who set themselves up as unofficial interpreters of program and field requirements.

Certain students come to library education programs with clear career goals in terms of type of service (reference, technical services, outreach, and so on), service population (adults, young adults, children, special populations) and type of library/information center (academic, public, school, special, independent broker). Other students clarify their goals after taking a number of courses. In both cases the faculty advisor's role is to clarify the necessary course experience for each career option considered.

While we may expect continued personnel needs in the future in several areas, such as children's/youth service and technical service, there has been a recent increase in the literature on "alternative careers." Some individuals enter information production and processing-distribution careers, often because traditional posts are unavailable. In certain countries, there seems to be a decline in traditional public and school library jobs. Because alternative careers often demand skills in journalism, packaging, production, and broadcasting (audio and video), as well as marketing of information products, the interested student must be advised to take courses and gain experience outside the traditional library education curriculum.

The student advisement process is complex because in many career areas students must satisfy not only university degree requirements but also the certification requirements of state governments or professional associations. As an example, U.S. students who wish to become school librarians must satisfy the requirements of state department of education certifying boards. Typically, they require specific course contents, titles, or competencies related to the role of the school librarian. In addition, many states require institutional recommendations from the library education program and school library media field experience, as well as background education courses. This may increase the number of courses far beyond those required for the library science degree.

T. Matsumura describes a similar set of external requirements and the resultant confusing variety of entry-level qualifications for Japanese librarians. J. Annastasiou defines three specific types of library operations and recruitment/education pathways for Swedish librarians, which result in different training and employment options for those who wish to work in public, academic, or special libraries.[9]

Occasionally, the faculty advisor must deal with the student who tries to prepare for work in all types of library settings. However, this is a difficult ambition. Conversations between library managers and educators often involve serious disagreement about the specific job skills and the amount of theory that should be included in preservice education. In these circumstances the faculty advisor should help the student to clarify specific career goals, select courses, and become involved in field experience that will lead to further clarification of career choices.

Obviously, the adequacy of faculty advisement with regard to courses and essential skills will depend on whether or not the instructor maintains close contact with the library/information world. He or she needs to know the kinds of decisions and problems facing practicing librarians. R. D. Stueart stresses the need for close cooperation to make the curriculum relevant to area personnel needs and to prepare students who will have the specific skills needed in the market.[10]

Another advisement problem concerns the student who is academically qualified but does not have the requisite skills for working with people in a library. Some prospective students, having undergone inter- or intrapersonal difficulties previously, see library/information work as a way of avoiding human interaction. Besides, they love books! Such situations are particularly distressing when the prospective student has been advised by his or her former employer to seek the safety of library/information work. The need for essential human relations skills in library work should be recognized.

STUDENT AND ALUMNI PLACEMENT SERVICE

Placement service for graduating students and alumni varies widely from informal contacts with potential employers, often by telephone, to more formal resumé service or job notice files and newsletters. Advising students approaching graduation should include (1) introduction to the job-hunting process, including sources of job vacancy information; preparation of a professional resumé; and training in the interviewing process as well as interview followup.

The job-hunting process begins with an understanding of job information sources. Formal sources include position vacancy announcements in library publications as well as a host of job information telephone numbers. (See *American Libraries* or the *Bowker Annual of Library and Book Trade Information* in the United States.) Many library education programs routinely receive published vacancy announcements from employing agencies.

In certain countries placement service is the responsibility not of the library education program but of the larger social order. In the People's Republic of China library program graduates are said to be assigned to libraries by the government according to the national need. M. N. Maack describes the French system in which nearly half of the students were admitted by examination in the *élèves-fonctionnaires*, received a stipend while they studied, and were obliged to serve for ten years in the French National Library Corps.[11]

V. S. Lesokhina describes the Soviet Union's program of specialist training for library workers as follows:

The state not only absorbs all expenses of specialist and advanced training, but it provides jobs to all graduates of higher and secondary institutions as well. [The state] must provide young specialists with the necessary living conditions, must materially and morally encourage their good works, and must provide conditions for the continuous rise of the general educational and professional level.[12]

N. D. Lane cites Australian studies of the number and types of vacancies as related to the number of library education program graduates.[13] She also notes the number of nonlibrary workforce career options advertised.

Placement services useful to the graduating student can include advising students on resumé preparations; training in job-seeking and interviewing skills; informing students about job information sources; maintaining files of job announcements and lists; distributing biographical sketches of recent graduates to prospective employers; visiting prospective employers to promote employment opportunities; and providing facilities and service so that prospective employers can interview graduating students at the university or at library meetings.

Training in formal resumé preparation will be essential for students lacking previous work experience. Certain universities maintain career guidance and placement offices that routinely sponsor resumé-writing and career orientation programs. In other settings the library education program must provide these activities on a regular basis.

Resumés play a crucial role in the employment-seeking process. Because of the large number of library position applicants, it is unlikely that every resumé receives careful attention. Students should be taught how to prepare a resumé which will:

1. Present the essential qualifications *relevant to the position advertised.*
2. List essential career goals and qualifications in a one-page "cover sheet."
3. Give the impression of careful, professional work.

Guidelines for building a resumé should be given, and a resumé-writing and job-hunting bibliography provided. The resumé should be planned for a specific job. It should show that the student has thought through career goals and has developed specific objectives in seeking a position. There is no such thing as a "good general resumé" Resumés must contain only the truth.

Individuals seeking positions in other countries should be particularly careful that their academic and employment histories are understood in the context of the potential employer's culture. Copies of academic awards are often requested. In many situations, a variety of government forms—both in the country of origin and the country of prospective employment—must be filed. Considerable time should be allowed for these forms to be processed.

Preparation for interviews can be helpful as students seek employment. Interview training may include sources of information about the prospective employer; advice on appearance, including dress and attitude; recommendations on information which the applicant should have available for the employer; questions which the interviewer can "legally" ask; and questions which the interviewees will want to ask.

Workshops can be useful in developing job interviewing skills. They can include information on what employers are seeking, often presented by a panel of library personnel officers. Successful techniques include use of videotaped interviews with critiques, role-playing, and sending students out to interview for jobs and report to the class.

ALUMNI FOLLOWUP

Followup of graduates is important. If a school knows what its recent graduates are facing in terms of skills required, adequacy of library education in those skill areas, and new challenges, then it can improve curriculum evaluation and student advisement. In a time when institutional accreditation evaluation has moved from measuring "inputs" to "outputs" or "products," one of the major "output" measures should be alumni career success as measured by the alumni *and* their employers.

Two of the self-study questions used by the ALA Committee on Accreditation are, how does the school learn of the success or failure of its graduates in the library profession, and how is this information used in the school's planning for the future?

Curriculum planning based in part on alumni and employer evaluation will not only provide better student preparation but also serve as a major recruiting device. Followup is part of a cyclical process involving the identification of competency requirements, determination of education and training requirements, design and implementation of curricula for competency attainment, and demonstration of competency achievement through performance.

As schools modify their programs to meet new needs, they will attract prospective students by disseminating program brochures and catalogs. This effect can be seen in the emphasis on "information management" in the publicity issued by certain schools and the rapid change of school names to include the terms *information studies, communication,* or *informatics.*

CONCLUSION

The advisement-placement process occurs in the wider context of the larger society. Because of the vast societal differences, the library education process varies widely around the world. Equivalance and reciprocity of qualifications seem to be far off. However, the rate of technological change and worldwide information dissemination is accelerating rapidly. The dream of being able to recruit, educate, and place students freely throughout the world may be closer than we realize.

NOTES

1. "Our Professional Destiny: A Global Librarianship," in R. Krzys and G. Litton, *World Librarianship: A Comparative Study* (New York: Marcel Dekker, 1983), p. 202.

2. M. J. Lynch, *Survey of Librarian Salaries* (Chicago: American Library Association, 1984).

3. K. A. Schmidt, "The Other Librarians," *Journal of Education for Librarianship* 24 (Spring 1984), pp. 223–232.

4. Association for Library and Information Science Education, *Library and Information Science Education Statistical Report, 1984* (State College, Pa.: ALISE, 1984).

5. J. D. Lockwood, *Employers' Expectations of Recent Library School Graduates: A Review of the Recent Literature* (ERIC Document Reproduction Services, 1975, no. ED 114 079); M. D. Cooper, "Projections of the Demand for Librarians in the United States," *Library Quarterly* 54 (October 1983), pp. 331–367.

6. S. Rothstein, "The 97 year-old Mystery Solved At Last: Why People Really Hate Library Schools," *Library Journal* 110 (1985), pp. 41–48.

7. D. Gleave, "Structural Change Within the Information Profession," *ASLIB Proceedings* 37 (1985), p. 117.

8. J. C. Colson, "Professional Ideals and Social Realities," *Journal of Education for Librarianship* 21 (Winter 1980), p. 91–108.

9. T. Matsumura, "The Development of Library and Information Education in Japan," *Journal of Education for Librarianship* 23 (Fall 1982), pp. 43–54; J. Annastasiou, "Training for Library Work in Sweden," *Special Libraries* 69 (1978), pp. 71–76.

10. R. D. Stueart, *Cooperation Between Library Schools and the Profession* (ERIC Document Reproduction Services, 1975, ED 116646).

11. M. N. Maack, "Library Education in France," *Journal of Education for Librarianship* 24 (January 1984), pp. 283–286.

12. V. S. Lesokhina, "Problems of Training Library Personnel in the USSR," *Journal of Education for Library and Information Science* 25 (Spring 1985), pp. 200–206.

13. N. D. Lane, "Education for Information Professionals in Australia," *Journal of Education for Library and Information Science* 25 (Summer 1985), pp. 326–332.

BIBLIOGRAPHY

American Library Association. *Realities: Educational Reform in a Learning Society.* Chicago: American Library Association, n.d.

Morris, L. R. "The Rise and Fall of the Library Job Market." *American Libraries* 12 (September 1981), pp. 557–558.

Myers, M. "Guide to Library Placement Sources." In *Bowker Annual of Library and Book Trade Information.* New York: R. R. Bowker Co., 1985, pp. 340–356 (an annual article).

Stueart, R. D. "Great Expectations: Library and Information Science at the Crossroads." *Library Journal* 106 (1981), pp. 1989–1992.

7
TOWARD A FACULTY SUPPORT PROGRAM FOR INTERNATIONALIZING LIBRARY EDUCATION

Edwin S. Gleaves

Many faculty concerns are international. To a point, therefore, it is unnecessary to speak of an international dimension to library education. Many aspects of a faculty and support staff program for internationalizing library education are difficult to distinguish from the normal concerns that characterize any occupational teaching program. On the other hand, any program that does not recognize the universality of professional concerns runs the risk of operating within a national vacuum and thereby cuts itself off from certain of the main currents of thought and practice in its field. On the surface, this recognition seems to come at the cognitive level, that is, the teaching of courses that are international in character.

Internationalizing library education is essentially a process through which an occupational school must go to achieve a dimension transcending the purely national. Such a process involves internationalizing the curriculum and all other school facets. It also requires a strong faculty support program characterized by the following practices:

1. Advertising vacancies worldwide.
2. Selecting from a worldwide candidate pool.
3. Identifyng faculty members with an international interest.
4. Promoting cooperative international exchanges and faculty projects.
5. Supporting foreign assignments for faculty members.
6. Rewarding international activities in promotion and tenure.

ADVERTISING VACANCIES AND SELECTING FROM A GLOBAL CANDIDATE POOL

Library schools traditionally employ two kinds of "foreign" faculty members: (1) those who normally live and work in other countries and

(2) those who originate from other countries but are permanent residents of the host country. Both categories present excellent potential for enriching the faculty (and staff) of any school intent on achieving an international dimension.

North American schools have made significant progress in hiring foreign (non-American and non-Canadian) faculty, particularly those from other English-speaking countries such as Great Britain and Australia. Because Anglo-American names are not distinctive among faculty rolls, without conducting a full survey it is difficult to ascertain how many faculty fall into this category.

Canadian schools have utilized a higher percentage of colleagues from other countries than have American schools, and at least three of them (Dalhousie, McGill, and Western Ontario) have had foreign-born deans/directors. Among the American schools, at least six (California-Berkeley, Chicago, Oklahoma, Pratt, Rosary, and Wisconsin-Milwaukee) have recently had deans/directors of other national origins. Instructors come from a number of nations, including Australia, Austria, Bangladesh, Egypt, France, Great Britain, Hungary, India, Iran, Ireland, Mexico, Russia, Taiwan, West Germany, and Yugoslavia.

Notably few have been the representatives of Third World countries. Even the University of Puerto Rico, an associate member of the Association for Library and Information Science Education (ALISE), has relied most heavily for faculty on native Puerto Ricans, North Americans, and Spaniards.

Temporary and part-time lecturers can also contribute to a program. A number of programs in Europe, Latin America, and North America have invited professors from abroad to teach during a limited time period or for a year or more. For example, over the past decade, Peabody College has contracted with visiting faculty from Australia, Colombia, and Great Britain for summer teaching assignments. The University of Guanajuato in Mexico has also invited a number of professors for short-term assignments.

Visiting international faculty require special attention to ensure that their courses relate to the overall program while providing new perspectives to students. Someone new to a country may not be aware of many cultural and linguistic subtleties that can often lead to embarrassing situations. Teaching methodologies and standards for grading also requires agreement between instructor and faculty.

The University of Pittsburgh has made notable progress in internationalizing its faculty and student body. Its international aspects are summarized in the following letter:

Both the faculty and the student body reflect a strong international aspect. The seven-member founding faculty included distinguished librarians from Australia, England, Austria, and Iran. Over the years, instruction has been enriched by a succession of visiting lecturers and scholars from abroad.[1]

The present twenty-eight member permanent faculty of the University of Pittsburgh includes six who were born and/or educated outside the United States and fifteen individuals with significant teaching or consulting experience in Europe, Latin America, Asia, Africa, or the Middle East. In recent years, the school has engaged in major research and development projects in Spain, Saudi Arabia, Iran, and the People's Republic of China.

Approximately 15 percent of the school's graduate student body is drawn from other countries. In 1984–1985 this group comprised sixty-one Master's and doctoral students from twenty-eight foreign countries. In the most recent curriculum revision leading to the Master of Library Science degree, the faculty adopted the following as one of the eight specific program objectives: "In order to provide students with a unified interdisciplinary curriculum which is more than an aggregate of courses, the MLS program will incorporate . . . an international dimension which reflects intercultural and cross cultural perspectives.[2] It is unlikely that any other library school in the world—with the possible exception of the College of Librarianship, Wales—has developed such a broad international dimension.

IDENTIFYING FACULTY MEMBERS WITH
INTERNATIONAL INTERESTS

Most of the qualifications expected of an international instructor apply to all other instructors as well: (1) academic preparation; (2) teaching experience and ability; (3) previous professional experience; and (4) ability to carry out relevant research.

It is more difficult to identify the qualifications that mark a person as being especially well qualified to work in international projects. Except for history and occasional language courses, few faculty members have had formal course work in any aspect of international relations. Usually, persons interested in international affairs have gravitated in that direction because of other professional concerns which can be advanced through international contacts. Examples of such concerns include international standards, acquisition of foreign material, bibliography and the publishing trade in other nations, and international projects of special import (such as UNESCO National Information Systems).

Indeed, the community of "internationalists" is highly fragmented along special interest lines, and many persons with common international interests are unknown to each other. They may meet in certain organizations such as the Seminar of the Acquisition of Latin American

Materials, the International Federation for Documentation, the International Federation of Library Associations and Institutions, the International Board on Books for Young People, and the national library association committee.

ALISE has addressed the issue of bringing together faculty members with an international interest. Following a successful 1981 inter-American conference, ALISE established an International Committee. Among its early (and most notable) activities was a pre-conference workshop on "Education for Research and Research for Education" at the 1982 IFLA conference. The workshop brought together library education researchers from Argentina, Brazil, Chile, Colombia, Costa Rica, Haiti, Jamaica, Mexico, Paraguay, Venezuela, Canada, and the United States.

Another International Committee project attempted to identify American and Canadian faculty with good language fluency. In each directory issue, the *Journal for Library and Information Science Education* lists those "Faculty Members Qualified to Teach Library and Information Science in a Foreign Language." The latest list includes 24 languages spoken by approximately 100 instructors. Other faculty members interested in international librarianship can be identified through publications, consultant reports, membership in international library organizations, and direct contact with librarians in other countries.

Although possession of these interests may not be a criterion for all school faculty members, certainly any school that aspires to develop a significant international dimension should, within legal limits, consider prospective faculty members who are themselves "international" or who, through education or experience, evince a strong international librarianship interest. Such faculty can contribute to the educational program in several ways. In addition to teaching such courses as international and comparative librarianship, they can provide an international perspective on all courses and activities. A visiting professor can also serve as a consultant to the regular instructor in developing new course material and teaching strategies.

Joint research projects are often easier to implement than teaching assignments. Frequently, United States' Fulbright lecturers have carried out research projects in addition to teaching. These activities can also lead to international exchange of material such as the cooperative program between the University of Western Ontario and the University of Guanajuato.[3]

PROMOTING INTERNATIONAL EXCHANGES AND COOPERATIVE FACULTY PROJECTS

International exchanges are difficult to arrange because of (1) different salaries and living standards from one country to another; (2) different academic calendars; (3) different faculty academic qualifications and teaching requirements; (4) different languages; and (5) different philosophies and styles of teaching.

Professional exchange programs are rare. Only one North American school has maintained an international faculty exchange program: the University of Montreal with the Superior Normal School for Librarians in Villeurbanne, Lyons—as well as infrequent exchanges with schools in Senegal and Switzerland. To my knowledge, the only inter-American exchange has been made between the University of Western Ontario and two Caribbean universities: the University of the West Indies and the University of Puerto Rico. Since 1972, thirteen Western Ontario instructors have taught courses in the West Indies, while three from each one of the Caribbean universities have taught at Western Ontario.

However difficult to arrange, the prospect for international exchanges stays alive. The International and Comparative Group of the Library Association has established the Bureau for International Library Staff Exchange at the College of Librarianship, Wales, to facilitate exchange programs. The American Library Association International Relations Round Table and the International Relations Committee are exploring bases for exchanges with other countries.

Vanderbilt University's Peabody College has developed a set of exchange guidelines that attempts to address certain of the difficulties inherent in exchanges by putting greater responsibilities on the home (sending) institution than on the host (receiving) institution.[4] (See Appendix I.) The unique aspect of these guidelines relates to student research and study. Careful arrangements are made for the type of activity in which the student is to engage. It is the home institution's responsibility to grant academic credit, and this usually involves blanket provision for giving a certain number of credits.

Participants are assisted in developing a schedule of audited course work or research overseas that becomes a regular part of a program leading to the Master's, specialist, or doctoral degree. Most students plan to spend a concentrated term or summer overseas. The Peabody faculty has agreed to permit up to twelve semester hours of credit for study abroad during one semester, provided both parties agree to the particulars in advance through a letter of understanding.

Peabody provides student travel grants for overseas study and research. Awards are keyed to the extra travel costs directly associated with the field within an overseas setting and to the amount of time devoted to study and research. Applicants registered for at least twelve hours are eligible for up to $1,500 of airfare assistance. Occasional travel grants are made to faculty members in lieu of stipends for outstanding performance in teaching, publishing, or administration.

SUPPORTING FACULTY MEMBERS' FOREIGN ASSIGNMENTS

Another means of achieving an international dimension is through foreign assignments for regular full-time faculty members. Library educators have had ample opportunity to contribute to development in other countries through a panoply of international programs. For example, over the past twenty-five years, Peabody faculty members have been significantly involved in developing library programs in Brazil, Colombia, Costa Rica, Japan, Korea, Mexico, Sierra Leone, Taiwan, and Venezuela.

The sponsoring agencies for these assignments, ranging from a few weeks to two years, were the Fulbright Program and the United States Information Agency (USIA), the Organization of American States (OAS), UNESCO, and various national organizations such as the National Council on Science and Technology of Mexico and the National Library and Information System of Venezuela. These and other agencies are important sources of funding for the citizens of many countries. The OAS Library Development Program has sponsored numerous projects, including library education program support in Brazil, Colombia, Costa Rica, Jamaica, Mexico, and Paraguay, with special interest in the Inter-American Library School, Medellín, Colombia. Many national faculty of these schools have studied in North America with OAS support, and OAS has sent a number of North American instructors to those schools. UNESCO has supported many Third World information-related activities, most notably through the UNISIST program and its fellowships and study grants. The United Nations (UN) sponsors both a graduate study program and a graduate student intern program to provide means of better understanding the UN and related agencies.

The British Council supports library development in many Commonwealth countries, with particular success in Jamaica, Ghana, Nigeria, Kenya, Singapore, Sri Lanka, and India. Other developing countries have received technical and financial assistance from the United Kingdom Ministry of Overseas Development.

The International Graduate Summer School at the College of Librarianship, Wales, provides education and training in a worldwide context. Academic credit is offered by both the College and the University of Pittsburgh. Financial support is often provided through UN agencies, the Commonwealth Foundation, the Africa Educational Trust, and British Council representatives.

Certain agencies provide support for citizens of many countries to study, travel, and/or conduct research abroad. Eisenhower Fellowships enable non-U.S. citizens to undertake a period of professional observation in the United States that will benefit their country. Various Institute of International Education (IIE) programs promote educational and cultural exchanges at all levels; for example, 800 leaders and specialists visit the United States annually through IIE, which also provides administrative support to 1,000 researchers and advisors on technical assistance projects in other countries. The Fulbright-Hayes Student Program provides support for 600 graduate students per year to live and study abroad.

The Fulbright program finances educational exchange by making grants for U.S. citizens and for nationals of other countries to cover university lecturing, advanced research, graduate study, and elementary and secondary school teaching. USIA administers the program with the help of binational educational commissions and U.S. embassies in 120 countries. Country schools can request lecturers and suggest the fields needed. In a typical year there are about ten announcements for library science teaching and research for Americans.

For 1986–1987, Fulbright awards in library science were announced in Bangladesh, Brazil, the People's Republic of China, Finland, Indonesia, Jamaica, Spain, and Sri Lanka. Other special lecturing and research awards are available from time to time, such as the Expanded Research and Lecturing Program with the Republics of Central America, which for 1986–1987 listed two additional awards in library science. Selection of Fulbright senior scholars and researchers is handled by the Council on the International Exchange of Scholars. (A guide to exchange literature appears in Appendix II.)

REWARDING INTERNATIONAL ACTIVITIES THROUGH PROMOTION AND TENURE

In certain countries, such as Australia, international activities are valued highly by educational administrators, and university faculty are encouraged to take their sabbatical leaves abroad. In many Third World countries, a degree from a European or a North American university is a favorable indication of an instructor's willingness to travel and study abroad.

Few American universities give special consideration for international service except in areas in which such service is expected: language programs, international and comparative education, and so on. International meetings may bring special recognition, but teaching for a year in a distant country, for example, may be viewed unfavorably by American university administrators.

Although the international element may reflect favorably on the university, often administrators simply do not know how to evaluate such an experience. The instructor who teaches in a developing country is sometimes thought of as an academic missionary whose zeal may have outrun good judgment. And the fact that certain less effective instructors choose to teach abroad does not improve the image of the rest of the field. If, on the other hand, the assignment is made through a prestigious granting organization which involves a high level of competition, then the overseas instructor can become an asset to the university.

The school can deal with this problem in at least two ways. First, if internationalizing the program is indeed a goal, then that goal should be included in the formal statement of school goals and objectives. When recognition is given for international activities, it should have a philosophical base on which to rest. Secondly, the school should include international activities, explicitly stated, in its own criteria for promotion and tenure and, to the extent possible, have those criteria reviewed and approved by the university administration. Even if the university-wide criteria do not deal explicitly with international contributions, the fact that the school has its own criteria recognizing them should give credence to its recommendations.

CONCLUSION: EDUCATING FOR THE GLOBAL VIEW

Internationalizing the faculty should result in a school in which faculty, staff, and students maintain a global view of the field. The ultimate goal of global education is "to build a world society in which we can live politically as well as scientifically. Most serious world affairs students agree that we are long past the time when such education was an ideal; it is now an imperative for survival."[5]

In no area is a global view more essential than in the information sciences. This begins with the simple need to see the world and see it whole through library collections. If tomorrow's librarians are to broaden their perspectives, then they must first be exposed to faculty with an international viewpoint, one that cannot be gained without looking beyond national borders. Such a perspective should be the goal of library education programs throughout the world.

NOTES

1. Letter from Thomas Galvin to Edwin S. Gleaves, July 24, 1985, updating a previous letter to Laverne Carroll quoted in "Library Education," in John F. Harvey, ed., *Comparative and International Library Science* (Metuchen, N.J.: Scarecrow Press, 1977), p. 153.

2. Ibid.

3. Edwin S. Gleaves, "La Investigación en las Escuelas de Bibliotecología y Ciencias de la Información en América Latina y Norteamérica: Modelos de Cooperación," *Revista Interamericana de Bibliotecología* 6 (January-December 1983), p. 45.

4. The guidelines were modeled in part on "Exchanges of Staff Between

Melbourne State College and Other Tertiary Education Institutions" (Melbourne: Melbourne State College, n.d.).

5. See Edwin S. Gleaves, "All in One Boat: Educating for the Global View," *Proceedings of the Sixty-second Annual Meeting of the Tennessee College Association* (Nashville, Tenn.: Vanderbilt University, 1984), pp. 15–21.

BIBLIOGRAPHY

ALA World Encyclopedia of Library and Information Services. Chicago: American Library Association, 1980.
Bowden, Russell. "Improving Library Education in the Developing Countries." *UNESCO Bulletin for Libraries* 30 (September-October 1976), pp. 255–261.
Jackson, Miles M., Jr., ed., *Comparative and International Librarianship.* Westport, Conn.: Greenwood Press, 1970.
Jackson, Miles M., ed. *International Handbook of Contemporary Developments in Librarianship.* Westport, Conn.: Greenwood Press, 1981.
Krzys, Richard and Gaston Litton. *World Librarianship: A Comparative Study.* New York: Marcel Dekker, 1983.
Library Times International. Vol. 1. Oshgosh, Wis.: 1984–   .

APPENDIX I:
PRINCIPLES OF AGREEMENT GOVERNING THE COOPERATIVE RELATIONSHIP BETWEEN GEORGE PEABODY COLLEGE FOR TEACHERS OF VANDERBILT UNIVERSITY
AND

We believe that the cause of education and the pursuit of scholarly inquiry may be well served when faculty and students from one institution become more closely acquainted with the work of colleagues in sister institutions of higher education. The goals may be accomplished through exchange of faculty and students, visits between the campuses, and extension of other courtesies. Toward this end, official representatives of the institutions named above have drafted this nonbinding agreement of cooperation.

GENERAL GUIDELINES

I. Faculty Exchanges

Faculty exchanges will be considered on an individual basis. In some cases a faculty member from one institution may wish to visit colleagues at the cooperating institution and merely desires the courtesies of assistance with visas, housing, and scheduled appointments. Such visits may be enhanced by meetings with departments, seminars, receptions, or other opportunities for exchanging ideas. If the faculty member is to teach or conduct research on a regular basis, more formal arrangements will be made. The two cooperating institutions may seek assistance from third parties to fund visiting scholars or arrange faculty exchanges.

II. Student Research and Study

Student overseas research and study plans also will be arranged on an individual basis. A student who wishes to spend time on the campus of the overseas cooperating institution must apply through his or her institution. In consultation with faculty advisors, the student will develop a comprehensive plan for study and research.

Management. Appropriate arrangements for student research and study shall be made between the cooperating institutions. The host institution will review the tentative plan for study and/or research, designate a faculty member to work with the student, and, to the extent permitted by law, forward periodic reports concerning student progress. In addition to faculty advisors, each institution will designate one faculty member to coordinate the overall program. The Coordinator will be the contact for sending inquiries about faculty members or students who would like to participate in the program. The Coordinator will also serve as the institution's continuing link between visitors, faculty advisors, administrative offices, and the community.

Plan of Study. A plan of study for research must be approved by both institutions. Copies of the plan will be made available to the institutions for dissemination to appropriate faculty members and administrators. While subject to modification, the approved plan will constitute the general outline of expected goals and activities for the time the student is studying or conducting research in the host country.

Tuition and Fees. If the student desires credit for the activity, the credit will normally be in the form of individual study, field experience, or research credit *from his or her own institution*. Thus, there may be no need for matriculation or tuition and fee payment to the overseas institution. If permitted by the two institutions, the student may include in this plan the auditing of courses or seminars on the host campus. If the student wishes to receive official credit from the host institution, he or she will need to make application, be admitted, and pay appropriate tuition and fees to that institution.

III. Travel and Living Expenses

Costs of travel, living expenses, and incidentals will be the individual responsibility of the faculty member or student who participates in the program. In some cases, the home institution may wish to assist with these expenses. A third party, such as a governmental agency or international foundation, may be approached for financial assistance. The host institution may provide non-financial assistance in arranging for housing, informal course auditing, setting up appointments and research contacts, and serving as a base of operations for the visiting faculty member or student.

IV. Information Exchanges

The respective Deans, International Coordinators, faculty advisors, and others who are concerned with the program will endeavor to meet regularly. These progress and planning meetings may occur at either institution. In addition, in years when there have been exchange of faculty or students, a written summary of the activity will be prepared for each institution. The institutions will supplement these reports and sharing activities by forwarding copies of the college catalogs, newsletters, research reports, announcements, and other printed matter that would be of interest to faculty members and student scholars at the cooperating institution.

V. Special Conferences

A major purpose of the cooperative arrangement is to further the dissemination and exchange of knowledge. Therefore, opportunities for special international conferences to share results of faculty and student research, to plan for cross-cultural studies and other joint ventures, and to promote closer relationships between the two institutions may be sought. When the means are available, such special conferences and research seminars will be held alternately on the two campuses. Administrators and scholars from the two institutions also may seek opportunities where their joint research endeavors can be presented in special sessions at conferences sponsored by international organizations.

LIMITATIONS

These principles of cooperation are intended as an informal set of guidelines without the force of contract or law. They represent the desire of two institutions to engage in cooperative exchange of faculty, students, and ideas to improve and extend scholarly inquiry. If either institution feels that the principles of cooperation should be ended or modified, a formal letter of explanation should be sent to the cooperating institution. In the event of such change, however, it is expected that courtesies extended to faculty or students currently at an overseas location will be extended in a way that will not be detrimental to them or to their work.

In compliance with U.S. federal law, including the provisions of Title IX of the Education Amendments of 1972 and Sections 503 and 504 of the Rehabilitation Act of 1973, Vanderbilt University does not discriminate on the basis of race, sex, religion, color, natural or ethnic origin, age, handicap, or military service in its administration of educational policies, programs, or activities; its admissions policies; scholarships and loan programs; athletic and other University-administered programs; or employment.

AFFIRMATION OF PRINCIPLES OF AGREEMENT

As an affirmation of the principles of cooperation outlined in the sections above, we hereby sign in behalf of our respective organizations, subject to the stated limitations.

Signature and Title	Institution	Date

APPENDIX II:
SOURCES OF INFORMATION FOR WORK AND STUDY ABROAD

A useful source of information on study abroad is *Study Abroad/Etudes à l'Étranger/Estudios en el extranjero*, vol. 1– , 1948– (Paris: UNESCO). In 2,600 entries, this work lists programs in many academic and professional fields in 115 countries. Part I lists international scholarships and other forms of financial aid, and Part II lists international study programs. This work is in English, French, and Spanish. Consisting of over 1,000 pages, it is designed primarily for the student and not the instructor.

Opportunities for teaching abroad are more difficult to locate. One would do well to get on the mailing lists of those organizations that sponsor instructors and scholars. A useful general source is *Intercultural Education: An Information Service of Education and World Affairs* (New York: Education and World Affairs, 1969). A promising new work is *International Funding Guide: Resources and Funds for International Activities at Colleges and Universities* (Washington, D.C.: American Association of State Colleges and Universities, 1985).

An old standby is the *Annual Register of Grant Support: A Directory of Funding Sources* (Chicago: Marquis, 1984), for nonrepayable financial support from a great variety of agencies. It focuses on programs that accept applicants from the United States or Canada or directly benefit those two countries.

Of more direct interest for library educators is Diane Stine's *Librarian's Directory of Exchange Programs/Study Tours/Funding Sources and Job Opportunities Outside of the United States* (Chicago: American Library Association, 1982). The section on job opportunities is useful for persons who wish to continue their careers abroad. A summary of exchange programs is also provided.

8

AN INTERNATIONAL DATA AND INFORMATION COLLECTION AND RESEARCH PROGRAM

Jashu Patel, Frank L. Schick, and John F. Harvey

In order to make a positive contribution to international information management, or library and information science, each information or library school should maintain an international research program. To maintain a research program, each school must operate a cooperative international data and information collection program to provide the raw material for research programs. This chapter will describe research methods and programs and the statistical and information collection programs to support them. The collection programs will cover all national and international subfields, but the research programs described will cover only international research.

INTERNATIONAL RESEARCH PROGRAM COOPERATION

The international research program objectives of the information school should be to make a strong positive contribution to knowledge in appropriate subject fields and to educate students in research methods and evaluation. Research findings should be used to improve information management and form the basis for further research. Interest in these projects should be stimulated.

The school research program should be organized around topics useful in increasing its international and regional contributions. They are usually more significant than national or local topics. A large variety of appropriate topics is available. Some represent the extension of national problems onto a regional basis, problems existing within many nations, while others represent problems existing between nations.

Student research projects should use varied international sources, especially the raw material assembled in the school's data and information collections. The research and the data and information collection programs must be closely integrated, since the data and information collection program will serve the research program and must be directly responsive to changes in it.

Faculty members in conference with perceptive practitioners and theorists should identify useful international research projects. Many projects will require a series of discussions and studies to identify their composition, what substudies to carry out, and in what order before a useful approach can be designed. As part of these discussions, the group must identify the fundamental question(s) on which each project rests. The search for fuller understanding of national and international problems should be the guiding principle of all projects.

As an eventual part of their research and service program, schools should cooperatively allocate subject specialization responsibility among them according to faculty and student interests and strengths. Allocation should be made on an international networking basis with each nation's schools taking responsibility first for national and then for international research topics. For instance, perhaps Soviet Union schools will take responsibility for children's service research and Iranian schools for religious information service, at least for Islamic mosque libraries, because of each nation's emphases.

All possible information subfields should be included in these allocations. Certain topics, such as public library use, will probably interest many schools, while others, such as art collection acquisitions, will interest few. Some schools may participate in many fields while others select only a few. The extent and quality of the school's research collection may influence its choice of subfield. Along with topic acceptance will go responsibility to collect data and information comprehensively in that subfield.

The degree of school interest and of the national information field's involvement in a subject area should be considered. In addition, the ability to fund large projects should influence subfield choice. The participating schools should agree on sharing data and information use without limitation, and on using uniform, internationally standardized data and information formats and definitions.

An international clearinghouse that lists accepted thesis and dissertation research topics should be developed as part of this cooperative program. It should list all projects by researcher, topic, subtopic, and school in a computer file and publish the indexed printout quarterly. Thesis topic duplication can then be avoided and similar projects coordinated. Partial journal lists of accepted academic research and doctoral dissertation proposals are available.[1]

Cooperative international research projects must be prioritized, which can be done by using several criteria. First is the importance of the question to world information management—its significance—and second is its independent versus dependent position vis-à-vis related projects. The number of nations in which this problem is significant is also important.

An international research subject allocation plan may appear to assume that every nation's schools teach the same information subfield theory and practice, faculty strength being the only difference among them. While there must be much similarity among world schools, no doubt much difference still remains, only part of which depends on national political philosophy differences. To the extent that school-to-school differences are significant, then research program adaptations and compromises must be made and subcategories established to accommodate them.

In contrast to some high-level schools in developed countries, a cooperative international approach may be impractical for certain nations because school development level enables it to carry out very little research. However, still other nations may be working on an intermediate level and can start by establishing a subject division of responsibility among national schools. Experience in doing that will be useful when cooperation can be extended to the international level.

RESEARCH METHODS

In identifying and discussing research problems, certain terms must be clearly defined.[2] In addition Douglas Waples advises researchers to outline the proposed investigation through the following elements: (1) title and full problem statement, (2) definition of terms and scope limitation, (3) previous studies in the field, (4) analysis of subproblems and hypotheses, (5) designation and evaluation of sources, (6) types of evidence desired and methods of obtaining data from appropriate sources, (7) rough topical manuscript organization, (8) cost estimate, and (9) tentative time schedule.[3]

Richard Krzys and Gaston Litton have enumerated seven methods for serious international researchers: (1) historical, (2) survey, (3) case, (4) statistical, (5) experimental, (6) composite methods (which include any of those above), and (7) the comparative method. In planning, researchers must identify practical projects. They should consider the strengths and weaknesses in their backgrounds in education, experience, financial assistance, and time. And which library school is best qualified to carry out a specific project?[4]

Empirical investigations are conducted to learn something about the world. Motivations for research studies vary, with some researchers wanting to learn something new, others to solve an immediate problem, and still others to test a theory or determine whether something until now only hypothesized actually exists.[5] Researchers may wish to investigate international topics because of their mutual concern.

Since 1960 many educators have predicted a rise in interest in internationalized library education. Nasser Sharify has written: " 'As technology expands even further in the future, interest in international information will continue to grow rapidly.' "[6]

The Comparative Research Method

In support of the comparative research method, Thomas Galvin made the following observation: "we have much to learn from colleagues in other countries because in many cases their achievements in developing service are far more significant than our own (USA). I think, for example, of the achievement in conservation and preservation in Spain and of that of Jamaica public libraries in adult literacy."[7]

After selecting a comparative research topic, the researcher must plan a literature search. Certain educators have designed checklists for a total approach to a country's librarianship.[8] With regard to sources useful for dissertations, U.S. library literature should be freed from its parochialism. Because of its objectives, scope, coverage, files, collections, services, and potential uses, UNESCO's International Information System on Research in Documentation represents an international research clearinghouse.[9] *Dissertation Abstracts International* lists U.S. dissertations, and provides information on purposes, methodology, conclusions, and further research suggestions. Dissertation lists from the United Kingdom are also available.[10]

Krzys and Litton have advocated that researchers rigorously employ the comparative method, a procedure that facilitates the study of data concerning two or more comparable library phenomena, collected through any of the seven methods described above, juxtaposed, and analyzed to formulate logical hypotheses and conclusions.

J. Periam Danton discusses the meaning of comparative and international library science and suggests that a study in comparative librarianship must include: (1) a cross-societal or cross-cultural element, which does *not* necessarily mean a cross-country/cross-national element; (2) actual comparisons, which involve more than simply the juxtaposition of like data from the two or more societies being studied; and (3) explanation, or at least discussion, of the observed similarities and differences.[11] He adds that points (2) and (3) suggest elaboration. The goal of the comparativist is analysis of the phenomena which are to be observed in order to try to determine not *how* things are, but *why*.

Sylvia Simsova believes that comparative librarianship is firmly established in schools of librarianship as a method of training, and that greater emphasis should be placed in developing doctoral programs. Comparative librarianship should seek to establish contacts in two directions: with other comparative disciplines and with research in librarianship.[12] According to Anthony Thompson, Simsova "distinguishes two kinds of comparative studies and defines them: (1) area study equals a study of the whole field in one geographical area; (2) problem case study equals a study of a problem in one geographical area."[13]

More research studies based on the comparative method are needed for scholarly investigation, because, according to Danton, most of the literature described as comparative librarianship is thin, largely narrative and descriptive, and often neither comparative nor in conformity with even minimal scholarly investigation standards.

In carrying out the project, the student must (1) state the problem being investigated, and (2) formulate a hypothesis which "is the best statement one can make at the beginning of a study as to the relationship thought to exist between two or more designated variables."[14] It is vital, therefore, that research methods instructors include a comparative study unit. The unit should include comparative studies definitions and explanations, comparative method examples—general and specific—and case studies.

Data Collection

Danton explains that data collection has been confused with research and, when cross-societal, with comparison. Data collection, whether done by the investigator or by someone else, is an indispensable research step essential in testing any hypothesis. But mere compilation is not research. It is the analysis and treatment of facts, and the conclusions and explanations that this analysis enables one to draw that, together, justify speaking of a piece of research.

A "framework" is required within which the data may be collected: In making a comparative study data collection and analysis must be organized so that systematic relations become clear. Having set up a hypothesis about the possible results, we begin with a framework within which to collect information. This will not at first be elaborate, little more than a general conception of the problem. It will crystallize into framework as we learn more.[15]

The researcher should develop a data collection program based on scientific research characteristics: an awareness of the presence of hypotheses and assumptions, careful definition of terms, insistence on evidence rather than opinion, limitations, causal element, universal application, and results. In investigating public libraries, for instance, it is important to seek a better understanding of their genesis and to understand why public libraries developed more rapidly in some environments than in others. The different forms and specific features in various cultural zones must be studied and finally we must ascertain how to insure their development.[16]

The Role of the Faculty Member

With regard to the faculty member's research role, A. Neelameghan makes the following suggestions:

1. Adopt measures to orient the trainee's thinking to systematic methods conducive to research work at a later stage.
2. Intimately study each trainee's aptitudes and handicaps through personal contact.
3. Organize tutorials, group study, and colloquia to encourage and facilitate cooperative endeavor and learning productive library use.
4. Introduce small piece investigation—as class assignment, term paper, or dissertation—to help the trainee's first research steps.
5. Introduce the trainee at the appropriate stages to different methods of approach in finding problem solutions.
6. Use all opportunities within and outside the classroom to inculcate in the trainee the right spirit and correct attitude toward research.
7. Guide and encourage the trainee's research efforts.
8. Continue to give such guidance and encouragement appropriately even after the trainee has left the library school.[17]

DATA AND INFORMATION COLLECTION AND SERVICE DEVELOPMENT

Students and faculty members can be expected to teach and carry out comparative and other international research projects. Hence, the objective of a library and information collection program should be to provide as much as possible of the material on which these user groups will depend. Both statistical data and prose material describing information service will be needed for many projects.

A clear distinction should be made between (1) collecting statistical data through information service and publishing figures, usually portrayed in tabular form and in certain cases stored in computer data bases in the school statistical laboratory, and (2) collecting information in the form of textual descriptions in print or microform reports, journals, books, manuscripts, indexes, and abstracts housed in the school's information center or library.

Most statistical data and information will be found in printed material stored in the information center. The data housed in the statistical laboratory will be limited to the material stored in the computer data base, certain of which will arrive in machine readable form.

In addition, another category exists of (3) nonprint images on slides, transparencies, films, cassettes, records, and floor plans normally housed in the school media center, where the microform collection may also be housed. The three centers can be combined into one, or each one can be separate but preferably in close proximity to the others, since they should be closely coordinated to maximize service effectiveness. Each center may have its own head, or all may be supervised by the school information center director. In any case, the statistical laboratory will need one or more assistants of its own to assist and instruct users, supervise computer use, prepare class material, file, and shelve.

All three of these collections may need upgrading and deserve discussion, but this chapter will concentrate on the first two, especially the data collection. For historical research projects, information must be collected primarily through scholarly books and journals, while for other kinds of projects statistical and tabular material will often be requested. Information management research seems to be moving strongly toward objective analyses requiring statistical and mathematical material—hence this section's data collection interest.

The collection will never meet all needs, and certain students will prefer to collect most project information independently. The rest, however, should be able to locate much helpful material in the statistical laboratory and information center.

The school must maintain a steady inflow of new and useful data and information if its research program is to prosper. Many dependable sources of material supply must be developed, probably many more than are presently accessed. The school must also develop a comprehensive development plan and timetable to implement the material collection responsibility. The plan must show specifically what subject subfield information and data are to be collected, from what sources, through what organizations, at what frequency, and in what manner.

Standard university library material selection and acquisition policies can be used to guide the center in obtaining textual material. Though similar, statistical data selection and acquisition policies are not as widely discussed and understood as those for textual material. Certain "grey literature area" policies must be used here.

Statistical reports issued by information centers are often hard to identify and locate, are published in informal fashion, and are often enclosed in other reports, with limited and localized distribution, irregular coverage and frequency, and poorly defined categories. In some cases, they are considered to be confidential and therefore unavailable to foreigners.

These problems must be dealt with by attempting to improve the quality of both the product and the methods of obtaining it. In any case, once started, most reports will continue to arrive regularly for many years.

Another problem is that few current and comprehensive statistical report bibliographies exist. An information center must therefore compile its own before selection can proceed. Lists of serial titles covered by international and national information management indexing services will provide a good starting place.

The development plan should list the countries from which data and information should be sought, the four main kinds of information centers, and the kinds of work and the subject subfields in which the faculty is interested. It should list possible material sources, report frequency, and institutional, geographic, and chronological coverage. Whether the material is primarily statistical data or information may be shown.

Close cooperation in both material collection and use can be expected with many information management data and information centers. Collection may be extensive for eighty or selective for forty countries, or else chosen from among countries strong in subject areas close to the school's research program.

Possible contributors include all types of information centers, especially national, state, and provincial ministry offices, national and international statistical centers, information associations, schools, and book, journal, media, and report publishers. The U.S. National Education Statistics Center, Statistics Canada, and UNESCO's Division on Statistics should be included.

Many serial titles must be obtained directly from the source institution, while others can be obtained through an intermediary, a national library, or a national information association which has collected and analyzed data and information, or else through a local book dealer. In many specialized subject areas, such as law librarianship, few nations collect data nationally, and so they must be collected from individual centers. Ways of identifying and locating this material must be developed.

Faculty members should compile a basic list of data items wanted from each source, whether use, acquisitions, budget, or other subfield. For any information center group, the list should resemble that of the UNESCO data collection list but with more detail. The school's own data collection form may be sent to the source organization with the hope of obtaining more data than those which the organization's own form provides. Degree of report accuracy, uniformity, and standardization should be checked, and definitions should be identified.

Data can be found either in a collective report (such as data on all public libraries) or, most often, in a single leading organization's report, but in a variety of formats. Much less frequently found are longitudinal reports. Gift and exchange arrangements between schools and information centers can often be arranged.

A few foreign and national off campus users can be expected to pay contract fees for accessing the school's data and information collections, particularly the abstracting and indexing data bases. Occasional financial support may come from private foundations or government agencies. The school should stimulate the interest of its national government library or office in assisting the program.

No doubt some data and information are already being received and must be coordinated with the collection program. In addition, perhaps certain textual titles are already being indexed in order to increase accessibility. If so, the statistical data collection should be included in this indexing program. Indexing coverage should be both extensive and intensive using subject and geographic approaches. These data and their indexes should be stored in a computer data base, and a thesaurus should accompany the programming software. For example, a specific information school in the German Democratic Republic might collect the Bulgarian National Library annual report as well as prose and statistical reports from the Ministry of Culture on public libraries, ten large trade union information centers, five universities, and the Ministry of Education school library report. For each center, the report should include at least the annual acquisitions figures broken down by Dewey call numbers in the hundreds, personnel complement figures, an expenditure breakdown, and circulation and reference use figures by Dewey call number.

Further Bulgarian subfields may include music for which additional information can be requested, such as bibliographies compiled, cassette and record players available, sheet music titles available, staff departmentalization, and serial indexing and abstracting services available from ten music libraries. In addition, by exchange or paid subscription three Bulgarian information management and two publishing journals may be received annually, along with twenty books. The German school's information center will send appropriate tabular and textual material to the Bulgarian center to provide a fair exchange.

In summary, in addition to the school files of printed textual material, (1) a selection and acquisitions program should be developed to collect useful statistical reports; (2) while most will be housed with printed material, certain data reports should be located in computer data bases for easier manipulation and trend spotting; and (3) special indexing should be carried out to facilitate statistical collection use. Considerable school initiative and continuity will be required to carry out this ambitious program.

To house, manage, and service part of the data collection and provide other services, the modern information school needs a statistical laboratory and data and information processing center where equipment items and terminals are available on which users can carry out both class and research projects. It should be a school teaching laboratory, a workroom, a production center, and a storage center. The center's international objectives should be to house and service foreign and national information for both foreign and national information centers.

Introductory hands-on experience should be obtainable with a large variety of the equipment used in modern information center service. Human-machine interface and competing equipment pieces can also be studied. Equipment should be usable with a minimum of intermediary instruction. User self-instruction programs should be readily available, and languages should be user-friendly.

The laboratory equipment inventory will vary by school and should include both foreign and national hardware. Several mini- and microcomputers and their terminals and peripheral equipment will be needed as well as calculators. Terminals of the university-wide main frame computer system and of the university library data base system should be included.

Disc, cassette, video and aural tape, radio, television, at least two photocopiers, and teaching machines may be accommodated and serviced here. Equipment used in the history of printing as well as all other courses may be located here. Noteworthy statistical laboratories are found at Drexel University, Philadelphia, Pa, USA, and at Rutgers University, New Brunswick, NJ, USA.

INTERNATIONAL STATISTICAL COLLECTION PROGRAMS

Librarianship has been internationalized through bilateral and multinational gift and exchange agreements for material and personnel. During the last fifty years, statistical and other research programs have been initiated through international conferences and relevant meetings arranged by international associations and organizations.

Before World War II, the League of Nations maintained a library project office. Starting in 1946, the United Nations and UNESCO formed both committees and their own organizational units to deal with librarianship. The idea of compiling library statistics originated in 1853 at the First International Statistics Congress in Brussels. Participants felt that library data would be among the few tangible national assets to provide information regarding national educational developments and intellectual resources.[18] Today all international associations foster research and statistical collection.

The International Climate

During the 1960s and 1970s, international library and information-related organizations in the developed countries learned to cooperate through conferences and student and faculty exchanges. These activities fostered the development of international research, statistical data collection and analysis, and standardization, exemplified by the adoption of internationally accepted standard definitions and terminology for statistics and other subjects.

Starting in the mid–1970s, in a natural evolution, developing countries began participating increasingly in these activities. As a consequence, the emphasis in international librarianship shifted considerably from experience and methodology exchange among the developed countries to introducing the developing countries to these new concepts.

In spite of the progressive politicization of international agencies during the late 1970s and early 1980s, UNESCO continued to provide an international government level forum for cooperation in statistical data collection and research. In addition, nongovernmental international organizations through their less formal programs and publications also helped improve world information service.

During the early 1980s, U.S. foreign policy and diplomacy reflected a decline of confidence and reduced support for participation in multinational organizations. Partly for this reason, international research must be simultaneously maintained through governmental agencies such as UNESCO and the foreign offices of member states, nongovernmental international associations, such as the International Federation of Library Associations and Institutions (IFLA) and the International Standards Organization (ISO), and large professional organizations such as the United Kingdom's Library Association and the American Library Association (ALA).

As a result of the emphasis on including developing countries during the last decade, cooperation and information exchange among developed countries has declined, particularly at UNESCO where the staff member balance has shifted from developed to developing countries. UNESCO's increasing concern with issues between developed and developing countries exemplifies the shift from an East-West to a North-South polarization.

In a recent report Galvin summarized UNESCO's General Information Program (PGI). The current PGI program has five principal themes relating to the development of (1) information policies and plans, (2) methods, norms, and standards of information systems, (3) information infrastructures, (4) specialized information systems, and (5) education and training of information specialists and users. PGI maintains close working relationships with major international nongovernmental organizations.[19]

As a result of the worldwide economic recession during 1981–1983 and a funding reduction for international library activities, a period of stocktaking has replaced the 1965–1980 period of rapid advance in international library statistics and research. If the current period is used for evaluation and improvement, the next decade should provide opportunities for strengthening existing dissemination channels and information service advances by assessing their progress through research and statistics.

An International Library Statistics Data System

Statistical surveys, especially on a worldwide basis, are labor-intensive and therefore expensive. They require a highly competent statistical staff, the mailing out of thousands of questionnaires, followup and editing of returns, arrangement, tabulation, and data analysis, and printing and dissemination of the resulting publication. Nongovernmental national and international organizations cannot afford such an undertaking which can be handled far more effectively by international governmental cooperation through UNESCO.

Among the functions best carried out by an international association is standards development. UNESCO established an International Publishing Statistics Standard in 1964 and library statistics and terminology standards in 1970. Preparation of these standards was undertaken through cooperation by librarians from many countries who worked effectively on the IFLA and ISO Statistics Committees between 1965 and 1969. The committees' decisions were brought before the ISO and IFLA annual meeting general memberships, and the recommendations were published jointly.[20]

The international professional organizations developed and submitted the standards in a final report to the 1970 UNESCO Paris Conference which adopted them. A further report recommended that data collection be undertaken every third year, specified the data elements to be included in the newly developed questionnaire, and established standardized terminology.

Consequently, UNESCO's Division on Statistics mailed a survey instrument to its members nations in 1972, 1975, 1978, and 1984. The same kind of survey form was sent to various types of libraries—national, public, higher education, and special—and the terms used were identical or compatible. No survey was conducted in 1981.

Survey results were published in the *UNESCO Statistical Yearbook*, but data analysis or text were not provided. Without IFLA and ISO/TC46 and the cooperation of Eastern, Western, and Third World countries, the adoption of this international statistics program would have been impossible. The question remains whether the program is now worth as much as was hoped for when it was established.

The surveys were not as productive as expected because many countries did not respond at all and others responded only in part. The 1978 survey results indicated that 137 out of 161 countries responded (85 percent). Some countries did not have certain types of libraries, and others did not want to make certain admissions regarding their libraries' condition. Some respondents may not have had all the necessary data or a staff adequate to respond. The results consisted entirely of tabulated data; it is hoped that IFLA or ISO/TC46 can provide data analysis and at least some text in the future.

Future Research and Statistics Developments

Until UNESCO's role stabilizes in the next five years, the importance of nongovernmental organizations will increase, and they will need to spearhead research and statistics advances. IFLA programs indicate the scope of its concerns; its activities operate on a larger and more general base than do those of the other library-related nongovernmental organizations. Its plans are officially stated by the Professional Board.[21] The desirability of close cooperation between IFLA and UNESCO is stressed, especially with UNESCO's PGI and the Division for Book Promotion and International Exchanges.

CONCLUSIONS

During the 1984 ALA Midwinter Meeting, the Executive Board adopted Committee on Research recommendations for Office for Research goals, namely (1) to collect and/or promote statistics collection about libraries and librarians, so that ALA and other organizations will have pertinent and consistent data available, and (2) to monitor ongoing library research and disseminate information about studies to the field. Another call for library research was made in 1984.[22] It stressed defining information-seeking skills and education for librarians, and promoting adult literacy and learning. These topics are equally applicable to the international library community.

International research and statistics efforts have been a binding element making librarianship cooperate across borders and engage in large-scale problem-solving. Library problems, regardless of location, are easily understood by all librarians who have participated in national and international meetings.

International research can only be carried out through dedicated persons who work on committees where professionalism operates on a comparatively high level and politics on a comparatively low level. UNESCO's working conditions have frequently been the reverse of this in the past decade. It is vital that future cooperation between nongovernmental international organization members overcome political obstacles and continue to achieve international cooperation and progress.

NOTES

1. Examples are the *Journal of Education for Library and Information Science, Library Science with a Slant to Documentation*, and *Current Research in Library and Information Science*.

2. See Heartsill Young, ed., *ALA Glossary of Library and Information Science*, (Chicago: American Library Association, 1983), and Anthony Thompson, "Multi-culturalism, Libraries and International Terminology," in John F. Harvey, ed., *Comparative and International Library Science* (Metuchen, N.J.: Scarecrow Press, 1977).

3. Quoted in Richard Krzys and Gaston Litton, *World Librarianship: A Comparative Study* (New York: Marcel Dekker, 1983), p. 32.

4. See Patricia Layzell Ward, ed., *Introductory Guide to Research in Library and Information Studies in the U.K.* (London: Library Association, 1975).

5. Jeffrey Katzer, "Understanding the Research Process: An Analysis of Error," Charles H. Busha, ed., *A Library Science Research Reader and Bibliographic Guide* (Littleton, Colo.: Libraries Unlimited, 1981).

6. Quoted in Harvey, ed., *Comparative and International Library Science*, p. 177.

7. R. N. Sharma, "Interview with Thomas Galvin," *Library Times International* 1 (January 1985), p. 62.

8. See J. Periam Danton, *The Dimensions of Comparative Librarianship* (Chicago: American Library Association, 1973), pp. 159–166.

9. S. Seetharama, "Library and Information Science Research in India: An Analytical Study Based on the Input to ISORID," *Library Science with a Slant to Documentation* (September 1976), p. 122.

10. Penelope Biggs, "Research in International and Comparative Librarianship" in A. Whatley, ed., *International and Comparative Librarianship Group Handbook* (London: Library Association, 1971), pp. 160–171.

11. J. Periam Danton, "Definitions of Comparative and International Library Science," in Harvey, ed., *Comparative and International Library Science*, pp. 3–4.

12. Sylvia Simsova, "A Delphi Survey of Comparative Librarianship," *International Library Review* 7 (October 1975), p. 425.

13. Anthony Thompson, "Towards International Comparative Librarianship," *Journal of Librarianship* 4 (January 1972), p. 68.

14. Herbert Goldhor, *An Introduction to Scientific Research in Librarianship* (Urbana: University of Illinois Graduate School of Library Science, 1969).

15. D. J. Foskett, "Discovery of Essence," in B. C. Bloomfield, ed., *Middle East Studies and Libraries* (London: Mansell, 1980), p. 65.

16. Jean Hassenforder, "Comparative Studies and the Development of Public Libraries," *UNESCO Bulletin for Libraries* 22 (January-February 1968), p. 15. Suggested research topics are as follows:

- British reference course internationalization level.
- Russian versus Australian children's literature course foreign title coverage.
- An East versus West European school library objectives analysis.
- An international introduction to a library science course syllabus.
- Public library collection internationalization analysis: Spain versus Latin America.
- Biography of Marietta Shepard, internationalist.
- American science data base use in Europe.
- Canadian information science versus cataloging citation internationalization.
- Comparative roles: International Association of Agriculture Librarians and International Association of Orientalist Librarians.
- Career profiles: Twenty Canadian librarians who studied abroad versus twenty who studied in Canada.
- Women library administrators: Japan versus Yugoslavia.
- Foreign language facility of West African reference librarians.
- An academic library internationalization manual.

17. A. Neelameghan. "Research in Library Science: The Why and the How," *Herald of Library Science* 6 (April-July 1967), pp. 116–117.

18. Frank L. Schick, "Library Statistics," in *Encyclopedia of Library and Information Science* (New York: Marcel Dekker, 1975), vol. 16, p. 63.

19. Thomas J. Galvin, "Trends and Issues in the International Library and Information Communities," *Bowker Annual of Library and Book Trade Information* (New York: R. R. Bowker Co., 1985), pp. 69–75.

20. The International Standardization of Library Statistics: A Progress Report (London: IFLA, ISO, 1968); UNESCO, International Standardization of Library Statistics, Final Report, Paris, February 26, 1970; and "Recommendations Concerning the International Standardization of Library Statistics, Final Report, Paris, February 26, 1970" and "Recommendations Concerning the International Standardization of Library Statistics, Paris, November 13, 1970," *UNESCO Bulletin for Libraries* 25 (January 1971).

21. International Federation of Library Associations and Institutions, *Medium-Term Programme 1986–1991* (The Hague: 1985).

22. U.S. Department of Education, "Alliance for Excellence; Librarians Respond to 'A Nation at Risk'" (Washington, D.C.: Government Printing Office, 1984), p. 33.

BIBLIOGRAPHY

Carroll, Frances Laverne. "Internationalism in Education for Librarianship." *International Library Review* 4 (April 1972), pp. 102–126.

Carroll, Frances Laverne. "Library Education." In John F. Harvey, ed. *Comparative and International Library Science*. Metuchen, N.J.: Scarecrow Press, 1977, pp. 155–156.

Foskett, D. J. "Palabras: A Decade of Comparisons." In Library Association,

"International and Comparative Librarianship Group. 10th Anniversary Conference. London: Library Association, 1979.

Foskett, D. J. *Reader in Comparative Librarianship.* Englewood, Colo.: Information Handling Services, 1976.

Harvey, John F. "Toward a Definition of International and Comparative Library Science." *International Library Review* 5 (July 1973). pp. 289–319.

Patel, Jashu. "International Problems in South Asian Bibliographical Information Services." *International Library Review* 15 (January 1983), pp. 95–103.

Sharify, Nasser. "Beyond the National Frontiers: The International Dimension of Changing Library Education for a Changing World." Brooklyn: Graduate School of Library and Information Science, Pratt Institute, 1973.

Sharify, Nasser. "The Need for Change in Present Library Science Education." In Larry Earl Bone, ed., *Library Education: An International Survey.* Champaign, Ill.: Illini Union Bookstore, 1967, pp. 171–196.

9

AN INFORMATION SCHOOL RESEARCH AND SERVICE CENTER PROGRAM

John F. Harvey and John Wilkinson

An information school service center is more often called a research center, but its service is not limited to research. Rather, the service center may provide a rich variety of service: data collection and analysis; research; development and implementation; system library and information school surveys; campus library research service; experimental, pilot, and demonstration projects; equipment and supply testing; service and technical standard development; computer and media system design; information provision; advisory, referral, and bibliographic work; literature searches and analysis; abstracting and indexing; selective dissemination of information; state of the art studies; critiquing and evaluating; clearinghouse operation; building programming; management consulting; publication; fund-raising and grant management; and translation service.

A service center is an administrative unit or division within an information school for developing, managing, and coordinating a variety of specific noninstructional services, mostly directed to an off campus clientele. The center should be client-oriented, service-oriented, and, to a considerable extent, research- and development-oriented. It should be active and aggressive. Probably no center now or in the future will carry out all of the services discussed here, but all centers (and most schools) carry out certain of them now and all services described herein fit logically into the center concept.

Many Western libraries, consortia, associations, and government agencies carry out research, and some even operate service centers. Locating the center in a university and occupational school setting with access to communication, computer, library, and research staff facilities should become more common in the information field if it is to move toward research respectability.

These services can be carried out through a variety of school organization patterns. They may be assigned to an assistant dean or an administrative assistant, for instance. The formally organized center is probably justified only when the volume of service work reaches a level that cannot be handled easily by the existing administrative staff. Normally, the larger and more research-oriented schools establish such centers before smaller schools do, but the smaller schools should think about centralizing these services in a part-time center.

Center tasks can be contrasted both with those focused on the regular campus student teaching program and those focused on student recruitment, admissions, counseling, placement, and alumni relations. The teaching program can be managed by the dean's office directly or by an assistant dean, while the recruitment-alumni program can be managed by the school's personnel officer. In turn, the service center can be subdivided between research and development on the one hand, and consulting and literature services on the other hand, if desirable.

There are at least four kinds of information research and service centers: (1) multi-subject field (mostly within the information field) and multi-function, (2) multi-subject and specialized function, (3) specialized subject and multi-function, and (4) specialized subject and specialized function. The ERIC Clearinghouse for Information Resources is an example of (1), the University of Chicago Center for Children's Books (concentration on bibliography and book reviewing) of (2), the University of Sheffield Center for Research on User Studies of (3), and the Library Association Bureau of International Library Staff Exchange of (4). Information on these and other currently active centers can be found in the final section of this chapter. Over half of the centers described there were affiliated with information schools.

Probably categories (1) and (2) contain the most common and the longest lived centers, including most of the socialist methodological centers. On certain campuses, a single research office carries out research and development management for all schools. On any campus, certain projects may need to be spun off from multi-subject or multi-function into semi-independent specialized centers.

The service organization pattern used is of only secondary importance. The one adopted will depend on the number of staff personnel available and obtainable and on their time constraints as well as on clientele interests. The service center pattern is suggested as a systematic and efficient method of focusing project management. Each center is unique and has its own patterns of service which it has learned to perform well and can market successfully to the clientele. These must be considered to be permanent units.

The center should be heavily involved with the off campus information world and should be one of the school's primary liaison agencies with practicing information personnel. Several managerial and support staff members and several years of dedicated effort will be required before a strong center can be developed.

SERVICE

The center should be active in providing the various types and subtypes of useful service listed above to many different clientele groups:

1. The school and center can design and implement a comprehensive program to collect useful statistics on information service institutions. Each center needs a source of varied and comprehensive input and output data for research use, and this program can provide it. Student theses and dissertations and current activity analysis by institutional staffs, state and national libraries can be supported. A logical design, practical plan, timetable, systematic data definition, collection, computer storage, analysis, and dissemination program are needed. The objective of the *data collection and analysis program* is to provide the data needed to improve institutional understanding. The University of Illinois Library Research Center has performed such a role in part for Illinois public libraries.

2. The center can be directly involved with both applied and basic *research projects* and with school research papers, theses, and dissertations. Research to discover new knowledge and relationships is a primary focus of many centers, though others carry on none of it. A research agenda can be drawn up and implemented over a decade. Certain projects can be initiated within the center and others in the field. Many research methods can be used—survey, statistical analysis, comparative, case study, system design, bibliographic, theoretical, experimental, historical, and content anaysis.

Although funding them will be difficult, the center can attempt to establish projects to develop a research-based and universally relevant information service theory or philosophy. Theory should have the generalizability necessary for internationalization and export, which practice lacks.[1]

3. *Development and implementation projects* have a high priority in many centers—what John Wilkinson calls applied community service of practical and immediate benefit to specific community groups. These projects exploit old and new ideas and improve and expand existing systems. They dominate monthly work lists and represent the only kind of project which the typical practitioner will pay for. Extending a computer-based catalog system to the circulation department is an example.

4. *System library surveys* are needed to discover national or local information system characteristics. Extensive survey data collection and analysis against sets of criteria can precede national and local system planning.[2] The center can assemble a staff, collect and evaluate data, and recommend action in a variety of fields.

5. The strong center can *advise other information schools*. Either a comprehensive survey with recommendations for a new school against national personnel requirements or a specialized analysis of a school's archive management curric-

ulum, for instance, can be produced. The center should bring information on new concepts and trends to the school. The center should be especially well qualified to advise on school and center research and development (R and D), consulting, continuing education, and internationalization programs.

6. *The campus university library* needs *institutional research service* in order to understand and improve its operation. Analysis of service point use, processing times, reference failure, catalog versus index use, supplier service comparisons, and serial cancellation formula application are examples. Certain studies can form part of the library's quality control program. The center can replace an inhouse research office as the library's research arm.

7. Certain projects require *experiments* under controlled conditions, such as comparing subject classification systems for retrieval efficiency. A few centers can perform this kind of research, and its popularity should grow. *Pilot* projects may be needed in order to test a new idea or system in operation, such as a new abstracting title reader opinion survey. *Demonstration projects* can also be mounted to publicize a new idea.

Library supply, equipment, and furniture company testing programs are not new. Product comparison, new item testing, user acceptance, simplification, ease of operation, motorization studies, and forms control systems can be realized. The efficiency, durability, and marketability of new and existing products can be tested. Support can be gained through (a) charging manufacturer or dealer testing fees, or (b) publishing a library consumer bulletin of equipment and supply evaluation reports.

8. Work with information associations is needed to prepare *service standards* and with individual libraries and groups to prepare *technical standards*. Specialized associations can be assisted in preparing appropriate and fully researched sets of input and outut service standards for their members. Few of these groups have researched standards that facilitate institutional comparison and progress.

In cooperation with the national standards agency and the International Standards Organization, the center can provide the study and research needed to prepare technical standards appropriate for various information work areas. Staff members at the Tehran Book Processing Centre have assisted with standards projects for many years.

9. *Information association and government agency service* can take several other forms: regular data collection and analysis, clearinghouse operation, continuing education (CE), conference organization, and publication service, for instance. Most associations lack the skilled staff and time—and often the funds—to perform these services themselves, but the center can produce what the association or government office will pay for. While government project contracts may be easy to obtain, they may also pay the lowest overhead rates.

10. *Computer and media system design* is becoming popular. Many information centers need this service in order to use mini- or microcomputer capabilities. Full exploitation of a computer in all department systems is not yet widely understood so that the center can make a useful contribution. Computer capabilities, as well as the system and the design concept, must be explained. Many types of media systems are used in information center and classroom applica-

tions. A coordinated media, textbook, and supplementary reading system can teach students more than older methods through careful design, preparation, and testing.

11. *Information provision, reference, advisory, referral, and bibliographic work* fit together well and can be provided by skilled reference librarians in cooperation with a large library reference department. Advisory service requires strong subject and bibliographic knowledge to choose the most suitable among book titles, but referral service requires primarily a comprehensive directory and list collection in sending the user to the most fruitful source.

12. The Georgia Institute of Technology Science Information Research Center has carried out retrospective and current computer-based and manual *literature searches and analyses* to discover what is already known about each one of its projects. Many users search for themselves, but others hire skilled specialists to perform this task. Searching and analysis require more subject matter and subject literature knowledge, data base understanding, and searching skill than most users possess.

13. A number of service centers produce formal or informal secondary *abstracting and indexing* journals for specialized fields. Both abstracting and indexing demand superior subject knowledge, and abstracting requires writing skill, also in order to bring the flood of material under control. Each one of these complex fields requires full understanding of its techniques and subfields.

14. *Selective dissemination of information service* builds on the work of other information personnel to provide citations and documents fitting the interest and needs of specific individuals or institutions. It should be increasingly popular as the information explosion continues. The Institute for Scientific Information in Philadelphia performs this service by mail for a customer group whose interest profiles are matched with current publication output.

15. *A state of the art study* involves literature study and evaluation in order to produce a mature assessment of a specific subject's current development state. It requires a professional specialist's subject field understanding and a reference librarian's ability to assemble citations and photocopies. A center consultant may be asked to critique a proposal or plan, such as one for a staff training program. Constructive suggestions, revisions, and alternatives may also be expected. Critiquing can be applied to any concept, design, or plan.

16. A *clearinghouse* concentrating on service to a single target group can be established for a specific set of printed and media material, probably composed mostly of serials and research reports. This organization is an information collection, analysis, and dissemination center serving a discrete clientele identified by the contractor. It requires personnel sophisticated in dealing with material and people in a specific subject field. From such a center will often come an abstracting and indexing serial. An example is provided by the University of Chicago Center for Children's Books.

17. *Program preparation for new buildings*, wings, and renovations has long been a popular North American consulting activity and can be carried out by well-qualified architects, interior decorators, and librarians. This can become one of the center's popular and lucrative services. A team of specialists can carry out

these assignments, most of them hired by the project. A reference collection of printed and media material is needed to support this service.

18. Much the same situation exists in *library management,* another popular North American *consulting* field. Personnel evaluation and training, cost reduction, service expansion, organization adjustment, branch service retrenchment, and book approval plans plague librarians and lead them to consultants. A management consultant team is needed to handle these assignments; most of them are hired by the project. Many of these contracts can lead to continuing education requests.

19. All research results should be publishable. The objectives of the *publication program* are to communicate center findings and progress to a wide audience. This program must be integrated with the curriculum, research, and CE programs. The center can publish school and center annual reports and alumni placement newsletters. Papers delivered at certain conferences can be collected, edited, and published in a monograph series. Course material can be published for classroom instructors and students.

Lecture series can be collected for publication, and course syllabi, teaching materials, media, textbooks, and recruiting materials can be published. School catalogs and guides must also be issued. The Illinois Library Research Center has a good publication record, and its school Publication Office, with a self-supporting staff of four, can serve as a program model.[3]

20. *School and alumni fund-raising, grant, and gift management* can be assigned to the center. It can manage grants and gifts of all kinds, their planning, proposal preparation, solicitation, and use. Fund-raising is needed to supplement small school and center budgets. The center is a natural place for these activities because it is already managing its own R and D solicitation program. It can also assist university development office fund-raising with school groups and individuals.

In cooperation with the alumni association, each school can ask its alumni to contribute annually to its quest for excellence through a scholarship, fellowship, or general purpose fund. Furthermore, the school and center can make an annual appeal for business and corporate support. Bookstores, book, serial, and media publishers, book wholesalers, library binderies, supply, equipment, and furniture manufacturers and dealers can be approached.

21. *Translation service* can be provided for the campus and the information school. Without knowledge of the foreign material on certain topics, the client cannot place them in more than a national context. A team of part-time translators can be assembled to provide this service by the project.

OBJECTIVES AND JUSTIFICATIONS

The primary objective of the center is to coordinate and maximize off campus noncurricular and nonpersonnel school service to the information field, especially those institutions and persons in the primary catchment area. The center should considerably extend the school service range beyond the typical concentration on elementary level instruction and extend the range of information specialists and geographical areas reached. It should also significantly enhance its clientele's decision-making capabilities.

Justifications of center operation depend on the importance and usefulness of its service and the effectiveness of its organization. The strongest argument is that a center should extend and improve the school's usefulness to its field and practitioners' respect for it. A center can be justified by practitioners' need for the service which it provides and the service's practical nature. Few information centers employ personnel sufficiently qualified to carry out specialized projects, nor can they find these services well performed and readily available elsewhere. The ineffectiveness of most information centers, in terms of user service and market penetration, for instance, shows the need for service center assistance.[4]

In the past decade, British information school R and D has progressed rapidly, but in the United States it has dwindled. Wilkinson quotes Lloyd Houser's statement to the effect that library science has no active research fronts in the sense that Garfield has developed that phrase.[5] An increasing amount of American information R and D has been conducted by commercial organizations staffed primarily by nonlibrarians.

Wilkinson makes the important point that before an R and D center (research or service center) can exist on a solid and well-justified foundation, relevant local and national government departments, and the national library, must recognize it as their information R and D arm. That recognition underlies the success of the British Library Research and Development Department. Recognition may be more feasible in a country like Sweden with a single national information school than in Canada where information service responsibility is decentralized.

The information field must be recognized to be among the disciplines qualified for national and local, public, private, and university funding agency grants. Information skills must be seen as relevant to dissemination and transfer which itself is already recognized as being socially important. Universities must recognize that information R and D is important across a broad subject field spectrum. The information field's interdisciplinary nature alone should justify establishing an R and D center.

Few North American government agencies see the information field as requiring an R and D base. Until information workers themselves demonstrate that research and a theoretical framework are essential to management decision-making—that information work is more than a clerical field—they should not expect outside agencies to adopt that view. Few North American information workers or students now regard library science R and D findings as being important or interesting.[6] Center staffs must justify information field R and D persuasively when requesting institutional funding for it.

PERSONNEL, FINANCE, AND QUARTERS

Most centers contain a variety of staff members:

1. An advisory board is needed to advise, provide creative suggestions, and serve as liaison between center and clientele. Board members can be chosen for their interest in the center's programs and their familiarity with information R and D service and support. Guidance in policy, practice, and planning can be provided.

2. Director: A full- or part-time manager is needed who reports to the school dean. The director should be a well-organized person, persuasive, skilled in market development, research proposal preparation, budget management, and preferably should have a strong reputation as a consultant or researcher. Preferably, but not necessarily, the director should be a faculty member. Service center management can be combined with part-time teaching, if needed.

3. In larger centers, an assistant director, research director, or research assistant may be needed to share administrative tasks and supervise certain projects.

4. Senior staff members consist of full- and part-time faculty members from the information school and other university schools plus outside consultants. Faculty members should be expected to carry out all their funded research through the center, and they can work on an overtime or released time basis. Center staff members should teach the school research methods courses and should be oriented as much to the research as to the teaching program. Often center projects are more important to the school's clientele than is the teaching program.

If available, the best person to carry out each project should be hired, no matter whether or not that person is already on the faculty. A considerable variety of well-qualified information specialists can be used for specific projects. Practicing consultants can be used for such projects as a management training session or public library branch program, persons who can be persuaded to institutionalize their consulting.

5. Junior level research assistants are graduate and undergraduate students in the information and other university schools. Certain assistants will work on specific projects on the subprofessional level for standard campus rate pay.

Financial support is a key center area and is difficult to develop. Long-term university operation support should cover the director's and secretary's salaries, though the director may be able to bring in enough direct and indirect funding to cover those salaries. A travel budget of some size will be needed. Financial record-keeping can be handled by the university business office.

Clearly, outside support is essential to develop a viable center. There are thousands of potential funding sources, and locating funds is a year-round job for not merely the director but all senior staff members. The director must get on government bid specification mailing lists and must be alert to developing an extensive knowledge of funding sources. The university research office can help to locate funding and bid opportunities.

In certain cases, for instance the British Library's R and D centers, the entire center is given minimum funding by an outside agency, and supplementary funding may be sought from additional sources. In these cases, the entire project must be "sold" to the sponsoring agency. In other situations, each part must be funded one by one from a variety of sources and probably with some variation in arrangements.

In addition to all direct costs, project budget proposals should list an overhead or indirect cost allowance to cover *university expenses* connected with payroll maintenance, cleaning buildings, utility costs, campus security, library use, and research office time, for instance; and *center expenses* for equipment, terminal use, managerial and clerical salaries, and supplies, for instance.

It is difficult to say what portions of center expenses should be covered (a) on a sustaining basis by the university and school, or by project (b) indirect and (c) direct charges. As much as possible should be covered by (a) and then by (b), but pressure will often be strongly in the opposite direction.

Normally, university overhead charges run 15 to 50 percent of direct charges, depending on the project and the institution, as compared with 60 to 100 percent in commercial institutions. Some percentage of the overhead income should be returned to the center. Project bids must conform to university research office requirements and overhead charges.

Funding sources will be client institution budgets, local, national, and international government agencies, associations, commercial firms, and private foundations. Proposal writing to obtain government and foundation funding is an art that must be mastered. Scholarship funds can be used to support graduate students while they carry out a project. Business and industrial firms are excellent support sources.[7] Both large and small firms contract out many information services. This service often involves literature analyses and abstracting and indexing bulletin publications for specialized subject fields.

The commercial and industrial world of Europe and North America is a more dependable funding source than government agencies and foundations, except in socialist countries, of course. In fact, the information science and media fields generally should provide more project funding than the library science and archive fields. Since both the direct and indirect costs of the university are usually lower than those of commercial competitors, university centers can often outbid commercial rivals for contracts.

PROGRAM PLANNING, COORDINATION, AND MARKETING

Before embarking on a service program, development must be carefully planned. Initially, a five-year development period can be projected, budgeted, and staffed. The plan can explain center organization, direction and finance, goals and measurable objectives. The development strategy can be divisible into annual segments to facilitate objective evaluation. The plan can be integrated with university and school instruction and R and D program plans. The services to be provided, their justification and planning, can be covered. These services can reflect the information world's problem areas in which assistance is needed, for which funding can be found and a competent project director hired.

Close and continuing coordination with certain related organizations can be expected:

1. The center should organize its work to support the school curriculum. A research requirement can be included in all graduate degree curricula, for instance. The school can follow the pattern of most university graduate schools and require for graduation statistical and resarch methods courses as well as a thesis, dissertation, or research paper. Research participation is essential to the proper intellectual development of graduate students. Only course work and direct experience can produce a mature understanding of research. Both the University of Chicago and the University of California at Los Angeles require a Master's degree research paper or thesis.

2. Coordination in project seeking can be expected with other campus R and D centers. The center can cooperate in bidding, subcontracting, and mutual alerting to contract opportunities.

3. Coordination with information school R and D centers in other states and provinces can be recommended. Sharing project plans, funding, and personnel performance information can improve each one's service record. Joint bidding is possible as well as compilation of lists showing each center's special strengths.

4. Fund-raising must be coordinated to avoid competition with university development office and alumni fund office activity. Identification of special information field business, corporate, and personal donor possibilities is needed, as well as ensuring that the school receives full benefits from these programs.

5. Coordination with the local university press can be encouraged to spell out clearly each organization's activity field and to identify profitable cooperative activity. Getting the press to market center publications could lead to larger sales.

An initial challenge is to develop the market for center service in a setting that is frequently not very encouraging. In the West, developing the market requires indefatigible and persuasive education of potential clients over a long time period. The Institute for Scientific Information provides a helpful example of high-level and intensive international market development. In socialist countries, however, less promotion is required because centers are established with government subsidy and service market built into the system.

Various methods can be used to convince the audience both intellectually and emotionally of center value. Successful early project completion is one of them. Another relates to the quality of the consultants used. Still another requires full discussion of significant reports in government and association publications and conferences.

The center should operate an active public relations program. Regular news releases can be issued to announce new contracts and appointments, project completions, and findings to the world information press. Annual reports and newsletters can be distributed selectively.

INTERNATIONALIZATION

A research and service center can be internationalized through its objectives, personnel, information flow, projects, and funding. The following specific measures can be taken:

1. Objectives can be adopted to infuse the center's program with international awareness and provide its service to an international market. The center can both take information and staff from and return service to the global information community. So far are we now from internationalizing the service and research of most schools that their area of relevance only rarely reaches beyond a specific region or information group. Theory has failed to transcend institutional limitations.

2. The advisory board can include several foreign members who attend international conferences and are likely to hear about R and D projects and funding opportunities. In addition to the board, with a little initiative and imagination both senior and junior staff members can be internationalized, perhaps through faculty exchanges.

3. Many campuses have an international project office that develops and manages curricular, consulting, and R and D projects in cooperation with foreign institutions, government agencies, and private foundations. Close cooperation with this office can be expected. On certain campuses, all center international projects must be processed through that office and conform to its requirements.

4. Opportunities can be sought to bid on foreign and international contracts for research or service. The U.S. Agency for International Development, other national government international bureaus, and international semi-government agencies can provide helpful information.

5. Most service center projects will probably be local or national. However, by adding nearby nations to a data collection and analysis project, its conclusions

may gain regional implications, broader and more significant than those of a national project. International Federation of Library Associations and Institutions (IFLA) interest and Council on Library Resources (CLR) support can be sought. Analyses can include province versus province, nation versus nation, and region versus region.

6. Recommendations can be sent to the local university information school library and international information center to subscribe to several foreign information indexing and abstracting serials and to a selection of the journals covered so that fuller literature searches can be carried out. In addition, foreign dissertations, monographs, and reports are needed to support projects from a selection of nations.

7. The international information center is a collection of material or information service in other countries which can be maintained under the supervision of the information school library. It should cover all subject fields in this broad area and material in a variety of forms—serials, monographs, technical reports, and microforms.

8. A publication program with international objectives is needed to take school and center findings and ideas around the world. Serial publications can include a journal with an international advisory board, contents, and contributors, and an international information center newsletter. Newsletters, journals, and annual reports can be sent on exchange to foreign colleagues. News releases and review copies of new monographs and reports can be sent to a foreign journal mailing list.

9. Active participation in IFLA and the International Federation for Documentation (FID) can be recommended, especially their conferences which can provide information on useful personnel and projects. The IFLA Library Education and Research Section can be especially recommended. FID technical committees encourage research in their area.

10. Several kinds of international CE possibilities exist. The College of Librarianship, Wales, has provided many examples. Several schools have sponsored summer library study tours in Europe for credit. Special seminars for groups of international information visitors have been held by the University of Pittsburgh with U.S. government sponsorship. An annual international summer session similar to the Wales program is needed for non-English-speaking countries, for example, one each in Spanish, French, German, Russian, and Chinese.

11. The school and center can work out a partnership agreement with a school abroad. In this agreement, the two institutions can exchange faculty members, students, and teaching and library material, and can work closely together on dissertations, extension, and internationalization projects.

12. Work directly with foreign information research and service centers can be recommended. Project supervisors can ask several foreign centers to collect data locally for analysis at the project's home center. Possibilities exist for subcontracting projects with other centers.

13. Much of the serious thinking being done currently in information circles occurs in system, consulting, UNESCO/ICSU Science Information System (UNISIST), National Information System (NATIS), or national library headquarters,

in the public or private sectors. And often their thinking needs supplementing by well-organized R and D work.

14. International funding sources can be sought through international foundations; information associations; banks; semi-government agencies; national governments; and embassy cultural programs.

DATA AND RESEARCH NEEDED

Little is known internationally about information school research and service centers, their extensiveness, how they are organized, commercial versus university versus government centers, their projects, funding, staff size, and composition, their effectiveness, and their principal accomplishments. With such data available, center characteristics can be identified. Data are needed on these centers for analysis, comparison, and generalization. Research can be carried out to ascertain the most successful projects and the most productive organization patterns used in each country.

INFORMATION RESEARCH AND SERVICE CENTERS

1. All-Union Institute of Scientific and Technical Information (VINITI), Balaijskaja ul. 14, Moscow A214, USSR, A. I. Mikhailov, Director. The leading Soviet center for information science (informatics) study, research, and publication.

2. All-Union Scientific Methodological Center for Library Education, Moscow, USSR. This organization develops new information curricula and teaching departments after investigation.[8] The Soviet Institutes of Culture, in which the leading information schools are located, have improved research organization in recent years.

3. American Library Association (ALA), Office of Research, 50 E. Huron Street, Chicago, Illinois 60611 USA, Mary Jo Lynch, Director. An information center representing ALA to other research groups. The office assists the ALA in research proposal preparation and organizes and manages certain projects. It also monitors and encourages research activity and advises researchers.

4. Becker and Hayes, Inc., Suite 100, 2800 Olympic Boulevard, Santa Monica, California 90404 USA, Joseph Becker, President. A commercial library and information science research and development consulting center. It carries out computer and information service design and planning projects for business, government, and education clients.

5. Bibliographic Center for Research, Inc., Rocky Mountain Region, Suite G–150, 1777 South Bellaire Street, Denver, Colorado 80222 USA, David H. Buncil, Executive Director. Founded in 1935. Staff of twenty-two. Nonprofit, multi-state cooperative. Develops improved library techniques, means of document delivery, and information retrieval systems.

6. British Library Research and Development Department, 2 Sheraton Street, London WIV 4BH, England, which has funded six centers:

    a. Association of Special Libraries and Information Bureaus (ASLIB), Research and Consulting Department, 26/27 Boswell Street, London WC1N 3JZ, M. Slater, Director. Current interests are personnel, library and information science education and training, user and nonuser studies, and the public image.

    b. Center for Catalogue Research, Bath University, Claverton Down, Bath BA2 7AY.

    c. Centre for Library and Information Management, Loughborough University, Loughborough, Leicestershire LE11 3TU.

    d. Center for Research on User Studies, University of Sheffield, Sheffield S10 2TN, Colin Harris, Director. Publishes a semi-annual newsletter. The centre received UK£299750 for three years funding, 1982–1984. Now, funding comes primarily from Sheffield.

    e. National Reprographic Centre for documentation, Hatfield Polytechnic, Bayfordbury, Hertfordshire, AG13 BLD.

    f. Primary Communications Research Centre, Leicester University, Leicester L8T 7RH.

7. Clarion State University College of Library Science Center for the Study of Rural Librarianship, Clarion, Pennsylvania 16214 USA, Barnard Vavrek, Director. Founded in 1978. Covers all major library types. Its objectives, related to rural American library service problems, are to stimulate imaginative thinking, identify endemic problems, provide consultation in designing new service patterns, conduct research, stimulate continuing education, coordinate physical and human resources to analyze service, and collect data. Conducts workshops, research, offers internships, provides a speakers' bureau, and publishes bibliographies, conference papers, a newsletter, and a journal.

8. Center for Information in Information Science, IBICT—CNPQ, SCRN—Q 708/709—Bloco B. Loja 18, ne 30, 70.740 Brasilia, D. F., Brazil, Mrs. Yone Sepulveda Chastinet, Director. A department of the Brazilian Institute of Information in Science and Technology, the Center collects, analyzes, stores, retrieves, and disseminates information published in Spanish and Portuguese. It offers a variety of current awareness and research serial and monograph information science services.

9. Clearinghouse on Information Education and Training Material, Lehrstuhl für Bibliothekswissenschaft der Universität, Universitätsstrasse 33, D–5000 Cologne 41, West Germany, Professor P. Kaegbein, Director. This clearinghouse in the German language is similar in purpose and activities to the FID clearinghouse described below and the Brazilian clearinghouse above and operates by networking and referrals.

10. College of Librarianship, Wales, Llanbadarn Fawr, Aberystwyth, Dyfed

SY23 3AS, United Kingdom, Frank N. Hogg, Principal. Founded in 1964. One of the most internationally organized information schools in the world. Close study of its international service will repay any school. The College works with government and universities in several countries to develop and implement education programs with British Council and local funding. The Library Association Bureau of International Library Staff Exchange is located here. It studies and provides information on librarian exchange opportunities in the European Economic Community countries, Commonwealth countries, Austria, Switzerland, Arab countries, and the United States.

11. College of Physicians Medical Documentation Service, 19 S. 22d Street, Philadelphia, Pennsylvania 19103 USA, Alberta D. Berton, director. Founded in 1953 and associated with a 600,000-volume library. Provides referral and reference service, searches, translations, writing, abstracting, indexing, data analysis, and research.

12. Cyril and Methodius National Library Research Institute in Library Science, Bibliography and Bibliology, Blvd. Tolbuhin 11, 1504 Sofia, Bulgaria. Serves as the national librarianship research center.

13. Documentation Research and Training Centre (DRTC), Indian Statistical Institute, Bangalore 560001, India, G. Bhattacharya, Head. DRTC manages not only to include the word "research" in its title, but also to combine research and information education in one organization. It is heavily involved in research related to the instructional program in cataloging, indexing, classification, mechanization, and bibliographic problems.

14. Drexel University College of Information Studies Center for Information Research, Philadelphia, Pennsylvania 19104 USA, Thomas Childers, Director. Founded in 1981, its mission is to perform research, development, and educational activities that advance the information-handling occupations. The faculty is prepared to study information needs, develop service plans, design automated systems, study use habits, design instruction in automated systems, produce workshops, and more.

15. Educational Resources Information Center (ERIC), Clearinghouse for Information Resources, School of Education, Syracuse University, Syracuse, New York 13210 USA, Donald Ely, Director. Founded in 1967, this clearinghouse selects, acquires, catalogs, abstracts, and indexes information field documents and papers, and provides interpretative service and annotated bibliographies.

16. Franklin Institute Research Laboratories, 20th and Parkway, Philadelphia, Pennsylvania 19103, USA, Richard T. Nalle, President. A large commercial and technical research center.

17. George Washington University Science Communication Studies, 2000 L Street, NW, Suite 301, Washington, D.C. 20036 USA, Linda Suiter, Director. Founded in 1960. Carries out research on life science information flow, information science communication, and other subjects.

18. Georgia Institute of Technology School of Information and Computer Science Information Research Center, Atlanta, Georgia 30332 USA, Richard

A. Demillo, Director. Founded in 1963. Studies scientific foundations of information science, theory, computer science, science information systems, and other subjects.

19. The German Research Association, Kennedy Allee 40, 5300 Bonn 2, Federal Republic of Germany, and the German Library Institute are the German leaders in carrying out research in academic librarianship. Projects exist in the fields of budgeting, staffing, work study, cost analysis, interlibrary loans, user studies, and library careers.

20. Humboldt University Institute for Library Sciences and Scientific Information, Unter den Linden 6, 1086 Berlin, German Democratic Republic. Plans and coordinates library science research nationally.[9] The results of many research projects are published as dissertations, theses, and reports. Concentrates on theoretical and methodological problems, information service effectiveness, user studies, and library structure and organization.

21. Institute for Scientific Information, 3501 Market Street, Philadelphia, Pennsylvania 19104 USA, Eugene Garfield, President. Founded in 1956. A publisher of bibliographic information in all subject fields. This firm carries out R and D projects routinely.

22. The Central Institute of Library Affairs is one of the scientific-methodological institutions established for the most important sectors of the German Democratic Republic library system. Part of its time is devoted to study of fundamental problems, library statistics collection, and standardization. The Methodological Center for Research Libraries and Information and Documentation Institutions has similar responsibilities.

23. International Federation for Documentation (FID) Education and Training Committee Clearinghouse on Information Education and Training Material, School of Information Studies, Syracuse University, Syracuse, New York 13210 USA, Marta Dosa, Director. Founded in 1974, this clearinghouse is a source of course material from education programs throughout the world, and its use in the school and center internationalization program can be strongly recommended.

24. International Federation of Library Associations and Institutions, Associations in Information Fields Resource Center, Graduate School of Library and Information Science, Simmons College, Boston, Massachusetts 02115 USA, Josephine Fang, Director. Collects, studies, and publishes information on international and national information associations.

25. International Federation of Library Associations and Institutions International Office for Universal Bibliographic Control (UBC); Office for Universal Availability of Publications (UAP), M. B. Line, Director; and Office for International Lending (IL), M. B. Line, Director, British Library, 2 Sheraton Street, London, W1V 4BH, England. With Council on Library Resources support and British Library assistance, these centers contain research and survey components and carry on active publication programs.

26. International Referral Centre for Information Handling Equipment, TRG, Marsala/ALA Titr, 3, P. O. Box 327, YU–41001 Zagreb, Yugoslavia, Mrs. Neva Tudor-Silovic, Director. Founded in 1971, the Centre collects data on

all aspects of information-handling equipment and its appropriate research, carries out bibliographic surveys, publishes a bulletin and directories, and offers tutorials.[10]

27. Kent State University School of Library Science, Center for Library Studies, Kent, Ohio 44242 USA. Founded in 1966. Staff of twelve. Studies alternatives to graduate education for libraries in Ohio; also studies public library funding sources and use.

28. Lenin State Library of the USSR Center for Library Research, 3 Prospect Kalinina, 101000 Moscow, USSR. This is the leading national center for information research and experimentation.[11] A Ministry of Culture advisory council has been established to coordinate research activity in the various subject field libraries and in the universities. In the tenth Five-Year Plan, research is concentrated on improved service for workers, service to scholars and specialists, psychology of reading, library centralization, reader requests, library economics, and library work effectiveness criteria.

The Lenin Library and the M. E. Saltykov-Shchedrin Public Library coordinate research activities in scientific libraries. In each library as well as in major republic libraries, a special research section exists. The various republic libraries serve as regional centers and clearinghouses for library research, training, and methodological work. They study, discuss, and carry out research on policies and technical matters in order to prepare recommendations for the many libraries working with them. Research results must be transmitted from republic libraries to regional methods centers.

29. Matica Slovenska Slovak National Library, 03652 Martin Hostihoha, Bratislava, Czechoslavakia. This library supervises all library research activity in Slovakia.[12]

30. National Library Institute for Books and Readers, Ulica Hanklewicza 1, Warsaw 00–973, Poland. Founded in 1935, this research center is divided into four sections: reader research, library science, training for librarianship, and a cataloging bureau.

31. National Szechenyi Library Centre for Library Science and Methodology, Muzeum utca 3, Budapest VIII, Hungary, Istvan Papp, Director. Established in 1959, the Centre is organized into the following departments: network development, library technology, reading research, holdings, training, information, and public relations.[13] Most of the research deals with national library policy decisions, the library system as a whole, and public librarianship in particular. Principal research subjects include the library and society, reading, documents, information storage and retrieval, mechanization, bibliographic system development, and historical research. Total staff includes fifty professional persons.

32. Ohio State University Mechanized Information Center, Columbus, Ohio 43210 USA, Bernard Bayer, Director. Founded in 1970. Studies mechanization, management, and dissemination of information. Provides current awareness and retrospective services.

33. Online Information Centre, ASLIB, 26/27 Boswell Street, London WC1N 3JZ, England. Established in 1979 by the British Library and the Department

of Industry. Provides publications, inquiry, and referral service on computer use in information organizations.

34. Royal School of Librarianship, Birketinget 6, 2300 Copenhagen S, Denmark. The School has a Research Committee and a Research Secretariat, the latter sounding much like a kind of research center. Fifteen percent of faculty time is spent on research, and the school has certain technical facilities and a publication fund.

35. Saltykov-Shchedrin State Public Library, D–69 Sadovaya ul. 18, Leningrad, USSR. This library maintains the national Bibliographic Research Center.[14] In addition, the library's research office studies the role of different libraries in the scientific information system, book selection and stock control, updating of subject card catalogs, efficient use of resources, and staff training.

36. Saudia Arabian National Center for Science and Technology, P. O. Box 6086, Riyadh, Saudia Arabia, Abdulralman A. Mazi, Director, Information Systems. Founded in 1977. Serves the science and technology community with the most modern information service available. Provides searches, publications, R and D projects, system design and surveys, consulting, CE programs, and other services.

    Similar service and research programs exist in many national science and technology documentation centers, for example, Australia, Bangladesh, Bolivia, Bulgaria, Canada, Denmark (for public libraries), Egypt, India, Indonesia, Iran, Iraq, Israel (two centers), Japan, Jordan (for school libraries), South Korea, Kuwait (an especially sophisticated center), Lebanon, Mexico, Pakistan, Philippines, Poland, Singapore, South Africa, Spain, Sudan, Sweden, Thailand, Turkey, United States, Yugoslavia, and Zambia.

37. Tehran Book Processing Centre, P. O. Box 11–1126, Tehran, Iran. Established in 1968 and now affiliated with the National Library.[15] Maintains a department to carry on research concerning cataloging and bibliographic problems.

38. University of Chicago Center for Children's Books, Chicago, Illinois 60637 USA, Mrs. Zena Sutherland, Director. Founded in 1945. Concentrates on children's book bibliography and evaluation, and publishes a book review bulletin.

39. University of Illinois Graduate School of Library and Information Science Library Research Center, Urbana, Illinois 60801 USA, Herbert Goldhor, Director. This not-for-profit center was established in 1960 and has carried out investigations of public, academic, and school library organization service—surveys, program evaluations, literature reviews and analyses, field experience, and many other studies. Illinois has worked with the Illinois State Library to study data from public library annual reports, conduct surveys, and carry out other projects. In addition, it has had a contract with the U.S. Army Corps of Engineers Construction Engineering Research Laboratory to build and maintain a machine-readable file of index entries and abstracts on environmental protection. All Center publications are available at reproduction cost. The Center has published the *Fact Book of the American*

Public Library and has prepared the quarterly Index of American Public Library Circulation.

40. University of Pittsburgh Graduate School of Library and Information Science International Library Information Center, Pittsburgh, Pennsylvania 15260 USA, Richard Krzys, Director. Founded in 1964. Provides comparative studies of book distribution, libraries, education for library science, as well as specialized studies and surveys of world librarianship.

41. University of Southern California School for Library and Information Management Community Analysis Research Institute, Los Angeles, California 90007 USA. Roger C. Greer, Director. Founded in 1977; staff of two. Provides community analysis for library planning; data base design and user studies.

42. University of Toronto Faculty of Library and Information Science Center for Research in Librarianship, 140 St. George Street, Toronto, Ontario M5S 1A1, Canada, Adele Fasick, Director. Founded in 1975. Wilkinson has described its goals as follows: (a) to further an understanding of the nature of librarianship by adding to the body of data on Canadian libraries, (b) to increase librarianship's visibility in terms of political and financial support, and (c) to provide a research and intellectual focus for librarians in Canada and other countries.

Center objectives are to (a) attract viable research projects and funding, (b) develop the Center fiscal and administrative structure necessary to encourage project implementation, (c) attract research fellows with their own sabbatical leave or other funding, and (d) provide the facilities for exchange of data and opinions among students, faculty, alumni, and other scholars.[16]

NOTES

1. See John Wilkinson, "A School Service Center Program," Unpublished Paper, 1983, pp. 2, 4.

2. J. Stephen Parker, ed., *Aspects of Library Development Planning* (London: Mansell Publishing, Ltd., 1983).

3. See "The GSLIS As Publisher," University of Illinois Graduate School of Library and Information Science *Newsletter*, Issue 4 (Fall 1981), pp. 1–2.

4. See Bluma C. Peritz, "The Methods of Library Science Research: Some Results from a Bibliometric Survey," *Library Research* 2 (Fall 1980), pp 251–268.

5. See Lloyd Houser and Alvin Schrader, *The Search for a Scientific Profession* (Metuchen, N. J.: Scarecrow Press, 1978), p. 125; and Eugene Garfield, "The 1981 Articles Most Cited in 1981 and 1982, Life Science," *Current Contents* 15 (September 19, 1983), pp. 5–15.

6. See also M. Slater, "Research and the Practitioner," *Social Science Information Studies* 3 (July 1983), pp. 165–171.

7. Bonnie Carroll and Betty F. Moskewitz, "Information Analysis Centers," *Annual Review of Information Science and Technology*, vol. 15 (1980), pp. 147–189.

8. Ivan Kaldor, "Union of Soviet Socialist Republics," in Miles M. Jackson, ed., *International Handbook of Contemporary Developments in Librarianship* (Westport, Conn.: Greenwood Press, 1981), pp. 459–480.

9. Wilfred Kern, "The Library System of the German Democratic Republic," *IFLA Journal* 7, No. 2 (1981), pp. 94–110.

10. See Neva Tudor-Silovic, "International Referral Centre for Information Handling Equipment—IRCIHE. The Concept and the Reality," *International Forum on Information and Documentation* 9 (January 1984), pp. 20–23.

11. See I. P. Osipova "Research and Scientific Work in the State Lenin Library of the USSR," *Zentrallblatt für Bibliothekswesen* 89 (April 1975), pp. 155–165.

12. H. Hogh, "The Organization of Research Work in the Field of Library Science in Slovakia: History and Current Problems," *Bibliotekovedenie i Bibliografiya za Rubezhom*, Number 62 (1977), pp. 3–13.

13. National Szechenyi Library, *Centre for Library Science and Methodology* (Budapest: 1980), 60 pp.; Istvan Papp, "Research in Library Science: The Hungarian Scene," *UNESCO Library Bulletin* 30 (July-August 1976), pp. 199–205.

14. See O. D. Golubeva, "Research Work at the M. E. Saltykov-Shchedrin State Public Library," *Sovetskow Bibliotekivedenie*, No. 2 (1977), pp. 27–35.

15. John F. Harvey, "Iran," in Jackson, ed., *International Handbook of Contemporary Developments in Librarianship*, pp. 135–56.

16. The authors would like to thank the following for assistance in preparing this chapter: Evridiki Mavrommatis, Eleni Mavridou, Memna Hadjiharou, Sue Banfield, Azar Ashraf, and Georgia Agapiou.

BIBLIOGRAPHY

Information Services on Research in Progress: A Worldwide Inventory. Washington D.C.: Smithsonian Science Information Exchange, Inc., UNESCO, 1982.

Library and Information Science Research. Norwood, N. J.: Ablex Publishing Corp.. Quarterly. Vol. 1, 1979-.

Newsletter on Education and Training Programs for Specialized Information Personnel. The Hague: FID. Quarterly. No. 1, 1974-.

R and D Projects In Documentation and Librarianship. The Hague: FID. Bimonthly. Vol. 1, 1970-. (A comprehensive directory of institutions and individuals listed in the bimonthly issues was published in 1981.)

Register of Education and Training Activities in Librarianship, Information Science and Archives. Paris: UNESCO, 1982.

Research Centers Directory. Detroit: Gale Publishing Co., latest edition. (Check under library science, information science, information dissemination, and information retrieval.)

Wilkinson, John. "The Legitimization of Librarianship." *Libri* 33, No. 1 (1983), pp. 37–44.

10
INTERNATIONALIZING LIBRARY
CONTINUING EDUCATION

Robert Berk

Continuing education is a topic of major interest since librarians must insure the quality of the products and services they deliver now and in the future. It has received much attention in the past decade. This chapter will show how international continuing education programs in library schools can be planned and mounted. Associations, government agencies, and individual libraries must share in this effort. Superimposed on this program is the individual librarian's responsibility to meet the requirements of lifelong learning for both occupational competence and personal growth.

What is being proposed here is a possible model for offering continuing library education activities on an international scale based primarily on my own experience, but E. W. Stone's extensive bibliography is a good starting place for a comprehensive literature review.[1] Stone revealed that continuing education reflected lifelong learning; updated a person's education; diversified a person to a new area within a field; was the basic responsibility of the individual; and consisted of educational activities beyond those necessary for entrance into the field.

DEFINITIONS

There is little standardization in continuing education terminology. For example, the concept of the workshop is familiar to many, but its definition varies greatly. Consequently, the terms and definitions used in this chapter will be those which the author has used previously. These terms include staff development, in-service training, continuing education, personal growth, and lifelong learning.

The most general and inclusive term is *staff development*. Staff development can be achieved by any type of educational activity that aids the individual in doing a better job. It also includes those activities that do not relate directly to the individual's position but give a broader insight leading to personal growth. Most organizations support staff development programs that improve job performance and organizational understanding.

In-service training is a type of staff development that is specifically aimed at improving one's performance for a particular job. This may be the individual's regular job or a new one. In-service training usually takes place within the organization and involves relatively few individuals at one time.

Whereas in-service training is the responsibility of the supervisor, continuing education is a shared responsibility of the individual, the organization, and the provider of the continuing education activity. Continuing education consists of those activities that enable one to grow within an organization. Some of these activities may bear directly on an individual's job and enable him or her to perform better. Others may have little relationship to the organization's work but instead promote the growth of the individual as a person. All of these activities contribute toward an individual's lifelong learning goals. The concept of lifelong learning reflects the short half-life of entry-level library education and the need to continue learning for as long as one practices.

The library field is changing continually, and one should never cease to learn. By extension, a lifelong learning program shows awareness of the need and provides a means for participating in a continuing learning process. The responsibility for lifelong learning rests with the individual who must judge what is relevant to his or her needs. Continuing education is the key to lifelong learning, and occupationally related learning is intricately entwined with the employer's organizational objectives.

In this chapter the concept of continuing education will be limited to continuing library education involving activities designed to improve an individual's job performance or understanding of the organization or the field at large. Most of the programs offered through library schools seek to provide new or to update existing information or skills. Individual job performances may be affected, but an improved understanding of librarianship and information science is its objective. The following activities might qualify:

Area Studies	Conferences
International Summer School	Workshops
Study Abroad Programs	Lecture Series
Distance Learning Opportunities	Library Tours
Regular Credit Courses	Self-Study Programs

Any one of these activities is a potential means through which a library school can provide continuing education for graduates and other librarians and information scientists. Any one of them can also be internationalized.

LIBRARY SCHOOL CONTINUING EDUCATION PROGRAMS

With regard to continuing education, V. S. Sessions has said: "One of the mysteries of professional education is why institutions which work so hard to turn out competent practitioners usually suspend their educational concern after handing over their degrees."[2] Library schools must serve the continuing education needs of *all* librarians and information scientists, not just those of their own graduates or countrymen and must consider a variety of formats to serve their clientele best. Clientele should be expanded with progression from a provincial to an internatioal approach. In the light of current financial pressures, Sessions has commented that if the Canadian library schools should experience declining enrollments, self-preservation may change their negative attitudes toward lifelong education.

U.S. and Canadian library schools offer a variety of continuing education activities.[3] Of sixty-nine schools surveyed in a questionnaire prepared by T. W. Sineath, sixty-six (96 percent) responded, and of these sixty-two (90 percent) offered activities in 1981–1982. A total of 618 activities were presented to 24,247 individuals and occupied 5,806 instructional hours. The types of activities consisted of institutes, seminars, workshops, conferences, forums, colloquia, short courses, and others. One suspects that the semantics involved in delineating them is confusing and that almost all could be termed workshops (with active participant involvement).

An encompassing type of activity is the lecture in which a passive audience receives instruction. Another is the short course held either for continuing education or for formal university credit. Normally, formal courses last longer than workshops or lectures and involve an academic calendar schedule.

Extension courses offered off campus or in another country are also considered to be a form of continuing education. It is cheaper to send an instructor to a distant site than to have twenty to thirty students travel to a central location. Advanced study or degree programs can also be used. Would practitioners who completed their own course work so long ago that their knowledge has become outdated benefit from courses? The sabbatical leave has long been useful for this purpose.

Lectures, workshops, and short courses may be the most difficult activities to address because of the lack of university recognition for continuing education and the lack of faculty members to plan or teach them.

However, they are clearly feasible for many schools. Such short-duration activities also appear to meet the "hygiene" factors which motivate attendance: they do not remove the individual from the library for an extended period, they may provide a concentrated learning experience, and they can be tailored to meet special group needs. These factors should motivate participation, which is important because most continuing education must be self-supporting financially. In addition, extra funds should be obtained to provide seed money for planning additional activities.

OBJECTIVES

A number of objectives underlie library school sponsorship of continuing education. The primary objective of continuing education is altruistic: to insure the continued competence of practitioners. The second objective may be to bring in outside revenue. Additional objectives may involve building the school's influence and prestige within the library community.

International continuing education objectives should also reflect the school's special competence in a particular field. This may be a faculty or subject area competence or a valuable geographical or cultural setting. International program planning differs little from local planning, but the following tasks must be carried out:

Determining target group continuing education needs

Planning the activity

Making local arrangements

Marketing

Evaluating the outcome

Maintaining required record systems

Determining Target Group Needs

A planning technique for determining the program subjects and methods is the needs assessment which requires input from potential consumers. The assumption is that programs developed in response to expressed needs are more likely to be successful than programs developed in some other way. In a needs assessment, one must clearly define concepts and pretest instruments to insure that useful data will be collected. A representative sample is also required. Occasional reports violate this rule and are useless because a representative sample was not obtained. (For additional information regarding needs assessments, see Barbara Conroy.)[4]

An extensive needs assessment survey should usually be omitted because of its expense. Even if an extensive survey is undertaken, librarians may be able only to identify specific job problems and not their needs. Instead, a representative group of practitioners can be asked about the topics and delivery formats needed.

The survey panel should be small for efficient use, consisting of no more than six or seven members, and be specialized either by topic or by general library area, depending on what is needed. The panel should be aware of unique needs beyond those held in common. It should prioritize the needs to be reached and identify the most suitable delivery modes. Certain library schools already have advisory groups which can perform this function. International representatives should provide input as well. Correspondence can supplement face-to-face contacts with international representatives.

Planning the Activity

Format and content must be chosen, and duration and leadership decisions must be made. Supportive material and physical facilities will be required. If a library school faculty member is to be the instructor, then that person should be free to determine content and methods. If an outsider is to instruct, then perhaps a faculty member should review content and method.

An individual should be named to coordinate and administer all continuing education programs in library schools. This individual can develop skill and continuity in all aspects of their administration. The University of Wales College of Librarianship in Aberystwyth has a Director of Liaison and Training Services with five assistants. In the United States many library schools designate part of one faculty member's time for continuing education coordination. This assignment frequently supplements a full teaching load. It is desirable that the position of coordinator be permanent and that it be adequately funded to release the person from other duties.

A faculty member or staff administrator of a library school should supervise each activity, arranging directly for physical facilities, meals, registration, audiovisual and public address equipment, and so on. On an international scale, the problems of moving people from one country to another, coordinating schedules, and allowing for different cultural expectations and possible language barriers will make the supervisor's job even more important.

The motivations and expectations of continuing education students differ from those of regular degree students. Those in a regular degree program are familiar with the classroom and expect a didactic approach and formal delivery. Their goal is to prepare for an entry-level position.

For the continuing education student the goal may be quite different. This person is already employed, is not as comfortable with a classroom setting, expects to be treated as an equal, and learns largely through self-motivation and personal interest. In addition, this person expects to obtain practical information that can be translated into improved job performance or understanding.

Making Local Arrangements

Arrangements for space, seating, meals, refreshments, water for speakers and participants, lighting, and parking must be made by the supervisor or a person on the spot in an off campus location. Supporting material must be sent to that person in advance. Negotiations may involve arrangements with motels or hotels that have meeting rooms. Sometimes such facilities can be secured at a lower cost if meals are also taken there. The meeting site may need to accommodate special requirements such as phone jacks for online demonstrations. Several visits to the meeting site may be required by the local arrangement supervisor. U.S. meeting supervisors are frequently said to exhibit poor execution. International activities provide even more chances for mishaps. If a foreign location is involved, then a conscientious national should supervise local arrangements.

Marketing

Marketing may be one of the most difficult aspects of mounting a continuing education activity. Mailing lists can be developed from association membership lists, past program attendance lists, expressed interest, and alumni lists. Marketing approaches should reach the greatest number of potential students in desired locales, local, national, or international, at the least possible cost.

One of the most effective methods of accomplishing this goal is to list the activity in sources regularly carrying continuing education information. Organizations such as the International Federation of Library Associations and Institutions, the International Federation for Documentation, the United Nations Educational, Scientific and Cultural Organization, the American Library Association, and the Association of Special Libraries and Information Bureaux publish journals, newsletters, and continuing education calendars. A very large mailing list should be avoided because of the international postage cost. Commercial journal advertising should also be considered.

Sufficient time must be allotted for the target group to be reached and to make leave, registration, travel, and other arrangements. This lead time may be eight to twelve months for international activities.

Planning must therefore precede the event by twelve to eighteen months. Word-of-mouth advertising by previous program participants should be encouraged. Each activity's participant file can be used in generating public relations releases, mailing lists, and statistical reports when marketing future offerings.

Evaluating the Outcome

Many activities are paid for by library employers as part of staff development programs. Hence, employers are interested in the activity's educational outcome. Was any learning and/or behavior modification achieved? In addition, individuals need evidence that they have gained something. However, adult students not only learn differently from younger students, but they are also affected differently by formal testing. Many adults will not attend activities that are formally evaluated.

Many continuing education leaders have used a pre- and a post-test to evaluate performance. Testing results have not been used to determine credit eligibility, and individuals have been recognized (usually in the form of a certificate and a number of credit hours) regardless of performance. However, employers are beginning to demand evidence of learning before committing staff members and funds to these activities.

Meaningful ways must be found to measure learning and behavior changes. Not only will employers be more likely to support successful activities, but also providers can use positive outcomes as a basis for developing additional programs. Innovative ways of measuring learning must be developed which offer data as conclusive as that produced by formalized test procedures.

Some activities may be suitable for producing a written paper, while other activities might lead to applications in a participant's library. For example, individuals who attended a library performance measurement workshop might return to install performance measures in certain areas of their library.

Certain subjects lend themselves to formal test procedures. For example, a program on PRECIS could be concluded with some actual monographs for analysis and subject assignment. The correctness of the subject headings assigned could determine individual success. Attendance certificates can continue to indicate participation, but we need something more concrete to show cognitive and behavioral gains.

Before planning an activity, perhaps one should learn what employers would like their employees to gain from it and how they would like this gain to be documented. Their ideas about the basis for granting continuing education credit can also be solicited. In this way, some participants complete a formal paper, some go through formal test procedures, and others only attend in order to acquire evidence of participation. For international continuing education programs, it may be more difficult to demand a minimum competence level before awarding credit.

Maintaining Required Record Systems

Library schools must provide a permanent record of continuing education activities. Many maintain such records in the school or university registrar's office. If formal academic credit is awarded, then the necessary recordkeeping will be part of the university's record system, and participants can request transcripts from the registrar. If the registrar's office cannot perform this function for noncredit activities, then the school must maintain records in another way. A simple system identifying the activity participant, type of activity, dates, and whether or not completion certificates were awarded should be sufficient.

A standard American means of reporting continuing education credit is based on the amount of time and effort involved in the activity. Another common measure reports participation in terms of instructor-student contact hours. Such credit is frequently provided in the form of semester or quarter hours of academic credit. Continuing education activites are generally of much shorter duration than formal degree courses. Contact hours reflect the time spent in the classroom or meeting in which actual instruction takes place; they do not include break or lunch time. The Continuing Education Unit (CEU) is frequently used to show continuing education credit.[5]

A problem is presented when the activity is not based on instructional time or contact hours. For example, a planned program of individual self-study may not involve contact or direct instruction. These activities can be converted to contact hours or CEUs, but such measurements become less meaningful as the activities move away from the strict definition of instructional time. Records should provide a clear explanation of the basis used in computing contact hours and credit for each activity, and this explanation should be sent to each inquirer.

INTERNATIONAL ACTIVITIES

The specialized programs that library schools might offer include area-studies activities, international summer schools, study-abroad programs, distance learning, academic credit courses, conferences, workshops, lecture series, library tours, and self-study programs.

Area Studies

Many schools offer bibliography and reference courses in a variety of subject areas, usually in the sciences, social sciences, and humanities.

Courses on special language material or subject matter are common. Many of them might also serve as continuing education activities for persons with international interests. They can be marketed to area studies students dealing with the bibliography of a particular area or language. For example, a library school might offer a course in Eastern European literature in the sciences. An extension course in Mexico City has been offered in English by the University of Arizona.

Whether or not such activities are marketed to an international audience, providers should consider international perspectives and content in their planning. A workshop on patent literature, for example, would suffer greatly were one to ignore the importance of the international scene. Similar approaches are also important when planning programs dealing with networking, the organization of material, and computer applications.

International Summer Schools

An international summer school is appealing to librarians who wish to combine continuing education with foreign travel. Librarians may study different educational approaches and library applications abroad. The College of Librarianship, Wales, has the best known program. Both Drexel and Oklahoma in the United States have sponsored summer European study programs for graduate credit. A 1973 European summer school for senior librarians was sponsored by the Liverpool Polytechnic Institute. This type of activity might serve as a model for international summer programs aimed at middle management.

Study-Abroad Programs

One of the best ways to internationalize is to attract foreign students to regular library school degree programs. The University of Pittsburgh has long attracted a large number of foreign students. Foreign student enrollment at the University of Missouri amounts to 10 percent of the student body. (For a comprehensive discussion of the study-abroad concept,[6] see F. L. Carroll.) With greater library education internationalization, a concomitant avenue to international continuing education will develop.

Funding is the major limiting factor in attracting international students, and may be overcome by transporting an offering (instructor, material, and so on) from country to country. A large local enrollment can spread the cost over a broad base and result in reasonable registration fees.

Distance Learning

Among the alternatives to international travel are correspondence courses, teleconferencing using telephones, and satellite transmission of audio and video content. Australia and the United States are at present experimenting with such programs together. Correspondence course work for continuing education credit may be an ideal way to test market new international education activities. The initial investment should be relatively small except for the instructor's time.

Distance learning presents unique problems and requires resourceful approaches. One approach is to combine it with correspondence course work. Another is to combine distance learning with residential school requirements and require students to attend certain sessions in a central location. This might be a useful approach for an activity requiring extensive study and independent research and could culminate with a session to discuss outcomes and evaluate the learning process.

Only a few reports of distance learning use for library education are available. The University of South Africa is the largest correspondence university in the world, with the Department of Library Science having 800 students. The problems of distance learning, including a 50 percent dropout rate, may have discouraged other library schools from utilizing this method. Still, there must be a market for activities that do not require absence from work, travel to distant locations, or a time frame.

The correspondence courses offered in the United States are offered primarily through institutions that do not have accredited Master's degree programs for library sciences. A review of a recent guide to such programs shows that ten schools offer between one and eight such correspondence courses. The bulk of these courses are in children's work and the organization of material.[7]

Library schools should devote some of their resources to planning and to testing such activities for international continuing education. The American Society for Information Science has sponsored the development of a distance learning instructional package on motivation at Catholic University, in Washington, D.C., USA. Ironically, the subject of motivation is perhaps the cause of the excessive dropout rate. More direct interaction with the instructor may reduce student dropouts.

Some distance learning success may be seen in West Germany where the Deutsches Bibliotheks-Institut is experimenting with centrally produced and distributed "home-study packs."[8] Their goal is to cover a wide range of library-related subjects and to make the packs available throughout the country at a low cost.

Currently, one unit on cataloging and another on information work are being tested. Study pack material includes those that are similar to traditional multimedia workshop offerings: tapes, booklets, reading lists, slides, charts, and so forth. The approach is similar to that of the British Open University but without the supporting radio broadcasts and academic credit.

Though technology distance learning may be able to provide many of the benefits of the more traditional continuing education activities which bring instructors and participants together. Teleconference activities using the telephone or television can duplicate virtually every condition present in traditional gatherings. Audio and video teleconferencing may link geographically dispersed groups in an interactive network. The success of these ventures, as well as steadily increasing travel costs, dictate that more technologically mediated activities be sponsored. Use of audio only presents a problem for students who miss instructor and student eye contact.[9]

Academic Credit Courses

Academic credit courses are usually offered for continuing education by scheduling them at times that are convenient for practitioners—late afternoon, evening, and weekends. Credit courses can be designed specifically to attract participants from other countries in a way similar to the Wales program.

The acquisition of a doctorate is a form of continuing education but apparently for only a limited number of librarians. In addition to the intellectual discipline that a research degree provides, it also serves as a useful midcareer refresher course. A research-oriented degree has international appeal and possibilities because data-gathering is important to international librarianship.

Conferences

The conference, one of the most popular continuing education activities, may be local, regional, national, or international. FID and IFLA sponsor conferences for a market that mirrors their international representatives. Library schools may also sponsor conferences; an example is the annual University of Illinois Data Processing Clinic. Many library school conferences would be interesting to international participants if that group were included in the initial planning.

Workshops

The workshop is probably the most ubiquitous continuing education activity in librarianship today. Needs assessments underscore the attractiveness of short-term learning experiences that occur outside the library and do not involve extensive travel. Activities that present new and

creative ideas and offer the chance to meet informally with colleagues
to discuss mutual problems are heavily favored. The one-, two-, or three-
day workshop appears to meet many of the librarian's needs. It may be
the easiest activity to plan and support, particularly if there is a university
continuing educating division to help with workshop details.

Such divisions can provide advice in planning, marketing, transporting, registering, evaluating, and recordkeeping. They frequently have
mailing lists that assist in reaching interested individuals, and they may
also have detailed information regarding international programs. While
relieving planners of many detailed responsibilities, these divisions must
also support themselves, so that the activity cost to participants may need
to be increased significantly to pay for division services.

A few references to library school workshops will illustrate their wide
appeal. Fifty American library schools reported holding workshops during 1981–1982. This was the most popular continuing education activity,
with colloquia, as the second most popular, being offered by twenty-
seven schools. The schools held a total of 239 workshops with a range
of 1 to 18 and a mean number of 4.3 per institution. Average enrollment
was thirty-four individuals. The increased popularity of workshops is
shown by the 1978–1979 total which was only 158. Total enrollment in
1978–1979 workshops was 6,229 individuals compared to the 1981–1982
figure of 8,138. Although the number of workshops increased by 51
percent between the two years, enrollment increased by only 31 percent.

Norman Horrocks has predicted that the popularity of broad-based
subjects of general interest will give way to more specialized subjects.[10]
In a report on a survey conducted to determine Canadian library school
activities, Sessions has reported that workshops seem to be as prevalent
there as in the United States. Unfortunately, in many cases, workshops
may be merely cosmetic efforts designed to fulfill only the most obvious
and vocal library community needs. In fact, the prevalence of such activities may prevent faculty members from using their imagination to
search beyond workshops to other staff development approaches.

Lecture Series

A lecture series provides a means by which a library school can easily
establish a limited continuing education program. The possibilities for
internationalizing such a series are excellent if the school is near main
travel thoroughfares on which visiting foreign librarians pass regularly
en route to other destinations.

Lecture series may be scheduled regularly in the form of colloquia
intended primarily for the student body, but there should also be a
standing invitation to local librarians to attend. ALA sponsors the annual
Carl Milam lecture series which funds the visit of a prominent foreign

librarian to several American library schools. These schools offered 123 colloquia in 1981–1982.

Lectures should be planned both as parts of a regularly scheduled colloquium series and as independent services. Even local speakers should be encouraged to consider the international aspects of their topics, so that participants will be exposed to a wide range of ideas and practices. A school with a regularly scheduled colloquium series should plan for at least a few of them to treat international topics.

Of course, Sessions and others have questioned the value of lectures. Although Sessions supports the concept that most lectures provide some educational value, she believes it to be small. The Medical Library Association does not grant recertification credit for lecture attendance. However, both lectures and reading professional literature should be considered legitimate continuing education forms.

Lecture series probably provide the best means for involvement in international librarianship. Library associations, government agencies, and colleagues can provide information regarding potential international lectures. The presence of such lectures on the campus may lead to arrangements for other types of international continuing education and may help to link the school to the lecturer's colleagues at home. Presentations by local librarians who have practiced abroad can lend international support to a lecture series.

Library Tours

Many librarians visit other libraries to learn new techniques and useful ideas. The benefits of learning from one's peers are widely recognized. Many informal visits are made, but tours may also be arranged in conjunction with library association meetings. For example, the American and Canadian chapters of the Special Libraries Association frequently visit local libraries as part of the conference program. Many library schools arrange for class tours of interesting libraries.

At least two different approaches can be used to internationalize library tours. One approach is to organize a tour in one's own country. It can easily be limited to the school's immediate city or region. The tour should probably be designed for a specific national audience. For example, an American library school can plan a tour of major Chicago area libraries for a group of British librarians one year, German librarians the next, and Scandinavian librarians the following year. Each tour can be tailored to the needs of a specific national group.

A second approach would require a school to plan a tour in a foreign country. Such a tour can be led by a national of that country or by a knowledgeable and bilingual faculty member of one's own school. A variety of prominent libraries, library schools, publishers, and dealers is usually covered. If costs can be kept down, library tours may well increase in popularity. Library tour contacts can lead to short-term exchanges of librarian positions.

Self-Study Programs

Types of self-study might include planned personal reading programs and the use of radio, television, or videotapes to receive continuing education programs at home. The least expensive, most flexible, and easiest activity to employ is an independent reading program. Every librarian should have such a program.

Reading programs are matters of individual concern because their success depends on personal motivation. Many librarians are encouraged to undertake such programs by free time provided at work. A concept used in other occupations involves the journal club. In this activity, librarians in the same locale can be assigned individual articles to read and prepare in advance for discussion at a regularly scheduled club meeting. Library schools can easily sponsor and host such meetings. The chances of internationalizing such activities are good if resources are available and bibliographies cite international material.

Library schools may use self-study through assigned reading in conjunction with other continuing education activities, most notably the workshop. Participants can be sent reading lists and be expected to master certain material prior to the workshop in an attempt to insure that all participants have a common knowledge base on the workshop topic. By increasing the number of foreign citations on these reading lists, participants come to the workshop with a greater appreciation for library practice throughout the world. This can only help to identify solutions to local and national problems. Home-study packs might serve the same function and could include other kinds of material, such as programmed texts.

Home study through televised courses has been popular in certain countries, particularly Britain. With public access to cable television, a library school can present an activity to the local market through this medium. In most cases, students will need to pay fees, be evaluated, and be granted some form of recognition. As Sessions has pointed out, because continuing education has a low priority on many university campuses, such activities may need to generate sufficient revenue to cover all expenses.

Another approach to international home study is to offer a continuing education activity by videotape. Such a tape can be produced from the cable television activity discussed above. Arrangements can be made to provide tape copies for use by library schools abroad. Participants can also gather at the school for discussion sessions.

If a philosophy of internationalization is present, then the means of mounting activities for this market can be found. Certain activities involve bringing library school resources to persons who need continuing education, and others can be pursued by individuals on their own. The school's role is central to the success of each activity. The university must recognize its responsibility for an active lifelong learning program, and library degree holders must recognize that continuing education has become a common way of life.

Cooperating Sponsors

A number of other organizations appear to be preeminent in their concern for international continuing education. Cooperation and co-sponsorship should be sought with them. One of them, FID, publishes the *Newsletter on Education and Training Programs for Information Personnel.*[11]

On the national level, each country has a library association interested in continuing education. Certain national associations are further structured into geographic groups that provide a series of continuing education activities throughout the year. Library schools may find the best opportunity for cooperation in program planning and sharing at the local level. More individuals are touched by activities there than at the regional and national levels.

The literature available on planning international activities concentrates primarily on details. T. I. Skripkina, for example, describes a government-organized structure. In addition, a plank in the tenth Soviet Five-Year Plan for 1976–1980 "provides for an extensive programme to improve the pre- and in service training of library staffs and to bring about further advances in the ideological and professional education of library specialists." The results of such efforts mean that "a comprehensive system of further library education has grown up in the USSR, designed to help the specialist continue his education beyond school or university."[12]

It would be helpful to colleagues in other countries if Soviet librarians could encourage their government to open such further training to an international audience. For its part, the United States could advance librarian exchange with the Soviet Union and other countries as a means of improving international librarianship. If the library field can begin to think in terms of a global community and plan continuing education activities accordingly, all librarians will gain.

NOTES

1. E. W. Stone, *Continuing Library and Information Science Education* (Washington, D.C.: Government Printing Office, 1974), Bibliography, pp. 1–83.

2. V. S. Sessions, "Continuing Education Courses Are Few and Disparate," *Canadian Library Journal* 36 (June 1979), pp. 101–105.

3. T. W. Sineath, "Continuing Professional Education," *Library and Information Science Education Statistical Report* (State College, Pa.: Association of Library and Information Science Education, 1983), p. CE–4.

4. Barbara Conroy, *Library Staff Development and Continuing Education* (Littleton, Colo.: Libraries Unlimited, 1978), pp. 7–26.

5. According to the National Task Force on the Continuing Education Unit, one continuing education unit is defined as 10 contact hours of participation in an organized continuing education experience under responsible sponsorship, capable direction, and qualified instruction. A contact hour is defined as a 50-minute classroom instructional session or its equivalent. Ten 50–minute contact hours equal one Continuing Education Unit (CEU). Thus, a two-day workshop (7 hours per day) might provide a participant with a total of 14 hours (840 minutes) of activity at the rate of 60 minutes per hour, but only 11.7 hours (700 minutes) of activity at the rate of 50 minutes per hour of contact or instruction time. The 11.7 contact hours would equal 1.17 CEUs. Because of their frequent and prolonged nature, semester academic courses would normally provide more than 30 contact hours or 3 plus CEUs.

6. F. L. Carroll, "International Education for Librarianship," *International Library Review* 2 (January 1970), pp. 19–39.

7. *Macmillan Guide to Correspondence Study* (New York: Macmillan, 1983).

8. Blaise Cronin, "Continuing Library Education—An Innovation," *Library Association Record* 83 (September 1981), p. 411.

9. R. A. Berk, "The Delivery of Continuing Education: Teleconferencing," *Bulletin of the Medical Library Association* 70 (January 1982), pp. 21–27.

10. Norman Horrocks, "Continuing Education—An Update on the Dalhousie School of Library Services Activities," *Atlantic Provinces Library Association Bulletin* 39 (1975), pp. 14–15.

11. Documentation Research and Training Centre, *Seminar on Library and Information Manpower Development* (Bangalore: 1976).

12. T. I. Skripkina, "Continuing Library Education in the USSR," *UNESCO Journal of Information Science, Librarianship and Archives Administration* 2 (July-September 1980), pp. 184–188.

BIBLIOGRAPHY

Alvarez, R. S. "Continuing Education for the Public Librarian." *California Librarian* 30 (July 1969), pp. 177–186.

Aransky, V. S., and G. V. Ivanova. "Further Training for Information Specialists in Soviet Public Education." *UNESCO Bulletin for Libraries* 32 (July-August 1978), pp. 284–287.

Carroll, F. L. "International Education for Librarianship." *International Library Review* 4 (April 1972), pp. 102–26.

Hoban, M. F. "An Activist's Approach to Continuing Education for Special Librarians." *Special Libraries* 70 (November 1979), pp. 471–478.

Jones, Noragh. "Continuing Education for Librarians." *Journal of Librarianship* 10 (January 1978), pp. 39–55.

Mounce, M. W. "The Education of Library Development Personnel." *Library Trends* 27 (Fall 1978), pp. 197–208.

Taylor, N. B. "The Role of State Library Agencies in Continuing Education," *Library Trends* 27 (Fall 1978), pp. 189–196.

11

LIBRARY RESOURCES AND SERVICES FOR INTERNATIONAL LIBRARY AND INFORMATION SCIENCE EDUCATION

Mae L. Furbeyre

Relative to library resources and services, internationalization at its best can be carried out by raising the collection development level to multinational dimensions and expanding and improving user services to facilitate international access, retrieval, and use.

The setting of this chapter is limited to the United States and thus all external areas are considered to be international. A further assumption is that the library school has already made a policy decision to infuse its educational program with international perspectives and that its library is expected to help in implementing the decision. Observations based on collection usage where research on international issues has been rare and faculty international interest sporadic are not considered. Other pertinent limitations not considered are: the inordinate amount of effort needed to develop primary international material files, and the cost and space constraints.[1] Only key international material titles can be discussed.

THE LIBRARY SUPPORT SYSTEM

The library school may have a separate library with a staff reporting to the dean and funded as a school component, or it may be placed entirely under the supervision of the central library system. A branch library service can be customized to an effective support level as long as deviations from standard practices can be harmonized without unreasonable system pressure. The library school's modest size, the need for subventions, and the wide range of information sources required to support the curriculum pose difficulties that could require cooperative arrangements.[2] Ultimately, however, the type of adaptation needed may depend on the extent of the compromise on centralization versus decentralization of functions.

A third organization pattern, integration of library and information science (LIS) collections with the central library system's general holdings, minimizes the discipline's visibility and the identity of its literature.

Collection and service integration patterns are still controversial.[3] No matter what the organizational structure, the librarian responsible for LIS collection development must be identified, and that person's role in developing, managing, and preserving collections must be clearly defined and understood. The presence of a "dedicated" or system-assigned librarian is essential to strengthen the international perspective of resources and services. Such a librarian not only serves as the communication link but also provides commitment, continuity, and focus to monitor the coordinative function.

The coordination of systemwide collection development has been a significant function. LIS librarians or subject bibliographers perform coordinative roles for their immediate clientele. Collection quality rests on adequate fiscal support and proper bibliographic tools.

Since the LIS librarian is essential in internationalizing material resources, it is appropriate to learn how the librarian's group has been identified by American Library Association accredited schools.[4] Of sixty-seven schools, forty-six (69 percent) furnished librarians' names. Among those named, twenty (43 percent) were responsible for collections and services integrated with other subject fields. Only twenty-six (39 percent) were found to have separate libraries.

LIBRARY AND INFORMATION SCIENCE LITERATURE AND BIBLIOGRAPHIC CONTROL

The librarian required to internationalize library holdings must proceed cautiously, learning what is on hand before seeking more. Since the field is inherently international, the material already found on the shelves may well be partially international.

The basic LIS bibliographic control sources are the guides to the literature—indexes, bibliographies, and abstracting services. They are helpful not only as assessment checklists but also as collection development guides. The universal bibliographic control concept is not new to librarians, but control of their own literature has not seemed urgent until recently.

In 1964 library science librarians in socialist countries met in Budapest to discuss international bibliographic control and to work out cooperative projects.[5] Strong concerns were evident during a similar conference in the United States in 1968.[6] Recommendations included broadening foreign material acquisition, improving the international coverage of abstracting and indexing services, and establishing a mechanism for monitoring the literature worldwide.

United Kingdom librarians have demonstrated a continuing interest in tracking the literature, in making comparative surveys of abstracting services, and in discussing the bibliographic problems of library literature control.[7] A literature search conducted in 1984 revealed no previous attempt to address directly the question of the internationalization level of the leading LIS indexing and abstracting journals.

Determining *Library Literature's* (LL) internationalization level posed quantification difficulties, but its list of periodicals indexed was an indicator of its scope.[8] The language and geographic distribution of the periodicals indexed were the most relevant elements to internationalism and most easily quantifiable. In the 1983 cumulation, 85 of 201 titles were published outside the country of publication, the United States. It was therefore considered to be 42 percent international, the lowest in this study. Twenty-eight countries were represented in LL, and 16 percent of the 201 titles were in languages other than English.

In addition to LL, four current LIS indexing and abstracting services were examined: the United States' *Information Science Abstracts* (ISA), the United Kingdom's *Library and Information Science Abstracts* (LISA), the USSR's *Informatics Abstracts* (IA), and France's *Bulletin Signalétique* 101 (BS). To be consistent in comparing and quantifying, only the 1983 cumulated title lists were used. Periodicals published outside the country where the service originated were identified and entries verified.[9] Tom Edwards obtained the following totals in 1973:[10]

Service	Periodical Titles Covered	Total Number of Abstracts/ Entries
LL	221	10,401
ISA	247	3,721
LISA	210	2,873
IA	331	4,524
BS	320	3,245

Table 11.1 considers the degree of internationalization of the five services mentioned above. The total number of periodical titles and abstracts is significantly different from Edwards' total, especially for ISA and LISA. ISA, overlapping only 55 with LL, appreciably supplemented it with 639 more titles. Other overlaps are displayed in Table 11.2. Twenty-eight journals were common to four services (see the Appendix). LISA had the highest overlap with LL but covered more archival work titles, added abstracts, and provided much more extensive international coverage.

ISA covers information and computer science extensively and in 1984 almost doubled its 1983 output and changed its frequency from bi-

Table 11.1
Statistical Profile of the 1983 Lists of Indexed Library & Information Science Periodicals[1]

Indexing & Abstracting Services	Total Number of Abstracts (2)	Language of the Abstract Text (3)	Total Number of Indexed/ Abstracted Periodicals	Number of English Language Titles	Number of Non-English Language Titles	Extent of International Coverage to Country Where Published (Titles)	Extent of Additional Coverage To LL Users (Titles) (4)
Library Literature (LL)	7,202	English	201	169	32	85 (42%)	639
Information Science Abstracts (ISA)			694	587	107	316 (46%)	639
Library & Information Science Abstracts (LISA)	6,778	English	473	360	113	382 (81%)	336

Informatics Abstracts (IA)	5,398	English	402	153	249	325 (81%)	335
Bulletin Signaletique (BS)	4,209	French	195	120	75	162 (83%)	131

1. Excluded are non-periodical serials when found interfiled; title changes when new title is also given; duplicate entries or variant forms of identical periodicals, e. g., abbreviations, etc.

2. Estimated to be 10,000 items annually by Purcell and Schlachter (1984).

3. No abstracts; however, foreign language entries are given with English translation of titles.

4. For LL overlap with other services, see Table 2.

Table 11.2
**Periodical Title Overlap Among Indexing & Abstracting Services of Library
& Information Science, 1983[a]**

	LL	ISA	LISA	IA	BS
LL	(201)[b]	55	137	67	64
ISA	55	(694)[b]	75	74	61
LISA	137	75	(473)[b]	96	92
IA	67	74	96	(402)[b]	62
BS	64	61	92	62	(195)[b]

a Overlap is represented by the number of identical periodical
   titles indexed/abstracted by the services intersecting.

b Total number of periodical titles indexed/abstracted.

Note: Twenty-nine LL indexed titles appeared in all four lists of
      the abstracting services. Without BS, the LL titles common
      to LISA, ISA, and IA were 37.

monthly to monthly. In 1983 ISA covered 316 international titles, 46 percent of its abstracting effort.

IA overlapped other services more for English-language journals than for those in other languages. For Soviet citizens its international coverage was 325 titles, 81 percent of its 1983 effort. Clearly, IA had an international view. BS offered twenty-four unique titles published in France. To the French, BS was 83 percent international in journal coverage, very strong. Overlap with LISA was high.[11] As selection aids, the lists of periodicals indexed by LL, LISA, ISA, IA, and BS as well as the Ulrich, FID, and Standard titles should be helpful in identifying core titles when building an international serial collection covering library education.

Overlap and uncoordinated coverage of titles can be resolved cooperatively. This will entail rising above national interests, opposing tradition, cutting local vendor income, and striving for "true cosmopolitanism." The technology is available to facilitate systematic and coordinated bibliographic control, and useful networking experience is beginning to accumulate. The situation requires that a library group take the initiative and persuade publishers to make changes.

In their study Purcell and Schlachter brought together 1,129 annotated reference titles.[12] The time frame they considered limited most inclusions to imprints from the 1900s to early 1980s, especially the last decade. A tally of titles by geographic and language distribution indicates a modest 43 percent international coverage.

General reference sources may fill in time and language gaps. Retrospective bibliographies of bibliographies and guides to reference books, such as Sheehy and Walford, can furnish citations to earlier and foreign titles.[13] National and trade bibliographies with subject approaches can also be searched. The printed catalogs of the Columbia University School of Library Service Library and the United Kingdom Library Association Library can be used.[14] The *International Bibliography of the Book Trade and Librarianship* was noteworthy, with the latest edition listing 9,826 titles from 106 countries.[15] It was extensive for German, United Kingdom, U.S. coverage, and the USSR, France, Africa, Asia, and Australia had more than 100 entries each.

A serial registry in an international data bank of over 150,000 serial records grew by 25,000 to 30,000 titles per year. The International Serials Data System (ISDS) file is maintained by the International Centre in Paris in cooperation with a network of forty-seven centers.

THE GRAY AREA OF LITERATURE

In the gray area of ephemeral material, sources are primarily outside commercial control, tend not to be cataloged, and are therefore a problem in internationalizing resources. The significance of gray literature for international library research has been recognized, however. The extent of the LIS gray publication area, though difficult to assess, cannot be overlooked, especially for developing countries.

Gray area items tend not to be listed by dealers. They are usually cheap or free, and their production is limited; in addition, they are not subjected to strict editing, they are bibliographically difficult to describe, and they are intended primarily for current use. Such organizations as the H. W. Wilson Company, National Technical Information Service, and the Educational Resources Information Center (ERIC) cover portions of this field.

The project of internationalizing gray area collections is a challenging one. Alternatives to normal acquisitions channels might be helpful, and the following strategies can be explored:

1. Joining international library groups and attending conferences where contacts with foreign librarians may help to establish exchange arrangements.

2. Writing to library school librarians and international organization libraries abroad to establish exchange relationships.

3. Writing to dealers that provide gray area material, especially those with network agents in Third World countries.

4. Maintaining an address file of school alumni working abroad as a list for distributing material and soliciting assistance in extending holdings.

5. Selecting and maintaining an organized file of duplicates of significant titles for exchange.

6. Keeping up with gift and exchange activities of university libraries and increasing and improving the available stock.

PRINT COLLECTION

Library collections can be divided between print and nonprint. Basic LIS reference sources include encyclopedias, dictionaries, bibliographies, indexes with or without abstracts, directories, handbooks, manuals, and yearbooks. Most of the field's monographs cover subjects inherent in the core and related to the fringes of the field. Serials form another group subdivided primarily by frequency: periodicals, continuations, and newspapers.

Government documents include technical reports and can either be a separate section or be integrated into the collection. Ephemera may or may not be processed fully and integrated into the collection, depending on use and significance. Subject authority files may be maintained by the staff, and user retrieval may be direct when immediate access is built into the file structure.

In certain cases the monograph collection includes a special juvenile book section to support courses in library work with children and young adults. Cataloging and classifying tools are sometimes shelved in a laboratory, with a practice collection representing the various types of material used in cataloging exercises.

A special historical children's collection and an archival file of official school records and papers are sometimes part of the library collection. Certain special centers might be administered by the library: a center for foreign language books for children and adults or an international LIS information center with primary source material, an audiovisual facility for production and service, and a computer laboratory for processing and online searching.

The physical form and organizational structure of the material must be considered. In determining the extent of internationalization, content was central and bibliographic records held the key to analysis. No basic material list for an LIS collection was found during the literature search. When considering the content of the field's collections, Joel M. Lee found "no truly efficient sources or means for exploring the resources in the field; the researcher must rely on a series of incomplete and inadequate published directories and on general guides to material and collections."[16] Evaluating existing collections was impossible because there was no descriptive information about them.

Attempting to locate noteworthy U.S. collections for international LIS education was difficult. A literature search revealed only two locations for possible verification, one at Pittsburgh and the other at Pratt. A questionnaire was mailed to sixty-two faculty members in forty-three U.S. and Canadian library schools, persons who were listed in the *Journal of Education for Librarianship* directory issue as teaching international and comparative LIS courses. Presumably they were qualified to evaluate international collections. The responses of thirty-three instructors (a 53 percent return) from thirty schools (a 70 percent return) indicated that no collection was self-contained in both published and unpublished material.

Eight faculty members (24 percent) used their own material collected from activities abroad to supplement the school's collection. Seven (21 percent) rated their school collections to be weak, three (9 percent) thought the collections were average for their own needs, and the rest (70 percent) considered holdings adequate for course work. Nevertheless, six (18 percent) of the last group expressed candid reservations in the areas of primary source material, foreign language journals, and Third World government documents. For doctoral research, two (6 percent) expected candidates to use resources widely.

Four (12 percent) thought that the strength of their collections came from the rich and comprehensive university holdings of foreign publications, augmented by the resources of cooperating research libraries. The interdisciplinary nature of international LIS was stressed. Ten forms (16 percent of sixty-two) were returned unanswered.

Faculty assessment of existing collections was limited to the perception of adequacy for one or two international courses, not for an international LIS education curriculum. No school had a center for international LIS information, three (9 percent) from other schools suggested checking the Pittsburgh school, and one suggested a national clearinghouse for international primary source material.

The University of Pittsburgh School of Library and Information Science International Library Information Center (ILIC), established in 1964, was intended to serve as a national clearinghouse, laboratory, research center, and "an interface between the United States and the rest of the world" in international and comparative librarianship.[17] A special collection of primary source material, ILIC was designed to collect information on the resources in librarianship, information science, book production, and related fields on a worldwide basis. It collects files of annual reports, surveys, library school programs, planning and development reports, and inhouse publications from developing countries, 22,000 items in all. Since 1979 the Center has had difficulty in maintaining and updating its collection. During a Fall 1984 visit, the collection was found to be not completely dormant, and occasional exchanges and gifts were being added by a part-time graduate assistant.

The Pratt Institute Graduate School of Library and Information Science offered two courses with an international perspective among seventy-two listed in the latest catalog (3 percent). International LIS was not currently listed among the school's six area specialties. Its modest collection could not be considered unique in international holdings. A separate international collection did not exist. We may conclude that neither the Pittsburgh nor the Pratt international collection was a strong and current research resource, though ILIC had extensive holdings for the period when it was active.

The College of Librarianship, Wales (CLW) Library had aggregate holdings of 115,000 volumes and 1,000 current periodical subscriptions, both estimated to be 80 percent international.[18] The library offered a translation service of many languages; online searching using DIALOG, BLAISE, and other hosts, including Teletext and Prestel; photocopying; varied media services; and a publication program. Selection/acquisition policies were intended to cover all English-language material in the field, and in foreign languages collection development was "comprehensively selective."

Traditionally, books for children and young adults have been part of the library school's instructional material. They were housed either as small noncirculating demonstration/laboratory or extensive historical and contemporary imprint collections.

Although impressive juvenile book holdings were found, they were predominantly American and English-language material and not necessarily centralized. A good case in point was Columbia University in New York City. The library school's children's books, mostly contemporary imprints, were not part of the Butler Library historical collection of 10,000 volumes in English and Western European languages. The Columbia Teachers College Milbank Memorial Library listed extensive holdings, including foreign elementary and secondary textbooks. Scattered titles of Japanese, Chinese, and Korean children's books were found in the East Asian Library.

Accessible to Columbia University scholars were the New York Public Library's rich resources of over 70,000 historical and contemporary titles in fifty languages.[19] The U.S. Committee for UNICEF Information Center on Children's Cultures, New York, contained both trade imprints and textbooks from Africa, Asia, and Latin America.

At the Texas Women's University (TWU) School of Library Science, Denton, was an unusual collection of more than 20,000 books, journals, and nonprint material for Spanish-speaking children and adults, known as the Proyecto LEER (Libros Elementales, Educativos y Recreativos). Among its objectives were those of training librarians and teachers in selecting and acquiring material for Spanish-speaking people, disseminating information through its *Bulletin*, and providing for Hispanic TWU library school students the experience of cataloging Spanish books, evaluation for collection development, and research. Proyecto LEER showed what other ambitious schools might do with other languages and geographic areas.

Internationalizing the juvenile collection may start with bibliographic sources such as *Children's Literature Awards and Winners*.[20] "Books of International Interest: Prize-Winning Books from Throughout the World" in the *Bookbird* should keep the collection current. *Phaedrus* includes extensive annotated entries of foreign language books and is invaluable for internationalizing collections. *The Index Translationum* can also be helpful for translations.

Nonprint Collections

In view of the changing work environments for which LIS schools must prepare students, nonprint collections must be open ended and fluid, and include a great variety of media. The International Council for Educational Media published monographs of comparative media §ervice among advanced and developing countries.

The sheer variety of nonprint forms, the difficulty in locating media, the numerous types and models of equipment required in conjunction with their use, the obsolescence rate, costs, and several other factors suggest that internationalization will be most challenging in this area. Personal observation during on-site tours revealed no noteworthy international media holdings.

PUBLIC SERVICE

Internationalization of LIS education programs may affect user services in several ways. An international awareness can extend reference work into new geographic regions, and it should be more geared than before to cope with foreign languages. Translation sources will be used more since the language barrier must be overcome.[21] Polycentrism at the reference desk may be forced on the service, and demand that the librarian's entrenched ethnocentric information work habits resulting from monolingual practices may have to be consciously overcome.

More referrals may be needed resulting from the expanded dimensions, whether at the micro or macro level. Service may not only require knowing which esoteric sources to use, if any special bibliographies cover the geographic area, but also knowing where to find available specific documents when their copy location has not been identified, particularly titles from developing countries.

The search may entail sending the investigator outside the library to locate leads. A campus area-studies program may be able to direct the information seeker to a likely source. International data bases may also be searched, since several LIS indexing services are covered therein. Of course, finding a promising citation introduces the element of availability which may be a problem. International interlibrary loans are useful but may increase complications and time consumed, though IFLA has drawn up guidelines for their use.[22]

An international program may attract many foreign students. The presence of foreign students not only creates an international atmosphere but may also promote local student interest in librarianship overseas which may in turn create a demand for material from abroad. If supervised field work or practicum is required, field service in the library school library may present many opportunities to the students and challenges to the library staff.

Translation work may be offered, if quality and continuity can be assured. The scope of current awareness service can be broadened with the expanded international emphasis of the educational program. Foreign student participation in book selection can bring more suggestions of foreign imprints. Library bulletin board displays, exhibits, and extracurricular activities might show intensified internationalism in themes and foreign student participation. An international student center might be given more responsive support by the library school. Overall, the public service staff should be constantly alert to provide sensitivity to foreign viewpoints.

International library school librarian exchange may be arranged through the LIBEX office operated by CLW. In addition, the librarian should strive to improve foreign language competency and knowledge of LIS abroad.

CONCLUSION

The concepts and mechanisms for a plan to internationalize library resources and services have been tried previously. Library support for area-studies programs has demonstrated what can be done on a worldwide scale. The grand concept of ILIC and the operation of ERIC including its document reproduction procedures can be dovetailed into a workable arrangement with proper fiscal support. UNESCO programs can be actively promoted by IFLA's Section for Library Schools in areas where these programs impinge on resources supporting LIS education. Library school librarians in IFLA member countries should be closely involved in IFLA activities.

The United States' Discussion Group of Librarians of Library Science Collections could bring together library school librarians for another useful conference aimed to increase cooperation and improve service among them.[23] It will take professional commitment, much time, and dedicated effort to find sources of support. Many library school librarians and concerned educators should be invited to participate. Internationalism as a theme would be appropriate indeed.

NOTES

1. Based on conversations with selected library and information science school librarians during on-site visits to forty-three research and academic libraries, September 14-November 2, 1984, United States and Canada.

2. William Robert Eshelman, "Erosion of Library Education," *Library Journal* 108 (July 1983), pp. 1309–1312.

3. Jean Kindlin, "Library School Libraries," in *Encyclopedia of Library and Information Science* (New York: Marcel Dekker, 1975), vol. 16, p. 13.

4. "Directory of the Association for Library and Information Science Education," *Journal of Education for Librarianship* 24 (Winter 1984), entire issue.

5. Pal Boday, *Die Zusammenarbeit der sozialistischen Länder auf dem Gebiet der bibliothekswissenschaftlichen Dokumentation und Information* (Budapest: Zentralstelle für Bibliothekswissenshaft und Methodik, 1964) English abstract in *Library Science Abstracts* 16 (1965), p. 102, entry no. 15184.

6. Conference on the Bibliographic Control of Library Science Literature, 1968, *Proceedings* (Bethesda: ERIC Document Reproduction Service, ED 050 738, 1970); see also Diane Butzin, ed., *Institute on the Role of the Library School Library in Education for Librarianship, 1971 (Proceedings)*, (Atlanta: Division of Librarianship, Emory University, 1973).

7. Herbert Coblans, "The Literature of Librarianship and Documentation," *Journal of Documentation* 28 (March 1972), pp. 56–66; Tom Edwards, *A Comparative Analysis of the Major Abstracting and Indexing Services for Library and Information Science* (Paris: UNESCO, 1975), COM–75/WS/25; and L. J. Taylor, "Library Science Literature," *Aslib Proceedings* 23 (September 1971), pp. 465–480.

8. Patricia Tegler, "The Indexes and Abstracts of Library and Information Science," *Drexel Library Quarterly* 15 (July 1979), pp. 2–23.

9. *Ulrich's International Periodicals Directory: A Classified Guide to Current Periodicals, Foreign and Domestic*, 22d ed. (New York: R. R. Bowker Co., 1983); Grazyna Janzing, comp., *Library, Documentation and Archives Serials*, 4th ed., FID Publication 532 (The Hague, Netherlands: International Federation for Docu-

mentation, 1975); and *Standard Periodical Directory*, 1983–1984, 8th ed. (New York: Oxbridge Communications, 1982).

10. Edwards, *A Comparative Analysis*.

11. See also *Fachbibliographischer Dienst: Bibliothekswissen* (Berlin: Deutsches Bibliotheksverband, 1965-), vol. 1. An annual but irregular library science indexing service of international scope, extensive on German material.

12. Gary R. Purcell and Gail Ann Schlachter, *Reference Sources in Library and Information Services* (Santa Barbara, Calif.: ABC-CLIO Information, 1984).

13. Eugene P. Sheehy, comp., *Guide to Reference Books*, 9th ed. (Chicago: American Library Association, 1976) and A. J. Walford, ed., *Guide to Reference Material*, 3d ed. (London: Library Association, 1977).

14. *Dictionary Catalog of the Library of the School of Library Service, Columbia University* (Boston: G. K. Hall, 1962), 7 vols:, First Supplement (Boston: G. K. Hall, 1976), 4 vols.; and *Catalog of the Library* (London: The Library Association, 1953).

15. *International Bibliography of the Book Trade and Librarianship/Fachliteratur zum Buch- und Bibliothekswesen*, 12th ed./12. Ausgabe 1976–1979 (München: K. G. Saur, 1981).

16. Joel M. Lee, "Collections in Librarianship and Information Science," *Drexel Library Quarterly* 15 (July 1979), p. 82. But see Carol S. Nielsen, comp., *Directory of Library Science Collections, 1977*, 2d ed. (Chicago: American Library Association, 1977).

17. International Library and Information Center, *Statement of Activities, Achievements and Future Programs* (Pittsburgh: Graduate School of Library and Information Science, April 1977), p. 1, typescript.

18. *College of Librarianship Wales Prospectus 1985–86* (Aberystwyth, U.K., May 1984), p. 15; "The Library and Its Resources: A Brief Guide" (Aberystwyth: College of Librarianship, Wales, July 1984), leaflet.

19. Carolyn W. Field, *Special Collections in Children's Literature* (Chicago: American Library Association, 1982).

20. Dolores Blythe Jones, *Children's Literature Awards and Winners: A Directory of Prizes, Authors, and Illustrators* (Detroit: Neal-Schuman Publishers, 1983).

21. James D. Anderson, "Foreign Language Barriers in Information Transfer," *Journal of Education for Librarianship* 14 (Winter 1974), pp. 171–175.

22. Valentin Wehefritz, *International Loan Services and Union Catalogues*, 2d ed., Zeitschrift für Bibliothekswesen und Bibliographie/Sonderheft 17 (Frankfurt: Vittorio Klostermann, 1980), pp. 5–33.

23. Jean Kindlin, Chairperson, Association of College and Research Libraries Library Science Librarians Discussion Group, Memo to Members, June 11, 1975; *Library Science Librarians' National Newsletter*, No. 1 (May 1976)—No. 17 (Spring 1984).

BIBLIOGRAPHY

Boyd, C., ed. *Library Science Libraries: A Quantitative Survey*. Philadelphia: Drexel University Libraries, 1974.

Burn, Barbara B., *Expanding the International Dimension of Higher Education*. San Francisco: Jossey-Bass, 1980.

Henige, David. "Acquisition of Foreign Materials from Africa." In Theodore Samore, ed. *Acquisition of Foreign Materials for U.S. Libraries.* Metuchen, N. J.: Scarecrow Press, 1982, pp. 109–117.

Jackson, Miles M., ed. *International Handbook of Contemporary Developments in Librarianship.* Westport, Conn.: Greenwood Press, 1981.

Kaser, David. "Library School Libraries." *Journal of Education for Librarianship* 5 (Summer 1965), pp. 17–19.

Nyren, Karl. ". . . A Report of a Conference on Bibliographical Control of Library Literature." *Library Journal* 93 (June 1, 1968), pp. 2215–2217.

Stevens, Rolland E. "Library Support of Area Study Programs." *College and Research Libraries* 24 (September 1963), pp. 383–391.

Taylor, Peter J., and Blaise Cronin, eds. *Information Management Research in Europe; Proceedings of the EURIM5 Conference, Palais des Congres, Versailles, France, May 1982.* London: Aslib, 1983.

Vosper, Robert. "IFLA and the Recent Growth of Organized International Librarianship." In *Advances in Librarianship.* Orlando, Fla.: Academic Press, 1984, Vol. 13, pp. 129–134.

Whatley, H. Allan. "The Bibliographical Control of Library Science Literature." *Library World* 70 (July 1968), pp. 19–21.

Whatley, H. Allan. *A Survey of the Major Abstracting and Indexing Services for Library Science and Documentation.* London: Library Association, 1966.

APPENDIX: *LIBRARY LITERATURE* INDEXED TITLES COMMON TO ISA, LISA, IA, AND BS

1. *Aslib Proceedings* (U.K.)

2. *College and Research Libraries* (U.S.)

3. *Documentaliste* (France)

4. *Documentation et Bibliotheques* (Canada)

5. *Drexel Library Quarterly* (U.S.)

6. *Government Publications Review* (U.S.)

7. *Information Processing and Management* (U.K.)

8. *Information Technology and Libraries* (U.S.)

9. *Interlending and Document Supply* (U.S.)

10. *International Classification* (West Germany)

11. *International Forum on Information and Documentation* (FID)

12. *International Library Review* (U.K.)

13. *Journal of Documentation* (U.K.)

14. *Journal of Information and Image Management* (U.S.)

15. *Journal of Information Science* (Netherlands)

16. *Journal of Librarianship* (U.K.)

17. *Journal of the American Society for Information Science* (U.S.)

18. *Library Acquisitions: Practice and Theory* (U.S.)
19. *Library Journal* (U.S.)
20. *Library Quarterly* (U.S.)
21. *Library Resources and Technical Services* (U.S.)
22. *Library Technology Reports* (U.S.)
23. *Library Trends* (U.S.)
24. *Microform Review* (U.S.)
25. *Nauchno-Teknicheskaia Informatsiia* (USSR)
26. *Online Review* (U.S.)
27. *Program* (U.K.)
28. *Special Libraries* (U.S.)

The following are eight more titles common to ISA, LISA, and IA which BS had not covered in 1983:

29. *Bulletin of the American Society for Information Science* (U.S.)
30. *Canadian Journal of Information Science* (Canada)
31. *Computer Equipment Review* (U.S.)
32. *Database* (U.S.)
33. *Journal of Academic Librarianship* (U.S.)
34. *L.A.S.I.E.* (Australia)
35. *Law Library Journal* (U.S.)
36. *RQ* (U.S.)

PART III

INTERNATIONALIZING THE CURRICULUM

12
CURRICULUM DEVELOPMENT POLICIES AND PRACTICES

John F. Harvey

This chapter deals with the management of general curriculum in an internationalization program for occupational schools and discusses the policies and opportunities in such a broadening project as well as explaining useful educational concepts and techniques. What is said about curriculum change applies equally to course and course unit change, though each one has its own context and perspective. The chapter assumes that the school has made a positive decision, approved at higher levels, to internationalize its curriculum.

CURRICULUM CHANGE PLANNING

Strategy for making curriculum change, namely, the ways in which appropriate changes are selected, screened, coordinated, and implemented, should be clarified early in the planning process.[1] A series of school faculty and staff meetings should be held throughout the change process, step by step, report by report. Sufficient time should be allowed for proper discussion; individual curriculum change suggestions should be integrated with group considerations; and curriculum content change proposals should be listed and clarified for consideration. The result should be a "reborn" curriculum. Figure 12.1 lists project steps which may instead be expressed in a flowchart if the educator prefers.

Systematic and comprehensive curriculum building is needed—not the older and more limited "tinkering" with a few courses, minor additions and subtractions, which in the past often resulted in a hodgepodge. The curriculum design is the heart of the plan. If it is done well, the process of selecting and organizing content in preparation for teaching a course is simplified and the pattern of emphases can be noted.

The design process requires changing the curriculum in what the faculty believes to be positive directions.

Figure 12.1
Major Curriculum Change Project Steps

Planning and Collecting Information	*Establishing Content*	*Implementation*
Plan entire curriculum change project	Analyze existing strengths and weaknesses	Prepare new curriculum, course, and unit outlines
Establish decision-making process	Study and discuss framework data to develop content change suggestions	Prepare new units in full for all affected courses
Evaluate and update curriculum objectives	Pretest new suggestions in the classroom	Prepare new class and outside exercise assignment schedules
Develop set of curriculum evaluation criteria	Design new curriculum, then courses, and then units	Select and list appropriate reading assignments
Collect and assess new curriculum-related information	Present alternative versions of each unit	Prepare personal teaching material
Collect and assess new field-related information	List decisions to be made	Prepare individualized teaching modules
Conduct appropriate literature searches	Apply evaluation criteria	Two years later—reevaluate new curriculum and prepare to revise it
Prepare curriculum framework data base	Choose best alternatives	

The faculty should gain a new perspective on the entire curriculum and upgrade it. Planning must consider both the intellectual and emotional aspects of change. A major transformation can be expected. Change implementation should start with the curriculum viewed comprehensively, before it is considered in parts, by course and then by unit. A reexamination point should be built into the system at a specified future time. The curriculum should be placed in a biennial revision cycle, for one that is static is dying.

Curriculum change involves policy formulation and decision-making.[2] First, policy statements about curriculum content and priorities must be established to guide changes that require decision-making. Second, the educator must establish a decision-making process and then collect and assess appropriate information from various sources. Curriculum and course policy decisions enable the faculty to shape and emphasize topics and are biding on unit development. Less important but numerous decisions about course content changes will be made and then implemented for each unit. Decisions should be made only after listing all possible items that might be added or subtracted from that unit. The nature of each decision must be understood fully before a choice is made. Almost all decision alternatives have their trade-offs; when cost exceeds benefit, the decision must be negative.

Who should participate in curriculum change discussions? Certainly all school faculty members, both full- and part-time, and all senior administrators. In addition, consultants on curriculum development as well as on internationalization can add much to faculty and staff understanding. In many schools, policy decisions are made democratically by faculty members as administrative advisors. Later, these decisions will be confirmed or denied at a higher university administrative level.

Curriculum change must be a cooperative endeavor involving many persons. Faculty members will play a leading intellectual role and must do the course preparation; managers will prepare reports, expedite paper work, and locate funds and staff members; students will be the direct target group; and alumni will work with the program's products. In some situations, decisions are made by a government ministry office with or without faculty advice. Implementation decisions are usually made by faculty members and school administrators acting collectively or individually, depending on the situation, while classroom decisions are made by individual faculty members.

A decision-making process should clarify just who will be responsible for researching possible changes at each curricular level (unit, course, or curriculum) and for each occupational subcurriculum, as well as who will make the decisions at each academic level (undergraduate versus graduate). Normally, unit decisions will be researched and made by cach instructor for his or her own courses. Course decisions will be researched by the primary instructor, and curriculum decisions by one to three designated faculty members. Course and curriculum decisions will be made by the faculty group as a whole. Course research should be discussed at weekly meetings at which detailed minutes must be taken, distributed, read, and acted on. Planning, data-collecting, and course-building will probably take a year or two of intensive effort as will implementation.

To continue down Figure 12.1, column 1, information or library school objectives must guide the curricular programs. A comprehensive set of measurable objectives should be developed, many of which bear on the curriculum. No curriculum design project can be started properly until a fully current set of objectives is in place. The objectives and curriculum must be examined to identify obligations and opportunities to change emphasis. As a consequence of changed or enlarged objectives, subcurricula and courses may be added, dropped, merged, or revised.

Before a decision can be made about proposed changes, a way must be found of evaluating them against curriculum objectives reflected in specific criteria. The criteria should be agreed on as fair, and change should begin and end with review and evaluation.[3] Evaluation of course changes must view the reorganized course in the context of the entire reorganized curriculum as well as the information practitioner's real world. To upgrade each course, evaluation should be vigorous and systematic. Lists similar to those shown in Figures 12.2 and 12.3 may be helpful.

Figure 12.2
Administrative Checklist of General Criteria for Judging a New Curriculum and Course

Describe existing constraints on school effectiveness
New curriculum supports school objectives
Availability of interested and skillful instructors with appropriate backgrounds
Availability of appropriate library and media support material and service
Availability of well-written teaching material to support curriculum
School budget sufficient to fund new curriculum
School physical facilities support new curriculum
Effect of curriculum on current students is positive
Job performance of curriculum graduates is positive
Employment opportunities available for graduates locally and abroad
School faculty and administration thoroughly discussed and approved new policies and practices
Students, alumni, and service area leaders discussed and approved new curriculum
University curricular authorities discussed and approved new curriculum
Government curricular authorities discussed and approved new curriculum
Were curriculum changes fully implemented?
Was curriculum development process carried out in full?

School resources must be used efficiently in order to achieve curriculum objectives, evaluate courses properly, and prepare new material for use. Figure 12.4 shows both the preparatory reports needed and their sources. It takes a comprehensive administrative view, but faculty members will find the information collected essential for specific courses as well. While it is desirable to obtain advice from many local and foreign sources, it is even more important for the instructor to *think* creatively about problems.

Figure 12.3
Course Unit Evaluation Criteria

Identify appropriate curriculum, course, and unit objectives and their components

Evaluate skill with which unit supports appropriate objectives

Concepts have been chosen

Concepts have been explained

Unit coordinates with and reinforces remainder of course

Dynamic and innovative teaching methods are used

Teaching policies and practices bring student understanding

Articulation, sequencing, and balance are carried out

Unit supports educational curriculum building concepts discussed later in this chapter

Appropriate illustrations and examples are used

Unit uses library material, media, individual teaching modules, and other special techniques

Classroom leadership is carried out

List improvements needed

New course and unit information needs must be identified. What information is required before a faculty member can plan course change? And where can this information be obtained? Figure 12.4 should answer these questions for the school as a whole, but a supplementary answer is needed for each individual faculty member and for each course and unit.

The data collection steps for Figure 12.4 should provide part of the input information needed for the Curriculum Framework Data Base which can be maintained in either machine-readable, printout, or typed form. This data base should contain reports from all sources bearing on the present curriculum revision. Changes should be based on the information contained therein. This easily usable tool, containing all Figure 12.4 and faculty-generated reports, can serve as the entire project's comprehensive foundation or springboard.

CURRICULUM CONTENT PATTERNS

Establishing new curriculum content requires carrying out the series of steps listed in the middle column of Figure 12.1. The data collected earlier must be analyzed, both to reveal the present curriculum's weaknesses and strengths and to develop practical changes. Discussion of these steps is divided into Curriculum Content Patterns, Internationalization, and Teaching Aids and Approaches.

Most instructors probably assume that the curriculum should be subject-centered in simple, logical, and straightforward sequences, that the

Figure 12.4
**Administrative Checklist of Curriculum Change Planning Information
Reports Needed**

Information needed	Sources
Individual introspection and brainstorming reports	Faculty members
Curriculum policies and practices from other campus occupational schools	School directors
Other national information school reports	School directors
Foreign information school reports	Faculty members or directors
University curriculum policies	Curriculum policy committee
Ministry of Education policies	Ministry policy group
Curriculum advisory report	School curriculum consultant
Internationalization report	School internationalization consultant
Curriculum change report	Student government officers
Curriculum change report	Alumni association officers
Curriculum change report	Service area practitioners
Budget adequacy for change	School director
Physical facilities needed for change	School director
Amount and character of new information already available for curriculum change	Faculty members
How far have new curriculum concepts been implemented already in course work?	Faculty members
Curriculum areas needing revision for other reasons	Faculty members
Curriculum areas most and least amenable to change	Faculty members
Higher and occupational education printed literature report	School director
Recent world information service education trends	School director

curriculum should present the field's cultural heritage, that this heritage can be usefully grouped into segments and subfields, and that, since this is an old and much used organizational pattern, emphasizing absorption and memorization, it must be the best one.

Since subject-centered lecture and exposition tend in practice to mean

Figure 12.5
Major Curricular Organization Patterns

Subject-centered (Traditional)	Common Core	Correlated	Integrated Core	Fused	Student-centered (Elective or Independent Study)

something similar to faculty member-centered curriculum, this too is bound to improve the instructor's opinion of this authoritarian pattern. In many schools in developing countries, all courses are required and are taught in the traditional manner. That is the subject-centered pattern's ultimate level, largely ignoring individual student interests. We may ask, however, need all curricula necessarily be narrowly subject-centered? Could certain of them just as well be student-centered? Probably many new and revised curricula will have certain characteristics taken from both extremes. Figure 12.5 shows a spectrum of pattern possibilities.

Much terminological confusion exists in the curriculum field, and each one of the terms in Figure 12.5 is used elsewhere to represent a different concept. However, this pattern fits the present situation. As a matter of fact, to compound the confusion, whereas Figure 12.5 suggests that gradual rightward movement means increasing student-centeredness, a large gap exists between student-centered and all the other concepts. The correlated and the fused merely represent ways of adjusting subject content somewhat to assist understanding.

In juxtaposition to the subject-centered curriculum, the student-centered stresses its freedom from the subject-centered's compartmentalization and its ability to adjust to student interests, to individual differences, and to current community information activities and problems. Furthermore, it can be very democratic, articulates well between subjects, and encourages individual thinking.

Compartmentalization is overcome by building a flexible and ever-changing program around student interests expressed actively. A student-centered curriculum can refer not only to a completely elective curriculum, but at its ultimate level also to one designed entirely in an independent study mode to suit individual student interests and without fixed courses or class meetings.

A fused, integrated, or broad-fields curriculum attempts to strengthen the relationship between subjects that are already closely related. For instance, a reference resources course that combines rather than separates subject areas could represent a fused course. It blends together subjects as do North American undergraduate survey courses in Western civilization. The fused curriculum may blend together subfields of one major field, or less commonly, subfields of two or more major fields. Ideally, the fused organizes course units by large theme rather than by minor subject division. Fusing is said to make learning more meaningful and to broaden the student's topical view as well as to make it shallower.

The correlated and fused curricula differ primarily in degree of correlation. As a compromise between extremes, a correlated curriculum tries to articulate all subjects closely by sequencing them appropriately, queuing topical order and emphasizing contact points between subjects. An example would be to correlate course work in selection of material and reference sources as each course moves through each subject matter field.

Few information schools have been sufficiently bold and imaginative to develop correlated or fused curricula, although several have correlated or fused specific courses. None apparently has a student-centered curriculum. Instead, many North American schools have become so subject-specialized that the trend is toward proliferation in ever smaller specialties (or else newly developing subfields), a faculty-centered approach. Perhaps these schools have now become subcurriculum subject-centered.

Another compromise is the common core curriculum which divides the entire course list into two groups: (1) those few courses that are introductory and essential, so essential that students in all subcurricula must take them (including such courses as introductory cataloging, bibliography and reference sources, and material selection), and (2) those elective courses, much larger in number, which are more specialized or advanced and less essential in providing a common background.

Apparently, many world schools that are not purely subject-centered use the core curriculum. In recent years, however, as a result of the growing demand of burgeoning subcurricula (or the core's increasing centrifugal weakness) and other reasons, many U.S. schools have changed their introductory course emphases and have considerably reduced the number of required core courses. Certain U.S. schools require only one to three core courses. Counseling, the course numbering system, and prerequisite course requirements are commonly used to channel student course selection. In contrast, a few schools still require up to nine out of ten to thirteen courses for the degree.

Many schools have compressed the core in this already fractionated field. Thus, a pressing question in the United States has been how long students should be held in the core before being allowed into their primary subcurricular interest area. Or, on the other hand, the question may be, is almost nothing held in common now among information studies subcurricula students?

The required core program is only somewhat student-centered, being merely a way of corraling every student into certain introductory courses. The recent freedom from the core requirement makes the curriculum more student-centered in giving students more freedom of choice, but little or no curriculum correlation or fusing is occurring. In contrast, individualized instructional modules are being used in certain schools. They permit students to move through at least certain course material at their own speed and represent a more positive step in the direction of student-centered education.

Curriculum designers have developed several additional approaches that can be helpful to educators. All items listed in Figure 12.6 should be included in a course, varying in proportion by topic.

Figure 12.6
Course Content Checklist

History: Description of past events and conceptual origins
Concepts or theories: Abstract ideas guiding service organization and explaining why something is done
Principles or laws: Fundamental service rules interpreting theories
Institutional policies: Specific statements guiding practice
Trends: Significant long- or short-term institutional or market statistical index changes
Personal attitudes: opinions, guesses, biases, intellectual postures
Practices or routines: Policy implementation or how something is done
Description of facts: Statements about practice or existing situations

Teaching should endeavor to integrate the theoretical and practical aspects of each topic in the proportions needed. They must be coordinated within each course and between courses. We are teaching primarily *why* and, secondarily, *how* action is taken in the field. The course unit is where most of this information is used and where most change projects succeed or fail.

A second set of educational concepts relates to Figure 12.7. Perhaps a concept should be introduced only after the need for it has been explained through a problem situation. Sequencing deals with new idea arrangement. In sequencing, the chronological approach suggests teaching older or historical material before tackling recent concepts. The geographical approach suggests teaching first the near and then the far. Other instructors teach the easier concepts and course first and the more difficult ones later, and similarly, the simple before the complex, the introductory before the advanced, and the concrete before the abstract.

Horizontal articulation deals with the tightness of relationships between the separate presentations of related ideas and demonstrates the need to consider the curriculum and the field in an intradisciplinary context. Knowledge of the units taught in other courses is essential. Continuity is correlation between introductory and advanced subjects. Both gaps and overlaps must be reduced. The entire curriculum should be viewed as one closely interlocking and synergistic system, with the positioning of each unit and course carefully planned.

Each new concept should be given to a student in an order reflecting development and facilitating learning. It should emerge logically from the concepts preceding it. This is called the Developmental Curriculum approach and grows out of sequence, articulation, and continuity. Prerequisite courses should be completed before admission to intermediate work. Nonsequential or discontinuous course development implies a willful teaching sequence based on faculty preference and convenience rather than student need or readiness.

Figure 12.7
Curriculum Concept Selection and Organization Checklist

Scope: What concepts are to be taught
Sequence: Queuing, prioritizing new concepts
Frequency: How often should a concept be discussed?
Duration: How much time should be spent on each concept?
Articulation (Horizontal): Correlated concurrent conceptual relationships
Continuity (Vertical Articulation): Correlated concurrent conceptual relationships between introductory and advanced levels
Balance: Having proper curriculum proportions

Balance is also important but difficult to judge. It refers to assigning the proper amount of attention to each subject field, to the avoidance of curricular extremes, and to reasonableness in the course emphasis of each student.

Third, dynamic, innovative, and experimental teaching approaches must be considered. A dynamic, vigorous approach, one full of personality, should arouse interest and markedly increase student participation. Introducing old concepts in innovative ways is desirable, and introducing new concepts into a course may be a kind of innovation itself. Innovation, trying a new approach, will often intrigue the instructor as well as the student.

A carefully planned and controlled teaching experiment can carry much interest. One in which groups of students are given separate assignments as a way of checking its effectiveness can be an example. Pretesting educational approaches before implementation is a sensible procedure. An innovative experiment can invite the student's contribution to an exciting venture. Of course, curriculum internationalization is an experiment of its own and can have strong educational appeal.

Fourth, two concepts can be recommended for inclusion among course changes: interdisciplinism and futurism. They have become increasingly important in occupational education. Interdisciplinary approaches require using varied concepts from related subject fields. In order to find subjects with which to correlate, information schools should seek closer ties with other occupational schools and with traditional university curricular areas. Information education should anticipate its future. Course changes in occupational schools should be designed to prepare students to function well in a subfield a decade hence. Future study is usually done by analyzing current social and institutional statistical trends to predict the near term. Today's students need to study futurism itslf so that they can anticipate changes continuously.

The final topic is good classroom course presentation. Teaching is partly an art, and the approach of each skillful instructor is somewhat different. The classroom is a human relations center, and this view should guide thinking. While individual differences among students must be recognized, all students should be exposed to similar ideas. A loud and clear voice, clear thinking, a friendly and likable but firm and commanding personality, articulation skill, sympathetic understanding of students, and the ability to view instruction from the learner's seat are helpful.

A good sense of pacing and of each student's progress level are needed as the course evolves. Variety and wit are desirable, and so also are a strong sense of organization and mastery over unit detail. An additional talent for simplification and succinctness will be helpful. The student should be able to sense the instructor's dedication and hard work on course construction and presentation. Instructors should regard themselves as primarily student-learning facilitators, not as classroom oracles. The final gift of this paragon must be compassion—the instructor must *care* that each learner learn.

INTERNATIONALIZATION

As part of the curricular change program shown in Figure 12.1, we have now come to the heart of the chapter. Both adjectival uses of the word "international" are important here: use that refers (1) to other countries, and (2) to multinational institutions and organizations such as the Asian Development Bank in Manila. Two additional uses of the words "foreign" and "international" can be identified. Many instructors will describe foreign only in order to compare it with national information service, but foreign service can also reasonably be studied as an end in itself.

The need for internationalization may be checked in the field for confirmation and detailed information, as suggested in Figure 12.1. Even though the change is gradual, we assume that the local information officer's job requires an increasing knowledge of the publications and information policies and practices of other countries. If asked, the more alert practitioners and information management human resources planners may recommend increasing attention to internationalism.

The role of alumni in challenging positions may be examined in order to isolate common international characteristics. Such studies should show how much and what kind of internationalism is needed, information about which few hard facts exist now. As an example, the characteristics of institutional material handled should be considered. Recently, Martin Runkle calculated that 70 percent of the material added annually to the University of Chicago Library was in foreign languages.[4] Does that figure suggest a need for internationalism in the education of his potential staff members?

As an increasing proportion of information personnel is involved with foreign ideas, oral and written feedback on these workplace shifts must be transmitted to educators. Their sensitivity to these user need and interest changes must be developed.

Course recasting and reformatting require reorienting faculty thinking. Curriculum improvement necessitates "people-changing," which is a very difficult exercise. Faculty minds must be retrained and broadened, at least in certain cases, until they can grasp the significance of the international mode. They must move away from the short-term provincial approaches to a more critical and long-term view of the information officer's task which must ultimately have a world perspective. Present faculty international interest varies greatly, but we can hope for at least one strong advocate per school. A formal decision to internationalize commits every faculty member on the plus side, to restudy each course in order to maximize student benefit.

Curricular internationalism is introduced primarily by modifying or adding specific course units and perhaps by adding one or more new courses, rather than by initiating many new courses or necessarily by fusing, combining, or coring any of them. Internationalism can exist in any one of the six major curriculum organization patterns (See Figure 12.5).

Traditional information study schools with few electives will have fewer opportunities than others to internationalize because the possibility to add new courses is likely to be absent. Otherwise, their approach can resemble that of other schools if their conservatism toward change can be overcome. Those schools dedicated to the core concept may wish to start changes there. Of course, change will vary by the faculty member's understanding of the course and by subject field. Internationalizing will probably be somewhat easier and more strongly needed for specialized than for core courses.

Fritz Veit mentions two basic ways of organizing material in an internationalized course: either divide the course (or the course unit) into two major sections, national versus international, or else introduce the international material wherever appropriate.[5] These can be called the bifurcated and the ad lib approaches.

Students must be exposed to a variety of national service system patterns. Socialist countries emphasize a centrally coordinated national information system, as in Albania. Capitalist countries may have a decentralized system, such as in India, a provincial system such as in the United States, or a combination as in the Republic of Cyprus. Information service differs by country primarily according to differences in educational and political organization and in financial status, rather than by differences originating within the information center itself. The context controls the center.

In teaching national differences, external factors are usually less obvious but more significant than internal factors. Countries and information systems can usefully be divided into groups by many other indices as well. Each instructor can develop his or her own groupings.

There is also the regional, the problem, and the type of institution approach to course organization, according to Rosemary Du Mont.[6] The regional can be used in a situation where one's own country is compared with selected regional countries, such as the Republic of Cyprus with Syria and Jordan. The problem approach permits us to examine certain questions, such as the contrasting roles of the popular church library in the religious life of two countries, Poland and Zimbabwe. The type of institution approach allows us to compare the objectives and activities of two libraries of the same type, university medical libraries, for instance, between two countries, such as Libya and India.

In each course, which should be taught first, the international or the national? The general or the specific? Information service education has traditionally been taught by country or province without having higher aspirations. There may be variations by subject, but in general, the idea of broader significance should have priority and the remaining time should be given to less significant national and provincial material. The way in which this decision is made for provincial material may separate professional from paraprofessional students.

First, the instructor should teach those information service features that are found in all or most countries. The next level down from the universal is the regional; then may come distinctive subregions, certainly in the case of the Scandinavian countries as a Western European subregion; next come countries, each one being different from its neighbors; and finally, distinctive provinces. Of course, to label information concepts as provincial, national, regional, and international is an oversimplification. Often the history and breadth of a concept's use can be determined only after some exploration. If the origin and early development are traced, for most countries and concepts that probably occurred abroad and long ago. Ancient centers had simple ideas of shelf arrangement, for example.

In addition, the instructor should recognize that of several alternative information management techniques used locally, the foreign picture may differ only in emphasis, not in essence. For instance, in medium-sized and large information centers a minicomputer terminal is being used widely now in U.S. book charging systems, but the older manual Newark system is still found in smaller centers. In Cyprus, the one card manual Newark system dominates the picture, and computers are used rarely. The two countries are not basically different, but emphasis and complexities differ. Many basic information service ideas are quite old, but the history of new techniques is quite short, individualistic, and nationalistic.

Therefore, three kinds of international and one kind of national ideas can be distinguished here. First is the idea or technique which originated abroad but is now used nationally through a major or minor adaptation. If instructors explain both the older original and the newer national use, they are explaining both the foreign and national idea or technique. An example is the Dewey Decimal Classification (DDC), which originated in the United States in the late nineteenth century and was adapted for use in Iran in certain schedules in the 1970s.

Second, there are international ideas that have been used nationally, but without adaptation. An example is the DDC used locally without change in the Republic of Cyprus. Third, other foreign or international principles and concepts exist abroad which have almost never been used except nationally. An example is the USSR Lenin Library Classification system unused in Cyprus. In certain countries, a fourth category exists: national policies and practices that have been adapted abroad. Certain national policies can be identified and questioned in class because of their contrast with foreign policies.

Curricular proportions among the four categories are impossible to predict. Should the student be asked to study a concept in its original form or modified for national use? Or both? Certainly, the original form should be mentioned, but the modified should be studied more carefully. In internationalization, use of the first and second categories will cause fewer course changes than many instructors expect. The second is probably the largest category in number of examples and the most intriguing as well, and so it provides a fine opportunity for use.

This explanation should not be interpreted as a justification for teaching primarily national material that has been adapted from foreign precedents. Such a policy would not then enable the instructor to enrich the course with new foreign descriptions and ideas not yet known locally.

A distinction should be made between (1) teaching the concept of internationalism, and (2) simply using concepts in class that have a foreign origin. The second type can impregnate the course with internationalism if the foreign nature of the ideas is called to the students' attention; if not, the student will assume mistakenly that these are national ideas.

In order to meet internationalization requirements, both the international and domestic history of the ideas should be summarized for the students. In addition, the philosophy of internationalism must be explained before we can say that the course has been internationalized. Thus, internationalizing a course requires the following steps: (1) the philosophy of internationalism must be clarified and discussed in order to provide the proper context for the ideas introduced; (2) international and foreign concepts must constitute an important part of the course; and (3) they must be properly labeled as such.

Should the course cover a few foreign countries in detail or many briefly? Generally, concentration on three to four countries can be recommended to allow the instructor to treat them in some depth. Material should not be introduced for its curiosity value but for its educational value. Discussing the ideas peculiar to a single foreign country is not as useful educationally as discussing those popular in a group of countries. And certain instructors will prefer to discuss ideas which they believe their own national information system should move toward, while others will concentrate on those of their own regional family of nations.

In course reorganization, should the instructor enlarge the course by adding new information or merely substitute new for old material? Each approach will be used at different times, but many courses are now "full" and can tolerate no more additions. Existing material may be eliminated for other reasons—being obsolete, inaccurate, misleading, out of scope, or of decreasing importance, for instance—rather than just to make room for new concepts.

In certain cases, the national ideas of a few years ago have now given way to international ideas, such as the widespread use of Machine Readable Cataloging (MARC) tapes and the *Anglo-American Cataloging Rules*. This will happen with many other ideas in the future. In other cases the national situation is changing to resemble that of certain other nations.

Shall we internationalize every course and course unit or merely specific parts of certain courses? All change gradations should be considered. Probably each course shall include some internationalism, and certain units will be easy to internationalize. A fundamental approach is to broaden the frame of reference. Many units will be made more general in their application to encompass both international and national ideas.

Should the reorganization try to saturate each course with internationalism or to add it selectively? Should internationally used concepts, policies, and principles be emphasized or only practices, descriptions, and examples? Of course, the answer is to use what is most apropriate to the particular course unit. Generally, international descriptions and examples are more interesting, but concepts and policies are more important. Often, however, the international descriptions should accompany the information on concepts and policies.

A number of formal curricular approaches can be used in internationalization, and they are listed in Figure 12.8. A program can be developed with a subcurriculum or major giving a concentration in area studies or international information studies.[7] Each area-studies program can be tailor-made for students to emphasize that world area and those subject fields in which they are most interested. Students can also be encouraged to write papers, compile bibliographies, and carry out other assignments with an area emphasis. The area-studies subcurriculum can contain three to five courses taken outside the information school, as well as seven to nine information studies courses for the degree. It can be developed to improve the school's ability to accommodate international interests. A variation of this program can require *every* student to obtain an area-studies major as a graduation requirement in order to produce students with some qualifications for international work.

Several U.S. schools offer a variation on the area-studies concentration: the dual degree program. In each case, the student receives two Master's degrees after completing the entire program. The University of California Graduate School of Library and Information Science lists a specialization area in Latin America taken outside the school. Through this program, the student can obtain a Master's degree in library and information science and a Master's in Latin American Studies on the same graduation day after a three-year study period. The University of Chicago Graduate Library School has a combined 2.25 year program leading to two Master's degrees through internal library science study and South Asian studies in the academic department of that name.

Many of the larger information studies schools offer the student a choice of several subcurricula within the school for the elective work beyond the core courses. International information service can become one of them. Study can consist of any combination of the courses offered in the international area, not more than one-fourth to one-half of all degree requirements, or three to six information studies courses, depending on degree requirements.

The international information service subcurriculum can consist of information school courses with a strong international emphasis; the second column in Figure 12.8 lists several of them. In addition, the subcurriculum might include an international thesis. The idea of a major

Figure 12.8
Formal Curricular Internationalization Alternatives

Area-studies subcurriculum	Internationalism Courses:
Area-studies graduation requirement	International book trade course
Dual area-studies degree program	International book trade language course
Internationalism subcurriculum	International cataloging and classification course
Area information studies subcurriculum	International information service organization and administration course
Semester abroad program	International bibliography course
International internship program	International government publication course
Cooperative international internship program	International information organizations and publications course
Comprehensive examination questions	International information science course
Doctoral program language examination	International archive management course
Required thesis or dissertation on an international subject	Comparative research methods course
Required international library and information science course	International library and information science seminar

inside the school contrasts with and supplements the idea of internationalizing the entire curriculum but still states clearly the school's international dedication. The subcurriculum is an alternative to pervasive internationalism, one that may be easier for the faculty to cope with.

In another possibility, a subcurriculum may be offered within the school in a specialized rather than a general international area. As an example, the University of Texas Graduate School of Library and Information Science has a bilingual Latin American Studies information specialization *within the school*. It represents a combination of an area-studies subcurriculum with an international information subcurriculum since its six courses focus on several aspects of library material and service in Latin America. The same thing can be done for other geographic areas as well.

Another variation is the semester or year-abroad program. This subcurriculum requires spending half or a full year as part of a home country program in residence in a foreign information school. The program can be fitted into the degree curriculum in any of several ways. The time spent abroad may be occupied with a research project, a foreign information service project, a formal course work program, a personal thematic study program, or an internship.[8]

The internship course should be useful to emphasize either national or international concepts. If the internship is held within national borders, then it can teach certain national concepts given less than full curriculum attention. If held abroad, it can teach those foreign concepts that have been previously omitted. A program in which two students alternate semesters in a job and in school study can also provide useful foreign experience.

Another idea is to add an international section to the comprehensive examination which each graduating student must pass on many campuses. Questions can have an international basis or require an answer based on international policies, activities, or material. Most doctoral programs in information schools already contain one internationalism element, the requirement of passing one or two foreign-language examinations.

Another way of stressing internationalism is to require each information school thesis or dissertation to be written on an international subject. Such a requirement would in turn demand that the course work preparing students to write them be well internationalized. It should not limit the student's subject matter but merely move it into an international area.

Many schools offer a special introductory course in the international field, sometimes with the title, "International Library and Information Science.[9] It should study foreign and international information institutions, organizations, policies, and services. As yet another alternative, this course may be *required* of all students in order to expose them to the field's introductory ideas.

In conclusion, Figure 12.9 shows several administrative ideas that are useful in the internationalization program. If not already done as a preliminary step, internationalism should be added to the list of school curricular objectives. It should become a major school theme, and its influence should penetrate every course and service project.

Each information studies school should endeavor to establish a formal cooperative relationship with an information studies school located abroad. Varied cooperation projects can be undertaken for mutual benefit. Each school should collect material from abroad: course outlines and assignment lists, media, term report topics, textbooks, journals, the school catalog, and faculty meeting minutes. Material is also needed on information service policies and practices. Such cooperative arrangements may be established with several schools.

Figure 12.9
Internationalization Administrative Alternatives

An internationalization curriculum objective

Cooperative curriculum material collection with foreign information schools

Faculty exchange program

Scholarships for foreign students

Scholarships for interested domestic students

Faculty foreign conference travel fund

Student foreign travel fund

Implementation of certain curricular changes will require budgetary adjustments that should be recognized at the outset. In certain cases, a reduced teaching load will be required for one semester in order to allow an instructor the time to study specific course change possibilities. A substitute instructor will be needed for that semester. On campuses where strict school and departmental budgetary control is maintained, the student who takes area-studies course work in other departments may thereby reduce information school income. The semester or year-abroad program may remove potential income from the information school in the same way.

TEACHING AIDS AND APPROACHES

Several suggestions can be made about teaching approaches and details helpful in implementing curriculum internationalization programs. (They fit into the implementation program summarized in Figure 12.1, column 3.) Instructors who try to teach without making a detailed course outline are incompletely prepared, for the outline covering all units enables them to see all major and minor course divisions in succinct form and to check and adjust articulation, balance, and sequencing. Students need such a document in order to gain perspective and plan their work.

The outline should include each lecture and discussion topic, thereby enabling the student to follow closely as the class develops. It should show what will occur at every class meeting, including examinations, field trips, review sessions, visiting speakers, quizzes, and other events. Some instructors use an alternative, the traditional syllabus, which is an expanded outline with several paragraphs introducing or summarizing each unit. Depending on its fullness, a syllabus can be quite useful.

Another useful document is a complete course assignment list and bibliography covering all outside work and showing dates due. It should also clarify precisely what each student is expected to learn from each assignment. Still another document is a suggested course term paper topic list. These documents should be distributed to the students at the beginning of the term.

Many instructors depend heavily on a textbook for succinct presentation of basic ideas, whereas others assign varied reading material in a variety of media. Unfortunately, few textbooks now cover international situations, and so the instructor must cover them in other ways.[10] The field needs new textbooks that introduce both interdisciplinary and international approaches with a strong future sense.

Media are being used increasingly but still at a relatively unsophisticated level. Instructors may need to shoot their own films and tape their own interviews abroad for class use. Surely thay can collect information center picture postcards when abroad. Short wave radio broadcasts can give the student a taste of a country's political and social situation, and occasional introductory programs on libraries can be taped for later use. A bibliography of appropriate international media titles available for class use should be compiled and in addition, internationalized information service games, puzzles, and computer quizzes can be developed.

Instruction in course internationalism should be individualized as much as possible in order to stimulate student interest and understanding. If sufficient material to reward the student's search is available in the school information center, then the term paper can be a useful vehicle for bringing international ideas to the class in some depth. A list of topics that emphasizes international approaches can be offered for student choice; small comparative research projects can be carried out; and the oral report can also be individualized.

Visiting speakers and professors can be recommended. The foreign information leader who can teach for a semester can make a major contribution to the student's understanding of information service. Team teaching with a national content can improve international content of any course. A series of visitors can add to the curriculum, and if videotaped, the addition can be longterm.

With a flexible curriculum, the school can profit from the presence of the foreign visiting professor by offering a special seminar on information service in his or her own country. This occasion should provide an opportunity to focus both narrowly and in depth on service in one other country or perhaps on an entire region.

For a few information schools located very near another country, field trips by car to visit libraries and information centers there are possible. Examples are five Canadian and three U.S. schools that are close enough to the other country (less than 200 kilometers) for a one-day round trip. Other examples are one Irish and two British schools; Belgium, Dutch, and North German schools; Viennese, Hungarian, and Czechoslovakian; Singapore and Malaysian; Nairobi and Tanzanian schools.

A problem-centered approach to teaching must emphasize multinational situations and should be based on real-life problems in the countries covered. Solutions should require insight into national or regional information service principles and policies. Problems can be collected through correspondence and personal visits.

Controversial questions such as (1) university information service centralization versus decentralization, (2) material selection by college information center staff members versus faculty members, (3) expatriot versus national information center employees, (4) the national "scholar" information specialist versus the educated information specialist, and (5) traditional national versus international information policies can make interesting international study topics.

Wherever possible the instructor should choose for inclusion topics with cross-cultural, not just foreign, dimensions, those that reflect a contrasting heritage and way of life, as well as policies used in several countries. In addition, the instructor should emphasize fundamental cross-country similarities, not just superficial differences. Studying the information service *standards* of other countries can be a useful way of learning more about service there. In this connection, a similar approach, the case study, can be used to enable each student to report on service in one influential information center abroad. The case study adopts a micro view and zeros in on typical institutions, leaders, cities, or national publications in an effort to learn the essence of a situation.

Foreign information systems that cannot be studied directly can be analyzed through simulation, mathematical, or tabular modeling by placing the foreign and domestic side by side in abstract system or model form. This form of teaching is done through the use of outlines or abstracts. Increasingly, instruction should move toward an international approach in which portrayals are expressed in terms of mathematical formulas that demand exact supporting data and lead to the development of laws explaining information service behavior.

Each course may teach students about the information-related associations and organizations that exist in other countries as well as giving them an introduction to the country's literature. Unit bibliographies should cite a variety of international information service journals. However, there is a severe shortage of information about information service in most countries, even in the local language. Probably most countries publish no information service journals, pamphlets, or books in a typical year.[11] This shortage exists primarily in countries outside Eastern and

Western Europe, Australia, and North America. Language problems will plague the instructor studying foreign information service material, hence, material must be translated for use.

DATA COLLECTION AND RESEARCH

Since internationalism has not been widely and consciously taught in information schools, few data are available on its extensiveness, its curricular organization, and the course and unit methods used. Instructors need this information to aid course development. A number of action research projects should be developed to study this activity. Collecting and analyzing information on current practice and comparing it with certain theoretical models is a desirable project, perhaps one for several doctoral students. Or perhaps an international organization like UNESCO or IFLA should collect and publish this information regularly.

What do faculty members need to know about internationalized information education? The extent of international concept use should be studied, primarily the activities and material used in representative curricula. Is it true, as John Harvey claims, that many curricula are already 10 percent or more internationalized? That a start in internationalization has been made in all schools and that most schools in developing countries are teaching primarily foreign and international service without necessarily describing internationalism? Which courses are the most extensively internationalized? In which course units and exercises is internationalism most often used? And how? Which the least? How does internationalism in information schools vary by country? By undergraduate, graduate, and doctoral level? By subcurriculum?

An agenda should be developed to explore this area in world information schools. What facts and ideas should be explored initially? The agenda must start with data collection and publication. We need the facts, school by school, before we can picture situations comprehensively and evaluate them against objectives and standards and before a model can be made of the ideal situation for comparison with a specific school's model. A country-by-country or subcurriculum-by-subcurriculum approach can also be used for study, but only after the objectives of internationalism and its application to information education have been clarified.

Tracing the development of an information service idea through historical periods and geographic areas is needed. Is it possible to trace a concept's use from its origin long ago in one country, such as the United Kingdom, through modification and travel to another country, such as Bermuda? How does school context relate to internationalization? Politically? Economically? What about school size or age, or being in an independent (developed) or dependent (developing) country?

On the other hand, what is the minimum necessary national content of a course? At what point does a course's nationalistic content dip so low and its international content move so high that the course is of little value to a student planning to work locally? Or is such a point ever reached? These are only a few of the questions to which objective answers are needed before we can begin to understand curricular internationalization in information studies schools.

NOTES

1. The author found the following education titles helpful: Curtis R. Finch and John A. Crunkilton, *Curriculum Development in Vocational and Technical Education* (Boston: Allyn & Bacon, 1979); and Albert I. Oliver, *Curriculum Improvement, a Guide to Problems, Principles, and Procedures* (New York: Dodd, Mead & Co., 1965).

2. Elizabeth T. Dresang, "An Application of Decision-making Theory to Curriculum Change in Library Education," *Journal of Education for Librarianship* 20 (Winter 1980), pp. 184–197.

3. Felicia Antonelli Holton, "Where the Door Can't Open Too Soon or Close Too Late," *University of Chicago Magazine* 77 (Winter 1985), p. 16.

4. Ibid.

5. The author is grateful to several authors in this book whose chapters were helpful in preparing this one, especially Harold Borko and Eileen Goldstein, Emilia Bernal, Rosemary Du Mont, Donald Ely and Walter Stone, Robin Guy, Sigrun Hannesdottir, Richard Krzys, and Fritz Veit.

6. See note 5.

7. Howard Winger, "Education for Area Studies Librarianship," *Library Quarterly* 35 (October 1965), pp. 361–372; and Beverly J. Brewster, "Area Bibliography Program in U.S. Library Schools," *International Library Review* 9 (January 1977), pp. 3–18.

8. Frances Laverne Carroll, *Feasibility Study for Incorporating a Year Abroad in the Library Science Curriculum* (Norman: School of Library Science, University of Oklahoma, 1969); and Frances Laverne Carroll, "International Education for Librarianship," *International Library Review* 2 (January 1970), pp. 19–39.

9. See Martha Boaz, "The Comparative and International Library Science Course in American Library Schools," in John F. Harvey, ed., *Comparative and International Library Science* (Metuchen, N. J.: Scarecrow Press, 1977), pp. 169–175.

10. But see A. Robert Rogers and Kathryn McChesney, *The Library in Society* (Littleton, Colo.: Libraries Unlimited, 1985).

11. But see A. H. Huq and M. H. Aman, *Librarianship and the Third World: An Annotated Bibliography of Selected Literature on Developing Nations, 1960–75* (New York: Garland Publishing Co., 1977); and M. Mackee, *A Handbook of Comparative Librarianship* (London: Bingley, 1983).

BIBLIOGRAPHY

ALA World Encyclopedia of Library and Information Services. Ed. by Robert Wedgworth. (Chicago: American Library Association, 1980).

Campbell, H. C. "Internationalism in U.S. Library School Curricula." *International Library Review* 2 (April 1970), pp. 183–186.

Curriculum Change for the Nineties: A Report of the Curriculum Development Project on Library and Information Work (by) E. P. Dudley. Boston Spa: British Library, 1983.

Curriculum Development in Librarianship and Information Science; Proceedings of a Workshop. Research and Development Report 5439. London: British Library, 1979.

Hayes, Robert M. "The Core Curriculum for Library and Information Science Education." Unpublished Paper Presented at the IFLA Conference, 1980, Manila, Philippines. 22 pp.

Hoyle, Eric. "How Does Curriculum Change?" In A. A. Baellach and H. M. Kliebard, eds. *Curriculum and Evaluation*. Berkeley, Calif.: McCuthran, 1977, pp. 517–527.

Janis, I. L., and L. Mann. *Decision-making*. New York: Free Press, 1977.

Kirst, M. W., and D. L. Walker. "Analysis of Curriculum Policy-making." In A. A. Baellach and H. M. Kliebard, eds. *Curriculum and Evaluation*. Berkeley, Calif.: McCuthran, 1977, pp. 538–568.

Magrill, R. M. "Curriculum." In M. B. Cassata and H. L. Totten, eds. *The Administrative Aspects of Education for Librarianship: A Symposium*. Metuchen, N. J.: Scarecrow Press, 1975, pp. 140–152.

Parr, E., and E. J. Wainwright. *Curriculum Design in Librarianship, an International Approach*. Perth: Wait Aid, 1974.

Sharify, Nasser. "The Need for Change in Present Library Science Curricula." In Larry A. Bone, ed. *Library Education: An International Survey*. Urbana, Ill.: University of Illinois, 1968, pp. 171–196.

Toffler, Alvin. *Learning for Tomorrow, the Role of the Future in Education*. New York: Random House, 1974.

13
INTRODUCTION TO LIBRARY SCIENCE COURSES

Robin Frederick Guy

The distinctiveness of each occupational group is created in part by the degree of common activity among its members. If a common thread is lacking, a specific occupational label cannot be assigned to the group. In the late twentieth century, various forces threaten to fracture whatever cohesion exists in librarianship. Indeed, it could be argued that total fracturing has already occurred in the split between library and information science. In Britain, for example, the existence of two separate bodies, the Institute of Information Scientists and the Library Association, seems to provide concrete evidence that two distinct fields exist. It is worth noting, however, that certain individuals are members of *both* bodies and by implication both fields.

Technology is rapidly changing librarianship. The impact has taken many forms: on the one hand, a tendency has developed to create both a technically aware elite and a much less well-informed mass while simultaneously certain "traditional" librarians have become active users of "sophisticated" technology, for example, with online information service. The general effect of technology spread has been to increase the number of specializations within the field.

The existence of many specializations does not necessarily mean, however, that there is no core from which the specializations spring. One has just to think of medicine to refute this idea. A criterion that defines an occupational field is "a central knowledge base."[1] Specializations emanate from this knowledge and suggest that one must pass through the core before reaching a specialty. Following this principle in education means that the central knowledge core should be mastered before studying a specialty.

The core curriculum has been defined as "that fundamental segment of the library school program which is pertinent to all types of libraries and which ought to be mastered by all library students."[2] It has been a perennial issue in library education. D. J. Grogan has outlined the historical controversy surrounding the core concept and concludes that the concept still persists despite experimentation to omit it and that a remarkable degree of unanimity exists about its content.[3]

In Britain and North America, for example, different educational structures have required different approaches to the core. As a rule, British universities do not use a modular approach but extend courses over an entire academic year. Students take longer and fewer courses, with most of them being required rather than optional. In library education this has meant required courses in information storage and retrieval, reference work, and management, together with certain optional courses. Even after the Library Association relinquished authority for setting examinations to the universities and polytechnics, the "new" courses were not radically different from the old ones.

The modular course structure in American institutions has created core curriculum problems since four or five courses must be taken simultaneously. If specialties are offshoots of a central knowledge body, then that body, or at least its important principles, should be learned before work commences on the specialties as a developmental curriculum requires. If time is to be spent pursuing basic knowledge within each specialization, then repetition between courses and fragmentation of material may occur. The only sensible way out of this dilemma may be to concentrate core teaching and to arrange for it to *precede* all specialist teaching.

Introduction to Library and Information Science courses can fulfill a number of functions: they can (1) provide all students with the field's basic principles, (2) integrate the disparate parts of the basic knowledge, and (3) bring all students to a similar awareness level. Students entering librarianship manifest a considerable degree of heterogeneity. They may wish to enter a particular type of library work which may or may not be based on their previous experience, or they may be unsure about their preferred area.

Students entering medical schools will, however, have a science background and little or no previous medical experience, and must undertake core medical course work before embarking on specialized courses. An introductory course can help to smooth out these student variations by providing a broad and common course experience.

Perhaps the introductory course should be referred to as a foundation or fundamental course since the term *introduction* often suggests one that is superficial or elementary. Foundation or fundamental courses are introductory, but these words suggest a degree of substance lacking in the other title. The rest of this chapter will consider foundation courses that are usually compulsory; precede other courses (although there may be overlap); and purport to cover a core curriculum subject that should be mastered before proceeding to specialized subjects.

EXAMPLES OF EXISTING COURSES

Several examples of foundation courses have been described in the literature. The University of South Carolina offers three core foundation courses, one a six-semester credit hour course (normally meeting six hours per week for a sixteen-week semester) and two three-credit courses. At the University of North Carolina the course comprises a block of six unequal units that totals twelve semester hours. The Drexel University course comprises approximately forty class sessions for three credits. The eight-week University of Illinois course, "Foundations of Librarianship," was designed to replace four courses previously prerquisite for graduate program entrance. Case Western Reserve University provided a six-credit course prerequisite to all other courses.

Certain course objectives may be described. For Illinois, it is stated that the foundations course (1) provides an integrated overview of the field and gives students a better idea of what branch of the profession they want to prepare for and which courses they should take to provide such preparation; and having a standardized content, ensures that each student moves into the advanced courses with the same level of preparation and that the instructors in these courses will know what students have been exposed to.[4]

Drexel's course objectives are to:

1. Present an integrated view of the activities that take place in the library and information science field and provide a conceptual framework that relates these activities as they are found in libraries and information centers of all types.

2. Acquaint students with the major institutional settings in which these activities are carried out and demonstrate the similarities, differences, and relationships of these institutions.

3. Introduce students to the range of skills and the techniques that underlie these skills; and provide students with a basis for the later development of distinctive competencies in their chosen area of specialization.

4. Relate library and information services to the needs of users; instill a critical and evaluative attitude in students toward the operation and function of such services; and identify some major factors determining their effectiveness for users.

5. Describe the roles and functions of information professionals in relation to the environments in which they operate and review the nature of the responsibilities that are inherent in professional performances.[5]

Jesse Shera states that the objectives of the foundations course should be to

1. Provide the student with a generalized overview of librarianship in a way that will make clear the interrelationships and interdependencies of the variant forms and specializations of the field.
2. Present a theoretical structure of librarianship that will make clear these relationships.
3. Give something of the historical development of librarianship in relation to the communication processes of society and the emergence of the library as a social instrumentality.
4. Make reasonably certain that all students have a common background of understanding of the field prior to their entry on their library specialty.
5. Relieve the subsequent courses of much of the technical detail, terminology, and standard procedures that must be mastered by recruits before they can progress very far in their quest for competence.
6. Provide those students who have not at the time of matriculation in the library school decided on a specific area of activity some bases for making a rational choice in terms of their competencies and interests.[6]

A considerable degree of unanimity exists among the three lists in terms of basic objectives. All state the need to (a) demonstrate the nature of the library field, in particular showing the relationships between the various parts, and (b) ensure that all students achieve a standard preparation level before taking additional courses.

COURSE INTERNATIONALIZATION

The importance of adopting an international perspective in the foundation course must be emphasized. This course is compulsory and is the student's first formal contact with library education. Therefore, it provides a prime mechanism for propagating international ideals. If international attitudes can be inculcated at the beginning of an educational program, there is some chance that, with reinforcement, they will prevail throughout the program and the career. At the same time, this course offers an excellent place in which to stimulate an international perspective. The course is global in intent and emphasizes breadth rather than depth. It tries to establish frameworks and to identify relationships between parts.

Internationalization Methods

The difficult objective of creating a genuine international perspective can be achieved by using a variety of methods: examples from a range of situations, case studies including role-playing, seminars, term papers, guest lectures, and media.

Examples are useful methods of illustrating particular points. They can help to clarify and elucidate a particular point by enabling the student to visualize what is meant and are vital in assisting understanding. They help to provide hooks on which theory can be hung by creating mental pictures. In terms of developing an international perspective, the instructor should choose examples of practices in different countries to illustrate existing differences.

Case studies are extensions of examples and can assist students to analyze, in depth, approaches to problem-solving and decision-making. At their simplest, background information about a particular situation is supplied, and based on this information, together with a methodology applicable to the overall aspect under consideration, the student is required to produce a sensible solution to the problem in hand.

To create an international dimension, the situation to be analyzed can be centered in an overseas country: if so, the background notes must state any social or behavioral factors that apply. Alternatively, the students could work out a solution to the problem appropriate to their own country and then be supplied with notes about the solution(s) for other countries. Role-playing can help to increase understanding in suitable situations.

Seminars are ideal vehicles for exposing students to other viewpoints and encouraging them to defend their own. Either case studies or student papers can act as discussion catalysts. If group members represent several nations, the seminar can benefit the student in two ways: an examination of published and unpublished literature will provide background and detailed information, while the act of writing should help ideas to crystallize and expose any limitations in thinking.

Guest lectures from overseas can help, provided the students have achieved a defined level of understanding about a particular topic against which the lecturer can pinpoint national variations. To achieve genuine understanding of another country without visiting or living in that country is difficult.

Media (films, tape/slides, and so forth) can support general teaching by providing pictorial and other evidence. For example, it is difficult for those who have never visited it to appreciate the size of the Library of Congress collection. A film can help to put across the scale of the operation. In the same way, Western Europeans are unlikely to have any concept of what rural Africa is like, let alone any idea of libraries placed therein. A film, videotape, and the like can create a pictorial and factual context that can be helpful.

Faculty

Providing a course that sets out (a) to show connections between the various parts of the subject area and (b) to provide an international perspective imposes substantial demands on the instructor. Faculty members are thereby forced to move out of their familiar specialization areas into a more general context. To many faculty members comfortable in, for example, library management, the prospect of having to grapple with, say, cataloging policies, is unappealing. Yet for an intergrated course to succeed the instructor must cross the boundaries.

While course preparation may be done primarily by one instructor, in a number of institutions preparation may involve all faculty members. One reason for this is that preparation will involve a considerable amount of work, notably in syllabus or course book production, and it is only fair to share it. However, more fundamental benefits exist. For example, at Drexel, endless discussion on basic content and effective methods of teaching have forced faculty to learn each other's strengths and to expose themselves to peer review.

The wish to impose an international perspective on teaching places further demands on the faculty. If they have little knowledge either from working in, studying, or visiting other countries, they will have difficulty in introducing examples and case studies. Thus, the term teaching approach can be beneficial. This general problem, however, focuses on the importance for all faculty members of acquiring international knowledge.

Course Evaluation

Evaluation has two aspects, namely, that of the student's progress and that of the course itself. Student evaluation must be rigorously carried out, and the student should perform to a satisfactory level in *all* foundation course modules. This, however, is not to suggest that the student evaluation needs to be a dramatic once and for all pass or fail situation. At Illinois, for example, while students must complete the course work in the time available, they can submit work until it is judged acceptable.

The type of evaluation used will be determined by the practice of particular parent institutions. Some institutions base evaluation entirely on course work, and others (although a small and declining group) on written examinations. The nature of this course strongly suggests a high degree of project-type work, but it is important to keep such work in balance. If assessment is entirely project-based, there can be a tendency to concentrate all efforts on the project(s) leading to a neglect of the remaining areas.

The evaluation of the course as a whole is important, especially when new ideas are being tried. The classic way of achieving this is by using end-of-session questionnaires. To help provide some balance in this process, both faculty members and students should be involved. It is also important to see evaluation as a continuing process and to avoid too hasty a reaction to critical comment.[7]

Course Structure

The challenge of creating a unified course for a field which many feel to be one of four or five interlocking subprofessions is considerable. However, a surprising degree of agreement exists among those who have grappled with the problem. Helen M. Focke has suggested that a foundation library science course be built around five key areas:

1. *People* and their needs and methods of communication, with special emphasis on the use of recorded material.

2. *Material* generated by people in trying to communicate, covering a brief history of various types, both book and nonbook, production, and distribution.[8]

3. *Institutions* which have developed to handle and house the material and serve the people's needs; their history, types, and common external and internal administrative problems.

4. *The services offered by libraries and information centers* to bring the material and the people together.

5. An introduction to the basic *tools* with which a librarian works for the identification, selection, acquisition, and use of the material.

Jesse Shera adopted this structure for (a) people and communication; (b) material: history, types, distribution; (c) tools for access to material: bibliographic organization; (d) tools for access to material: information sources; (e) the institutionalization of the library; (f) services; and (g) research in librarianship. Harlow has suggested the following areas:

1. Generation, organization, and storage of the record (collection building, bibliographic organization creating the appropriate file or "store").

2. Interface between the record and user (mediation, question negotiation identifying the character and level of information needed).

3. Retrieval of information (search strategy, finding, analyzing, and evaluating data) and its transmission.

4. Evaluation of output in terms of satisfying users' needs in learning decision-making and human behavior and as feedback for systems adjustment.[9]

The 1981 course at Illinois strongly reflects the structures suggested by Focke and Shera: the profession; concepts including communication models, history and types of libraries; material; services and operations; management; and summary. The North Carolina course has the following structure: library and environment including communication process and role of library—history of libraries and communication media; automatic information processing; library service and material; research;

planning for libraries and administering them; and librarianship as a profession.

Drexel's course was divided into the following units: introduction to library and information science; information needs of clients and service provided; building collections and information files; identification and control of documents and information; document organization and retrieval; management and research process.

The rest of this chapter will consider individual courses within the following overall structure: historical perspective, type of libraries, resources, processes, library management, and international aspects. This structure is only a convenient one for considering the wide range of possible variations. Curriculum planners must choose a structure appropriate to their own priorities and resource availability. The kinds of individual units that could be included within each section will be considered. No suggestion is being made that all units would necessarily be taught; rather, this is the range from which a suitable selection should be made. Suggestions on how internationalization may be achieved are made at the end of each section.

Historical and Sociological Perspective

The following units are included: history of writing, book and printing history, world library history, library and society, and history of communication. Historical courses are a contentious issue. Many persons argue that at best they are a waste of time and at worst they alienate many students. Too often they are a mere enumeration of events and assume that libraries originated in a social vacuum.

This suggests that the content of history of libraries courses should be broadly sociological and that a more all-embracing title should be the development of libraries in a sociohistorical content. Certainly, some schools emphasize the sociological content of their courses by calling them Library and Society. Regardless of the exact title, the point is that history is not mere arid facts but must acknowledge social developments and how they influenced factors. In his plan for a sociology of communication foundation course, K. J. McGarry provides a helpful syllabus on communication history.[10]

INTERNATIONALIZATION

This section offers obvious opportunities to create an international perspective. Writing, book, and printing history must be taught from an international viewpoint because that is the way things happened. So, for example, one can move from the earliest known Egyptian hieroglyphic writing and papyrus use to the first public library in Athens, through to Germany and Gutenberg. Although many library history courses tend to concentrate on national developments after the earliest world history has been sketched in, the international context must be preserved through to modern times. The argument that the present can only be properly understood in the context of the past must be applied to other countries.

Obviously, all countries cannot be considered, but a small number can be studied and their historical development compared with that of the home country. For the various regions, teaching can be based on case studies that raise questions and require students to use research material on specific countries. Study countries must be selected to ensure that adequate published material exists locally in the student's language.

Types of Libraries

This module should provide a broad overview of the range of libraries to bring out the wide variety that exists. Units that could be included are school, public, academic, special, and national libraries, and information centers. This module will outline the various library types. Individual units offer an opportunity to explore the unique characteristics of the different library types. There are quite a few problems in teaching this module in a foundation course. Very little student knowledge can be assumed for each library type, but at the same time, the student must be taught enough to make a career decision about the preferred type of library.

Teaching must be based on trends rather than on detail. This means concentrating on the key differences among types of libraries in terms of the user community—emphasizing differences of background, needs, and information-seeking behavior. At times this may lead to a simplistic and crude analysis, but its purpose is to clarify by highlighting, not to confuse with many qualifications and caveats.

INTERNATIONALIZATION

This module offers considerable opportunity to create an international perspective but also creates considerable problems. Superficial similarities exist between types of libraries in different countries. More profoundly, however, considerable variation can exist between apparently similar types. The same nomenclature is often used to describe types of libraries that differ radically in practice. Of course, the same point applies to libraries of the same type across national frontiers.

Library types are also strongly rooted to their socioeconomic backgrounds which must be fully understood. Students cannot be expected to possess this kind of knowledge for more than a few countries. Considerable demand will therefore be placed on the faculty to provide sufficient background for valid comparisons to be made.

The following approaches are possible:

1. General introduction to types of libraries which highlights the essential differences among them.
2. Sessions devoted to the different library types. First, look at the generalized idea of a particular type of library by drawing out significant features. Follow this by examining the appropriate national context and studying the type in selected areas.

So, for example, for the public library sessions, library school students in the United Kingdom can study the current British system by building on the historical aspects considered in the history module. Structure and overall philosophy can then be contrasted with the situation in France and Africa. International comparisons cannot merely be made to state differences but to attempt to explain how and why they exist.

Resources

Although information is held in many forms, the association in the public mind between libraries and books is strong. The purpose of this module is to identify the types of material, to consider their purpose, and to discuss how they should be handled and their relationships. The following units can comprise it: primary, secondary, and tertiary publications, reference sources, and bibliographic control.

The distinction between primary, secondary, and tertiary publications is not always obvious. Primary publications contain the author's original work, secondary publications contain second-hand reports of events and comments, while tertiary publications provide access to primary and secondary material. Primary material includes research monographs, government publications, and reports. Secondary publications include textbooks, encyclopedias, newspapers, and reviews, while tertiary publications include abstracting and indexing services and bibliographies. Reference sources include dictionaries, encyclopedias, yearbooks, and almanacs. Sometimes reference sources are grouped with secondary and tertiary sources.

INTERNATIONALIZATION

There is considerable emphasis in this module on learning about the various reference sources. This should not involve committing long lists to memory but rather should involve handling and using material. There is great potential, therefore, to develop the international perspective.

While categories of material published in various countries possess many common characteristics, national differences exist which can be identified by examination of the material. This approach can be applied to all material, although the exercise is likely to be more successful with some types such as government publications than with others.

Although many abstracting and indexing journals have international coverage, others do not. Interesting exercises can be established to explore the extent of international coverage, for example, by the journals indexed. A study of the national bibliographies of several countries can put the national context into perspective. Within the reference sources category, many insights can be gained by examining statistical sources which can reveal valuable comparative information.

Because the concept of bibliographic control has no meaning except in an international context, the international dimension must be covered. Study of Universal Availability of Publications and Machine Readable Cataloging transcend national frontiers, while several national bibliographies can reveal local problems.

Processes

This module provides an overview of the various kinds of library technical operations and includes acquisitions, cataloging, classification, circulation control, library lending, and data processing. These activities are self-explanatory. Data processing refers to a course on the fundamentals of this topic. Consideration of computer application to library processes, however, is best done without the context of the process itself.

All housekeeping activities can be carried out manually, but increasingly libraries are using computers. A data processing course is therefore an important adjunct to these courses. Essentially, the data processing course should deal with the fundamentals of computer hardware, software, and systems analysis and design. The objective is to provide sufficient background knowledge on these aspects so that the computerization of particular processes can be considered in adequate depth.

INTERNATIONALIZATION

These activities are carried out to a greater or lesser degree in most libraries in all countries. Existing variations are not so much between countries as between types of libraries. Certain varied aspects can be brought out in teaching. The English-speaking world bases its cataloging on the *Anglo-American Cataloging Rules*. whereas libraries in other countries use other rules. Similarly, the Dewey and Library of Congress classification schemes dominate in many countries; yet certain other schemes are widely used, especially the Universal Decimal Classification Scheme. Care must be taken, however, not to teach too many additional codes, for they may confuse the student. Less familiar approaches should be introduced only after basic systems have been mastered.

Interlibrary lending systems are well suited to international comparisons. For example, it is instructive to compare the British system, which centers on the British Library Lending Division, with the U.S. system which is decentralized and depends on many large research and public libraries. Furthermore, it is important for students in the First World to be made aware that computers are not prevalent in the Second and Third Worlds and that manual systems will continue to exist for many years.

Management

The purpose of this module is to introduce basic management concepts and to examine varied organizational structures within libraries and information centers. The following units might be included: personnel, finance, departmentation, position levels, and building. Management programs are often criticized for being too theoretical and too far removed from likely events in the early career years. These criticisms are often applied to the final degree courses and must have even greater validity for foundation courses.

As with all elements in the foundation program, excessive detail must be avoided. To laboriously study the administrative structures in many libraries is much less desirable than considering the most common structures. Similarly, how libraries have arrived at their stated goals and objectives need be studied in only a few of them.

Many believe it is important that practical management skills such as budgeting be taught in information schools. Many graduates will be required to demonstrate competency in these areas and often to do so early in their careers. The main question to consider here is the depth of treatment possible in a foundation course. It is reasonable to suggest that basic budgeting policies be taught in the foundation course and that more detailed study take place in specialized management courses.

INTERNATIONALIZATION

Imposing an international perspective on management is not easy to implement because of the nature of management as a discipline. Scientific management implies that particular rules can be applied with expectation of particular results. Common sense shows that people do not react according to predefined formulas. The problem is further complicated by the fact that much of the behavior with which management is concerned is culture-bound. The practice of certain management principles must therefore take into account the personality and background of those being managed.

The understanding of particular principles can be deepened by considering closely how the context, for example, the political context between capitalist and totalitarian states, affects the result. Even such activities as financial control, which might appear to be similar in every country, can be quite different. There will be differences in the way libraries are financed as between central and local financing. In fact, not all libraries will be dependent on government or central body finance. This would include not only libraries of commercial organizations but also libraries that generate income by, for example, the sale of services.

The International Scene

The international aspects of each module have been discussed, and this module may be unnecessary. However, two reasons can be given for including it: several important agencies will not have been mentioned because they did not fit into any module, and it is helpful to draw together the many threads of internationalism. This short unit could include: agencies (such as IFLA, FID, and UNESCO), information networks (such as AGRIS), standards (such as MARC), and education for librarianship. Although factual information about agencies must be provided, major emphasis should be on the successes and failures of international ventures, their problems, and how they may be overcome.

CONCLUSIONS

Two of the major problems in internationalizing foundation courses are the international understanding of teaching staff and the availability of teaching material. Many institutions arrange regular exchanges; for example, Birmingham Polytechnic (United Kingdom) and the University of Texas at Austin have had several staff exchanges. The idea of a clearing-house for international teaching material has been suggested, but it is difficult to envisage such a venture as being successful.[11] The many faculty members who are reluctant to distribute teaching material to colleagues are unlikely to send them to a national or international clearinghouse.

NOTES

1. K. J. McGarry, "The Sociology of Communication as a Foundation Course in the Education of the Librarian" (M.Lib Thesis, University of Wales, 1974), p. 18.

2. Guy Marco, "Recent Adventures of the American Core Curriculum," *UNESCO Bulletin for Libraries* 32 (July-August 1978), p. 279.

3. D. J. Grogan, "Education for Librarianship: Some Persistent Issues," *Education for Information* 1 (March 1983), pp. 21–42.

4. Walter C. Allen and F. Wilfrid Lancaster, "A Directed Independent Study Approach to a Foundations Course," *Journal of Education for Librarianship* 21 (Spring 1981), pp. 313–326.

5. A. Kathryn Oller, "The Nature of the Course," *Drexel Library Quarterly* 10 (July 1974), pp. 19–33.

6. Jesse H. Shera, *The Foundations of Education for Librarianship* (New York: John Wiley, 1972), p. 368.

7. Thomas Childers, "Evaluation of the Fundamentals Course," *Drexel Library Quarterly* 10 (July 1974), pp. 47–45.

8. Helen M. Focke, "Foundations of Library Science," *Journal of Education for Librarianship* 8 (Spring 1981), pp. 241–250.

9. Neal Harlow, "Changing the Curriculum," *Journal of Education for Librarianship* 10 (Fall 1969), p. 81.

10. McGarry, p. 187.

11. H. C. Campbell, "Internationalization in U.S. Library School Curricula," *International Library Review* 2 (April 1970), p. 184.

BIBLIOGRAPHY

Types of Library

Anthony, L. J., ed. *Handbook of Special Librarianship and Information Science.* 5th ed. London: Aslib, 1982.

Higham, N. *The Library in the University: Observations on a Service.* London: Deutsch, 1980.

Jefferson, G., ed. *The College Library: A Collection of Essays.* London: Bingley, 1978.

Kumar, K. *Research Libraries in Developing Countries.* Delhi: Vikas, 1973.

Line, M. B., ed. *National Libraries.* London: Aslib, 1979.

Mount, E. *Special Libraries and Information Centers: An Introductory Text.* New York: Special Libraries Association, 1983.

Robbins-Carter, J. *Public Librarianship: A Reader.* Littleton, Colo.: Libraries Unlimited, 1982.

Totterdell, B., ed. *Public Library Purpose: A Reader.* London: Bingley, 1978.

Historical and Social Aspects

Benge, R. C. *Libraries and Cultural Change.* London: Bingley, 1970.

Dunlap, L. W. *Readings in Library History.* New York: R. R. Bowker, 1972.

Johnson, E. D. *History of Libraries in the Western World.* Metuchen, N. J.: Scarecrow Press, 1976.

McGarry, K. J. *The Changing Context of Information: An Introductory Analysis.* London: Bingley, 1981.

Processing

Boss, R. W. *Automating Library Acquisitions*. White Plains, N. Y.: Knowledge Industry Publications, 1982.

Hayes, A. C. *The Subject Approach to Information*. 4th ed. London: Bingley, 1982.

Hayes, E. J., and K. G. B. Bakewell. *Cataloguing*. 2 ed. London: Bingley, 1982.

Lancaster, F. W. *Information Retrieval Systems: Characteristics, Testing and Evaluation*. 2d ed. New York: John Wiley, 1979.

Malinconico, S. *The Future of the Catalog: The Library's Choice*. White Plains, N. Y.: Knowledge Industry Publications, 1979.

Maltby, A. *Sayers' Manual of Classification for Librarians*. London: Deutsch, 1975.

Stueart, R. D., and G. B. Miller, eds. *Collection Development in Libraries: A Treatise*. Greenwich, Conn.: JAI Press, 1980. 2 vols.

Management

Brown, R. *Public Library Administration*. London: Bingley, 1979.

Corbett, E. V. *Fundamentals of Library Organisation and Administration: A Practical Guide*. London: Library Association, 1978.

Cowley, J. *Personnel Management in Libraries*. London: Bingley, 1982.

Shimmon, R., ed. *A Reader in Library Management*. London: Bingley, 1976. 2d ed. Littleton, Colo: Libraries Unlimited, 1981.

Stueart, R. D. and J. T. Eastlick. *Library Management*. 2nd ed. Littleton, Colo.: Libraries Unlimited, 1981.

Resources

REFERENCE BOOKS

Higgens, G., ed. *Printed Reference Material*. London: Library Association, 1980.

Katz, W. A. *Introduction to Reference Work*. New York: McGraw-Hill, 1982.

Walford, A. J. ed. *Guide to Reference Material*. 3 vols. London: Library Association, 1980.

REFERENCE WORK AND SERVICES

Davinson, D. *Reference Service*. London: Bingley, 1980.

Grogan, D. J. *Practical Reference Work*. London: Bingley, 1979.

INTERNATIONAL ASPECTS

Harvey, J. F., ed. *Comparative and International Library Science*. Metuchen, N. J.: Scarecrow Press, 1977.

Huq, A. M. Abdul, and M. H. Aman. *Librarianship and the Third World: An Annotated Bibliography, 1960–1975*. New York: Garland, 1977.

Jackson, M. M., ed. *Comparative and International Librarianship*. Westport, Conn.: Greenwood Press, 1970.

Krzys, R., and Gaston Litton. *World Librarianship: A Comparative Study*. New York: Marcel Dekker, 1983.

Mackee, M. *A Handbook of Comparative Librarianship*. 3d ed. London: Bingley, 1983.

14

COLLECTION DEVELOPMENT COURSES

Richard Krzys

Internationalizing the collection development course, or expanding its knowledge, attitude, and skill components to include concepts that transcend national boundaries represents another evolutionary change in library education. After library schools were established, courses in this area were first called book selection, then material selection, and presently collection development. Each title change indicated an expansion in material from books, to audiovisuals, to all types of media. Today's counterpart course must encompass a global outline of collection subjects, and the teaching methodologies employed must also reflect diversity.

This expansion of course content and teaching methodology results from the change in access to information. Today internationalism is as close to us as our radio and television newscasts and the international students we teach. At the flick of a switch we see news events from around the world, and we are continually reminded of the international dimension by our students' varied backgrounds. In most cases international students have come to library school only after overcoming serious problems, among which may be an overly nationalistic collection development course.

Lester Asheim has described the dangers inherent in library education that has not been internationalized:

A first concern (of professional leaders in other countries who must decide whether or not to give permission to the student to travel abroad for professional education) is that the overseas experience, especially for the young or immature student, will contribute to a kind of denationalization which could be harmful. The student who is not sufficiently flexible to distinguish between what is applicable and what is not may well return with expectations unsuited to the capacities of the native land.[1]

We shall concentrate on two objectives in this chapter: (1) to expand collection development topics or concepts, wherever possible, to international dimensions, and (2) to include international topics or concepts not mentioned in traditional selection courses. The principles discussed are more than a prescription for internationalizing this course; they may be used as philosophical guidelines for designing the entire gamut of courses taught within a school's resources and bibliography area. That area usually includes a general development course as well as separate courses in the humanities, social sciences, and the natural and applied sciences.

PLANNING THE INTERNATIONAL COURSE

At least three types of planning are possible for the internationalized collection course: planning (1) by the instructor alone, (2) with a committee, and (3) within the course itself.

Planning by the instructor alone draws on the instructor's experience in teaching the traditional collection course and allows the opportunity to delete, modify, elaborate, or add concepts that require attention. Because of the limited nature of this type of planning, due to lack of experience in other countries, it is less useful than other approaches.

Planning with a committee is more promising and should produce superior understanding of the expected knowledge, attitude, and skill components of the internationalized collection development course. It may utilize the basic course outline by Ruth Warncke.[2] Our first task is to consider the rational underlying the traditional collection course in terms of its description, purpose, objectives, outline, and requirements. After discussing these items as units, we can then divide them up as search topics. We can proceed to utilize whatever means seems promising to further our objective—literature searching, conversing and corresponding with colleagues, individual planning, and finally collaborating to produce a mutually acceptable syllabus.

Planning within the course itself combines the two processes just described as well as the additional phase of integrating student opinion into the course. Prior to designing the internationalized version of his present course, the author queried colleagues and searched the literature for opinions on the paper topic. The most useful reply was, "Design the best possible collection development course and then internationalize it, but be sufficiently flexible to add material and use pruning shears on content that exceeds traditional semester limits."[3]

BASIC COURSE UNIT CHANGE

The traditional collection development or core collection course outline follows:

Basic Traditional Course Outline

Course Introduction

Description	Outline
Objectives	Requirements

Historical Background of Books and Libraries

Types of Libraries and Their Communities

Library Material

Nature	Use
Categories	Organization and Arrangement

Publishers and Publishing

Nature	Functions
History and Development	Types

Selection of Material

Purpose	Selection Aids
Community Analysis	Format
Principles	Subjects
Policies	Censorship

Acquisition of Material

Principles	Annotation Writing
Examination and Evaluation of Material	Book Talks

Collection Evaluation

Storage	Preservation
Weeding	Replacement

Conclusions of Course Participants[4]

Warncke stated the traditional course objectives as follows: To develop (a) knowledge of the sources of information or assistance in the selection of books and other material; (b) understanding of the principles of establishing, developing, and evaluating collections; (c) knowledge of the channels of the book trade; (d) understanding of the principles of the selection process, from the application of the criteria to single titles through procedures and policies, as applied to all types of material; and (e) a philosophy of selection as the sum total of the above.

Three objectives may be added to the traditional course: To develop

(1) the skill to write annotations, (2) the skill to give talks, and (3) the attitude of impartiality in material selection. Now that we have identified the raw material—the barest minimum of concepts essential to internationalizing a collection course—we will, by examples, demonstrate other principles through which such a course can be developed.

Flexibility of teaching style is essential. The instructor should be aware that the class is composed of nationals from a variety of countries. The teacher of the internationalized course must make it meaningful and useful to students with varied backgrounds. How can we teach a course that is valid for all groups? The answer lies in our willingness—teacher and students—to formulate course objectives together. We as instructors must be willing to sacrifice our objectives to a process of scrutiny in the first class session.

A special approach may be required for the first day of class. The instructor should begin the course by stating with conviction: "This collection development course can be one of the most fascinating of your entire education if we take the time now to formulate together its objectives carefully and precisely. The objectives that we formulate will differ necessarily from those of any other course because you are here." Bearing in mind that the purpose of internationalizing the course is to enable students from the home country and abroad to derive maximum benefit from it, the instructor should ask the students to identify their countries of origin.

In expanding the topics to international dimensions, the items might be as follows: (1) the characteristics of national librarianship, (2) the sacred quality of the book in Middle Eastern and Asian countries, (3) Ranganathan's "Five Laws of Library Science," (4) the nature of publishing in other countries, (5) book pirating, (6) selection policies in the socialist and nonsocialist worlds, (7) foreign literature inclusion in the collection, (8) preservation of the oral tradition, and (9) attitudes toward weeding throughout the world.

After the instructor and students have agreed on the objectives and topics of the internationalized course, the instructor should prepare a final topical outline. The course outline should emerge as a product of the student-instructor discussion and should take into account the decisions made by class participants. Of course, the instructors, by virtue of their superior knowledge and broader collection development experience, should make all final decisions.

THE CHARACTERISTICS OF NATIONAL LIBRARIANSHIP

The instructor must impart a clear perception of the characteristics of home country librarianship in order to provide a frame of reference for discussion of situations in other countries. Another approach might be to discuss the nature of library service in the nine world regions, namely (1) the Middle East; (2) Central, South, and Southeast Asia; (3) Africa; (4) Western Europe; (5) Union of Soviet Socialist Republics; (6) Eastern Europe; (7) Latin America; (8) United States and Canada; and (9) Australia, New Zealand, and Oceania.[5]

Examples of these listings, drawn arbitrarily here, might provide insight into how these characteristics can serve as principles on which collection development is built with a region. For the Middle East, we might postulate the following characteristics: (1) A high esteem exists for learning and the book; (2) the centuries-old library development tradition tends to delay modernization of services, technology, and techniques; (3) the philosophy of librarianship has traditionally favored library use by royalty as well as religious and political leaders and the elite classes, but current philosophy is moving toward providing service to the ever-increasing educated masses; (4) lack of understanding exists among government officials of the necessary role of libraries in educational and technological advancement; and (5) the level of library consciousness among government officials is more influential than the enormous wealth of the area in causing progressive change in library development.

If the above characteristics are used as discussion items, the instructor and students may gain greater insight into the collection development situation in the Middle East than if the instructor merely lectures on the subject. The class should consider students from the region's countries as resource people.

As an additional illustration of this concept, the collection development characteristics of Soviet librarianship may be discussed. These characteristics are: (1) Soviet library practice is based on the Communist party principles devised by V. I. Lenin; (2) these principles reflect the party spirit in all library activities and state the concept of freedom of access to libraries and the planned character of library development; (3) the socialist socioeconomic system, based on the social ownership of the means of production and the goal of a balanced development of the national economy, includes library development; (4) the main task of Soviet libraries is to carry on active support for the policy pursued by the Communist party and the Soviet state; (5) underlying library planning is the assumption that libraries will expand and play an increasingly active role in the national economy and culture; (6) librarianship is a profession that enjoys widespread respect; (7) activities, collections, and the nature of the librarians' work are affected by the multinational composition of Soviet activity; and (8) library development plans take into account local conditions and national characteristics as well as approved state five-year plans and allocations to develop cultural and educational institutions.

Understanding the importance given to libraries and to collection development within the USSR becomes easier when one realizes that Lenin understood library functions and vigorously supported library service. Certainly the fact that his wife, Nadezhda Konstantinovna Krupskaya, was a librarian contributed to Lenin's understanding of library potential.

The characteristics of Middle Eastern and Soviet librarianship can then be contrasted with those of the United States. Ray Swank identified the six characteristics of U.S. librarianship as (1) the conception of the library as an organization of books; (2) the evolution of a library occupation; (3) the attitude of service; (4) the function of the library as an educational institution; (5) the role of the library in the advancement of intellectual freedom; and (6) the conception of organized information as a public resource and responsibility.[6] These characteristics still retain their validity, but one other can be added to bring them up to date. U.S. librarianship incorporates standardization of procedures and technology, including computerization, into its operation.

Once these characteristics are discussed and understood, they will provide deeper understanding of the intellectual foundations of collection development as well as permitting tolerance for varying international attitudes toward the book.

THE SACRED QUALITY OF THE BOOK IN MIDDLE EASTERN AND ASIAN COUNTRIES

Asheim and Kaser have discussed international attitudes toward the book. Asheim states, "In most of the foreign libraries I have been including in my generalizations, the book is more important than its user. The system that has been devised is designed primarily to protect the book and preserve it; in some cases this is the entire end of librarianship."[7] Kaser attributes a similar characteristic to Asian librarianship and even widened the concept when he stated, "Perhaps the key trait affecting libraries is a widely held esteem for books and learning".[8]

Students more clearly understand varying roles of the book in world librarianship when they compare the Middle Eastern and Asian view with its role in the United States: "In the United States, we tend to feel a loyalty to the reader more than to the book. We open our shelves even while knowing that some books will be stolen or mutilated."[9] Given multinational class composition, the instructor should expect to explain the reasons underlying these conditions.

Asheim attributes this phenomenon, which he labels "the philosophy of primacy of the book over the reader," to a variety of causes, including political beliefs that urge all citizens to accept their particular given place in society and a philosophy that encourages the librarians' custodial function. However, the present author attributes the primacy of the book to societies where books are scarce, expensive, and used mostly for transmitting religious beliefs. In such societies, more than scarce and expensive, the book, too, becomes sacred.

RANGANATHAN'S "FIVE LAWS OF LIBRARY SCIENCE"

Bearing in mind the desirability of interpreting collection development concepts in their world contexts, the instructor should relate the "primacy of the book philosophy" to an international measure like Ranganathan's "Five Laws of Library Science." From Asia have come two philosophies of librarianship: (1) the "primacy of the book philosophy" dating back to ancient times when the sacred books of the Jews, early Christians, and Muslims were the only ones they knew and therefore contributed to the sacred quality of books in general; and (2) the concept of the reader having supremacy over the book, which was formulated by India's S. R. Ranganathan.[10] An Asian student might be asked to report on these concepts.

THE NATURE OF PUBLISHING IN OTHER COUNTRIES

The student emerging from an internationalized course should understand the contrasting nature of publishing in both the developed and developing countries. The developed countries have a system of publishers, wholesalers, and dealers that enables librarians to select books easily. In developing countries the situation is different, according to Asheim:

Book selection in our terms is infrequently encountered. In many developing countries, a great part of the collection depends upon gifts and exchanges. Where book budgets are available, they are usually quite limited, and in any case the selector is seldom the librarian. In universities and schools, selection is completely in faculty hands, often with final authority resting with a dean's committee. Purchasing is done primarily through the local bookstore. In the usual situation, the selector must check the bookstore shelves periodically in the hope of running down what he wants and getting it before private purchases have picked over the stock; in the worst situations, a blanket order is given to the lowest bidder who may substitute as much as 15 per cent of an order with rejects and slow sellers he wants to unload. So the actual selection is made by the bookseller whose objectives are seldom those of a serious librarian.[11]

Students from abroad should concentrate on acquainting themselves with the publishing industry in their own country as a term project. Information on functional selection procedures may be obtained from library literature or correspondence with practicing librarians in the country. Reports on these situations can be presented in a group discussion about three-quarters of the way through the course.

BOOK PIRATING

An intriguing topic is the book piracy practiced in many countries. Piracy involves using an already published book from one country and publishing it in another with modification to make the book more acceptable. Such pirating is common, not only for fiction but also for textbooks. In the case of textbooks printers avoid the high cost of author royalties.

More important than the description of book pirating is an explanation of its effects and solutions. When printers translate and duplicate world literature and textbooks at a fraction of the cost of publishing an original book, they have a harmful effect on the local writers who might produce original manuscripts. From such facts it is desirable that students form their own conclusions, for example, why countries should comply with international copyright laws. The need for local publishing has been summarized by Krzys and Litton as follows:

While resorting to the expedient use of textbooks from his own country, an English-speaking instructor, for example, may find himself having to explain in the language of the host country the concepts that his students have already read and only partially understood. Or the instructor may purchase textbooks from a country whose language is the same as that of the host country. Saudi Arabians, for example, have for years been using Arabic library science textbooks published in Egypt.

Unfortunately, neither situation is satisfactory because in the first case, that of the library science texts in foreign languages, the student is compelled to study an unfamiliar language. And even in cases where the language is the same, as in the case with Saudi Arabia and Egypt, the underlying assumptions of the textbooks, their legal systems and social customs, may be quite different.[12]

SELECTION POLICIES IN THE SOCIALIST AND NONSOCIALIST WORLDS

If international practice variants are not discussed, the instructor runs the risk of making the course content doctrinaire. This tendency can become especially difficult to avoid in areas like acquisitions where the student may believe that the procedure used locally is used throughout the world. Selecting material to illustrate all viewpoints of a controversial national question may also be thought of as universal policy, even though it may be more extensive in democracies than in totalitarian countries.

Asheim explains the philosophical basis for educational decisions, including material selection, in the following terms: "The kind of education that any nation offers is based on its own beliefs and institutions, and formal education in a class-conscious society tends to confirm the belief of the educated that they possess particular natural qualifications which are absent in others."[13]

FOREIGN LITERATURE INCLUSION IN THE COLLECTION

As we espouse internationalism for the collection development course, we must ask the question: Internationalize for what purpose? Ultimately, we should aim to broaden readers' perspectives. No better way to do this exists than to include examples of recent foreign literature translations. We should include foreign literature in library collections and use national literary prizes as guides to selecting foreign fiction.

PRESERVATION OF THE ORAL TRADITION

Within certain black African countries there is almost no image of the book because many of the local languages have not been transcribed in written formats. Because these languages are still in the oral stage, preserving that oral tradition is necessary if the people are eventually to enjoy authentic stories from their own culture in written form. For such situations the audio/video recorder is the necessary tool for anyone attempting to preserve this tradition. Once such material has been properly recorded, it can be used by authors and illustrators who wish to preserve their countries' culture. For library school students coming from such cultures, stressing the need for attaining audio/visual proficiency is important.

ATTITUDES TOWARD WEEDING THROUGHOUT THE WORLD

The obverse of the selection process is weeding, or removing books from the collection because they are outdated, erroneous, or physically worn out. Although weeding is an accepted procedure in many countries, within certain developing countries books are seldom retired from the collection. The explanation for this practice relates again to the "philosophy of the primacy of the book over the reader." If the book is sacred, as many people believe, the attitude toward weeding must be negative. Because of this opposition to removing books from the collection, the internationalizing course instructor must disucss the rationale underlying weeding.

ATTITUDES AND SKILLS

Up to this point we have been considering the cognitive aspects of the internationalized collection development course. Also important are attitudinal and skill considerations. Prominent among the attitudes to be explored are certain negative beliefs among students. Among the skill concepts to be explored are acquisitions in countries with poorly developed book trades, as well as the traditionally valuable skills of annotation writing and giving book talks. Within these time-honored practices some variations necessary for internationalizing the collection course will be discussed.

Attitudinal Learning

The instructor must try to inculcate various attitudes. A positive and negative example may illustrate the point. Foremost among positive attitudes should be the U.S. principle of developing collections impartially. The instructor must teach that when libraries select they select for other people. We must select to represent the needs of our community, not ourselves. This philosophy of collection development can result in quite a different type of collection, however, if the national government defines the needs of the community.

Turning now to the negative attitudes that the instructor must attempt to eradicate, we focus on one attitude that is common to international students. Many people believe that students who come from a developing country have little to contribute to class discussion. What the instructor should attempt to elicit from each student is a description of the national scene and a review of the strategies used by librarians attempting to cope with their problems. Class participants can cooperate in devising new strategies for coping with acquisitions problems in countries without publishers or jobbers.

Among the attitudes that merit investigating are philosophies of librarianship that derive from the writings of world librarianship leaders, for example, Ranganathan, the Spanish philosopher Jose Ortega y Gasset, and V. I. Lenin. From the discussion of Ranganathan's "Five Laws of Library Science," the reader should realize the necessity of educating students about the philosophy that books are for use rather than for purposes of conservation or ornamentation.

From Ortega y Gasset we become aware of the librarian's responsibility to exercise extreme discretion in selecting from the plethora of titles available. Since Ortega y Gasset expressed that conviction in 1934, we should realize the implication of his words. Books have become even more abundant than they were then. He stated:

...the book is indispensable at this stage in history, but the book is in danger because it has become a danger for man. Up until the present, the librarian has been principally occupied with the book as a material object. Now he must give his attention to the book as a living function. He must become a policeman, master of the raging book. The gravest negative attributes that we begin to perceive today in the book are the following: 1. There are already too many books. 2. They are being produced every day in torrential abundance. Is it too utopian to imagine librarians held responsible by society for regulating book production? 3. Furthermore, the librarian of the future must direct the non-specialized reader through the *selva selvaggia* of books.[14]

The writings of V. I. Lenin can help the collection development librarian. In 1913 he wrote:

The glory and the pride of a public library does not depend on the number of its rare books, sixteenth-century editions or tenth-century manuscripts, but on how widely books are circulated among the people, how many new readers are enrolled, how rapidly book requests arre filled, how many books are borrowed, and how many children become interested in reading books and using libraries.[15]

Learning Skills

An important part of the internationalized collection development course is learning to write book annotations and deliver book talks. After showing students excellent annotations, the instructor should teach them to write such annotations. The instructor should also demonstrate the use of annotations to acquaint readers, especially those in public libraries, with the contents of a collection. Many students have recognized the value of book talk skills, once they have learned to present them in their own libraries. In fact, alumni sometimes write that learning to give effective book talks was one of the most valuable skills they learned in library school.

POTENTIAL DANGERS WITHIN THE INTERNATIONALIZED COURSE

Within this type of course lurks a potentially harmful pedagogical problem. Cultural bias can manifest itself in course content and examinations. Regarding content, the instructor should be aware of the danger of overemphasizing one's own culture in resources courses. Foreign students may endure a course whose outline reads like the table of contents from a Western civilization textbook, but no justification from such an orientation exists. Fortunately, the instructor is guided toward an eclectic approach by a recent textbook with a broad cultural viewpont.[16]

CONCLUSIONS

Following the attempt to internationalize the collection development course, this author arrived at the following conclusions:

1. The course requires a special type of instructor.

2. Student participation assists in describing course objectives.

3. A collection of world librarianship material is needed.

4. Theoretical concepts of world librarianship should be added.

5. The principles of course modification can be applied to other resource courses.

6. Evaluation should be continuous throughout the course.

1. *The internationalized course requires a special type of instructor.* Implementing the planning assumptions of the internationalized collection development course will require not only content changes but also changes in administrative decisions and teaching methods. The library school administration must decide whether or not the instructor who taught the traditional version is capable of teaching the internationalized course.

What kind of instructor does the internationalized course require? Two attributes are residence abroad and flexibility of teaching style. Such residence should instill the attitude that we have a great deal to learn from each other in collection development theory and practice.

2. *Student participation is important in formulating course objectives.* The attempt to obtain student opinion is imperative.

3. *A working collection of course realia should be available for classroom demonstration and evaluation.* This collection is useful to show international material, such as examples of books published abroad.

4. *Theoretical concepts of world librarianship should be added.* The course should affirm the following beliefs: (a) library science has a small body of theoretical knowledge which is expressed in the language of theory in its formative state, that is, definitions, principles, and hypotheses, and (b) the scant quantity of such incipient theory makes it incumbent upon library educators to introduce it wherever relevant. We should transform the course from mere national rules of thumb to one incorporating universally relevant theoretical knowledge and information. This suggestion refers to the four laws of world librarianship: (1) the Law of Appropriateness, (b) the Law of Interdependence, (c) the Law of Partial Convergence, and (d) the Law of Total Convergence.

The Law of Appropriateness

Successful aspects of librarianship, for example, legislation, literature, and services, that satisfy national needs, must be planned in accordance with country realities, including historical background, economic conditions, political situations, and cultural content. When planning a new variant of a library aspect, the planner can control its success through correct application of the historical, economic, political, and cultural factors. When adapting a variant from one context to another, its success can be controlled through modifying variant constituents from one context to the historical, political, economic, and cultural factors of the host context.

The Law of Interdependence

All librarianship aspects in one context are interdependent. The qualities of one aspect will be reflected in all other aspects; the strength of a context's educational agencies will contribute to the strength of all other aspects; conversely, the weaknesses of a country's library legislation will reflect in all other aspects of the context, especially its bibliographic control. The success of the aspects can be controlled through modifying, strengthening, or weakening constituent elements.

The Law of Partial Convergence

As library aspects cross national boundaries, they require constituent element modification in order to create element standardization. Success will be controlled by the preciseness by which the various elements are standardized.

The Law of Total Convergence

Eventually, all world variants of librarianship will, through standardization, converge to form a global librarianship. Global librarianship success will be controlled by the preciseness by which all elements are standardized.

5. *The principles of course modification can be applied to other resource courses.* These courses include offerings in the humanities, social sciences, and science and technology, along with the more specialized courses, for example, government documents or resources in chemistry. Of course, the danger of chauvinism is less in science and technology than in the other areas. In each case, the instructor should be sensitive to covering international as well as national content.

6. *Course evaluation should be continuous in order to be of maximum student*

usefulness. Rather than the approach of present New York Mayor Edward Koch, "How am I doing?," this author advocates following the approach of the late Library School Dean Louis Shores who advised never to become so enamored of methodology that one forgets to ask: "How are my students doing?"

NOTES

1. Lester Asheim, *Librarianship in Developing Countries* (Urbana: University of Illinois Press, 1966), p. 69.

2. Ruth Warncke, "The Core Book Selection Course," *Journal of Education for Librarianship* 4 (Spring 1964), p. 209.

3. Correspondence from John F. Harvey to Richard Krzys, July 12, 1983.

4. Richard Krzys, *Developing and Using Library Collections* (Pittsburgh: University of Pittsburgh Press, 1983), p. 4.

5. Richard Krzys and Gaston Litton, *World Librarianship: A Comparative Study* (New York: Marcel Dekker, 1983), p. 47.

6. Quoted in Asheim, p. 78.

7. Ibid.

8. David Kaser, "Library Development in Asia," in "Library," *The Encyclopedia Americana* (New York: Americana Corporation, 1977), Vol. 17, p. 324.

9. Asheim, p. 29.

10. S. R. Ranganathan, *The Five Laws of Library Science* (Bombay: Asia Publishing House, 1963).

11. Asheim, pp. 16–17.

12. Krzys and Litton, pp. 192–193.

13. Asheim, p. 36.

14. José Ortega y Gasset, *The Mission of the Librarian* (Boston: G. K. Hall, 1961), pp. 16–24.

15. Paul L. Horecky, *Libraries and Bibliographic Centers in the Soviet Union* (Bloomington: Indiana University Research Center in Anthropology, Folklore and Linguistics, 1959), p. 1.

16. Robert A. Rogers, *The Humanities: A Selective Guide to Information Sources* (Littleton, Colo.: Libraries Unlimited, 1979).

BIBLIOGRAPHY

Carnovsky, Leon. "The Foreign Student in the American Library School. I." *Library Quarterly* 43 (April 1973), pp. 103–125.

Carnovsky, Leon. "The Foreign Student in the American Library School. II." *Library Quarterly* 43 (July 1973), pp. 199–214.

Gollnick, Donna M. and Philip C. Chinn. *Multicultural Education in a Pluralistic Society.* (St. Louis: C. V. Mosby, 1983).

Marco, Guy. "An International Structure for Library Education." *International Library Review* 13 (October 1981), pp. 357–363.

Rovelstad, Mathilde V. "A New International Librarianship: A Challenge." *UNESCO Bulletin for Libraries* 32 (May-June 1978), pp. 136–143.

15
INTRODUCTION TO REFERENCE SOURCES: AN INTERNATIONAL VIEWPONT

Antonio Rodriguez-Buckingham

This chapter seeks to provide the philosophical framework for a reference course different from those normally offered. The course is based on a global view of information and library science.

DEFINITIONS

A *reference book* is designed by its arrangement and treatment to be consulted for definite items of information rather than to be read consecutively. The term *reference material(s)* applies interchangeably to books, audiovisual items, and software and hardware designed to answer reference questions. *Reference and information service* is the personal assistance provided to library users pursuing information and has three major aspects: (1) information service, (2) instruction in library use, and (3) guidance in choosing appropriate material.

The *reference field* includes the entire spectrum of reference material and service, including research, teaching, and practice. The reference field is subdivided into *data (or information) retrieval systems* and *document retrieval sources*. The first provides answers to specific questions, while the second deals with reference material retrieval.

A *reference component* is a set of introductory and advanced courses which incorporates the curriculum's entire spectrum of reference knowledge and skills. A core curriculum is assumed to have a reference component consisting of an introductory course followed by subject courses, often dealing with the humanities, social sciences, and sciences.

Internationalization is the quality of library and information work which, by intent, is not confined to the material and service of any specific geographic boundary. Most academicians subscribe to teaching free from ethnocentrism or geographic bias. However, a perusal of catalogs shows that U.S. library science courses lean heavily toward the use of sources, the teaching of practice, and the projection of perceptions which, if not overwhelmingly American, are almost exclusively limited to the English-speaking world. This practice has at least two deleterious effects: first, it projects the false impression that the fundamental value of information as a building-block of knowledge and progress is not understood beyond the confines of the English-speaking world; and, second, it limits preparation of well-rounded reference librarians.

ASSUMPTIONS

The first assumption is that a reference course is the most appropriate place to start library school internationalization. The second is that internationalization will be facilitated if we can widen the angle from which we observe the information process and consider information as a phenomenon of universal dimensions.

It is specifically assumed here that (a) data retrieval systems and document retrieval sources often cross space and time boundaries and therefore are bound to be international; (b) since it is a complex skill requiring technical and subject knowlege, document retrieval often becomes subject bibliography that is inseparable from research; and (c) an introductory course should include a balanced interplay between data retrieval and that aspect of document retrieval which leans towards internationalized subject bibliography.

The proposed course should answer the following questions: (a) How can we internationalize reference course instruction; and (b) how will reference course internationalization affect librarianship?

METHODS AND TECHNIQUES OF TEACHING REFERENCE

The diversity of methods used in teaching reference is so large that only a few of them can be mentioned here. Several major themes have appeared, one of which has been that of theory versus practice. Some instructors believe that reference courses should be practical and simple, oriented toward teaching students specific jobs since library science is an applied science. In this view, teaching principles makes sense only if they are presented together with their practical applications. The need to provide a combination of theory and practice has been argued for many years, with the pendulum swinging back and forth.

This theme takes on a different shade when the argument focuses on the rote learning of facts—titles—as opposed to principles. Louise Shores' approach to reference teaching is a combination of title study and on-the-job experience. With that combination, an environment is created wherein reference is related to information retrieval, censorship, and comparative bibliography.[1]

Today people ask the same question: Is computer technology fostering a greater emphasis on theory or on practice? Advocates of information science curricula may be more in need of practical experience than traditionalists. Joe Morehead leans toward combining classroom work and field experience.[2] Title approach critics point out that it separates the study of sources from the entire scenario involved in answering reference questions. These arguments usher in the third theme pointing out the importance of the reference interview. A fourth major theme has been the approach by the "type" of source in which information is found in contrast with the title or subject.

These themes have shaped teaching methodology. Reaction to concentration on sources led to problem-oriented instruction and the case method. Thomas J. Galvin has recommended this approach for all reference courses, where interviews might be conducted in the classroom by students who later attempted to locate the information requested by simulated users.[3] Use of pathfinders—narrow, in-depth guides to information on specific subjects—is another popular method of teaching reference. Because of its in-depth quality, however, this method is most effective when the environment provides a substantial bibliographic apparatus.

The computer has stimulated computer-assisted instruction. As early as 1970, Thomas Slavens applied the technique of simulated reference situations dealt with via the computer. Other techniques include role-playing; the flowchart to study research strategy and the decision-making process; the self-study approach; and the subject-interest method wherein students select a subject of interest and prepare a project or paper.

A major problem with applying these methods to the model proposed here is the acute lack of means—a compass—to guide instructor and student. A balance between principles and practical experience, coupled with class discussions of assignments and oral and written presentations, will be the most effective means to derive maximum benefits from the model.

PLANNING AND IMPLEMENTING A BASIC REFERENCE COURSE

The general objective of reference courses is to introduce students to the complex bibliographic and informational apparatus available to answer reference questions. The general objective of the present course is to provide a framework on which instructors and students can base the relationship of reference, research, and internationalism. (See the Appendix for the course outline.) Computer technology and its application to information storage and processing have placed at the disposal of librarians "an armamentarium of bibliographical and informational aids," the knowledge of which requires the broadest view possible of both the context and dimension of the field of reference work.[4]

The specific objectives of the present course are to enable students (a) to develop a view of the context and dimension of the field of reference work that will transcend local borders; (b) to examine and critically discuss the reference and information services available from international sources; (c) to apply new technology to reference work; (d) to associate information needs with sources regardless of geographic and/or ethnic relationships; and (e) to develop a philosophy based on the recognition of information's universal dimensions. The intended learning outcomes should be based on the diversity of formats in which reference material comes—data bases, encyclopedias, handbooks, dictionaries, and the like.

Objective 1: To furnish the student with a view of the context and dimension of the field of reference work that will transcend national borders. (a) Make students aware of the universal quality of information through a combination of class discussions and reports on reading assignments on the information revolution. (b) Present information-related problems from unexpected sources through reading assignments that lead to recognition of these problems. For example, do bureaucracies emerge because of information-related problems?

Objective 2: To critically examine and discuss reference and information service available from national and international sources. (a) Assign reference material by type concurrent with discussion of cluster material. (b) Assign information service by type concurrent with discussion of cluster material.

Objective 3: To familiarize the student with the application of new technology to reference work. (a) Provide hands-on assignments of data base searching. (b) Relate intended learning outcomes to electronic data systems and information reference sources locally and internationally. (c) Relate intended learning outcomes to information networks.

Objective 4: To associate information needs with sources. (a) Relate intended learning outcomes to elements in the social milieu shaping information needs. (b) Discuss appropriate information sources for specific cultural or social needs.

Objective 5: To develop a philosophy along the lines of the universal dimensions of information. (a) Focus on the universality of information. Give examples of its diversity and the methods for retrieving information over time and space. (b) Identify principles.

Intended learning outcomes should be directed to understanding principles and learning skills related to those principles. This assumes that the course will be taught with a strategy that balances theory and practice. Situations should be created that inherently provide student feedback. An effective way of obtaining feedback is by combining principle and practice. The feedback system should be aimed at students monitoring their own progress rather than involving constant instructor evaluation.

A cluster of intended learning outcomes should be dedicated to the analysis of government information policies in various world areas. The information apparatus can be explained by approaching it from its origin in the sociopolitical structure. For example, the information transfer process and information policies have different structures in First, Second, and Third World nationals. The configuration of their retrieval mechanisms—reference tools—is also different.

Many library schools accept the transfer of credit hours which students have accumulated in other disciplines. While this does not constitute interdisciplinary studies, these credit hours can be used in selecting students with experience in area studies, foreign languages, or other international disciplines. A more formalized way to internationalize curricula is through double degree programs. Learning consists of complex stages that may take a long time to master. Assignments should give students direct contact with material. Assignment discussion and evaluation should aim at encouraging students to take reasonable risks and learn from their errors.

As agencies of information dissemination and control, national libraries can be used to introduce students to reference work at the international level. This step may be coupled with the information technology applications that are well developed in Europe, for example, videotex and teletext. A combined view of systems and sources may be presented in clusters of intended learning outcomes. Teaching reference material by subject is in certain ways logical. In most instances, there is a commonality between subjects in various parts of the world, but there are sufficient discrepancies to justify a preference for teaching reference sources by type of material.

DATA COLLECTING AND RESEARCH

Anyone attempting to internationalize reference teaching faces serious problems involved in collecting and selecting the necessary data and sources. Edwin S. Gleaves has suggested that research in the 1980s will be dominated by information science, with greater emphasis on the library education practicum component, on new continuing education methods, and on coordinating specializations.[5] While certain U.S. library schools have avoided language requirements, library work makes language knowledge unavoidable. A 1982 survey to assess the position of foreign language requirements in public, academic, and special libraries showed that language was needed in two-thirds of the libraries answering the questionnaire.[6] It is disheartening to note, however, that in the last twenty years, many U.S. library schools have followed their universities' lead and have replaced human languages with computer languages. The intent is likely to have been part of the overall effort to increase enrollment.

This policy is tragic because it reflects ignorance of the very reasons for which languages were once required. The purpose was not to learn to decode one set of conventional symbols into another—though this is also important, especially for librarians—but rather to employ language as a vehicle by which we can penetrate a culture. By denying this knowledge, library schools denied students the opportunity to know the bibliographic apparatus of other countries and took a large step toward intellectual and cultural isolationism.

CONCLUSIONS

The two questions posed at the beginning of this chapter have been answered as follows. To internationalize reference course teaching, we must view information not as the exclusive result of the high technology characteristics of First World nations, but rather as an entity with its own behavior and dynamics which occurs in every aspect of human history. This view enables us to conceive of the information apparatus of any culture as attempts to control the information generated by that society's technology.

Reference people must concentrate on the information apparatus and the social order that produces it. Clusters of information based on themes are to be offered in a combined theory and practice mode. The first is provided by the central concept of information universality advanced in this chapter, and the second through assignments for class discussion and evaluation. A characteristic of the reference field must be singled out to determine how the internationalization of reference courses can affect librarianship. Data and document retrieval are so interwoven in research that they suggest conducting the information search outside national boundaries. Therefore, reference work is a natural subject for internationalization.

NOTES

1. Louis Shores, "We Who Teach Reference," *Journal of Education for Librarianship* 5 (Spring, 1965), pp. 238–247.

2. Joe Morehead, *Theory and Practice in Library Education* (Littleton, Colo.: Libraries Unlimited, 1980), pp. 108–109; Thomas Gwinup, "The Reference Course: Theory, Method, and Motivation," *Journal of Education for Librarianship*

11 (Winter 1971), pp. 231–242; Wallace J. Bonk, "A Reference Encounter; How Reference Should be Taught, An Interview," *Library Journal* 90 (April 15, 1965), pp. 1813–1824.

3. Thomas J. Galvin, *The Case Method in Library Education and In-Service Training* (Metuchen, N.J.: Scarecrow Press, 1973).

4. Thomas J. Galvin, "The Education of the New Reference Librarian," *Library Journal* 100 (April 15, 1975), pp. 727–730.

5. Edwin S. Gleaves, "Library Education: Issues for the Eighties," *Journal of Education for Librarianship* 22 (Spring, 1982), p. 271.

6. Rachel L. Crary, "Foreign Language and the Librarian," *Journal of Education for Librarianship* 23 (Fall 1982), pp. 110–124.

BIBLIOGRAPHY

Carroll, Frances Laverne. "Internationalism in Education for Librarianship." *International Library Review* 4 (April 1972), pp. 102–126.

Cheney, Francis Neel, and Wiley J. Williams. *Fundamental Reference Sources*. Chicago: American Library Association, 1980.

Katz, William A. *Introduction to Reference Work*. 2 vols. New York: McGraw-Hill Book Co., 1982.

Katz, William A., and Anne Crawford. *Reference and Information Services: A New Reader*. Metuchen, N.J.: Scarecrow Press, 1982.

Posner, George J., and Alan N. Rudnitsky. *Course Design: A Guide to Curriculum Development for Teachers*. New York: Longman 1982.

APPENDIX: COURSE OUTLINE AND INTENDED LEARNING OUTCOMES

Cluster I: The Reference Process

A. Procedures
   1. Steps
   2. Problems of communication
      a. Face-to-face contact
      b. Attitudes: interest in and comfort with the user's questions; body language; user feedback
      c. Telephone use
      d. Communicating with foreign language speakers; differences in cultural attitudes
B. The reference interview
   1. Question-negotiating skills
   2. Information and confidentiality; differences in cultural attitudes

Cluster II: Sources and Systems

A. Search strategy
   1. Conducting a search
   2. Literature searching
   3. Handling traced information

　　　4. The response
　　　5. Maintenance of records
　B. The importance of national and foreign sources and systems

Cluster III: The Diversity of Information Sources

A. Information sources
　　　1. Internal versus external information sources
　　　2. Referral
B. An overview of types of information sources
　　　1. Individuals
　　　2. Organizations
　　　3. Bibliographies
　　　4. Catalogs
　　　5. Abstracting, indexing services
　　　6. Thesauri
　　　7. Encyclopedias
　　　8. Dictionaries
　　　9. Directories
　　10. Yearbooks
　　11. Handbooks
　　12. Manuals
　　13. Guides
　　14. Digests
　　15. Quotation collections
　　16. Gazetteers, Periodicals
　　17. Reports
　　18. Theses
　　19. Trade literature
　　20. Patent specifications
　　21. Reviews
　　22. Statistics compendia
　　23. Biographical sources
　　24. Monographs
　　25. Newspapers
　　26. Atlases
　　27. Microforms
　　28. Media
　　29. Government publications

Cluster IV: Associating Information Needs with Sources

A. Categorization of inquiries and selection of sources
　　　1. Dates
　　　2. Events
　　　3. Illustrations
　　　4. Organizations
　　　5. Persons
　　　6. Geographical information
　　　7. Numerical information

       a. Properties
       b. Statistics
   8. Publications and bibliographic information
       a. Citations
       b. Abstracts and annotations
       c. Verification
   9. Terms and language
       a. Abbreviations and acronyms
       b. Words, phrases, definitions, and quotations
  10. General or background information
  11. Unspecified or other information

Cluster V: Examination of Sources I

A. Coverage of work
   1. Direct source of information or guide to sources
   2. Subjects
   3. Language
   4. Country
   5. Bibliographic details
   6. Time
   7. Selective or comprehensive
   8. Level
B. Content of entry
   1. Data
   2. Names and addresses
   3. Narrative
   4. Illustrations
   5. Reviews
   6. Extracts
   7. Abstracts
   8. Bibliographic references
C. Purpose of work
D. Source
   1. Publisher
   2. Methodology of compilation
E. Organization
   1. Topic
   2. Name
   3. Date
   4. Place
   5. Retrieval mechanisms

Cluster VI: Examination of Sources II

National Bibliographies and National Libraries

National libraries are usually entrusted with the provision of policy and service at the national level, and this trust is ensured through acts of parliament or the legislature.

A. The role of national bibliographies and libraries in the national language

B. Services
    1. Bibliographic
    2. Lending
    3. Information provision
    4. Resource-sharing networks
    5. Research and development
    6. International information systems
C. Bibliographic services are provided in the form of national bibliographies

Cluster VII: Examination of Sources III

The British Library

A. British Museum
B. National Central Library
C. National Lending Library for Science and Technology
D. British National Bibliography
E. Reference Division
F. Science Reference Library
G. Library Association Library

Cluster VIII: Examination of Sources IV

The Bibliographic Role of Other National Libraries

A. Africa
    1. Ghana, attempts at establishing a national library
    2. Kenya, Book Development Council
    3. Liberia
    4. Nigeria
    5. Tanzania, the National Central Library
    6. Republic of South Africa, the national libraries and information services
B. The Middle East
    1. Iran
        a. National libraries
        b. Iranian Documentation Centre (IRANDOC)
        c. Tehran Book Processing Centre (TEBROC)
    2. Arab Countries
    3. Israel
        a. National libraries
        b. Institute for Hebrew Bibliography
        c. Institute for Microfilmed Hebrew Manuscripts
        d. Center of Scientific and Technical Information
        e. Special libraries and information centers
C. Asia
    1. Bangladesh
    2. India
    3. Japan
    4. Korea
    5. Malaysia
    6. Pakistan
    7. People's Republic of China

8. Philippines
9. Singapore

Cluster IX: Examination of Sources

The Bibliographic Role of National Libraries

A. Oceania
    1. Australia
    2. New Zealand
        a. National Library
        b. National Bibliography
    3. The Pacific Islands
B. North America and the Caribbean
C. Central America
    1. Guatemala
    2. Nicaragua
    3. El Salvador
    4. Costa Rica
D. South America
    1. Brazil
    2. Venezuela
    3. Peru
    4. Colombia
    5. Ecuador
    6. Bolivia
    7. Argentina
    8. Uruguay
    9. Chile
  10. Paraguay

Cluster X: Examination of Sources VI

The Bibliographic Role of National Libraries

A. Western Europe
    1. Denmark
    2. Federal Republic of Germany
    3. France
    4. Italy
    5. Spain
B. Socialist Nations
    1. The Union of Soviet Socialist Republics
    2. Poland
    3. Hungary

Cluster XI: Information Service and Modern Technology

Lending and Information Service

A. Lending and information service at national level
    1. Books and periodicals
    2. Other reference material
    3. Films

      4. Phonograph records
      5. Prints
      6. Maps
      7. Photographs
      8. Manuscripts
      9. Microforms
    10. Music Scores
B. National and international interlibrary lending systems
C. Advisory and/or research and development responsibilities
D. Computer-based information service
      1. Science and technology
      2. Medicine
      3. Industry
      4. Social science
      5. Education
      6. Law
      7. Humanities
      8. The arts
E. Interlending networks of the British Library
F. The British Library Lending Division

Cluster XII: Universal Bibliographic Control

A. Universal Bibliographic Control (UBC)
B. European adoption of such videotex systems as ANTIOPE, CEEFAX, OR-
ACLE, and TELIDON
C. Videotex development in other countries

Cluster XIII: European Library and Information Networks

A. Germany: unpublished catalogs from Nordheim-Westphalia, Cologne;
Baden-Wurttemberg, Stuttgart; and Bavarian Central Catalog, Munich
B. The Netherlands
      1. Netherlands Central Catalog, the Royal Library
      2. Central Catalog of Periodicals
      3. University of Delft Library as a major source of information for Dutch
         industry
C. France: Bibliotheque Nationale's Union Catalog

Cluster XIV: North American Information Networks

A. American and Canadian information networks: national union catalogs
B. Smaller networks
      1. Rocky Mountain Bibliographic Center for Research
      2. Pacific Northwest Bibliographic Center
      3. Midwest Interlibrary Center in Chicago
      4. Illinois Regional Library Council
      5. Others

Cluster XV: Cooperative Cataloging Networks

A. Overseas cooperative cataloging schemes and their implications for reference
work

    1. BLAISE (British Library Automated Information Service)
    2. SCOLCAP of the National Library of Scotland
B. Online networks
    1. ESANET (European Space Agency Network)
    2. Euronet/DIANE
    3. SCANNET
    4. TYMNET

Cluster XVI: Referral Center Networks

A. National Referral Center, U.S. Library of Congress
B. British Library's Research in British Universities, Polytechnics and Colleges, Aslib Directory

Cluster XVII: Information Control

A. Information explosion
B. Control of information
    1. Indexing languages
    2. Newspaper indices
       a. The United States
       b. Great Britain
    3. Card catalog
    4. Book catalogs
    5. Classification schemes
    6. Abstracting services
    7. Thesauri
    8. General concordances
    9. Concordances of American and English themes
   10. Concordances in English about world literature

Cluster XVIII: The National Character of Information Control Sources I

A. Nationalism and general world encyclopedias
    1. Russia
    2. Germany
    3. Italy
    4. France
    5. Spain
B. The everlasting prestige of knowledge
    1. Earlier editions of the *Britannica*
    2. The modern *Britannica*
    3. The modern *Americana*
C. Information patterns
D. The accumulation of information
    1. Subject encyclopedias
    2. One- and two-volume encyclopedias
    3. Yearbooks

Cluster XIX: The National Character of Information Control Sources II

A. The power of the word, the pride of languages, and the great dictionaries
    1. English language

   2. French lanugage
   3. Spanish language
   4. German language
   5. Italian language
B. The royal academies
C. Unabridged dictionaries
D. Historical dictionaries
E. Specialized dictionaries
F. Bi- or multilingual dictionaries

Cluster XX: Evaluations and Overviews

A. Evaluation of reference service
   1. Interviews
   2. Direct observation
   3. Sampling
   4. Questionnaires
   5. Case studies
B. Evaluation of reference sources, an overview
C. Overview of internationalism and reference sources
D. Evaluation of the goals, objectives, and intended learning outcomes of the course

16
CATALOGING AND CLASSIFICATION COURSES

Emilia Bernal

Cataloging and classification (or just cataloging) courses have been part of library education since it moved from learning a library's routines inhouse to learning diverse topics in a formalized setting. Several of their characteristics can be identified and are probably related to their enduring importance:

1. A cataloging and classification course has been a part of the core curriculum since Dewey started formal library education. *The Standards for Library Schools, 1976*, approved by the International Federation of Library Associations and Institutions (IFLA) Section of Library Schools, included cataloging as part of the prescribed core courses.[1]

2. Cataloging and classification is a possible specialization area. Besides the core course, additional cataloging courses are described in many library school catalogs.

3. Because of their technical nature, the cataloging courses have been significantly influenced by the theory versus practice controversy. Although Dewey initiated formal library education, teaching at his school was practical and followed apprenticeship routines. Cataloging teaching in the 1920s was described as "the memorization of cataloging rules and Dewey classification numbers."[2] With the impact of the Williamson report and the establishment of the University of Chicago Graduate Library School, conditions began to change.

In the 1950s apparently most library schools attempted to include both technique and theory in these courses. In 1956 Shera emphasized developing a theoretical foundation on which practical applications could rest. The foundation suggested was broad and encompassed the theory and principles of bibliographic organization of which the catalog was a part. Seymour Lubetzky also wrote in favor of the theory and principles behind routines and code interpretation.[3]

Library education is still dealing with the theory-practice issue. A recent survey shows that library catalog department heads agree on needing both theory and practice, but that the amount of practical knowledge received by students is inadequate.[4]

4. The practicum and internship programs are likewise closely related to the theory-practice issue. Edwin S. Gleaves mentions the possibility of a "practicum component in library education during the eighties,"[5] specifically online cataloging and online bibliographic information retrieval as areas in which theory and practice could be blended successfully. The catalog department heads consider practicum courses to be beneficial.

5. Technology is permeating cataloging and classification courses, and the catalog may soon be altered drastically. More libraries are using centralized cataloging utilities and are reducing to a minimum the amount of original cataloging done inhouse. Course work, therefore, confronts a changing field and must adjust to prepare students for the future.

CATALOGING AND CLASSIFICATION COURSES RECONSIDERED

In 1965, anticipating publication of the *Anglo-American Cataloging Rules* (AACR) and the consequent catalog changes expected, Lubetzky called for a pause to consider the implications for cataloging teaching. After publication, the rules were incorporated into the courses, and apparently that was all that happened.

Twenty years later, more than a pause and an incorporation of a new set of rules seems to be necessary. Centralized processing has led to a controversy over the cataloger's function, since fewer catalogers may be needed. Michael Gorman talks of "doing away with the technical departments" and claims that 80 percent of the cataloging will be done by centralized processing.[6] Yet, a 1984 Nebraska library survey showed that enough original cataloging was done locally to keep catalogers busy.[7]

What better time, then, to examine, evaluate, and improve cataloging education? Going a step further, why not try at the same time to answer within the context of cataloging courses certain of library education's perennial questions? Can there be a proper balance between theory and practice in course content?

The best possible way to make cataloging courses more meaningful is to move from a narrow, mainly nationalistic to an international approach in which study of the subject areas advances from the particular or national to the general and universal. Now, we are aware of the interdependence of all people. The worldwide communication network has made the world small, and independent action may be detrimental to all.

There are more specific, and perhaps more practical, reasons for internationalizing cataloging courses:

1. The capacity to make the right decisions and select the best options is increased if the librarian knows the whole panorama of possibilities, such as a variety of classification schemes when a choice is needed.
2. Participation and leadership in regional and international activities are open to librarians who are well prepared for them.
3. When librarians maintain international contact, national library interests are advanced in standardization, cooperative and other activities.
4. With a broad background, international job mobility is possible.
5. A librarian with an international outlook is more versatile than most colleagues and may be better prepared to adjust to different work environments.
6. The graduate of an international curriculum will be better prepared than others to serve a pluralistic society. A cataloger will select the best codes and classification schemes to meet community needs.

Before going into cataloging, course internationalization assumptions will be explained about the library school program of which they could be part. The assumptions are as follows:

1. The courses are part of a one-year tertiary education, full-time program leading to a first professional degree.
2. The program will prepare librarians to work at national and international levels. Graduates will be committed to world librarianship but without excluding a national emphasis that could consider specific problems and solutions.
3. One objective of the school is, to paraphrase Lubetzky: to cultivate not only practitioners but also thinkers and critics, not only followers but also leaders—librarians who will not only carry on but also advance the art of the profession.

Specific curriculum assumptions are as follows:

1. The core curriculum is not integrated but composed of individual courses.
2. A thesis is not a requisite for the first professional degree.

The following definitions were applied:

1. World librarianship: That librarianship whose relationships and activities quantitatively surpass a majority of the known nations, which recognizes in that range of nations major political ideologies and economic systems, and whose purposes are relationships and activities of such a nature as to be of worth and interest to the wider spectrum of nations as described.[8]
2. Internationalization of the courses: applying the perspective of world librarianship to the course content.

Two or preferably three cataloging courses are necessary to enable students to concentrate on it. The introductory course will be part of the required core curriculum. It will include bibliographic control fundamentals and the catalog as a component; it will introduce different types of catalogs, descriptive cataloging, main entry determination, and subject cataloging; and it will emphasize the codes and tools most widely used and technology's impact.

The one or two advanced courses will develop what the first course could only initiate. If there are two, one advanced course will expand descriptive cataloging and main entry determination and concentrate on different types of material, such as periodicals and media, and on the problems which their descriptive cataloging and main entry determination might present with varied approaches to solutions.

The second advanced course will cover subject cataloging through classification and subject description. Classification theory and systems will be studied, moving from the enumerative to the faceted, analytico-synthetic scheme. Linguistic problems will be examined: natural languages versus controlled vocabulary through subject heading lists and thesauri. Indexing systems and their role in bibliographic control will be included.

COURSE INTERNATIONALIZATION

The whole school program must be committed to internationalization. Changes in cataloging courses should follow curriculum and school changes, including those of the school's goals and objectives. Individual course objectives must also be revised.

Maurice F. Tauber has identified "the essential objectives" in cataloging and classification teaching as:

1. Inculcating basic knowledge in the fields and the general competence to use this knowledge.

2. Developing ability in orderly, analytical thinking on a professional level, so that sound conclusions will be reached in situations requiring decisions.

3. Providing the cataloger with the desire to grow in knowledge and keep abreast of the changing current of work.

4. Adjusting the philosophical viewpoint, basic knowledge, and feeling for values, so that the cataloger will understand the economic and service aspects of problems.

5. Nurturing an understanding that will use professional background when dealing with library-wide problems.[9]

Tauber discussed the objectives in terms of a particular program: what could be considered basic knowledge, how it was practically impossible to develop in a year "ability in orderly, analytic thinking" in certain students, and the difficulties in expressing in measurable activities what the students should learn in a specific course.[10] These difficulties are still with us. Let us consider how certain of Tauber's objectives could be changed either in content or interpretation to reflect the new international characteristic that courses should have:

1. *Inculcating basic knowledge.* What constitutes "basic knowledge" should be broadened from Tauber's terms to show emphasis on international principles.
2. *Desire to grow in knowledge and keep abreast of change.* Tauber urges continuing education to keep abreast of the field. If the outlook is national, the knowledge is incomplete and the ability to meet changes defective. A broad knowledge base is our best resource to improve methods.

Besides the goals and objectives, other aspects of the program must be examined and changes implemented. Faculty members must complete preparation in several areas:

1. Examples of topics that might require restudying are:
   a. Cataloging and classification systems in use in other nations.
   b. International library organizations and their cataloging activities.
   c. Historical approaches to national and regional bibliographic systems. Faculty activities include increased involvement with international organizations and attendance at international meetings.
2. Library school library holdings must be carefully studied to determine how well they will support course changes. The extent of pertinent foreign language material must be considered as well as the translation problem.
3. More visual aids illustrating differences in codes, classification systems, and other topics can be prepared.
4. Faculty members should meet foreign catalogers who can be invited to discuss certain topics that present special difficulties. Foreign librarians can also help the instructor in clarifying issues and difficult areas. Foreign students can be important class work resources.

The process of internationalizing cataloging courses can be carried out through the following approaches:

1. Consideration of what is best for the world community and how nations can work toward attaining it.
2. Less emphasis on traditional institutions and methods and consideration of information transfer channels and needs in other world areas.
3. Consideration of the needs and problems of different community sectors—business, industry, science, and the humanities, for example—in developed and developing nations.
4. Consideration of the impact of international activity on national and/or institutional interests.

5. Testing the fundamentals and principles at the universal level. By moving into the international realm, it may be possible to distinguish what is transitory from what is basic.

6. A historical perspective will help in answering this question: Is this the best way to do this, or is it only a possible way at this time, in this place, with the resources available? Is it the only way we know from historical sources?

7. Consideration of different approaches to doing things, based on the availability or lack thereof of financial, mechanical, and human resources.

8. Performance of comparative analyses of national and regional systems and codes now used.

9. Study of how national or regional codes and systems treat other nations. Foreign librarians should be asked how successful code and system transfer has been.

10. Study of international programs and organizations active in the cataloging field.

INTERNATIONALIZING COURSE AREAS

This section examines cataloging and classification course areas as well as the activities and considerations to be used in internationalizing them. The points under each area will be incorporated into it and developed through reading, class discussion, reports, exercises, comparative study, and other activities. (See also the Appendix.)

Area: *The Catalog and Bibliographic Control*

A. *Bibliographic control.* Components: bibliographies, indexes, and catalogs
(1) Discuss how national can lead to Universal Bibliographic Control (UBC).
(2) Consider several UBC aspects: (a) UBC's importance to the international community; (b) barriers to UBC: political, economic, sociological, and cultural; (c) national library and bibliographic center functions in UBC; and (d) IFLA initiatives and UBC work.
(3) Other international activities that should be studied: International Standard Book Number and International Standard Serial Number.

B. *The Catalog as an element in bibliographic control*: Functions, history, policies
(1) Catalog functions are: (a) finding function, a narrow institutional or system function; (b) bibliographic function, a broad national or international function. The importance of both functions could be discussed by using the functions statement included in Cutter's *Rules for a Dictionary Catalog*. At the international level, a statement of catalog functions can be found in the *Statement of Principles* adopted at the International Conference on Cataloguing Principles, Paris, 1961.
(2) Historical development: The purpose of the catalog has been constant through time. Physical form has varied, as have content and types of access offered, but the need for a record of the collection and the expression of it have endured.

(3) Institutional policies: Discuss their possible effect on the use of cataloging records generated outside the institution, e.g., Library of Congress (LC) cataloging records; also, on the possibility of national and international cooperation.

C. *Kinds of catalogs*: Author, Subject, Title, Dictionary, Classified, Shelf list, Union

(1) Author, Title, and Subject Catalogs: Historical development shows that use of one or more of these catalogs to describe a collection has depended on: (a) the function(s) of the specific catalog; (b) publication characteristics at a specific time, e.g., no title page in the publication or title more important than author; and (c) publication shelf arrangement at the specific library.

(2) Dictionary catalog versus Classified catalog: Study the characteristics of both and their relation to the catalog's purpose.

A point of international significance is that the classified catalog uses a notation to express subject matter. Shera and Egan's book, *The Classified Catalog*, considered this an advantage for a community where more than one language is spoken.[11] It can also be important in international information exchange. A hybrid, the alphabetico-classed catalog, should also be studied since it may be the form of the future.

(3) Shelf list catalog: This could be considered a limited classified catalog. It could develop from its present function as an administrative record to become a component of the collection's subject access and be a tool in computerized national and international information exchange.

(4) Union catalog: National or international functions: (a) title identification and location for interlibrary lending, and (b) bibliographic function in information exchange. The usefulness of the union catalog will depend on system input quality and the universality of the rules used in recording bibliographic information.

Record computerization has made possible online access, book form publication, and Computer Output Microforms (COM) format, therefore allowing international use.

D. *Codes*

(1) Emphasize the *Anglo-American Cataloging Rules*, 2d ed. (AACR2), its development, interpretation, and application. Discuss its international importance.

(2) Historical approach: Consider the impact of codes in cataloging development. Important nineteenth-century codes are: *The British Museum Code of Ninety-One Rules* and Cutter's *Rules for a Dictionary Catalog*. Other codes and their influence should also be studied.

An outstanding twentieth-century cataloging event was the International Conference on Cataloguing Principles, Paris, which generated the Paris Principles. A list of the national or regional codes based on or adapted to the Paris Principles is included in the annotated edition of their *Statement*. Throughout the commentaries, "post-Paris code" interpretations or departures from the Principles are explained.

Another international cataloging meeting that should be discussed is the International Meeting of Cataloguing Experts, Copenhagen, 1969. It continued earlier standardization. AACR revision and AACR2 implementation should be included.

(3) Discuss the problems of harmonizing local needs with national and international considerations in applying the codes as well.

(4) Online catalogs and the codes: If the trend toward the online catalog is developed, will the present codes become obsolete? If so, how will this affect international standardization and cataloging cooperation?

E. *Physical forms of the catalog*

(1) Historical development: The catalog's physical form has depended mainly on resources available at the time and in the area, for example, tablets at Assurbanipal and the book form in the Middle Ages.

(2) Discuss the modern catalog's diversity of physical forms: book catalog, card catalog, COM catalog, online catalog. Consider for each form: (a) relevant material retrieval possibilities offered, and (b) effect on international information exchange.

(3) Should we strive toward one uniform physical form? Would online catalogs be best for all libraries, all users? If form is standardized nationally, how would that affect the international level and cooperation possibilities?

Area: *Descriptive Cataloging*

A. *Main entry*: Entry verification, added entries, unit card

(1) Examples and discussion in the Paris Principles annotated edition can show the difficulty in reaching consensus even on such basic matters as definitions of author, title, and corporate body. In addition, they can show efforts to systematize determination and form of main and added entries.

(2) Unit card development and use is an example of the impact of mechanization on library processes. With advanced card reproduction methods, the main entry has become the unit card with complete bibliographic information repeated on all added entries.

(3) The online catalog is challenging the main entry-added entries concept. The online catalog has no need to make this distinction, nor is the unit card concept needed. Will parallel sets of principles be needed: one for online catalogs and one for other types of catalogs? What effect will this have on national and international cooperation?

B. *Authority files*: Author, suject, corporate

Authority control is changing due to network and cooperative developments and computerized communication. Anderson predicted that this will be an area to which "major endeavors will be directed in the next decade."[12] National activity examples are the Name Authority Co-Op at LC and the Linked Authority Systems Project. In Canada, the Shared Authority File for name, subject, and series authority is of the same order. The work of the IFLA Working Group on an International Authority System should be considered.

C. *Descriptive paragraph*: Title and statement of responsibility, edition, imprint

(1) Consider AACR2 and the description of each work as well as the development and importance of International Standard Bibliographic Description (ISBD) formats, "not a cataloging code but a descriptive framework to which any cataloging code can be applied."[13]

(2) International differences in using terms to decribe a work from the title

page could constitute a problem. For example, in Spanish books the term *edition* (*edición*) is often used for a reprint, where content and format are unchanged.

(3) Local or national use might hamper the incorporation of international standards or codes like AACR2 or ISBD formats to cataloging practice, e.g., the lack of punctuation in Chinese cataloging.

(4) National and international script conversion standards should be discussed. LC and National Information Standards Organization (NISO Z39) activities in the Romanization of non-Roman alphabets should be considered. At the international level, the International Standards Organization is also issuing transliterating script standards.

D. *Cataloging by type of material*: Monograph, Periodical, Map, Microform, and others

(1) AACR2 deals with variations and problems for different types of material. They could deal with main entry determination or the information included in the descriptive paragraph. Uniform headings or form headings might be at issue here.

(2) ISBD formats have been developed for different types of material, e.g., ISBD(M)—for monographs, ISBD(S)—for serials, ISBD(CM)—for cartographic material, and ISBD(BM)—for nonbook material. There is also a general framework—ISBD(G).

E. *Cataloging by type of library*: School, public, academic, special

(1) International or national cooperation in exchanging cataloging records has been done mostly at the full cataloging, research-needs level. School and public libraries do not need detailed bibliographic description, close shelf classification, or many access points. Commercial cataloging services acknowledge this by offering simple or complex descriptive cataloging. LC does this by segmenting DDC numbers on cataloging records to provide longer or shorter call numbers.

There are abridged DDC and Universal Decimal Classification (UDC) editions in seventeen languages. In cataloging, AACR2 offers three description levels and instructs to base the choice of a description level on the purpose of the catalog.

(2) With online cataloging, a library may select a cataloging record of the complexity level most appropriate to its clientele. Cataloging cooperation for different types of libraries and users should be explored.

Area: *Subject Cataloging*

(1) Historical development: Discuss evolution from subject catalogs based on shelf arrangement to the present description of subject content and shelf location.

(2) Renewed subject access interest is due mostly to the possibilities and challenges presented by the online catalog.[14]

(3) Subject cataloging problems important in a national and international context are: (a) subjective determination of subject matter; (b) impact of cultural, regional differences; (c) variations in interpretation of subject heading lists and classification schemes.

A. *Subject headings*: Subject heading lists: *Library of Congress Subject Headings, Sears*
   (1) Historical development: Discuss subject headings and the dictionary catalog, subject heading use as example of precoordinated subject access in the
   printed catalog, and subject heading characteristics, problems, and structure.
   (2) Consider the lists as authority files and discuss principles in preparing
   and using them. Use *Library of Congress Subject Headings* (LCSH) and *Sears
   List of Subject Headings* as examples designed for different types of users;
   consider terminological differences and subject term complexity.
   (3) Discuss the possibility of cross-national use of a list prepared for national
   or institutional use and the adjustments and changes necessary.
   (4) Consider the translation and adaptaton of lists from one language to
   another, for example, the Université Laval translation and adaptation of
   LCSH to French.
   (5) Study lists prepared for use in several nations with a common language
   and adjustments.[15]
   (6) Discuss lists of equivalent subject terms in different languages and their
   use in subject cataloging exchange.
   (7) Discuss the treatment of peoples, groups, countries, events, and so on,
   by such lists.[16]
   (8) Consider computer use in storing, updating, and printing subject heading
   lists and use of subject heading lists online.

B. *Subject heading list versus thesauri*
   (1) Discuss similarities and differences in structure and function.
   (2) Consider online display of relationships in thesauri and possibilities due
   to hierarchical structure and display diversity.
   (3) Study post-coordinate subject searches in future online catalogs: Boolean
   logic, truncation, and other possibilities.
   (4) Consider multilingual approaches in thesaurus construction and regional
   and transnational thesauri.[17] Comparative studies of the *ERIC Thesaurus* and
   EUDISET Thesaurus could be done.

C. *Other Systems used to express subject content*: chain indexing, PRECIS (Preserved
   Context Indexing System)
   (1) Study the following points about each system: Characteristics and use of
   the system, solutions offered by the system to semantic and syntactic language
   problems.
   (2) Discuss extended international use of the PRECIS system.

D. *Classification*: History, theory, policies
   (1) Consider the history of the library's classification system use.
   (2) Discuss theoretical considerations in developing classification schemes:
   general and specialized systems as well as enumerative versus analytico-
   synthetic schemes.
   (3) Consider the work of the British Classification Research Group on: (a)
   limited or subject field classification, (b) faceted analysis and (c) development
   of a general classification.
   (4) Study the characteristics of a library classification system: notation, literary
   warrant, needed updating, and others. Compare how different schemes do
   this: LC, DDC, UDC, and Colon Classification (CC).

(5) Discuss the functions of a library classification scheme: (a) shelf arrangement for relative location, (b) subject description of content in the classified catalog common in Europe. Compare and analyze the differences in the classification system notation used for the two functions.

E. *Classification systems*: Dewey Decimal Classification, Library of Congress Classification, Universal Decimal Classification, Colon Classification, Bliss Bibliographic Classification, Bibliothekal-Bibliographical Classification (BBK), and Broad System of Ordering (BSO)

(1) Give emphasis to DDC and LC classifications, with less detailed discussion of the other systems covering characteristics, similarities, and differences.

(2) Use DDC as an example of a widely used classification which has influenced other systems; UDC as a universal classification system both in content and development; CC as the only completely synthetic general scheme. BBK is a universal system designed from a specific viewpont.[18] UNISIST's BSO is a broad, general classification developed in the 1970s.

F. *Classification by subject*: Philosophy, psychology, religion, social science, and other fields

(1) Consider problems in enumerative classifications and in faceted classifications due to multiple, changing, and ambiguous relationships. How are the disciplines or main classes organized? In relation to each other?

(2) Compare the subject areas in the humanities, science, technology, and the social sciences in different schemes. Discuss the use of auxiliary tables or the lack of them in different schemes.

(3) Consider and compare the treatment of people, countries, groups—religious, ethnic—in the schemes.

(4) Translation and adaptation of a general classification for regional or national use.

G. *Classification by type of material*: Monograph periodical, map, microform, and others

(1) How do classification systems treat form of publication? Compare in several schemes: generalia class, auxiliary tables, sections in classes and subclasses.

(2) Discuss library practice in relation to different types of material: separation of collections—documents, periodicals, microforms—and use of special classification schemes or arrangements for them. Materials, thus segregated, are usually not represented in the catalog. Discuss its importance for the catalog user and cooperative participation at the regional, national, or international level.

Area: *Other Cataloging Issues, Themes*

A. *Cooperative and centralized cataloging*

(1) Discuss the LC National Program for Acquisitions and Cataloging and its international importance.

(2) Consider development and adaptation of different LC Machine Readable Cataloging (MARC) formats: for language variations, e.g., MARCAL for Spanish material; for broader scope of information included, e.g., British MARC format includes subject headings and PRECIS strings; universal

MARC (UNIMARC). Discuss importance in cataloging data international exchange.

(3) Discuss and compare cataloging services: OCLC; Research Libraries Information Network; Washington Library Network; and University of Toronto Automatic Systems.

(4) Example of a cooperative project to create a data base for a specific type of material is the CONSER (Conversion of Serials) project, the purpose of which is to develop a national serials data base.

(5) Cataloging in Publication (CIP): By the end of 1981, it was reported that CIP was operating in at least nineteen countries. The recommendations of the IFLA meeting in Ottawa in August 1982 should be discussed.

B. *Minimal Level Cataloging (MLC)*

(1) Consider the effect of the availability of LC minimal level cataloging through online bibliographic utilities. Until now the ideal has been full cataloging. MLC is done for different types of material—microforms, theses, and so on—to solve arrearage problems.

(2) Discuss problems concerning MLC records: (a) Different standards are being used by different libraries, for example, LC MLC record, the AACR2 first level of description, and the OCLC K level. Standardization is needed. (b) How far is entry verification done when cataloging at the minimal level? (c) The importance of upgrading MLC records is that it would increase cataloging records available for different types of material which would be helpful to libraries in minimizing backlog.

C. *Leading catalogers*

Librarians from many countries who have contributed to the international development of cataloging will be discussed at the appropriate moment: Panizzi, Dewey, Ranganathan, Cutter, Lubetzky, and others.

D. *Organization, institutions*

Through the different topics, national and international organizations should be mentioned as active in different aspects of the nationalization and internationalization of cataloging and classification activities.[19]

This chapter has attempted to identify the reasons in favor of cataloging course internationalization and the issues and areas that can be studied in the process. It has tried to convey the topic's importance and the ways in which different librarianship levels—local, national, and international—touch and merge. Awareness of the need to convince librarians of the importance of international involvement increases when library school course internationalization is considered.

For a small segment of the field, international participation is already a fact, for example, LC and the Council on Library Resources. There is also a group of librarians with a strong interest in world librarianship. By studying their involvement alone, cataloging courses are already into partial internationalization. The school must be convinced of the importance of full commitment to world librarianship if it is to become a leader in cataloging instruction.

NOTES

1. "Standards for Library Schools, 1976," *IFLA Journal* 2 (1976), p. 219.
2. Ruth French Strout, "Cataloging in the GLS Curriculum," *Journal of Cataloging and Classification* 12 (July 1956), p. 123.
3. Jesse H. Shera, "On the Teaching of Cataloging," *Journal of Cataloging and Classification* 12 (July 1956), p. 131; and Seymour Lubetzky, "On Teaching Cataloging," *Journal of Education for Librarianship* 5 (Spring 1965), p. 257.
4. Cynthia C. Ryans, "Cataloging Administrators' Views on Cataloging Education," *Library Resources and Technical Services* 24 (Fall 1980), pp. 349, 350.
5. Edwin S. Gleaves, "Library Education: Issues for the Eighties," *Journal of Education for Librarianship* 22 (Spring 1982), p. 271.
6. Michael Gorman, "On Doing Away with Technical Services Departments," *American Libraries* 10 (July/August 1979), pp. 435, 436.
7. Carol Truett, "Is Cataloging a Passé Skill in Today's Technological Society?" *Library Resources and Technical Services* 28 (July/September 1984), p. 273.
8. Frances Laverne Carroll, "World Librarianship," *Encyclopedia of Library and Information Science* (New York: Marcel Dekker, 1982), Vol. 33, p. 252.
9. Maurice F. Tauber, "Introduction," *Library Trends* 2 (October 1953), p. 177.
10. Maurice F. Tauber, "Teaching of Cataloging," *Journal of Cataloging and Classification* 12 (July 1956), pp. 134–137.
11. Jesse H. Shera and Margaret E. Egan, *The Classified Catalog: Basic Principles and Practices* (Chicago: American Library Association, 1956).
12. Dorothy Anderson, *UBC: A Survey of Universal Bibliographic Control* (London: IFLA, 1982), p. 16.
13. Marybeth Milcetich, "The History and Impact of ISBD," *Library Resources and Technical Services* 26 (April/June 1982), p. 181.
14. *Books Are for Use*, a Report by Pauline Atherton Cochrane; Final Report of the Subject Access Project (SAP) (Syracuse, N.Y.: Syracuse University School of Information Studies, 1978).
15. Carmen Rovira Bertran y Jorge Aguayo, *Lista de Encabezamientos de Materia para Bibliotecas* (Washington, D.C.: Union Panamericana, 1967).
16. Joan K. Marshall, *On Equal Terms: A Thesaurus for Nonsexist Indexing and Cataloging* (New York: Neal-Schuman, 1977).
17. UNESCO, *Guidelines for the Establishment and Development of Multilingual Thesauri*, by Derek Austin and Janet Waters (Paris: 1980).
18. "Russia—U.S.S.R., Book Printing and Libraries," *Encyclopedia of Library and Information Science* (New York: Marcel Dekker, 1982), Vol. 26, p. 229.
19. Henriette D. Avram, Sally H. McCallum, and Mary S. Price, "Organizations Contributing to Development of Library Standards," *Library Trends* 31 (Fall 1982), pp. 197–223.

BIBLIOGRAPHY

ACM Conference on Management Issues in Automated Cataloging, Chicago, 1977. *Requiem for the Card Catalog: Management Issues in Automated Cataloging.* Edited by Daniel Gore. Westport, Conn.: Greenwood Press, 1979.

Auld, Larry. "Authority Control: An Eighty-Year Review." *Library Resources and Technical Services* 26 (October/December 1982), pp. 319–330.

Boaz, Martha. "The Role of Library Education for National and International Needs." In Martha Boaz, ed., *Current Concepts in Library Management*. Littleton, Colo.: Libraries Unlimited, 1979, p. 267–275.

The Card Catalog, Current Issues: Readings and Selected Bibliography. Cynthia C. Ryans, ed. Metuchen, N.J.: Scarecrow Press, 1981.

Carroll, Frances Laverne. "Internationalism in Education for Librarianship." *International Library Review* 4 (April 1972), pp. 103–126.

Carroll, Frances Laverne. "Library Education." In John F. Harvey, ed., *Comparative and International Library Science*. Metuchen, N.J.: Scarecrow Press, 1977, pp. 148–166.

Conant, Ralph. *The Conant Report: A Study of the Education of Librarians*. Cambridge, Mass.: MIT Press, 1980.

Extended Library Education Programs. Proceedings of a Conference held at the School of Library Service, Columbia University, March 13–14, 1980. Ed. by Richard L. Darling. New York: School of Library Service, Columbia University, 1980.

Holley, Robert P. "The Future of Catalogers and Cataloging." *Journal of Academic Librarianship* 7 (May 1981), pp. 90–93.

Line, Maurice B. "Requirements for Library and Information Work and the Role of Library Education." *Education for Information* 1 (March 1983), pp. 25–37.

Problems of Identifying Training Needs for Library and Information Services in a Predominantly Non-Literate Society. Papers presented at the FID/ET Technical Meeting, Ibadan, Nigeria, May 6–9, 1981, ed. by B. Olabimpe Aboyade. The Hague: Federation Internationale de Documentation, 1981.

Williamson, Nancy J. "Is There a Catalog in Your Future? Access to Information in the Year 2006." *Library Resources and Technical Services* 26 (April/June 1982), pp. 122–135.

APPENDIX: DETAILED OUTLINE OF CLASSIFICATION UNIT IN INTRODUCTORY COURSE

   I. Classification as a human activity
      A. Definition
      B. Importance
      C. Examples
  II. Classification systems
 III. Classification of library material
      A. Functions
         1. Shelf arrangement
         2. Subject description of content (Compare DDC, LC, and UDC as to possible functions.)
      B. Historical development
  IV. Classification systems for library material
      A. Types of systems

       1. General—Examples: DDC, LC, others

       2. Specialized—Examples: National Library of Medicine Classification, Classification of Library and Information Science

    B. Types by approach in development

       1. Outline of knowledge—DDC, UDC

       2. For and dependent on a specific collection—LC

    C. Types by relationships of subject areas

       1. Enumerative—LC

       2. Analytico-synthetic—UDC, CC

  V. Characteristics of classification systems for library material

    A. Provide a class for material that does not express subject matter—LC, DDC, UDC

    B. Provide for different levels of subject analysis—DDC, LC

    C. Express, if possible, form of presentation, treatment of material, level of complexity—DDC, LC

    D. Use of notation

       1. Types

          a. Pure—DDC

          b. Mixed—LC

       2. Characteristics

    E. Treatment of subject areas

       1. Use several subject areas as examples in DDC and LC

       2. Consider in LC and DDC treatment of peoples, groups, countries, and controversial events

    F. Hospitality of the schemes

    G. Updating the schemes (Use DDC, CC, LC, and UDC to discuss this point.)

 VI. Problems in application of schemes (Comparison between LC and DDC.)

VII. Call number: classification number plus author notation

    A. Function

    B. Characteristics

    C. Assignment of call number (Use Cutter or Cutter-Sanborn Author Tables with DDC; also, LC and its book number table.)

VIII. Exercises

The students should complete two or three sets of assignments with DDC and LC and their respective book numbers.

17

HISTORY OF BOOKS, PRINTING, AND LIBRARIES COURSES

Harry Clark

If the history of a subject is a chronological account of its development, then the history of books and printing must certainly be international. Every major civilization has originated or perfected some writing form, and all world alphabets came from one location in the Sinai Peninsula. The Greeks and Romans developed permanent iron gall ink to record information and ideas on papyrus (an Egyptian product) or parchment, a writing surface originating in a West Asian city. Parchment and vellum manuscripts sustained and recorded the culture of medieval Europe.

Paper traveled across Asia from China to Damascus, and from there through Islamic North Africa to Spain where it displaced parchment and vellum as a writing surface. Viscous oil-based paints and inks were developed by artists in The Netherlands, and the lead-tin-antimony type was first successfully cast in Mainz by the same hand that adapted the screw press to the craft of producing many identical inked impressions on parchment or paper.

Since the beginning of printing in Europe, book manufacture and trade have developed and changed, and the annals of printing have recorded contributions from printers and publishers in every country to the development of techniques and practices common to all. Historians have used these annals, however, in pursuing research for differing ends, and the aims of historical research have developed two well-recognized major national biases, British and French.

British bibliographers have used the history of the book as an ancilliary to textual criticism, the effort to clarify an author's meaning by discovering the most valid available copy of his or her work. Through records of printing practice and examination of available texts, analytical bibliography attempts to reconstruct a probable sequence of events and a probable group of people involved in the composition, makeup, and printing of the earliest edition of the author's work.

The spellings and mannerisms of individual compositors and the working habits of the printshop as a whole can be discovered by intensive study of the printed words on the pages they produced. The results of such study bring the bibliographer closer to the printing history of the individual work. Knowledge of the work's history is knowledge of the probable validity of the text and a foundation for further criticism.

The printing press has been more than a preserver or distorter of text, however. One of its most important functions has been to disseminate text in a volume never before possible, a function which, in the eyes of early modern historians, brought it into parity with the magnetic compass and gunpowder as one of the three most important inventions of its time. This concern with the social effects of the printing press has been most prominently discussed in this century by French bibliographers and historians following the publication of Febvre and Martin's *L'Apparition du Livre*.

Like the British, the French have tried to discover how business was conducted in various specific printing offices or bookstores, but their aim has been to trace the development of social concerns such as author-publisher relationships, the growth of popular literature, or the contributions of printers and their apprentices to the history of organized labor. As Robert Darnton has remarked: "They concentrated . . . on the most ordinary sort of books because they wanted to discover the literary experience of ordinary readers."[1] This is a concern of obvious importance to library science students.

In addition to the annals of technical developments in book production, the bibliographic reconstruction of texts, and the history of book and printing influence, the book is frequently considered to be an art form. From the fully illustrated guides to the underworld that once were buried with wealthy Egyptians, through early Hebrew, Byzantine, and Latin manuscripts to the exquisite Books of Hours of the high Gothic period, books contained and preserved the loveliest art of their times. Oil panel painting gave artists new channels of expression just when the printing press was changing the appearance and use of books, and the period in which the book was the chief repository of graphic art came to an end. The art of the book survived into modern times, and the development of design remains an active part of book history.

Those contemplating teaching book history are faced with a subject that is inescapably international in scope. They need only to bring together suitable portions of the history of technology, art, business, literature, and culture, and fit them into study units. Some trimming of this vast universe of information is vital to make course content fit present needs, but students must be made aware of all the aspects of book history that have been mentioned.

A little time may be saved by seriously restricting the study of forms of literature like cuneiform clay tablets, papyrus and parchment scrolls, sets of inscribed palm-leaves, and other book types that influence neither the form nor content of present-day books. These are museum artifacts, to be displayed in isolation under glass, untouchable and distant, as even the costliest Book of Hours is not.

The time saved by snipping away readings and discussions concerning shelves of clay tablets and jugs of papyrus scrolls must be used to study the vast changes in book production methods of the last thirty years. The movement from composition with raised metal type to composition with a word-processor; from printing from a chaise full of type or a stereotype to printing from a photolithographic plate is one of the major worldwide revolutions in book production and one that modern librarians should understand thoroughly.

Despite their international sources, the aspects of printing history mentioned above have been incorporated into the European-American tradition, and most of these aspects—technical, bibliographical, social, and artistic—should be considered in any basic book history course. The teacher who is seriously interested in internationalizing the subject will want to show the forms and influence of the book in non-Western cultures. Ideally, such internationalization should include Eastern Europe and cover cultures using the Cyrillic alphabet from the Byzantine to the modern Slavic. Persian and Islamic cultures employing the Arabic alphabet should also be considered, as should Hebraic works and books originating in India, Thailand, Burma, and Malaysia, the ideographic literature of China, and the mixed script of Japan.

Allusion to the literature of these parts of the world is essential, but bibliographic study of the works themselves should be restricted because of the unfamiliarity of the scripts to most Western students. Secondary writings in English or other Western European languages are generally available, however, and intensive comparisons of artistic style, technical innovations, and the social effects of books in one or more of these non-Western cultures are possible. Such comparisons will lead to an added understanding of the processes of cultural diffusion.

In summary, then, the objectives of internationalizing book history courses are to bring together the divergent threads of the art, techniques, and social aspects of book production in Western Europe and America and to follow these same threads in exploring the forms and influences of the book in other cultures.

The same objectives should hold for the development of libraries, which has naturally followed the historical course of the book, first as conservators of relatively rare and precious repositories of knowledge and imagination for the few who could afford and read books, later as retreats for scholars by wealthy and cultured rulers, and finally as information resources for a large and literate public. Buildings, facilities, organization, and staffing have accommodated themselves to this development and to the changing forms of the book itself—tablet, scroll, folio codex, octavo, fiche, or data bank.

To include all of its forms as mentioned above, a *book* must be defined as any form of sequential symbolic information preserved on some medium and designed for distribution. The most common symbols are alphabetic, set in sequence to form words, sentences, paragraphs, and chapters, and the most common medium is paper, but great variation is possible. To avoid unnecessary confusion, however, the word *book* will be used here in its conventional sense, a volume of folded leaves glued together on one edge and opened on the other three. Periodicals, newspapers, microfiche, and floppy discs, though forms of the book as most broadly defined, will be referred to by their popular names.

Printing consists of any method, except manual copying, of transferring images from a master copy (metal type, lithographic stone, stencil, typed page) to a suitable medium. A *library* may be defined as any storehouse of books (as broadly defined), systematically collected and organized, and intended for public or private use rather than sale. The definition includes private and public circulating and noncirculating collections whether the books are on parchment, paper, microfiche, tape, or discs. Bookstores and data banks, which are interested primarily in selling information, are not considered libraries within this definition.

A general assumption behind every attempt to record or teach the history of any subject is that knowledge of the background and development of any idea, object, or institution helps us to understand its influence within and beyond its field. Such understanding will help in predicting the future course of ideas and institutions and aid in planning for the future. The evolution of ideas, objects, and institutions is an international process reflecting contributions from every nation. As world nations become aware of sophisticated developments elsewhere, and of machines and processes useful to them, they may adapt these machines and processes rather than evolving similar ones indigenously.

Particular assumptions regarding the history of books and printing relate to the three major aspects of that study—technical, bibliographical, and cultural. Technical developments may come from any culture; they move toward speed and economy of book production and are rapidly adopted in the world wherever they may be useful. Media influence forms (as exemplified by the development of the Roman alphabet from stone-cut capitals through brush and reed writing to the cast type used in printing), but the influence of media is modified to minimize the unfamiliarity of new forms. Looking at former transitions in forms as affected by the media in which they were rendered will help us predict what new technologies will do. Because of the international nature of communication, national letter forms (such as fraktur in Germany) will not continue to develop.

Bibliographically, one may base several assumptions on the most general one: the copy that reaches the reader is not the text that leaves the author's hands. Acknowledging this, the study of printing house practice becomes particularly important, as haste, carelessness, and misunderstandings on the part of editors, compositors, and proofreaders affect text transmission between author and reader. If one understands printing procedures in any period, however, one can often determine, by examining many copies of a given work, what changes have been made in press and whether they represent proof corrections or content changes. Because of greater speed and simplicity in book production and increasing conscientiousness by editors and publishers, the more recent a work the more control the author has over its final form.

Cultural historians begin to study the history of books with several assumptions of their own. Backed up by accounts of the careers of prominent printer-publishers, historians can assume that booksellers and publishers are usually influenced by both the desire to contribute to learning or other aspects of culture and the desire to make profits. They must also assume that books which sell well or are widely circulated are read by the people who acquire them, and that popular reading reflects popular culture, that is, readers' needs and values. If historians include art in cultural study, they will acknowledge that fine illuminated manuscripts and printed books both reflect and influence the artistic taste of their times. In any case, their most basic assumption is that the study of books produced in any period and in any country helps one to understand the culture of the period and the country.

Although the source material for book history is preserved in libraries and archives, library history is not closely related to book history. Library history follows two tracks simultaneously: (1) institutional development—the growth of various collections, the provision of suitable buildings and facilities, and the careers of administrators; and (2) the social function of the library—the growth of library importance as a center for information, education and recreation, and the evolution of library service from collection-centered to client-centered activities.

Both tracks are international in scope unless artificially restricted, and the study of library social functions is closely related to the cultural history aspect of book history, but otherwise the history of books and of libraries covers divergent fields, permitting combination only on a superficial level. Type of library courses and type of service courses normally contain elements of both tracks mentioned above and are the normal places to teach library history.

History is customarily taught in at least two sections of an introductory course in librarianship. A discussion of library development is necessary to understand the library today, and such a discussion should stress the worldwide continuity of the concept of preserving the written communication of knowledge and ideas as well as the international lineage of libraries from ancient times to the present. Consideration of the selection and acquisition of library material should include a discussion of the invention and development of present-day formats (hardback, paperback, and microform books, as well as periodicals and newspapers), with due credit given to their country of origin. This same course section devoted to acquisition should cover the international booktrade.

Type of library courses usually include some account of the contributions of many countries to the development of the type covered by the course: public, school, academic, or special. They could easily be expanded to study common strands and contrasts in the development of the type of library studied, both in affluent countries and in the Third World.

General printing history surveys are offered by several library schools. Certain schools are able to offer studies of the book industry and trade in particular places and periods, such as Europe in the fifteenth century or America in the nineteenth and twentieth centuries. Analytical and descriptive bibliography is occasionally listed, as are courses related to books and culture such as studies of popular literature—pamphlets, periodicals, and newspapers. The art of the book is an important element in general survey courses and, in those schools fortunate enough to have a press, may be taught as a course in itself. Such courses cover developments in their fields in America, England, France, Germany, and Italy quite well because of the abundance of literature in English concerning those areas.

Securing a strong collection of reading and reference material for broadening the scope of history courses is a major problem for anyone who wants to internationalize these courses unless the entire curriculum is to be internationalized. Books and journals devoted to the rapidly expanding practical knowledge necessary to understand and direct today's automated libraries will often have library budget priority over culturally enriching studies. Library schools in larger universities, however, will often find a campus graduate institution concerned with the history, economics, and culture of a major area of the world—East Asia, Slavic Europe, Latin America, or Africa. Collections assembled for these institutes should offer challenging material for the study of printing or libraries in the area covered. Studying away from the library school collection also offers great benefits to students, since the cultural contact may stimulate the appreciation of foreign ways and attitudes that is so important for internationalization.

Except for the problem of strengthening the collection, the path of the instructor who wants to internationalize further the history of books is fairly smooth. Since it is less vocationally oriented than many library school courses, it could prove attractive to students in other disciplines and introduce them to the role of literature, literacy, and libraries in their own fields.

To internationalize the basic course in the history of books, the present emphasis on Western developments to the exclusion of Eastern European, Islamic, and other developments in art and technology must be corrected. The instructor must attempt to resolve the present division of emphasis among the technical, artistic, bibliographic, and social aspects of book history to give each one a place in the course, and there must be an increased emphasis on modern (post–1950) book production.

Basic book development elements that remain essential to any historical approach include the development of alphabets, and early writing material and media, including the invention of paper in China and its travel westward. Cultural developments such as monasticism which forwarded the preservation of knowledge in the West remain important, as do the beginnings of printing in China and Korea preceding its reinvention in Europe. General details of printing from the sixteenth to the nineteenth century in Europe and America—standard practices, technical innovations, and book design—cannot be neglected but should be set in place with their bibliographical and social consequences.

Books in English covering the major developments of book history in Western Europe to about 1950, some of which are listed in the select bibliography at the close of this chapter, are widely available. Most of them are replete with illustrations showing the appearance of books at various periods. Printing outside Europe is the subject of a valuable monograph series.[2] A selection of slides of manuscripts and other rare books is available from certain major libraries such as the Pierpont Morgan Library in New York and the British Library in London.

Books concerned with computer composition and modern high speed lithographic printing are more difficult to find than those dealing with earlier bookmaking processes. Because the field is developing so rapidly, such books quickly become obsolete. Some knowledge of these processes can be acquired through observation. It is frequently possible to take a class to a local press or printing plant for a look at modern book production by photolithography; it will be easier to find such a press than to locate a press still using metal type.

With regard to research in this area, it would be interesting to compare what is taught in history courses in various countries. Utilizing the available literature and bearing in mind possibilities for acquiring teaching aids such as slides and realia (hand-made paper, manuscript pens, metal type), an outline for a first course in the history of the book could be developed along the lines shown below.

COURSE OUTLINE FOR HISTORY OF THE BOOK

(Class size: six to twelve)

Goal: To lead students to heightened awareness of the role of the book in expressing and fostering culture throughout history. Expressing culture refers in this context primarily to the appearance of books, the arts of writing, lettering, and illustration involved in the production of manuscripts, and the technical developments of papermaking and of printing, engraving, and lithography involved in creating today's books. Fostering culture refers to the contents of books, the preservation of sacred and secular knowledge through carefully supervised copying of ancient texts during the manuscript period, and the dissemination of contemporary as well as traditional ideas through the ability to multiply copies by printing.

Objectives: (1) Students will become aware of the evolution of graphic communication symbols and be able to identify alphabetic and ideographic systems in use in various parts of the world. (2) Students will become familiar with the material and methods of book production in various parts of the world from the manuscript era to the present. (3) Students will be able to analyze aspects of external forces—social, political, religious, and artistic—that have affected the content and appearance of books in several specific parts of the world and the nature of these effects. (4) Students will understand the economic problems that have shaped methods of publishing and distributing books and be able to predict the effects of specific economic constraints. (5) Students will be able to attribute major technical and artistic developments in typography, book design, and book production to persons and nations originating these developments. (6) Students will develop standards for evaluating book design and construction.

Method: Lecture (with appropriate media), readings, student papers, discussion.

Evaluation: Students should be evaluated by the quality of their work outside of class as well as their powers of recall under the stress of examinations. Assigning short papers on manuscript development in various cultures and on the contrast in development of printing in Western and non-Western cultures will give students a chance to study particular areas of interest to them and to enrich the experience of their classmates through oral reports. Papers might be assigned on any aspect of history—technical, bibliographical, artistic, or social—of most general interest.

SCHEDULE OF CLASS MEETINGS

First Week *Introduction*

I. The power of writing
   A. Time-binding
   B. Preservation of formulas, incantations, instructions
   C. Preservation of agreements
   D. Communication over distance
II. The Evolution of book production
   A. Manuscripts
   B. Printing with the hand press
   C. Mechanization of printing
   D. Electronics in printing

   Communication in the Ancient World

I. Pre-alphabetic communication
   A. Pictographs
   B. Ideographic writing—hieroglyphics, cuneiform, modern Chinese
   C. Syllabic scripts
II. The alphabet
   A. Problems of origin
   B. The Phoenicians and the Greek alphabet—modern Cyrillic
   C. The Roman alphabet
   D. The Arabic alphabet
   E. Hebrew and other alphabets
III. Writing material
   A. Clay, stone, papyrus, and other early material
   B. Parchment and vellum—the codex
   C. Brushes, pens, and their influence on letter forms

Second Week *The manufacture of books in the Middle Ages*

I. Monasticism in the West
   A. Nature and function of monasteries
   B. St. Benedict and his rule
   C. Cassiodorus and the Vivarium
II. Scriptoria in West and East
   A. Goal: to preserve and disseminate texts
   B. Methods
      1. Copying and verifying
      2. Rubricating and illuminating
      3. Binding
III. Development of Islamic manuscripts
   A. Territorial spread of Islam, seventh to ninth centuries
   B. Importance of the Koran

    C. Islamic universities—development of mathematics and medicine
    D. Islamic literature
IV. Evolution of manuscript hands in Western Europe
    A. Quadrata to uncial and half-uncial
    B. Carolingian minuscule
    C. Gothic scripts
    D. Humanistic scripts

Third Week *Illumination and illustration* (slide lectures)

  I. Insular school, seventh-ninth centuries—The Book of Kells
 II. Carolingian and Ottonian illumination, ninth-tenth centuries
III. Romanesque illumination, eleventh-twelfth centuries
IV. Gothic illuminatin, thirteenth-fifteenth centuries, Book of Hours

Fourth Week *Illumination and illustration* (continued)

  I. Judaic manuscripts
 II. Islamic manuscripts
    A. Religious prohibition of human or animal forms
    B. Decoration with alphabetical and floral forms
III. Persian and Indian miniatures
IV. Student reports comparing Western European and other manuscripts

Fifth Week *Technological developments to the fifteenth century*

  I. Paper
    A. The invention of paper in China and its route to Europe
    B. The manufacture of paper by hand
    C. Identification of paper—watermarks
 II. Printing in Japan, China, and Korea before its discovery in Europe
III. Printed illustrations—Woodcuts
    A. Playing cards and devotional pictures
    B. Manuscript illustration
    C. Block books
IV. Problems of reproducing books mechanically
    A. Making letters
    B. Ink suitable for metal type
    C. Device for making impressions

Sixth Week *The introduction of printing in Europe*

  I. Printing in Mainz
    A. Gutenberg as the inventor of printing
    B. Early artifacts
      1. Papal indulgences
      2. The forty-two line Bible
      3. The Catholicon—first printing from type slugs
      4. The Fust-Schöffer Psalter
 II. The spread of printing
    A. Germany
    B. Rome and Venice
    C. Paris and Lyons

D. Netherlands and England
E. Spain
F. Russia
G. Balkins
H. Turkey

Seventh Week   *Printing in the fifteenth century*

  I. Economic aspects of printing
     A. The "perils of publishing"—supply and demand
        1. Notable failures: Gutenberg, Sweynheim, and Pannartz
        2. Notable successes: Fust, Koburger
     B. Protectors and patrons
        1. Alliances with merchants
        2. Universities
        3. The State
 II. Printing in Venice
     A. Commercial importance of Venice
     B. Proximity to paper mills
     C. High literacy and scholarship, influence of Greek refugees
     D. Prominent printers: Jenson, the Giunti
III. Changing styles in physical appearance
     A. Reproduction of Gothic scripts
     B. Early roman types
     C. The title page

Eighth Week—First Hour   *Examination*

Eighth Week—Second and Third Hours   *Bibliographies of incunabula*

   I. Hain-Coppinger
  II. Gesamtkatalog der Wiegendrucke
 III. British Museum
 IV. Pellechet

Ninth Week   *Sixteenth-century developments*

  I. Scholar printers and their innovations
     A. Western Europe: Venice, Basel, Paris, Geneva, Antwerp
     B. Eastern Europe
     C. The Hebrew Press
     D. Other cultures
 II. Design and illustration—dark Gothic to light Renaissance
III. Separation of the function of printer and founder
 IV. The Reformation, the Counter-Reformation, and censorship
  V. Piracy versus privilege—forerunner of copyright

Tenth Week   *Printing with the hand press*

  I. Composition and imposition
     A. Type and stick—setting type
     B. Imposing popular formats: quarto, octavo, duodecimo
     C. Signatures

   D. Proof and corrections
   E. Distributing type
 II. Printing
   A. The press and its parts
   B. Printer and apprentice
   C. The printing process
   D. Stop-press changes, cancels, and other irregularities
III. Management and labor in the printshop
   A. Master printers, journeymen, and apprentices
   B. Printers' chapels
   C. Labor relations
 IV. The description of hand-printed books

Eleventh Week   *Printing and society*

 I. Contributions of printing to knowledge
   A. Popular-priced classics
   B. Illustrated scientific works
 II. The growth of literacy and the growth of vernacular literature
   A. Vernacular translations of the Bible and other works
   B. Vernacular romance and adventure
III. Development of new popular publications
   A. Polemicist and pamphlets
   B. Essayists and periodicals
   C. Journalists and newspapers
 IV. The influence of the press
   A. The press and revolution
     1. Seventeenth-century England
     2. Eighteenth-century France
     3. Twentieth-century examples
   B. Movements to restrict the press
     1. State censorship
     2. State ownership
   C. The concept of freedom of the press

Twelfth Week   *Nineteenth-century developments* (two hours)

 I. Paper and presses
   A. Machine-made paper
   B. Paper from wood pulp
   C. Stronger hand presses
 II. Stereotyping and composing
   A. Stereotype and electrotype
   B. Composing machines
     1. Linotype
     2. Monotype
III. Power presses and equipment
   A. Hoe and the rotary press
   B. The web press
   C. Illustrations—half-tones, color processes

Student reports contrasting development of printing in Western and one non-Western culture (one hour)

Thirteenth Week   *Changes in book design*

I. Typographical design
  A. Italian, French, and Dutch types to the eighteenth century
  B. Major innovations in roman type design
    1. Caslon (old style)
    2. Baskerville (transitional)
    3. Didot and Bodoni (modern)
    4. Bauhaus influence (sans-serif)
  C. Arabic and Hebrew types
II. Illustration
  A. Intaglio processes
  B. Wood engraving
  C. Lithograph
III. Case binding
IV. Private presses
  A. Kelmscott, Doves, and Ashendene
  B. Twentieth-century presses
  C. Modern "rare books"—limited editions

Fourteenth Week   *Modern book production*

I. Cold type
  A. Offset photolithography
  B. Composition for lithography
    1. Photosetting—the "horseless carriage" approach
    2. Optical character recognition and word processing
    3. Computer-set type
  C. Simplicity of makeup
II. The third revolution in printing
  A. The movement from raised metal to cold type in the 1950s
  B. Implications for type design
  C. Bibliographic considerations
III. Modern book designers and their work

Fifteenth Week   *Printing and society today*

Student reports contrasting the social, educational, and political effects of printing in Europe with printing in the Third World.

NOTES

1. Robert Darnton, "What Is the History of Books?" *Daedalus* 111 (Summer 1982), p. 66.
2. Colin Clair, ed., *The Spread of Printing: A History of Printing Outside Europe in Monographs* (Amsterdam: Vangendt and Co., 1969–1973).

SELECT BIBLIOGRAPHY

Alphabets

Diringer, David. *The Alphabet: A Key to the History of Mankind.* London: Hutchinson, 1968. 2 vols.

Books—General History

McMurtrie, Douglas C. *The Book: The Story of Printing and Bookmaking.* New York: Oxford University Press, 1943.

Vervliet, Hendrik D.L. *The Book Through Five Thousand Years.* New York: Phaidon, 1972).

Book—History—Bibliography

Vervliet, Hendrik D.L., ed., *Annual Bibliography of the History of the Printed Book and Libraries,* 1970–. Amsterdam: Nijhof, 1973–   .

Manuscripts

Madan, Falconer. *Books in Manuscript; A Short Introduction to Their Study and Use.* New York: Haskett House, 1968. (Facsimile of 1927 revised edition.)

Printing—General History

Chappell, Warren. *A Short History of the Printed Word.* New York: Alfred A. Knopf, 1970.

Steinberg, S.H. *Five Hundred Years of Printing.* Baltimore: Penguin, 1974.

Printed Books—Guides

Stillwell, M.B. *Incunabula and Americana 1450–1800; A Key to Bibliographical Study.* New York: Coopers Square Publishers, 1961.

Book Design

Wilson, Adrian. *The Design of Books.* New York: Reinhold, 1967.

Illustrations

Harthan, John. *The Illustrated Book: The Western Tradition.* London: Thames and Hudson, 1981.

Type Design

Updike, Daniel Berkeley. *Printing Types: Their History, Form and Use—A Study in Survivals*. Cambridge, Mass.: Belknap Press of Harvard University Press, 1962. 2 vols.

Typefounding

Silver, Rollo. *Typefounding in America, 1787–1825*. Charlottesville: University of Virginia Press, 1965.

Printing—Bibliographic Aspects

Gaskell, Philip. *A New Introduction to Bibliography*. New York: Oxford University Press, 1972.

McKerrow, R.B. *An Introduction to Bibliography for Literary Students*. New York: Oxford University Press, 1928.

Printing—Social History

Febvre, Lucien. *The Coming of the Book: The Impact of Printing, 1450–1800*. Atlantic Highlands, N.J.: Humanities Press, 1976.

Printing—Bibliography

Besterman, Theodore. *Early Printed Books to the End of the Sixteenth Century: A Bibliography of Bibliographies*. Geneva: Societies Bibliographica, 1961.

Printing—General

Strauss, Victor. *The Printing Industry*. Washington, D. C.: Printing Industries of America, 1967.

Printing—Fifteenth Century

Haebler, Konrad. *Study of Incunabula*. New York: Grolier Club, 1933; Reprint—New York: Kraus Reprints, 1967.

Printing—Modern

Hattery, Lowell H., ed. *Technological Change in Printing and Publishing*. Rochelle Park, N.J.: Hayden Book Co., 1973.

Printing—Practical

Allen, Lewis M. *Printing with the Hand Press*. New York: Van Nostrand Reinhold, 1969.

Book Production

Jennett, Sean. *The Making of Books*. London: Faber and Faber, 1973.

Printing—Cyrillic

Zimmer, Szczepan K. *The Beginnings of Cyrillic Printing. Cracow, 1491 from the Orthodox Past in Poland*. New York: Columbia University Press, 1983.

Printing—Hebrew

The Hebrew Book: An Historical Survey. Ed. by Raphael Posner Ta Shema. Jerusalem: Kater Publishing House, 1975.

Printing—China

Tsien, Tsuen-Hsuin. *Written on Bamboo and Silk: The Beginnings of Chinese Books and Inscriptions*. Chicago: University of Chicago Press, 1962.

Printing—America

Lehmann-Haupt, Hellmut. *The Book in America*. New York: Bowker, 1952.

18

LIBRARY ADMINISTRATION COURSES

Rosemary Ruhig Du Mont

An international perspective of library management has practical interest and particular work relevance for three groups of people. First are the library management theorists, those who study and teach the subject. Second are the library field leaders who influence and are responsible for developing and maintaining national or local service. Third are all those persons who deliver library service. These groups constitute both the focus and audience of this chapter on teaching management from an international perspective.

No matter how successful a library program may be in a given context, these descriptions show us that it might evolve differently in responding to a community in quite another social, historical, or geographical context. For example, when transported to other countries, American library methods become adaptations based on unique needs rather than procedures favored by Americans for their own purposes.

Study of such adaptations can lead library science educators to look with new eyes at time-honored practices and to question what is centrally and what is locally and ephemerally important. We can learn from other countries and can help them as well, but it is difficult to do so without guidance from comparative study.[1]

THE COMPARATIVE STUDY OF LIBRARY MANAGEMENT

What then is the nature of comparative study in library management? Why should researchers engage in comparative study and educators teach it? Surely the two questions are related. Library management study is clearly related to librarianship in general, for, as Antonio Lemos has pointed out, "Managerial techniques have implications in all aspects of the provision of reading and information services."[2] Much that is written about librarianship from an international perspective relates to library management. Consequently, before proceeding, we must give a precise definition of "library management" as it is being used here. Many oft-quoted library literature definitions of management include goals and objectives which one particular culture has identified as desirable. These goals do not always span cultural boundaries since they may reflect value-judgments with which other cultures disagree.[3] Thus, "library management" needs to be expressed in terms of the aptitudes, skills, values, perspectives, and knowledge required of managers in various cultural settings.[4] These characteristics are related in a complex way to management tasks and environment; their connection to management education is shown in Figure 18.1.

Our underlying assumption is that managerial needs are traceable to a series of converging environmental influences that may vary from one culture to another. Culture is seen as a major variable in management study (see Figure 18.2). "Culture" is defined as that which includes the beliefs, expectations or behavior rules, and the explicit patterns of and for behavior: Management is a social function and is embedded in a culture—a society—a tradition of values, customs, and beliefs in government and political systems. Management is—and should be—culture-conditioned.[5]

J. Periam Danton has stated that no course could be more than a good beginning in preparing future comparative librarianship scholars. He suggests that a second stage of study is necessary for the "small and important group" who wish to work in the field in depth. Such study could investigate practical problems and questions cross-culturally. In management, presumably the studies could investigate such questions as the adoption of technology to library operation or establishing planning priorities.

A third stage of study could be concerned with the comparative research methodology itself. This methodology could be applied to the collection of relevant data to be used to develop more precise evaluation processes and to study cross-cultural relationships between libraries.

Important as it is to distinguish between levels and variations of purpose, the difficulty with identifying study stages is that separating them entirely is rarely possible. At any library management education level, the comparative or international perspective may be a totally new dimension to many students. They will need an introduction to the fact that many national management concepts are appropriate to one cultural setting but not to others.

Consequently, in an international context certain of these concepts must be discarded. Discarding concepts useful only in a particular geographic area means that the instructor must be knowledgeable not only

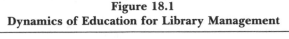

Figure 18.1
Dynamics of Education for Library Management

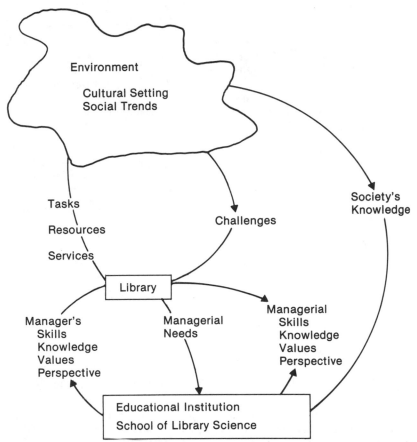

in management but in cross-cultural education as well. Team teaching is one way of dealing with this need. It may also mean that much of the material to be studied still has to be collected and classified.

Of the three study stages suggested—(1) securing awareness of the "comparative" viewpoint; (2) raising questions about pragmatic management issues in a comparative context; and (3) doing research in comparative management—most instructors will be concerned primarily with the first two. The consideration then becomes one of ascertaining what is practical to teach when only one three-credit hour comparative library management course is available?

The instructor may need to be satisfied with a limited investigation of international management issues and concentration on very few countries. Since the course should stress the relationship of the libraries to

Figure 18.2
The Impact of Culture on Management

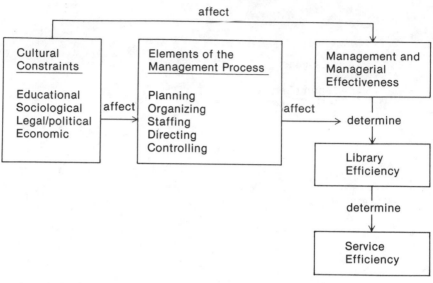

Adapted from Farmer and Richman, p. 35

the contemporary situation in the local environment, some time must be spent on the way they evolve to keep pace with changing demands on them.

Libraries cannot always be interpreted solely in terms of their own traditional aims and reference terms. By offering an international perspective, the instructor can aid students in widening horizons and thinking imaginatively about local institutions. Even without intending to reform local management practice, anyone can find foreign library administration study a fascinating exercise in organizational cause and effect.

TEACHING CROSS-CULTURAL LIBRARY MANAGEMENT

Textbook approaches to library management emphasize its content. That is, typically, such texts (and courses) are organized into distinctive activities, such as planning, staffing, directing, and budgeting. This activity focus might be called the *what* of a manager's job and would include such topics as developing strategic library operation plans and redesigning jobs. However, "the process of managing consists in getting things done for, with, and through people."[6] Therefore, management knowledge can be dealt with from a second perspective, that of the people who do the work. Here, attention is focused on *who*. Note is taken of individual and group behavior such as motivation, leadership, and attaining power. In traditional library education these behaviors are treated under such headings as organizational behavior or simply management.

Such an approach can be enhanced by investigating the large motivation and leadership differences possible among people in different cultures. Library workers can be viewed subjectively with personal drives, unique viewpoints, and individual skills peculiar to their personalities within a unique cultural context. Thus, management knowlege can be divided into two major segments: (1) knowledge about library work (encompassing tasks to be performed and interrelationships between tasks); and (2) knowledge about people within a cultural context (encompassing individual behavior and group behavior).

Understanding administrative practice requires knowledge of both segments. A relative emphasis on the cultural context of management would characterize a cross-cultural management course and distinguish it from a more conventional management process emphasis. A key goal in a cross-cultural management course would be to develop cultural awareness. Course content should clarify that human behavior in organizational settings differs because of its existence in particular cultural frameworks.

A number of alternative approaches can be attempted by persons wishing to pursue such a cross-cultural emphasis. To borrow from other disciplines using an international perspective, there is the regional, the problem, and the type of institution approach. The first one allows examination of the relationship between administrative practice and cultural background. Such an approach would emphasize one's own country with an international dimension included that would view selected "foreign" countries as contrast.

The problem approach allows us to examine "problems" cross-culturally. Library funding and the role of national libraries are examples. The type of institution study could prove valuable as a way of contrasting type-of-library objectives in selected countries. Then a study across cultural and geographic boundaries could examine the effectiveness of academic, public, or school library operation as attempts are made to reach objectives.

Another cross-cultural study approach is to identify the major factors that have encouraged the founding and support of libraries in different countries and then to separate out the kinds of adminstrative arrangements which libraries take in different cultures. In this way culture can

be examined as an environmental factor in its own right. A difficulty
with this approach is that the nature of "culture" is imprecise. The lack
of a precise definition can prevent the student from understanding the
logical development of course content.

An approach that eliminates this problem emphasizes management's
institutional aspect. The activity of apparently similar institutions can be
compared. This approach can be valuable if the instructor emphasizes
the contrasting significance of libraries in different cultural and social
settings.

Public libraries have quite different goals in the Soviet Union and the
United States, for example. Consequently, their administrative arrangements are likely to reflect that difference. It might prove valuable to
study the "leading" libraries in a given country or those that are considered "special" or "unique" by local people. Study of the operation of
significant libraries could provide valuable cross-cultural management
information.

Finally, two other approaches attempt to survey the field as an integrated whole. The first is the comparison of administrative patterns and
relationships among the various library service providers in given communities. Through this examination, attempts can be made to offer students
meaningful administrative arrangement and behavior categories.

The second approach draws and presents an entire taxonomy of library services and administrative arrangements internationally. By the
end of the course, students will have obtained much comparative systems
and service data in selected countries. However, the impact of such an
approach might be overwhelming to instructor and student alike.

Figure 18.3 outlines possible approaches in developing a cross-cultural
management course. Obviously, the figure's approaches can be refined,
and some of them can be combined in one course. They can be combined
to reveal similarities in cross-cultural managerial work; to explore the
differences among managers in different cultural environments; and to
consider the distinctions needed to account for these differences. These
approaches can also be used to compare managerial perceptions of demands, constraints, and choices in different countries.

IMPLICATIONS FOR COURSE CONTENT

The key point here is that to understand library management cross-
culturally, one must understand the nature of cultural influence, that is,
the choices possible within a cultural context. A course with this emphasis
can use lectures, discussion sessions, and case analysis to develop an
international perspective. Lectures can provide generalizations about the

Figure 18.3
Approaches to Developing a Course in Cross-Cultural Library Management

Cultural-specific approaches
(Emphasis on one country with international aspect for comparison)

1. Regional
   Focus on management as a response to culture
2. Problem
   Focus on management problems
3. Type of institution
   Focus on type-of-library goals and objectives

Cultural-nonspecific approaches
(International emphasis is paramount)

1. Administrative patterns
   Focus on cultural impact on administrative practice
2. Institutional emphasis
   Focus on administrative practice in types of libraries
3. Survey
   Focus on administrative arrangement and behavior
4. Taxonomy
   Focus on library systems and services

Figure 18.4
Topics in a Course in Cross-Cultural Library Management

Class topics

1. Libraries as organizations
   Nature and process of management
2. Nature of case analysis
3. Goals and objectives
4. Planning
5. Library's environment
6. Librarian's enviroment
7. Motivation
8. Decision-making and leadership
9. Group behavior and communication
10. Organizational control measures
11. Financial basis of the library
    Budgeting sytems
    Allocation of resources
12. Marketing
13. Organization politics
    Power
14. Library as a system

activities common to managerial positions and responsibilities. Case analyses will prevent overgeneralization about managerial work and provide examples accounting for behavioral variations and job differences in contrasting cutlural settings.[7] Figure 18.4 lists topics appropriate for the course.

Students should be able to demonstrate competence in the following
library service areas:

1. The nature of society; the physical and social environment of societal members as they affect administration
2. The basic administration principles and techniques
3. The basic techniques of measuring and evaluating service
4. The economic and political setting for service
5. The application of this information in promoting service

Competence in the first point would provide a basis for understanding
the differences between local and foreign culture and the need to modify
management approaches in different cultures. For example, job enrichment goals must be established in response to society's prevailing model
of humankind. In certain societies, enrichment leads to autonomy, letting
people make more of their own job decisions. In other societies, enrichment might take a different route—encouraging more group decision-
making and deemphasizing interindividual competition. Through all
five points listed here, there is the general theme of serving library users
effectively by being aware of environmental influences.

Such knowledge and insight are significant even for students who work
in a domestic setting. By understanding international management issues, the librarian can respond to a host of domestic management issues
as well. Knowledge about other cultures can help them respond to their
own polycultural environment and plan service that responds to the
diverse physical and cultural characteristics.

Understanding the administrative arrangements of service abroad will
enhance the librarian's ability to respond to foreign problems. Development planning, adoption of technology, and bibliographic control are
among those management problems begging for attention. The insights
obtained through a cross-cultural management perspective can be very
helpful in developing a management philosophy that respects the cultural sensitivities of both staff members and users.

The application of innovative practices developed abroad to domestic
library service must also be considered. Some countries have lessons to
teach about compromising with perfection, technological and otherwise,
so service can reach a greater number of users for a smaller investment.
Furthermore, recognition can be gained for the idea that planning strategies developed in other countries can be applied at home. In particular,

knowledge of foreign evaluation and research techniques may aid the programming efforts of local librarians. In addition, foreign programs dealing with such issues as the adoption of technology, bibliographic control, and cooperation may help us avoid others' mistakes and provide program guides.

The administration instructors must decide how to incorporate cross-cultural considerations into their course. However such a course is organized, it must be supported by material from abroad. The material must be sufficiently detailed to provide the context from which principles and conclusions can be drawn and case studies identified and discussed.

THE CASE STUDY APPROACH

Teaching is a function of individual style; however, a strong organizational framework is also necessary to support that style. The success of a course depends in part on the strength of its design and on clearly identified objectives. In particular, the selection and sequencing of material, the depth in which it is covered, the pace of instruction, and the nature of assignments must be determined.

In developing a course in cross-cultural library management, the instructor cannot assume that students have had any other course with an international emphasis. Consequently, initial lectures explaining this approach and background readings emphasizing it will probably be necessary.

Case material to follow must be carefully selected and sequenced. Students are likely to find short cases describing library situations in other countries most interesting when they reflect recent situations. In selecting material for study, the most significant problem is likely to be its availability. If the instructor underestimates the difficulty of finding appropriate information, course effectiveness is likely to suffer. A great deal of "lead time" will be necessary for the instructor to gather support material.

The instructors must, of course, have a thorough knowledge of the library situation to be discussed as a case. A careful reading of written material about the library and its cultural environment will allow the instructors to project a large number of significant dimensions of the case. But they must go beyond knowing the library situation well; they must also know about the country described in the case. Having someone from that country speak to the class about their homeland is an excellent way of gaining additional insight. Discussing the situation with colleagues who have visited that country or might be interested in the case situation may lead to other insights.

Analyzing the management situation in a library should be consistent with course and session objectives and should start with analysis of the library and its environment and build toward the end of the course when students will be required to make judgments and develop strategies for library development. The various components of the case analysis are useful "keys" to opening discussion about key concepts related to management procedures and policy.

In arranging the course, the case study can be divided into steps or stages; class sessions will be devoted to sequential steps in the analysis process. For example, Figure 18.4 lists the third major topic to be discussed as goals and objectives held by a particular library; differences in goals based on differences in cultural norms can be highlighted.

The fourth major topic is planning. In examining all of the various activities involved in the planning process, comparisons can be made cross-culturally. The opportunities and strengths, the threats and weaknesses, impacting on the planning of a library in one cultural setting are likely to be very different from those in another setting. One can move down the list in Figure 18.4 and note that cross-cultural comparisons can be made for each kind of management activity analyzed.

The resourceful instructor can prepare effective teaching material to aid in analyzing cases. The advantage of instructor-created material is that it is specific to individual student needs in terms of content presented and student knowledge level. If the instructor creates the material, students can be involved in producing it, which is an additional learning experience. Material can be used in different kinds of class activities. Case activities can be planned for use by the whole class, and other activities may be designed for independent study.

Obtaining material for cross-cultural library management issue study is a major challenge. Students can be invited to participate in collecting some of the material necessary for each study. Annual reports, planning documents, and government reports are some of the material desired. A vertical file might be started in the library to store material obtained. Obviously, the first group of students to participate in material collecting will not get as much use out of it as will later classes.

The course visualized can best be described as a time sequence model:

Stage 1: The beginning of the course will offer the knowledge and tools necessary for later case analysis. This knowledge can be imparted both by lectures and by discussion sessions.

Stage 2: The development of analytical and creative skills are the primary aims of Stage 2. Analytical skills are developed by practice in analysis of library problems and environmental change. The student of library management, by analyzing cases or problems and working on projects, becomes familiar with the ingredients and forces that make up the management process. Insights are developed by observing interrelationships and seeing the impact of model forces on institutional responses and outcomes.

Creative skills are developed by assessing situations and evaluating plans and programs and determining how operations are likely to evolve. These analytical and creative exercises present challenging problems to be studied. Students become highly motivated by sharing their findings with their peers and by investigating real-life situations.

Stage 3: Ideally, there is a stage 3 when students spend time in a reality environment. Many texts discussing international components in professional curricula emphasize that students learn most by visiting other countries and by observing what "it is really like." Simulated exercises and cases, while adequate, do not give a complete picture of foreign situations. Because of the financial burden associated with travel and study abroad, Stage 3 may seldom be possible.

NEEDED RESEARCH

Good research is needed to support any course. The present list of needed research projects is partial but indicates areas where information is scattered and needs synthesis. For convenience, the subject areas are listed under three headings:

1. Comparative studies: Much research in international library operation is merely descriptive; it describes and explains rather than compares. True comparative studies are also needed. For example, it should be possible for researchers to conduct comparative evaluation studies to aid in identifying performance measures useful worldwide.

2. Library service distribution and utilization: Much more information is needed about effective service distribution. Though not comparative, these studies would deal with service in a given country or region in order to hold many cultural factors constant. Without these studies, library organization and management ideas remain merely opinions rather than tested fact.

3. Comprehensive planning: The relation between library development and a country's overall development should be studied. These variables relate not only to setting realistic objectives but also to choosing administrative mechanisms to meet them in a given political and social context.

SUMMING UP

The key to any cross-cultural or international management study can be identified by examining the library as an organization on the one hand and the environment's effect on it on the other. They have a continuous mutual impact, and the link between them is management attitude or philosophy. This relationship is expressed diagrammatically in Figure 18.5.

In providing service, management's dominant motivating attitude might be economic, political, religious, social, or more narrowly specific. It will be influenced by the community's culture and outook. Dominant

Figure 18.5
Factors in a Course in Cultural Library Management

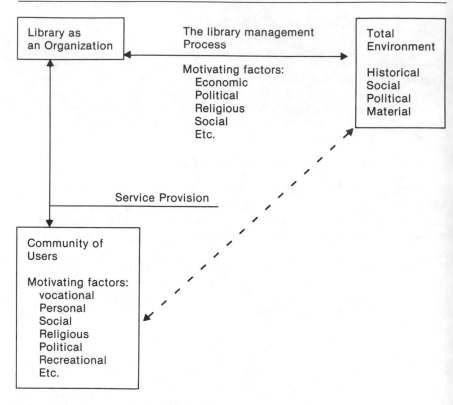

user motivations must also be considered; they may be vocational, personal, social, religious, political, or recreational. In turn, these needs will be influenced by the cultural setting and stimulated or discouraged by the community background.

An additional consideration is the total physical and social community environment, which includes the social and political background within which the community develops a library service pattern. Included in the material category are stable elements such as geography, climate, population, and land resources. More dynamic elements include communication patterns (including technology adoption for communication) and economic conditions, both of which are capable of influencing library provision and of being themselves influenced by libraries.

Among the political factors will be not only the philosophies of those powerful enough to make library service support decisions, but also the influence of the power structure itself. The historical factors include both slow trends and sudden developments in cultural values and community priorities and how these are translated into institutional arrangements. All of them are mutually interactive.

Thus, we have a three-dimensional network of closely related factors in which libraries attempt to provide services. Management's role is to be sensitive to these factors and to respond appropriately in moving the institution forward. International or cross-cultural management study must examine all of these factors and create an awareness of the philosophy of the library's community and the impact of environmental change.

NOTES

1. J. Periam Danton, *The Dimensions of Comparative Librarianship.* Chicago: American Library Association, 1973.

2. Antonio A. Briquet De Lemos, "Educational Needs for Library Management in Developing Countries," in Gilleon Holroyd, ed., *Studies in Library Management* (London: Clive Bingley, 1977), p. 13.

3. R. Farmer, "A Model for Research in Comparative Management," *California Management Review* 4 (February 1964), pp. 55–68.

4. H. Ingor Ansoff, "The Next Twenty Years in Management Education," in Herman H. Fussler, ed., *Management Education: Implications for Libraries and Library Schools* (Chicago: University of Chicago Press, 1973), p. 14.

5. Peter Drucker, *Management: Tasks, Responsibilities, Practices* (New York: Harper & Row, 1974), p. xii.

6. L. F. Urwick, "Papers in the Science of Administration," *Academy of Management Journal* 13 (December 1970), p. 365.

7. See Miriam H. Tees, "Is It Possible to Educate Librarians as Managers?" *Special Libraries* 75 (July 1984), pp. 173–182.

BIBLIOGRAPHY

Barrett, G. V. "Comparative Surveys of Managerial Attitudes and Behavior." In J. Boddewyn, ed., *Comparative Mangement: Teaching, Research and Training.* New York: Graduate School of Business Administration, 1970.

Bone, Larry Earl., ed. *Library Education: An International Survey.* Champaign: University of Illinois School of Library Science, 1968.

Bonn, George S., ed. *Library Education and Training in Developing Countries.* Honolulu: East-West Press, 1966.

Crozier, M. "The Cultural Determinants of Organizational Behavior." In Anant R. Negandhi, ed. *Environmental Settings in Organizational Functioning.* Kent, Ohio: Comparative Administrative Research Institute, Kent State University, 1973.

Davis, Stanley M. *Comparative Management: Cultural and Organizational Perspectives.* Englewood Cliffs, N.J.: Prentice-Hall, 1971.

Landsberger, Henry A. "A Framework for the Cross-Cultural Analysis of Formal Organizations." In Henry A. Lansberger, ed. *Comparative Perspectives on Formal Organizations.* Boston: Little, Brown, 1970.

Schollhammer, Hans. "Comparative Management Theory Jungle." *Academy of Management Journal* 12 (1969), pp. 91–97.

Seminar on the Role of University Libraries in the Information Systems of Developing Countries, Final Report: Dakar, 9–14 March 1981. Paris: UNESCO, 1981.

Sjoberg, G. "The Comparative Method in the Social Sciences." In A. Etzioni and F.L. Dubow, eds. *Comparative Perspectives: Theories and Methods*. Boston: Little, Brown, 1970.

Taylor, Weldon J. "Some Emerging Concepts in Education for Management." *AACSB Bulletin* 11 (October 1974), pp. 19–24.

Wasserman, Paul, and John R. Rizzo. *A Course in Administration for Managers of Information Services: Design, Implementation, and Topical Outline*. Paris: UNESCO, 1976 (Ed. 146 922).

19
INFORMATION SCIENCE COURSES

Harold Borko and Eileen Goldstein

A frequently cited definition of information science is: "an interdisciplinary science that investigates the properties and behavior of information, the forces that govern the flow of information, and the techniques, both manual and mechanical, of processing information for optimal storage, retrieval, and dissemination."[1] Three directions have emerged for information science, informatics (the term used in Eastern Europe), or documentation (the term used in certain other parts of the world):

1. The professional aspect concerned with information systems, services, and networks and with users and uses of information.
2. The technological applications of appropriate technologies to the processing, storage, and dissemination of information.
3. The scientific aspect concerned with theories and experimentation with communication and information processing systems.[2]

There are four basic views of the relationship between information science and library science:

1. Information science is a subdiscipline of library science.
2. Library science is a subdiscipline of information science.
3. Library science and information science are two distinct fields with an area of overlap between them.
4. Library science and information science are the same discipline which may appropriately be called *Library Information Science*.

The American Society for Information Science (ASIS) has published a directory of information science educational programs which indicates that courses were offered in a variety of settings, including American library schools, science departments, management and business schools, communication schools, and independent information science departments.[3] Jack Belzer has reported on the diversity of information science programs: forty-five schools responding to a questionnaire reported over 185 courses and 242 topics.[4] Not only did courses vary according to type of department, but also within the same type of department in different schools.

Belzer has identified seven courses that form the information science curriculum core: (1) introduction to information science; (2) systems theory and applications; (3) mathematical methods in information science; (4) computer organizations and programming systems; (5) abstracting/indexing/cataloging; (6) research methods; and (7) miscellaneous (all others).

Taking a different approach, Robert S. Taylor has identified six general information science curriculum subject areas: (1) information storage and retrieval; (2) information environment; (3) information media (communication); (4) systems and technologies; (5) research methods; and (6) information management[5]

Herbert Schur presents general topics for information science courses offered in six European countries: (1) generation and use of data; (2) data bases and their characteristics; (3) organization and dissemination of data; (4) Information, storage, and retrieval systems; (5) Theoretical and technical tools; and (6) Special topics.[6]

The topics noted by Belzer, Taylor, and Schur demonstrate the different ways in which information science courses are approached. However, whereas the lists differ in terminology, there is significant overlap in content and goals. The following information science education objectives taken from the Graduate School of Library and Information Science (GSLIS) catalog, University of California, Los Angeles (UCLA), might, with some modification, also apply to other library schools:

1. To provide an introduction to a variety of subjects that constitute information science and their relationship to libraries and other information centers.
2. To discuss systems analysis techniques and the application of data processing equipment to selected library operations.
3. To provide an introduction to information science development.
4. To provide an understanding of the changing roles and responsibilities of librarians and other information professionals in society.

INFORMATION SCIENCE TOPICAL OUTLINE

For this chapter, the categories presented by Belzer, Taylor, and Schur have been combined and generalized to cover those topics considered important on an international level within a library school setting. Information science courses are presently offered in many countries at different levels. For example, whereas in India information science is well incorporated into the general library school curricula, a minimal information science emphasis has been made in Pakistan and Bangladesh.[7]

The outline presented here may be used by schools initiating new information science curricula or by schools modifying existing curricula. Curricula will differ according to the accepted information science definition, the relationship between library science and information science, and each school's objectives. The number of courses in each area and the titles will need modification, depending on school emphasis, for what follows is a general subject outline and not a specific curriculum.

THE INFORMATION PROFESSIONS

Introduction

Information career options

Information science associations and journals

National information institutions

Activities of international organizations

UNESCO

International Federation of Library Associations and Institutions (IFLA)

Organization of American States (OAS)

International Federation for Documentation (FID)

International Standards

International Standard Bibliographic Description (ISBD)

International Standard Book Number (ISBN)

Universal Marc (UNIMARC)

BASIC FUNCTIONS OF LIBRARY INFORMATION SYSTEMS

Information storage and retrieval

Data bases

Search services

Primary, secondary, and tertiary information sources

Information generation, flow, transfer, and use

INTRODUCTION TO COMPUTER TECHNOLOGY

Functional organization of computer systems

Central processing unit

Internal and external memory

Input devices

    Punched cards, keyboard, light pen, tape, disc
  Output devices
    Video display, printer, tape, disc
Software
  Programming languages
  Software packages for operating systems and application programs
Types of computers and data processing systems
  Main frame, e.g., Maxi
  Mini and micro
  Turnkey systems
Batch versus interactive (online) processing

LIBRARY AUTOMATION

History
  Subsystem application
    Collection development
    Acquisition
    Cataloging
    Machine-readable catalog bases
    Circulation
    Reference
    Machine-readable reference service data bases and interactive searching
    Administration
  Type of library
    School
    Public
    Special
    Academic/Research

COMMUNICATION NETWORKS

  National, regional, and international planning
  Governance
  Television, Teletext, Viewdata
  Satellite communication

TOOLS

  Systems analysis
  Evaluation
    Systems design
    Bibliometeics

APPLICATIONS AND SPECIAL TOPICS

Abstracting

Types: descriptive, indicative, telegraphic

Full text versus abstract versus description

Indexing

Types: keyword, descriptor, citation, chain

Pre- and post-coordinate

Thesaurus versus subject headings

Natural versus controlled language

Question–answering systems

SPECIAL TOPICS

Artificial intelligence

Human-computer interaction

In many cases, information science students are encouraged to take elective courses in other schools, including philosophy, linguistics, education, sociology, mathematics, and computer science.

COURSE INTERNATIONALIZATION

Existing curricula for information science are nationally oriented and of limited application abroad. Information science can be understood only in the framework of social, political, economic, and cultural environments. However, an internationalized information science program should not be geared to a specific country or geographic area; a more general context is required. Nor should it be limited to examples from one country or region but rather to activities in many countries.

In general, as compared with national information science, international information science should have a much broader scope, expanded bibliographies, and flexible assignments. Its curricula should not be limited in application to one country or to one development stage. Less developed countries (LDCs) will find the internationalized curriculum as useful as developed countries. Since most developed countries already have information science curricula, this chapter provides several examples from LDCs for which information science curricula have been overlooked thus far.

For a broader scope, the course outline topics should draw on international examples and issues. Class discussions should encourage students to analyze similarities and differences in policies and practices in several countries. The applicability of principles to other countries should be questioned as well as the implication of their use.

For example, when considering the use of software packages, students should consider whether to adopt or adapt already existing packages or to write new programs. Local conditions should be taken into account. Are existing software packages appropriate for existing systems? Are experienced programmers available to assist in program adaptation or in writing new programs?

As another example, when discussing online interactive system use, the question should be raised as to the feasibility of online searching in LDCs. Alternatives, such as offline batch processing, can be discussed as can commercially available retrieval systems from other countries. The broadened scope will help LDC students to adopt or adapt ideas.

Online searching can explore data bases from various countries. The educational discount programs offered by certain American companies—Dialog Information Servies, Inc., and Systems Development Corporation Information Search Services—have been used to demonstrate online searching. Readers can explore the availability of educational discount programs from the online service organizations of various other countries, such as BLAISE (British Library) online service.

In addition, user manuals can be purchased from service organizations such as DIMDI (German Medical Information Systems) or QL Systems in Canada which provides access to data bases covering Canadian government information and other data bases.

The broadest scope of information science courses requires expanded bibliographies that should include material in several languages, and classroom discussions should present many foreign examples. The chapter bibliography provides examples that internationalize the reading list for certain basic information science areas. When expanding bibliographies, available collections must also be analyzed and modified to give an international perspective. Information science journals from various countries should be made available.

Student backgrounds should be taken into account for class assignments, thus allowing them to explore areas of particular interest by country. Students might address questions on the appropriateness of specific technologies for their countries; ways of adapting techniques, systems, or technologies to local conditions; and establishment of national information work priorities. These assignments will help to make the education more appropriate and useful when students try later to apply their learning.

CURRICULUM CHANGE PLANNING AND IMPLEMENTATION

Curriculum change is a complicated process. It begins and ends with a review and evaluation of the existing curriculum. Five areas should be considered when planning curriculum change and implementation:

needs and constraints of change; input sources for changing the curriculum; needed library resources; educational levels affected by change; and core and specialized courses. Changes in the library school's information science curriculum should be preceded by a survey of educational trends and the job market for graduates. In addition, the change from an industrial to an "Information Age" or "Post-Industrial" society influences the information science curriculum.

Although the full impact of the information age has not yet been felt in many countries, its effects cannot be overlooked anywhere. Post-industrial societies have made information central in economic planning, while pre-industrial societies consider information essential to their further development. Library information science program leaders can be consulted about their curriculum change experience as well as future plans and directions. Present library resources must be analyzed for appropriateness to the new curriculum. New material should be ordered well in advance of need.

The systems approach is recommended for implementing curricular change. The following steps summarize that process: (1) Planning—statement of goals, resources, and constraints; (2) analysis of the exisiting curriculum; (3) design of new curriculum—presentation of alternatives; (4) implementation of the new curriculum; (5) evaluation; and (6) iteration.

Two constraints should be considered when planning curriculum change. First, each school needs to consider the specialized abilities of its faculty members. It would be difficult to offer courses in an area without the necessary faculty competence. The second constraint is the financial one, that is, limitations in purchasing new equipment and hiring additional faculty members to meet new curriculum needs or helping existing faculty to obtain new skills.

Few schools offer library information science programs at all three educational levels—undergraduate, Master's, and Ph.D. Since the three levels vary in emphasis and objectives, changes at one level do not necessarily require changes at the other levels. Belzer suggests that the emphasis in programs for undergraduates, Masters, and Ph.Ds varies for theory, concepts, tools, and application.[8] In a bachelor's program, tools are the major emphasis, and applications are next in importance. The Master's level emphasizes applications with less concentration on concepts and theory. The Ph.D. level concentrates on theory with some emphasis on applications and minimal concentration on tools.

Different specialties may have different requirements. An information science specialization should include courses in computer technology, data base design, systems analysis, and managerial accounting. All specializations need to emphasize new, anticipated, and changing clientele needs, as well as to search for new applications and methods. Each educational institution should identify its core courses and prepare several specialization programs with appropriate course lists.

COURSE EXAMPLES

The following detailed outlines expand on specific elements of the general topical outline. Each one is intended for a single course lecture of two to four hours. The examples and issues presented illustrate internationalized information science courses.

LIBRARY AUTOMATION—SUBSYSTEMS APPLICATION
  Examples of subsystem applications
    Collection development
    Acquisition
    Cataloging
      Computer Output Microfiche (COM)
    Machine-readable cataloging data bases
      Utilities
        Online Computer Library Center, Inc. (OCLC) (United States)
        Australian Bibliographic Network (ABN)
      Data bases
        Machine Readable Cataloging (MARC)
        Canadian Marc (CAN/MARC)
        Latin American Marc (MARCAL)
        United Kingdom Marc (UKMARC)
        Brazil Marc (CALCO)
    Circulation
    Reference
      Reference Library Enhancement Systems—REFLES at UCLA
      Finland REFLINK
    Machine-readable reference and interactive searching
      Services
        Telesystems—Questel (France)
        Japan Information Center of Science and Technology
      Data bases
        International Information Systems for the Agricultural Sciences (AGRIS)
        Medical Literature Analysis and Retrieval Systems (MEDLARS) (United States)
    Subscriptions

Vendors

Perline—Blackwell Technical Services, Ltd. (England)

Datalinx—F. W. Faxon Co., Inc. (United States)

Inhouse

Administration

Data base management systems

Factors influencing library automation

Economic

Cost of hardware, software, and telecommunication

Technological

Feasibility

Manpower

Information personnel: librarians, information scientists, editors, computer programmers, translators

Information infrastructure

Definition

Political

Government priorities

Application

Developed countries

Less developed countries

Issues

Determining needs

Document procurement

Overall systems (examples)

Librunam—National Autonomous University of Mexico

National Library of Venezuela

OCLC (United States)

Available packages for inhouse use

CL Systems (United States)

PRODUCERS AND VENDORS OF ONLINE DATA BASES

Data base suppliers

Bibliographic data base publishers

New York Times Information Company (United States)

Bureau National des Données Oceaniques (France)

Producers of nonbibliographic data bases

Nomura Research Institute (Japan)

I. P. Sharp Associates (Canada)

Distributors of online data bases

    Online service organizations

        BRS, DIALOG, ORBIT (United States)

        European Space Agency—Information Retrieval Service (ESA-IRS)

    Time-sharing firms

        Data Resources, Inc. (United States)

        Computer Science of Australia Pty. Ltd. (Australia)

    Telecommunication networks

        National coverage

            Datapac (Canada)

            Finpak (Finland)

            PSS (United Kingdom)

        Multinational coverage

            Euronet (European Economic Community countries)

            Tymnet (International)

Producing and marketing online products

    Production concerns

    Pricing concerns

Online data base users

    Libraries/Information centers

    Information brokers

    End users

New Technologies

    Microcomputers

    Telecommunication

Videodiscs

INTERNATIONAL INFORMATION SYSTEMS

International cooperation

    Agreements between institutions or agencies

        Chemical Abstracts Service (CAS) in the United States with Germany and United Kingdom

    Intergovernmental action

        Eastern and Central Europe—International Centre of Scientific and Technical Information

        Latin America—Andres Bello Convenio

        Asia—ASEAN

    International nongovernment bodies

        International Federation of Library Associations and Institutions (IFLA)

International Federation for Information Processing (IFIP)

International information systems

    National in control with international coverage

        Chemical Abstracts Services (United States)

        INSPEC (United Kingdom)

    National in control with international coverage and input from other countries

        Medlars from National Library of Medicine (United States)

        Textile Information Treatment Users Service (TITUS) (France)

    Controlled by international body receiving input from many countries

        International Nuclear Information System (INIS) of the International Atomic Energy Agency (IAEA)

        International Information System for Agricultural Sciences and Technology (AGRIS) of the Food and Agricultural Organization (FAO)

Prerequisites for establishing international systems

    Technical

    Economic

    Political

United Nations role

Issues

    International standardization

    Future trends

SYSTEMS ANALYSIS—OVERVIEW

General

Analysis of special information problems and design solutions tailored to specific needs

Definition of systems analysis

Systems analysis uses

    Automation

    Reshelving

    Reclassification

    Bottlenecks

    Limitations

        Quantitative versus qualitative

        Decision-making

    Phases of a Systems Study

        Planning

Define problem and scope of work
Analysis
Describe existing sytems and interrelationships
New system design
Identify alternative configurations
Evaluate alternatives using a cost/performance/benefit analysis
Implementation of preferred design
Evaluation of new system
Iteration of system study
Techniques
Interviewing
Work flow analysis—flowcharting
Sampling
Critical path scheduling
Decision tables
Modeling
Mathematical programming

COMPATIBILITY OF RETRIEVAL LANGUAGES
The Question
To what extent are two retrieval languages compatible?
Importance of the question
Searching different data bases on one subject
Searching data bases in different natural languages
Translation
Degree to which translation can be automatic
History
Early 1960's—interest began
Switching language
One-to-one mapping
New interests
Present research and development
Russian conference
Other conferences
European achievements
Multilingual thesauri
Euronet
U.S. achievements

    University of Illinois—transparent systems

    Battelle Institute—vocabulary switching

    Massachusetts Institute of Technology—common command language

Some problems

    Few demonstrations of effectiveness

    Few cost justifications

DATA AND RESEARCH NEEDS

The topics for information science courses are not the same for developed and developing countries or for the United States and European countries. Empirical data on the relevance of American information science education to developing countries would be valuable in planning to modify existing curricula.

An informal pilot survey was conducted at UCLA in 1983 preparatory to developing an acceptable questionnaire for this purpose. While the pilot survey involved only nine students, the opinions voiced related to internationalizing information science courses. Students from developing countries felt that all courses were at least somewhat applicable to their home countries, even though emphasis was on the U.S. situation and usually disregarded cultural and linguistic differences. Research on the adequacy of library information science education in developed countries for foreign students is apparently deficient. A well-rounded study could include various viewpoints, and could include presently enrolled students as well as alumni.

Research is also needed on the factors influencing information science education. Factors including geography, politics, economy, religion, education, and language determine the information service patterns required in each country. However, it is unclear what role each factor plays and how the library information science curriculum is affected.

Library information science courses must keep abreast of technological advances in order to provide appropriate information service. The curriculum should present an international view. Since the information science definition as well as program objective will vary by school and country, no single curriculum can be used everywhere. Information science courses need to be reviewed and modified to become more appropriate for advanced technology as well as for national needs.

NOTES

1. Harold Borko, "Information Science: What Is It?" In Arthur W. Elias, ed., *Key Papers in Information Science* (Washington, D.C.: American Society for Information Science, 1971), p. 5.

2. Tefko Saracevic, "An Essay on the Past and Future of Information Science Education, Part I: Historical Overview," *Information Processing and Management* 15 (January/February 1979), pp. 1–15; and "Part II: Unresolved Problems of Externalities of Education," *Information Processing and Management* 15 (November/ December 1979), pp. 291–301.

3. Gerald Jahoda, "Education for Information Science," in Carlos A. Cuadra, ed., *Annual Review of Information Science and Technology* (Washington, D.C.: American Society for Information Science, 1973), Vol. 8, pp. 321–344.

4. Jack Belzer, et al., "Curricula for Information Science," *Journal of the American Society for Information Science* 22 (May/June 1971), p. 194.

5. Robert S. Taylor, "Areas of Information Science Curriculum," *Bulletin of the American Society for Information Science* 3 (August 1977), pp. 17–18.

6. Herbert Schur, *Education and Training of Information Specialists for the 1970s* (Paris: Organization for Economic Cooperation and Development, 1973) (ERIC ED 086178).

7. P. B. Mangla, "Library Education in India, Pakistan, and Bangladesh," in Michael Harris, ed., *Advances in Librarianship*, (New York: Academic Press, 1980), pp. 191–244.

8. Jack Belzer, et al., "Curricula in Information Science," *Journal of the American Society for Information Science* 26 (January/February 1975), pp. 17–32.

BIBLIOGRAPHY

Atherton, Pauline. "Putting Knowledge to Work in Today's Library Schools." *Special Libraries* 63 (January 1972), pp. 31–36.

Bousso, Amadou. "A Library Education Policy for the Developing Countries." *UNESCO Bulletin for Libraries* 22 (July/August 1968), pp. 173–188.

Ogunsheye, F. A. "Formal Program Development in Library Education in Nigeria." *Journal of Education for Librarianship* 19 (Fall 1978), pp. 140–150.

Roberts, Norman, and Gillian Bull. "Professional Education and Practice: A Survey of Past Students." *Journal of Librarianship* 15 (January 1983), pp. 29–46.

Saracevic, Tefko. "Information Science Education and Development." *UNESCO Bulletin for Libraries* 31 (May/June 1977), pp. 134–141.

Saracevic, Tefko. "Training and Education of Information Scientists in Latin America." *UNESCO Journal of Information Science, Librarianship and Archives Administration* 2 (July/September 1980), pp. 170–179.

Schur, Herbert. "The European Communities and the Harmonization of Educational and Professional Qualifications." *Journal of Librarianship* 7 (January 1975), pp. 49–65.

Sever, Shmuel. "Library Education in Israel." *Journal of Education for Librarianship* 21 (Winter 1981), pp. 208–234.

Whitten B., and Tom Minder. "Education for Librarianship in Developing Countries: The Hacettepe Experience." *Journal of Education for Librarianship* 14 (Spring 1974), pp. 220–234.

Internationalized Bibliography by Topic

INFORMATION FIELDS

Albertus, Ursula. "The Role of UNESCO/PGI in the Development of Information Systems and Services in Latin America." *UNESCO Journal of Information Science, Librarianship, and Archives Administration* 3 (April/June 1981), pp. 74–80.

Anderson, Dorothy. "IFLA's Programme for UBC: The Background and the Basis." *IFLA Journal* 1 (1975), pp. 4–8.

Keren, Carl, and L. Harmon. "Information Services in Less Developed Countries." In Martha Williams, ed., *Annual Review of Information Science and Technology*. White Plains, N.Y.: American Society for Information Science, 1980, Vol. 1, pp. 289–324.

Spiller, D. "International Organizations and Their Effect upon Libraries of Developing Countries." *International Library Review* 11 (July 1979), pp. 34–51.

LIBRARY AUTOMATION

Avram, Henrietta D. "International Standards for the Interchange of Bibliographic Records in Machine-Readable Form." *Library Resources and Technical Services* 20 (Winter 1976), pp. 25–35.

Bourne, Charles P. *Technology in Support of Library Science and Information Service.* Bangalore: Sarada Ranganathan Endowment for Library Science, 1980.

Lancaster, F. W., and John Martyn. "Assessing the Benefits and Promise of an International Information Program (AGRIS)." *Journal of the American Society for Information Science* 29 (November 1978), pp. 282–288.

Van Niel, Eloise. "Automation for Libraries in Developing Countries." *International Library Review* 6 (October 1974), pp. 373–386.

LIBRARY, INFORMATION, AND COMMUNICATION NETWORKS

Dubois, C.P.R. "Multilingual Information Systems: Some Criteria for the Choice of Specific Techniques." *Journal of Information Science* 1 (January 1979), pp. 5–12.

Tocatlian, Jacques. "International Information Systems." In Melvin J. Voigt, ed., *Advances in Librarianship*. New York: Academic Press, 1975, Vol. 5, pp. 1–60.

APPLICATIONS AND SPECIAL TOPICS

Wellisch, Hans. "Linguistic and Semantic Problems in the Use of English-language Information Services in Non-English-speaking Countries." *International Library Review* 5 (April 1973), pp. 147–162.

20
MEDIA STUDIES

Donald P. Ely and C. Walter Stone

This chapter seeks to help plan media instruction with an international perspective for use in library education programs. The chapter suggests what is and what should be taught, to whom, and (where appropriate) how.

The term *media* refers mainly to newer vehicles of communication (other than books and magazines) which usually require use of special equipment for viewing/listening. They include better known audiovisual media, that is, films, filmstrips, slides, audio recordings, and various combinations of them; newer telecommunication systems such as video recordings, cable and satellite delivery systems, and videotex; and print-oriented devices such as computers, microcomputers, and microforms (See appendixes at the end of this chapter).

Newer (nonprint) media are now common in libraries. This has led to library education course development which prepares initially or seeks to upgrade personnel for proper media handling in all library types. In general, library and information science media courses reflect current practice rather than preparation for the future.

Courses are organized in different ways. Some are centralized, with nonprint media emphasis placed on one or two courses. Others are decentralized with nonprint media components integrally built into traditional courses. Both designs are legitimate; hence, the authors' approach to chapter organization is topical rather than by course.

With more library education programs incorporating information science concepts, computer use has been given increasing emphasis. Most library schools offer separate courses dealing with specific computer applications. Topics suggested for inclusion in media courses relate to library clients rather than administrative use of microcomputers.

The computer, now central to many library management developments, is in certain ways an anomaly in this chapter since it simply stores, manipulates, and delivers print and graphic information. In this sense, it resembles microfilm, which also requires special equipment to develop printed information.

To some people internationalization means the extension of baseline topics that are not "culture-bound" but include cross-cultural dimensions. For example, a widespread recording study unit should go well beyond a simple description of content characteristics, costs, and applications to consider the various technical formats and standards used in different regions; important videotape sources in these regions might also be identified.

Major emphasis has been placed on libraries generally. Unfortunately, little hard and recent data appear to have been compiled regarding firm trends in media course development with library programs, and almost no related research is reported. For the most part, therefore, specific course data cited have been collected through an informal worldwide survey of knowledgeable persons and organizations. The separate experience and observation of the co-authors, however, represent the primary sources of recommendations.

While by chance working at the same time in Jakarta and having agreed after meeting to write this chapter, Ely and Stone sent a brief questionnaire to a selected group of library leaders, educators, and media service-related organizations (see Information Sources). The authors are grateful for the responses forwarded to them and for the particular support provided by Indonesian colleagues; ERIC Clearinghouse on Information Resources staff members; Singapore National Library; and Trans-Asia Engineering Associates, Inc. of the Resco Corporation. The authors are wholly responsible for any errors of data, interpretation, or judgment.

LIBRARY "MEDIA" SERVICE PROGRAMS

By the mid–1980s, professionally managed nonbook library service programs were being offered worldwide, albeit with varying degrees of sophistication and encountering various public and occupational acceptance levels. New media still constitute but minute fractions of most library holdings. Frequently, they have been acquired for special purposes, for example, to support given types of community adult education or semi-recreational programs.

A Definition of "Library Media"

Library responsibility for nonbook material provision has been much extended to include:

Sound, and/or visual material and machine-readable data files, fixed in any tangible medium of expression now known or later developed from which they can be perceived, reproduced, or otherwise communicated either directly or with the aid of a machine or device. Such materials include, among others the following—original art; chart; filmstrip; flash card; game; globe; kit; machine-readable data file; map, microform (e.g., aperture card, microfiche, microfilm, and micro-opaque); microscopic slide; model; motion picture; picture (e.g., art print, photograph, and poster); realia; slide; sound recording; technical drawing; transparency; video record . . . paintings; toys; etc.[1]

Knowledge of these media and of related equipment systems, as well as the ability to train others to use and, sometimes, even produce them, are today deemed to be the proper concerns of librarians.

Library Functions Being Redefined

It is the view of one prominent British colleague that, in all countries where the video revolution has happened, video is *by far* the most important medium, apart from the book; indeed, other audiovisuals are of very secondary interest to library users. The most important library media service is or will soon become "video reference and lending service."[2]

An American colleague has written quite bluntly that library concerns for "nonprint" media are now anachronistic—still useful but chiefly in classroom-like instructional settings. Libraries must give primary attention to a broadening range of new "information and communication products and technologies employing electronic equipment, communicative interfacing devices, [and] interactive and intelligent software."[3]

Of importance is the range of functions now performed increasingly by librarians as the consequence of expanding media service responsibilities and massive problems caused by "exploding" rates of knowledge growth and need for its control.[4] "Professional estimates suggest that, during the last three decades of this century, as much new technical knowledge will have been generated and reported as had been accumulated throughout the past history of mankind. The world is threatened with an eventual drowning in mountains of words and pictures."[5]

Traditional library responsibilities have included selection/evaluation, acquisition, cataloging and classification, storage, reference, and circulation. In the late 1980s more advanced libraries are expected to emphasize training service for new media individual, group, and staff use; design, production, and reproduction of various media forms and formats; diagnosis of information needs and "prescription" of procedures (or counseling), to be followed in meeting information needs; and the vital exercise of "screening," "criticism," and "feedback" functions, which concern both producers and consumers; as well as giving more attention to other special service needs, including media interpretation, translation, and abstracting.

In fulfilling these functions, the most important recent developments may be:

1. Those represented in library acquisition of computers.
2. Resource identification and sharing through electronic networking linkages.
3. Television-related services such as are represented in broadcast or interactive videotex systems and teletext.[6]

Needed today to manage such library media services are several well-established as well as some newer personnel categories, including specialists in communication analysis; production, packaging, and evaluation; systems designers and engineers; distributive program specialists; and a wide range of technicians.

Media Service Overview

Today, in most developed countries, leaders agree that the most important "nonprint" media services are computerized data bases and networks, microforms, and the telecommunication systems used to display and/or deliver them. In developing countries audiovisual media are regarded as the most important.

Among developed countries, the larger public libraries providing media service have usually departmentalized 16mm film service, recorded music and music archives, and oral history and speech collections; housed-microtext material by form, adjacent to serials or general reference areas; placed other material in special collections, dispersed as may be administratively convenient; and introduced computer service for users, first as adjuncts to management, planning, or business units, and later as "reader service" responsibilities. Media production service, apart from copy machine provision, is not normally available.

Smaller public libraries seek to share major resources through cooperative arrangements. Increasingly, libraries have generated computer-printed holdings catalogs.

Many school systems and academic libraries, notably in the United States, have established instructional media centers (IMCs), integrated media catalogs, and dispersed their collections to achieve optimally convenient storage and user access in study areas with "learning" carrels. Virtually all states issue school media program standards.

In January 1984 the American Association of School Librarians approved "Guidelines for School Library Media Education Programs." They call for personnel who have acquired specialized and demonstrated practical competencies in the selection and organization of material and in the use, production and management of all media required to meet educational needs.

Academic libraries access all types of microforms, which are frequently kept near periodical files. Computers are utilized to provide direct search service through separate use terminals. Online catalogs are emerging. Special libraries are oriented toward printed materials unless dedicated to other specific media, for example, films and various media combinations, or to subjects represented most importantly in particular nonprint media, such as music or drama. They do, however, now invest heavily in compressed information storage, research, and retrieval technologies and network participation agreements.

Developing countries exhibit uneven library growth patterns. Library-based nonbook service still exists in significant part only in unique collections. Among the least developed nations, unless they have an unusually aggressive national library program, nonbook service hardly exists at all. Indeed, even book-based service is minimal. Most of these nations look first to North America, Europe, and Australia for resources and leadership.

Although Japan has become a major producer of new instructional, information, and communication material and equipment, Japanese library initiatives do not yet appear to have greatly influenced developments elsewhere. Perhaps this is because of language differences, cultural goals, and Japan's recent opening up.

Finally, today, especially in the United States, United Kingdom, Canada, Australia, and Scandinavia, certain service programs incorporate the most advanced communication technology forms. In most developed countries, major libraries can now provide instantaneous access to an increasing number of rapidly expanding data banks via telecommunication networks.

Developing Country Aspirations

In marginal situations, for example, in Southeast Asian, African, and Latin American developing nations, most library media service programs are still limited to provision of simple photographs, slides, phonograph records or audio cassettes, a few maps and charts, and lending 16mm films. Yet, perhaps because of the greater need and awareness of it, certain of the least advantaged nations are among the most ambitious. Serious experimental attempts have been made to "leapfrog" the traditionally slow cultural improvement processes, as well as to enhance home public appreciation and international prestige for governments.

Such attempts have encouraged leading educators and information specialists in such countries to participate in local "glamor" technologies, such as space satellites, and to urge production of highly specialized, new public education slide-tape presentations, films, and videotapes as well as to create new distribution systems. Educational satellite projects such as the Satellite Instructional Television Experiment (SITE), India, Satellite Avançado das Commmunicasões Interdisciplinares—Brazil, 1972–1976 (Saci-Exern), the Indonesian domestic communication system, projected uses of the Palape Satellites Peacesat network inaugurated in 1971 to encourage teleconferencing in the Pacific area, and several U.S. Agency for International Development (USAID) rural development projects are planned or have already been launched recently.[7]

All of them involve significant potentials for library information storage, retrieval, and rapid long distance transfer service, as well as more direct instruction, for example, in "Open University" programs. Parenthetically, interest in such ventures is further stimulated by the rapidly growing presence in large cities, such as Jakarta, of commercial Video Tape Recorder (VTR) units and tapes.

There is an additional sign of changing times. Although unique among Association of South-East Asian Nations (ASEAN) libraries, in 1984 the Singapore National Library (SNL) began offering both teletext and VTR service, along with 7,000 books, 90 periodicals, tape/slide presentations, films, filmstrips and videocassettes, records and cassette tapes, 35mm transparencies, posters, and prints included in its Arts Resource Center.[8] In Brazil, Nigeria, India, the Phillipines, and Korea, new media programs have created an increasing demand for library personnel competent in the newer media.[9]

Current International Concerns

Librarians, especially those in developing countries, rely heavily for assistance on the Asia Foundation; British Council; U.S. Library of Congress; United Nations Educational, Scientific and Cultural Organization (UNESCO); USAID; World Bank; selected American, European, and Australian universities; sympathetic foreign colleagues; leading national libraries; and major national and international associations. Many libraries are hampered by the *lack* of international resource awareness aids, effective mutual agreements respecting media terminology use; service standards and optimal operating procedures; suitable copyright laws and practices; uninhibiting media import/export regulations; international resource-sharing mechanisms; cross-cultural media transfer studies; and research activity.

Given these needs, the probability of increasing international cooperation, and establishing more voluntary linkages into library "systems," it may be hoped that at least certain of the following activities will be actively supported in the future:

1. Frequent updating and wider distribution of comprehensive *international glossaries* of standard media terminology.

2. More regular preparation and publication of international *guides to significant media resources* and media management standards and practices.

3. Greater readiness to support *cataloging-at-source* (by the publisher).

4. Development of more workable and flexible *copyright conventions, bilateral treaties and multilateral agreements* needed to liberalize as well as continue protection for new media production and reproduction rights.

5. Identification and publication of technical standards on adaptation of foreign communication media and equipment.

6. Inauguration internationally of *improved media acquisition methods and systems* to ease and accelerate the deposit, purchases, loan, exchange, and use of shared-purchase arrangements, such as those proposed by the International Council for Educational Media, Paris (ICEM).

7. Co-sponsorship of more *research and experimentation* which anticipates international co-production of both "culture-free" and cross-cultural media.

8. A much broadened *international dissemination of technical and professional media journals.*

Some Unanswered Questions/Unresolved Issues

Respecting the establishment and operation of library media service programs, a number of questions remain:

1. Acknowledging the media's rising costs, what criteria should library budgets apply to accommodate these needs?

2. What administrative arrangements are best to administer library media departments, school-based IMCs, computer service units, microtext services, and so on? What facilities can be recommended?

3. What responsibility should libraries assume for distribution of unrecorded media such as live radio programs?

4. To what extent should media programs serve the handicapped, immigrants, and nonliterate groups known as the "underserved"?

Certain important issues remain unresolved:

1. To what extent should the functions suggested above be subdivided for *handling by different occupational groups and distribution agencies*?

2. Given suitably cost-conscious development, should it be agreed internationally that *library investments in new media programs* are judged most properly on the basis of unique media content presentation and distributive capacities, convenience of use, reaching powers (technological/psychological), user preferences, and physical availability, rather than on theoretical "alternative media" cost comparisons?

3. What practical steps may be initiated to encourage a greater *liberalization worldwide of library home loan versus on-site arrangements for newer media use?*

FORMAL MEDIA SERVICE PERSONNEL INSTRUCTION

The preservice professional education of library media service personnel is the responsibility of library schools and academic teaching departments, plus schools of education, information studies, computer science, and instructional technology. But whether these subjects are taught in separate courses or dispersed throughout curricula, in most developed countries there is a marked shift away from emphases given previously, that is, on films, slides, tapes, and so on, except in school library personnel courses. Formal library education is moving toward introducing more video products (tapes and disc), giving major attention to microcomputers (including accessories and software), introducing terminals for on-site use, and training computer users for data base search and networking functions.

What then are the most important new media-related knowledge and skills which should be taught, for example, to North American and British library school students? At Florida State University (as in most institutions queried), the answers of faculty representatives implied much use of lecture demonstrations and laboratory exercises with computers for data searching; visitation and field working experience in major computerized libraries to introduce their operation, management practice, policy and problems, and guided study in specialized course work.[10]

Florida State University regularly offered more than a half-dozen library school courses, for example, Information Science in Libraries, Computers in Libraries, Techniques and Management of On-Line Searching, Management of Library Non-Print Media, and Library Multi-Media Systems. In addition to an array of information science-related courses, the University of Wales offered "Audiovisual Studies for Libraries" which introduced in modular form a "core" program that first presented media soft- and hardware characteristics and later afforded opportunities for specialized study.

In the library schools of developing nations the situation was markedly different. At the University of Indonesia Department of Library Science, for example, which offered one optional undergraduate course in "Media Technology," the main topics stressed were audiovisual equipment familiarization, production of tapes, slides, and transparencies, and non-book media cataloging in accord with the *Anglo-American Cataloging Rules*. Some attention to media reference functions and information science was given in other University of Indonesia elective courses in documentation, data processing (emphasizing MARC records), and abstracting.

Where it does not simply represent the enthusiasms of individuals educated abroad or of donor agencies, library media education, which is offered in other ASEAN countries, Latin America, certain African nations, the Middle East, and Asia, appeared to be comprised of limited one- or two-course introductions to available media and some special training projects offered in association with other organizations.

At the MARA School of Library Science in Malaysia, however, one could also enroll in a series of optional courses on information storage and retrieval system functions and computer operations. At Sri Nakharinwirot University, Chulalongkorn and Thammassaet Universities in Thailand, as in Singapore, emphasis was given to information science aims, methods, technology, and resources.

In Singapore, a short, part-time "diploma-level" course on "Media Resources and Services" covered library media service roles; software and hardware characteristics, handling and use; service program organization, and simple material production. While audiovisual media were used widely in Latin America, a similar library education situation existed there.

The trends are clear. Whatever past practices may have been, although still not required of all, future librarians are expected to become media "literate." Most importantly, they are expected to address, as their primary professional interest, information science, communication technology, and computer system use.

Virtually all library schools provide at least some opportunities to study library automation, information storage, and retrieval functions. In varying degrees, they also introduce the basic approaches of systems analysis, programming, and interactive computer use. In ASEAN countries, continuing education programs feature information and computer technology and related administrative concerns.

The main patterns of media instruction worldwide are outlined later in this chapter. Two major patterns exist: as a separate course or courses, and as units within other courses. There are good arguments for following either approach. Content is the important element, and it can be organized either by topic *or* by competency. Choices must be made in relation to the nature of the curricula offered and teaching staff competencies.

Course Objectives

The paramount goal of traditional library curricula media components is to develop basic familiarity with a broad range of nonprint media. The media professional is expected to be able to undertake and properly supervise at least the following activities: describe unique roles which nonprint media play as information carriers; determine the media most appropriate to satisfy specific information needs; locate relevant media sources worldwide; use specific criteria to develop nonprint media collections; operate basic audiovisual equipment; produce simple graphic, photographic, and audio media; classify and catalog nonprint media; organize and manage nonprint media, and storage and circulation; and help others to select or produce and use media for specific activities.

Typical Assumptions

Since the time devoted to media education within most curricula is still minimal, most students acquire only rudimentary competencies. Specializations require study far beyond that outlined in this chapter. Properly trained technicians and paraprofessionals can often perform media operational tasks better than can librarians, but the librarian must have a basic knowledge of media and their uses.

The course outlines displayed below are based on nontechnical approaches. Where some technical knowledge/skills may be required, only a minimal amount is covered. Too often, general media courses are "catchalls" for media other than printed material. They usually omit detail on computers and microforms, which are often covered in separate courses.

Two specific generic outlines for library media study are presented later in this chapter. The first one has been organized by topic; the second lists competencies to be acquired. The authors' recommendations for internationalizing library media instruction have been advanced with general reference to these outlines.

Toward Internationalization

Media course internationalization has usually meant simply the extension of each topic to include ideas, sources, and approaches going beyond national borders. There are very few replacement materials to be recommended for special topics. Perhaps one critical element to be noted, however, is the global approach which can be followed by an instructor who, through example, reflects an international stance. Some believe that this one element can provide the best key to effective internationalization.

Conclusions

Library education worldwide is currently undergoing a major transition from simple familiarization and survey courses, which have introduced nonbook material and equipment, to the analysis and management of processes involving information storage, retrieval, and transfer functions. Major library education programs are seeking to make available—through formal classroom study, laboratory work, field experience, and participation in continuing education seminars—more opportunities to develop the specific competencies required to administer and use a broadening range of relatively new, chiefly electronic, ways and means of gathering, storing, searching, and delivering information.

Instruction

1. Media characteristics and their library use nomenclature
    1.1 Audio media—disc recordings, tape recordings
    1.2 Visual media—slides, filmstrips, photos, overhead transparencies
    1.3 Audiovisual media—videotape recordings, 8mm and 16mm motion pictures, slide or filmstrip/tapes
    1.4 Distribution systems—broadcast (including satellite), closed circuit (including cable)
    1.5 Computers (when feasible)—microcomputers and accessories
2. Major guides to and sources of media
    2.1. Producers
    2.2. Distributors
    2.3. Special media libraries
    2.4. Other agencies
        2.4.1 Government
        2.4.2 Private sector
        2.4.3 International organization
3. Evaluating and selecting nonprint media
    3.1 Developing and using criteria
    3.2 Using evaluation forms
    3.3 Organizing the evaluation process
    3.4 Published reviews
4. Evaluating and selecting audiovisual equipment
    4.1 Developing and using criteria
    4.2 Sources of equipment
    4.3 Published equipment descriptions and evaluations
5. Media procurement
    5.1 Standards
    5.2 Procedures/regulations/restrictions
6. Equipment operation (laboratory)
    6.1 Slide and filmstrip equipment
    6.2 Audio recorders
    6.3 Motion pricture equipment (including film splicing)
    6.4 Overhead and opaque projectors
    6.5 Microcomputers (basic keyboard operations)
7. Classifying and cataloging nonprint media (international standards)
8. Storing and maintaining nonprint media in libraries
9. Producing nonprint media (basic approaches/techniques)
    9.1 Planning audiovisual presentations; scripts and storyboards

   9.2 Simple graphics—lettering, layout, color, stick figures
   9.3 Photography—exteriors, interiors, copying
   9.4 Sound recording
   9.5 One-camera video
   9.6 Reprography
10. Organizing and administering library media service programs
   10.1 Functions, staffing
   10.2 Facilities
   10.3 Budgeting
11. Visual literacy
   11.1 Communicating with visual symbols and representations
   11.2 Cultural influence factors
12. Library application (International case studies)

Media Instruction (for selected competencies)

1. Selection/Evaluation
   1.1 Develops and applies criteria for evaluating and selecting a variety of material and equipment
   1.2 Establishes and administers processes for preview
   1.3 Uses review and evaluation tools to aid in selection
2. Design
   2.1 Considers alternative media formats and makes recommendations
3. Information retrieval
   3.1 Evaluates and establishes procedures for classifying and cataloging material and implements them
4. Instruction
   4.1 Instructs and supervises others in media design and production
   4.2 Develops learning programs to assist individuals to use media
5. Research
   5.1 Interprets research studies for media program development
6. Logistics
   6.1 Determines the most appropriate storage arrangements for all material and equipment
   6.2 Determines the most appropriate source for purchase or rental
   6.3 Inspects material and equipment to determine replacement, maintenance, and repair needs and makes appropriate arrangements
   6.4 Circulates media and equipment
   6.5 sets up and operates equipment
7. Production
   7.1 Develops and applies criteria when deciding whether to produce locally or to buy commercially available media
   7.2 Produces media for specialized objectives, including:
       7.2.1 Graphics (still photography, dry mounting, lettering)
       7.2.2 Sound (audio recording on discs, tapes, and cassettes)
       7.2.3 Videorecording (videotape—reel to reel, casette)
   7.3 Applies standards for evaluating locally produced media

   Note: These competencies come from several sources which advocate a competency-based education approach. Content and teaching techniques are derived from the behavior expected at the end of the education period. This is not a universally accepted approach, however.

RECENT SURVEY AND RESEARCH FINDINGS

Attempts to carry out international social science surveys are often fraught with problems. The informal survey undertaken for this chapter offers "indicators," but the findings show only the best information available to the authors. Two recent surveys touch on the subject.[11] Henry Ingle surveyed activities in forty-four countries to determine the status of information technologies as applied to education. Twenty-five countries responded, with fourteen indicating that they were applying computers to education, mostly in pilot projects. Of the remaining eleven, six mentioned video technology and five cited satellite communication use. Traditional audiovisual media were excluded from the survey.

Ann Irving's survey of fifty-six countries attempted to determine internationally relevant instructional material and research aimed at familiarizing school children with information concepts and skills.[12] The results were disappointing. Very few materials were fully described, and only a small proportion were considered internationally relevant. The bulk of identified material was produced in the United States, the United Kingdom, Australia, Scandinavia, and Canada.

For a more substantive look at media research, we must turn to educational media and technology research and cross-cultural use. Donald P. Ely reported on material developed for a North American context which was culturally translated for use in Iran and the Philippines, but not for Indonesia, The Netherlands, and Puerto Rico.[13] Insights gained from these uses offer guidelines for cross-cultural settings:

1. When material has been prepared for another audience in another culture and local participants must make their own translations, most people accept the differences as a challenge.

2. Participants would clearly prefer to have material in their own language and to use local examples.

3. Basic concepts and theories translate well. The examples and interpretations cause more difficulty.

4. A modest prestige element is felt among participants, especially in developing nations. Material from a more-developed culture carries some perceived value in that individuals who are going through an instructional development institute are receiving up-to-date information from an authoritative source.

Most media research has occurred in the developed nations. Current summaries of that research are helpful in assessing the state of the art.[14]

Wilbur Schramm's conclusion points the way for future research: "Students learn from any medium, in school or out, whether they intend to or not providing that the medium content leads them to pay attention to it."[15]

If any medium can be used effectively, than what questions should be addressed in selecting, using, and designing media for cross-cultural settings? Certian media seem to offer alternative and more effective communication than do conventional settings. After cost, availability, and user preference are considered, than the research questions should center on the qualitative aspects of media and the ways in which specific design elements are used.

Once objectives have been stated and a potential audience is defined, then questions about choice of optimum sensory stimuli, content density, pacing, redundancy, built-in responses, length, sound and optical effects, live/animated representation, photography versus graphic art, and other variables can be considered. If no one medium is best, the producer and user must determine the media design and use to achieve specific purposes with specific audiences.

Research would be helpful if producers and users knew audience predispositions toward one medium or another; the extent to which experience with a given medium is a determinant of its effective use; the extent of dissonance when media content is presented from the viewpoint of other cultures; and the extent to which attitudes toward a given medium (and its content and message design) affect learning and the attainment of cognitive objectives. Other questions are as follows: what qualities permit a medium to stand on its own without external assistance? Are certain mediated conventions universally understood? What are the ways in which audience response can be built in when such participation is desirable?

It may be a long time before research findings become available which help to answer certain of these questions. Meanwhile, certain indicators from existing research and observations may guide cross-cultural media designs:

1. Examples must show local personnel. Credibility is the issue. Individuals are unlikely to accept environments different from their own; such environments are dismissed as irrelevant or inappropriate.

2. The pacing of instruction must be consistent with local norms. The media assume a delivery rate that can be handled by average learners. Average learners in one culture usually do not equal average learners in another. One of the best ways to facilitate pacing is through multimedia redundancy. The same message presented by several media can greatly enchance learning.

3. Material must be carefully reviewed for cultural bias.

4. Material that calls for learner participation must prepare the individual for

this behavior, which is uncommon in many nations. Actually showing individual participation in a group serves as a model.

5. Live action motion is significantly better than animation.

6. There is no difference between color and black and white material when measured by learning effectiveness.

INTERNATIONALIZING LIBRARY MEDIA STUDIES

Instructional Goals

Each nation must depend increasingly on others to obtain important information. Indeed, one characteristic of national underdevelopment today is information deprivation. Knowledge is truly power, and specialists who effectively organize and make available information appropriately are required in every country. One continuing concern of Third World research and development is the need to provide access to educational opportunities and information.

During the past twenty years World Bank loans have been shifted from the support of infrastructural needs to meeting more "software" needs such as curriculum development, making more books available in schools, and supporting nonformal literacy programs. In this environment information plays a vital role. Those who handle it best, in all of its forms, are internationally oriented information specialists.

How is information to be approached internationally? Behind all techniques are substantive needs in virtually all fields. These needs have engendered a further need to broaden the concept of existing information agencies and institutions. Rather than think of a library as a place, perhaps it is most useful to think of it simply as one part of a system through which information may be collected from all parts of the world, organized for easy access, stored efficiently, retrieved accurately and quickly, and made available to users in appropriate formats.

Information service conceived so broadly must be truly international in concern and operation. Professional education courses reflecting this breadth of concern will be needed by those who one day will plan and manage international information service.

Even within one's own country, to achieve a proper cross-cultural stance librarians should begin this work "close to home." The need and potential for cross-cultural communication at home are broadly evident among ethnic minorities and immigrants, language groups, and the numerous cultural organizations. By meeting their needs and drawing on their diverse resources, it is possible to build up "at home" local, national, and even internationally significant network information services. This means expanding both the resources and services available.

The recommendations advanced below have been written with such

possibilities and capabilities in mind. Information service internationalization is no longer an option but a requirement for national integrity
and survival.

Basic Content Concerns

Library education media courses take a variety of shapes and forms:
media as storage vehicles and as delivery systems. No single course pattern has emerged, yet there is a consciousness and acceptance which
indicates continuation of media content in most library education
curricula.

When one contemplates the internationalization of such diverse approaches, it is difficult to present straightforward guidelines to fit all
circumstances. There seems to be, however, a series of recommendations
that might lead to a rational approach. The recommendations that follow
offer an agenda of unfinished business which should be pursued.

Respecting Definitions and Terminology

The deliberate ambiguity of the terms used in this chapter points up
the ambivalence of media people—audiovisual material, newer media,
nonprint media, nonbook resources, and so on. One of the surest ways
of facilitating communication is by agreement on terms and definitions.
A multilingual media term glossary would go far to facilitate consistent
terminology, but these terms must have conceptual definitions which
agree as well. Beyond standard terms and definitions is the need for
agreement on the field's scope.

Storage versus Delivery Media

Historically, libraries have been concerned with storing information.
Indeed, the book is the paramount example. This mindset will probably
continue as long as there are libraries. But the newer media are more
oriented to delivery, and librarians recognize the need to provide an
end product.

In any case the user cares only that the required document is delivered
in timely fashion. Information centers currently interested in cable television systems, electronic networks, online data base searching, and
other new technologies seem to focus more on delivery than on storage.
Probably this means that information service personnel must know how
to use these technologies but will not be involved with engineering
aspects.

New Competencies Requisite

As the functions of information professionals change, so must academic programs prepare for new times and assist incumbents to update knowledge. Lists of needed media competencies must be adapted for the "generalist" librarian who needs only "core" knowledge. Agreement on minimal media competencies is a better way to plan a course than simply to survey the trends or analyze new publication content.

A corollary issue relates to the extent to which media competencies ought to be acquired in library education programs if they can be obtained elsewhere. The thrust of this chapter causes one to ask if media competencies are universal, that is, international. Are there minimal competencies that should be expected worldwide?

Better Data Needed

It is difficult to discuss the library media's use of international dimensions with insufficient data. There appears to be little systematic data-gathering activity on media location, extent, and use in libraries. Neither individual countries nor international organizations seem to be collecting and reporting these data regularly. Developed countries are more likely to have these data than developing nations. Without such information, assumptions made or inferences drawn are often unwarranted.

Media Course Instructors

Responsibility for internationalizing media courses rests with their instructors. The instructor sets the tone for a course. If the course is international, then international concepts will permeate it. In any case, a course's international environment can probably be communicated most effectively by instructors who have worked abroad.

Knowledge about the international aspects of the media field falls into several categories: technical (country standards, international standards, and protocols); legal (copyright laws, import-export policies); and resource availability (what media are available from which international sources). There is no substitute for well-informed teaching personnel who not only have had experience but also know where to get information.

Case Studies

If any internationalized media course case studies exist, the authors were unable to find them. One source of help for planning new courses is the experience of others. Models offer starting places for new efforts.

The FID Clearinghouse at Syracuse University offers one mechanism for handling such information. Perhaps it can be encouraged to collect more case studies.

Study-Specific Recommendations

UNESCO personnel have striven actively to encourage three aspects of internationalizing library education: professional, cultural, and political.[16] Approaches have involved developing individual and association contacts and conducting joint projects with practitioners. Many bilateral conferences and programs involving national library development have been actively promoted. Library schools in many nations owe their origins in part to UNESCO's encouragement. UNESCO has given support to international survey work aimed at promoting standardization and upgrading service.

UNESCO's efforts have done much to revamp library education programs, with attention to sophisticated information handling in all formats and to introducing related computer techniques. UNESCO's continuing thrusts, especially among developing nations, have probably stimulated more concern for middle internationalization (and, indeed, for all library education) courses than have other international pressures.

The authors believe that virtually all library personnel today need some nonprint media orientation; that, excepting perhaps for school librarians, nonprint courses should not be oriented to particular types of libraries; that nonprint cataloging modes should generally be taught in basic or "core" courses; that a nonprint media laboratory is essential; that library education courses should reflect nonprint media service requirements; and that specific media education should be offered to all library personnel levels.[17]

These programs are justified on the grounds that all library staff who are expected to help users gather useful information must check information sources available internationally and become familiar with library practice elsewhere, especially in scientific and technical development areas. Anything less than global cognizance and a capacity to access information worldwide is now insufficient to support significant study, research, or management functions in any field.

Attaining the educational objectives implicit in the "internationalization" needs suggested requires that formal library media instruction, centralized or decentralized, assure the following:

1. Panoramic introductions to (a) the nature and operation of all new library media available and their technical possibilities for interface; (b) media reference and information availability worldwide, major network service and optimal library arrangements for new media organization, storage, preser-

vation, and use; (c) government and legal arrangements, for example, involving international treaties, procurement regulations, and copyright rules; (d) national characteristics of media production and presentation for films and television/cultural variations; and (e) basic production techniques for simple audiovisual media, for example, slide-tape presentations and overlay transparencies.

2. Development of at least a minimum level of "computer literacy."

3. A developing knowledge of new media terminology and of English and other foreign languages requisite for new media cataloging, searches, and so on.

4. Cultivation of the capacities needed to adapt and utilize effectively foreign media in terms of local expectations as well as to benefit from, interpret, and apply international standards to library media service program development.

A PARTIAL SUMMARY OF COURSE CONTENT RECOMMENDATIONS

The following is a very brief summary of selected recommendations implicit or advanced to internationalize media instruction:

1. Give particular attention to services offered and anticipated by libraries which involve *uses of computers*.

2. Explain the ways in which broadcast and wired *television-related services* may be utilized (including satellite communication).

3. Review the present and future nature of important *network services* and arrangements for library linkages.

4. Introduce, using practical and appropriate *laboratory facilities and techniques*, the various types of nonprint media and media presentation equipment now available, and locally relevant production/distribution methods.

5. Acquaint students with *primary reference tools* available which describe audiovisual media produced abroad and with the processes/conventions that pertain to their procurement.

6. Acquaint students with internationally recognized *cataloging/classification systems* now utilized for nonbook media.

7. Introduce known cultural *differences/characteristics* which influence the content of foreign material and their use.

8. Ensure that students become familiar with media *terminologies* and the best current glossaries and textbooks.

9. Familiarize students with significant *technical standards and limitations* (including costs) which will affect the local use (and/or adaptations) of foreign communication media and equipment.

10. Encourage media instruction, tailored appropriately for local situations, to develop very *specific competencies*.

11. Acquaint students (in appropriate terms) with the types of *media research* that bear on library service responsibilities.

12. Stress media as parts of a *total communication continuum* and not as separate entities; stress *multimedia interests/approaches.*

13. Give all students *"hands-on" experience with a minicomputer* and with principles underlining computer programming.

14. Review *services afforded to the media field* by various bilateral and international organizations such as UNESCO.

15. Encourage *language capability* development for efficient location, consultation, and home use of foreign media resources.

16. Where feasible/appropriate, *develop media instruction programs in partnerships* with local education schools/departments, communication instruction, and service programs.

17. Avoid imitating media instruction offered elsewhere except as relevant to local student needs and learning readiness.

18. Provide all students with a basic familiarization with *media selection, acquisition, storage, conservation and handling methods and techniques/facilities; hardware operations/maintenance procedures; organization/administration* of media service functions and *local library production/use/training for media use.*

19. Give interested students suitable opportunities for individual or small-group, special *project development* (e.g., planning a full media service program for a given library; local production of a multimedia presentation).

20. Seek to develop in students *a philosophy of library media service* as simply one aspect of the primary professional responsibility and an understanding that full library service can no longer be given properly anywhere without knowing and utilizing all types of information/recorded knowledge resources available from abroad as well as locally.

NOTES

1. "IFLA and Audiovisual Materials," *IFLA Journal* 7, No. 4 (1981), p. 331.

2. Personal letter from Anthony Thompson to C. W. Stone, March 5, 1984.

3. Personal letter from Patrick Penland to C. W. Stone, February 29, 1984.

4. *The Library in the Information Revolution* (Proceedings, Sixth Congress of Southern-Asia Librarians, Singapore, May 30 - June 3, 1983).

5. C. Walter Stone, "The Library Function Redefined," *Library Trends* 16 (October 1967), pp. 181–196.

6. Videotex is a generic term referring to any electronic system that makes computer-based information available via video display units to a dispersed and reasonably numerous audience.

7. *Learning at a Distance and the New Technology* (Vancouver, B.C.: Educational Research Institute of British Columbia, 1982), pp. 39–40.

8. During an interview on March 27, 1984, Mrs. Hedwig Anuar, Director, Singapore National Library, reviewed the present status of the Arts Center Project.

9. *Education and Training in Developed and Developing Countries; With Particular Attention to the ASEAN Region* (Papers presented at the International Federation

for Documentation [FID]/ET Workshop in Kowloon, Hong Kong, September 6–9, 1982.

10. Personal letter from Harold Goldstein to C. W. Stone, March 8, 1984.

11. Henry Ingle, "Preliminary Report of the New Information Technologies in Education"; *Educational Media International*, No. 1, 1983, pp. 3–7; and Ann Irving, ed., *Instructional Materials for Developing Information Concepts and Information-Handling Skills in Schoolchildren* (Paris: UNESCO, 1981).

12. Ann Irving, ed., *Instructional Materials for Developing Information Concepts and Information-Handling Skills in Schoolchildren: An International Study* (Paris: UNESCO, 1981), ERIC Document No. Ed 226 758 (microfiche only).

13. Donald P. Ely, "The Use of Educational Communication Media in Different Cultures," *Educational Media International*, No. 1, 1983.

14. R. E. Clark, "Reconsidering Research on Learning from Media," *Review of Educational Research* 53 (Winter 1983), pp. 445–459; P. Cohen, "A Media-analysis of Outcome Studies of Visual Based Instruction," *Educational Communications and Technology Journal* 29, No. 1 (1981), pp. 26–36; V. S. Gerlach, "Research" in J. W. Brown, *Trends in Instructional Technology* (Syracuse, N.Y.: ERIC Clearinghouse on Information Resources, 1984); D. J. Hesselgrave, "Dimensions of Cross Cultural Communications," *Practical Anthropology* 19, No. 1 (1972), pp. 25–34; R. A. Reiser, "Characteristics of Media Selection Models," *Review of Educational Research* 52 (Winter 1982), pp. 499–512; and Wilbur Schramm, *Big Media, Little Media* (Beverly Hills, Calif.: Sage, 1977), p. 267.

15. Wilbur Schramm, *Big Media, Little Media* (Beverly Hills, Calif.: Sage, 1977), p. 267.

16. M. Keresztesi, "UNESCO's Work in the Field of Library Education and Training: An Overview and Assessment," *International Library Review* 14 (October 1982), pp. 349–361.

17. Herbert L. Trotten has frequently expressed disappointment in the slowness of library media service development, for example, "Library Education and Non-Print Media: Where It's At," in Deidre Boyle, *Expanding Media* (Phoenix: Oryx Press, 1977), pp. 259–267.

BIBLIOGRAPHY

Baker, D. P. *The Library Media Program in the School.* Littleton, Colo.: Libraries Unlimited, 1983.

Brown, James W., and Shirley N. Brown, eds. *Educational Media Yearbook.* Littleton, Colo.: Libraries Unlimited, 1983.

Chisholm, Margaret, ed. *Reader in Media, Technology, and Libraries.* Englewood, Colo.: Microcard Editions Book, 1975, 530 pp.

Davies, Ruth Ann. *The School Library Media Program.* New York: R. R. Bowker, Co., 1979.

Eisenberg, Michael. *The Direct Use of Online Bibliographic Information Systems by Untrained End Users: A Review of Research.* Syracuse, N.Y.: ERIC Clearinghouse on Information Resources, 1983.

Fothergill, Richard. *Non-Book Materials in Libraries.* London: Bingley, 1984.

Griffiths, Jose-Marie. "Application of Minicomputers and Microcomputers to

Information Handling." Alexandria, Va.: Educational Document Reproduction Service, 1981.

Meadows, A. J., and M. Gordon Singleton. *A Dictionary of the New Information Technology*. London: Kogan Page, 1982.

Merrill, Irving R. *Criteria for Planning The College and University Learning Resources Center*. Washington, D.C.: Association for Educational Communications and Technology, 1977.

Rosenberg, Kenyon. *Dictionary of Library and Educational Technology*. Littleton, Colo.: Libraries Unlimited, 1983.

Voight, Melvin J., ed. *Advances in Librarianship*. New York: Academic Press, 1975, Vol. 5, entire volume.

Wilkinson, Gene H. *Media in Instruction: 60 Years of Research*. Washington, D.C.: Association for Educational Communications and Technology, 1980.

INFORMATION SOURCES

Aaron, Shirley L., Professor, School of Library and Information Studies, Florida State University, Tallahassee, Florida, USA

Anuar, Hedwig, Director, National Library, Singapore

Chisholm, Margaret E., Dean, School of Library and Information Science, University of Washington, Seattle, Washington, USA

Dosa, Marta, Professor, School of Information Studies, Syracuse University, Syracuse, New York, USA

Garrison, Guy, Dean, College of Information Studies, Drexel University, Philadelphia, Pennsylvania, USA

Goldstein, Harold, Dean, School of Library and Information Studies, Florida State University, Tallahassee, Florida, USA

Hammer, Donald P., Executive Director, Library and Information Technology Association, American Library Association, Chicago, Illinois, USA

Henry, Carol, International Federation of Library Associations and Institutions, The Hague, The Netherlands

Higgins, Norman, Professor, Department of Educational Technology and Library Science, Arizona State University, Tempe, Arizona, USA

Hogg, Frank N., Principal, College of Librarianship, University of Wales, Aberystwyth, United Kingdom

Horrocks, Norman, Director, School of Library Service, Dalhousie University, Halifax, Nova Scotia, Canada

Kalangie, A.A.M., Lecturer, University of Indonesia, Jakarta, Indonesia

Kurihara, Hitosshi, Secretary General, Japan Library Association, Tokyo, Japan

Lane, Nancy, Head, Department of Library Science, College of Advanced Education, Canberra, Australia

Lee, Bosco Wen R., Lecturer, National Taiwan University, Taipei

Loh, Alice, Reference Librarian, National Library, Singapore

Lowrie, Jean, Dean Emeritus, School of Librarianship, Western Michigan University, Kalamazoo, Michigan, USA

Myers, Margaret, Director, Office for Library Personnel Resources, American Library Association, Chicago, Illinois, USA

Penland, Patrick R., Professor of Education and Library Science, University of Pittsburgh, Pittsburgh, Pennsylvania, USA

Phillips, Janet, Association of Library and Information Science Education, State College, Pennsylvania, USA

Prakoso, Mastini Hardjo, Director, National Library, Jakarta, Indonesia

Royani, H. A., Lecturer, University of Indonesia, Jakarta, Indonesia

Soekarman, Director, Center for Indonesian Library Development, Jakarta, Indonesia

Somadikart, Lili, Head, Department of Library Science, Faculty of Letters, University of Indonesia, Jakarta, Indonesia

Thompson, Anthony Hugh, Senior Lecturer, College of Librarianship, University of Wales, Aberystwyth, United Kingdom

APPENDIX: MEDIA COURSE OUTLINES

Presented below are several outlines of library-related media courses currently being offered in various parts of the world.

UNIVERSITY OF SINGAPORE
POSTGRADUATE DIPLOMA COURSE III
LIBRARY AND INFORMATION SCIENCE (PART-TIME) 1982/83 SESSION
COURSE 209: MEDIA RESOURCES AND SERVICES

A. *Introduction*

The librarian is concerned primarily with information and its dissemination to the user. To be effective, the librarian must combine traditional printed information sources with an increasing range of audiovisual material, many of which require specialized facilities and equipment. The course is intended to provide an appreciation of audiovisual materials and their value in library users, to complement the students' knowledge of printed and other sources of information, and to give students a specialized knowledge to help them in developing and organizing multimedia collections.

B. *Syllabus*

1. The future role of the library
   a. Visual, aural, and print literacy
   b. Values of audiovisual material in libraries
2. The characteristics and implications of audiovisual materials and equipment; their physical control and exploitation.
   Materials—"software"
   a. General notes on storage and handling
   b. The range of media likely to be found in libraries
      (1) Physical format—standardization
      (2) Production details
      (3) Type of information carried
      (4) Handling, including preparation for library use
      (5) Storage
      (6) Conservation
      (7) Reproduction

(8) Library use

Media equipment—"hardware"

  c. Selection and maintenance

  d. Examination of equipment appropriate to each software type

    (1) Physical description—standardization

    (2) How it works (brief, nontechnical)

    (3) Use in the library context

    (4) Operational instructions

    (5) Maintenance

3. Organizing multimedia developments in libraries

  a. Attitudes to multimedia material

  b. Rationalization

  c. Exploitation

  d. Staff education and training

  e. User education and training

  f. Production, including Media Production Services, their role, development, and integration

  g. Physical planning

    (1) General (space, access, lighting temperature, and humidity

    (2) User facilities

    (3) Staff facilities

    (4) Building

    (5) Security

4. The librarian as producer. The need to produce audiovisual programs to fulfill a variety of educational needs

  a. The need for audiovisual programs

  b. Suitable audiovisual formats for inhouse production

  c. Program planning and production

  d. Presentation of audiovisual programs

UNIVERSITY OF WALES PG (XX), 1980: AUDIOVISUAL STUDIES FOR LIBRARIANS

The librarian is concerned primarily with information and its dissemination to the user. To be effective, the librarian must combine traditional printed and other sources of information with an increasing range of audiovisual materials, many of which require specialized processing, facilities, and equipment. The course begins with a core module, intended to provide an appreciation of audiovisual materials and their value to library users and to complement the students' knowledge of printed and other sources of information gained elsewhere in the postgraduate program. It is followed by a further study (chosen from either modules 2a or 2b listed below) intended to give students a specialized knowledge to help them in the development and organization of multimedia collections.

Module 1 Core study (Taken by all students in term 1)

    A study of characteristics and the implications of audiovisual materials and equipment; their physical control and exploitation in libraries. Practical workshop sessions are used to ensure familiarity with materials and equipment.

1. Media materials—"software"
   a. General notes on storage and handling
   b. A description of the range of media likely to be found in libraries and an examination of each one
      (1) Physical format—standardization
      (2) Production details in brief
      (3) Type of information carried
      (4) Handling, including preparation for library use
      (5) Storage
      (6) Conservation
      (7) Reproduction details in brief
      (8) Library uses
2. Media equipment—"hardware"
   a. Selection and evaluation—hardware advisory services
   b. An examination of equipment appropriate to each type of software, under the following headings
      (1) Physical description—standardization
      (2) How it works (brief, nontechnical)
      (3) Use in the library context
      (4) Operational instructions
      (5) Maintenance
      (6) Practical exercises for familiarization
   Sections 1 and 2 run concurrently.
3. Organized media development in libraries
   a. Needs and objectives—priorities—proportions
   b. User education
      (1) Staff education and training
      (2) User education
   c. Physical access to and exploitation of information
      (1) Browsable/nonbrowsable/integration
      (2) Loan
      (3) Presentation—individual and group
   d. Current and future developments
      (1) Roles of national organizations in the United Kingdom.
      (2) Technical developments

Module 2   Specialist studies (Students take ONE of the following in terms 2 and 3)

Module 2(a)   Aspects of Media Technology

Examines the means by which librarians can produce their own programs to fulfill a variety of library and educational needs. Consideration is given to the role, development, and integration of media production services in libraries of various kinds, and the provision of the specialized facilities necessary to allow users to consult audiovisual documents.

Workshop sessions familiarize the students with the practical production of audiovisual programs.

Course work in the production of an original audiovisual program.

1. The production and use of multimedia materials in the library.

2. Production methods for
   (a) Slides
   (b) Audio recordings
   (c) Tape-slide programs
   (d) Video programs
   (e) Overhead transparencics
3. Media Production Services, their role, development, and integration.
4. Planning implications
   a. Standards
   b. Planning requirements
      (1) Departmental/Centralized
      (2) General (space, lighting, etc.)
      (3) User facilities
      (4) Staff facilities
      (5) New buildings
5. Presentation methods
6. Exhibition of student projects

FLORIDA STATE UNIVERSITY
SCHOOL OF LIBRARY SCIENCE (SLS)
MANAGEMENT OF LIBRARY NONPRINT MEDIA
(2 Semester Hours)

Prerequisite: SLS Core Experience and Media Thread or undergraduate courses

Catalog Description: Theories and practices in organizing audiovisual resources and services in libraries

Course Objectives: Upon completion of this course, students should be able to do the following:

1. Use the audiovisual copyright rules and apply them to real-life situations.
2. Understand basic audiovisual organization premises and use.
3. Select from the various alternatives for organizing multimedia and apply them to various library settings.
4. Plan and design effective multimedia facilities as an integral part of the library.
5. Evaluate audiovisual programs as the basis for future planning.

Course Outline

I. Theories of multimedia organization

A. Integrated shelving
B. Organizing equipment systems

II. Basic premises of media services

A. Theories of multimedia utilization
B. Studies supporting nonprint media services

III. Copyright laws

A. Background of copyright for multimedia
B. Current laws
C. Application of copyright laws

IV. Planning and designing multimedia facilities

A. Background of current situation
B. Integrating multimedia facilities in libraries
C. Study of special areas
  1. Production labs
  2. Dark rooms
  3. Listening-viewing areas
  4. Television production and editing areas

V. Evaluation of library audiovisual systems

A. Methods used to evaluate audiovisual systems
B. Examination of new multimedia materials and equipment

21
GOVERNMENT PUBLICATION COURSES

Tze-chung Li

A government publication has been defined as "informational matter which is published as an individual document at government expense or as required by law."[1] Accordingly, any work published either by government authorization or expense is a government publication. Such publications cover all fields of human knowledge in different forms and for all walks of life. Certain of them have great reference value and are found in many libraries.

Librarians must possess the skill to use government publications effectively. National government publications refer to those of a native country; international government publications to those of international or supernational organizations, such as the United Nations (UN); and foreign government publications to publications of one or more foreign countries.

Most library schools include study of government publications in the curriculum. These publications are covered in the basic reference and bibliography course and in subject reference courses, such as those in the humanities, social sciences, science, and technology. A typical American reference and bibliography course includes government publication bibliographies and a few government information sources of high reference value.

The University of Illinois at Urbana was perhaps the first institution that offered a separate government publication course, in 1901. Worldwide course coverage has been developed in many schools, yet separate course development for international and foreign publications remains stagnant. Traditional library education aims at educating librarians for work within the country. In the United States, only two library schools claim to educate librarians at the international level—Hawaii and Pittsburgh.

Presently, a separate government publications course is offered in all accredited U.S. library schools, except one, but course coverage of international and foreign publications varies, as shown in Table 21.1.

Table 21.1
Coverage in U.S. Library School Government Publication Courses

Courses	Number of Schools	Percent
U.S. publications only	10	16
U.S. and international publications	20	33
U.S. international and foreign publications	27	44
U.S. and international/foreign separate courses	4	7
Totals	61	100

Source: Library school catalogs

Of the schools, twenty-seven or 44 percent offered courses which covered U.S., international, and foreign government publications. However, the foreign government publication coverage ranged from 18 percent to 30 percent in these courses. Foreign and international publications were often covered in a few weeks at the end of the single documents course—if there was time—and, in general, 80 percent of the course was devoted to U.S. publications. Only four schools offered separate and specialized courses: one for the United States and the other three devoted exclusively to international and foreign publications.

International and foreign government documents may be referred to in the comparative and international librarianship and the area bibliography courses. Twenty-seven U.S. schools offered one of these courses. It must be noted, however, that foreign and international government publications were only slightly touched on in most of these courses.

The international and comparative librarianship courses stressed types of libraries and library functions and services, not information source use. The area bibliography courses dealt with the selection, evaluation, and acquisition of area material by nation and subject, bibliographies, and managerial aspects of handling and organizing such material.[2] Coverage of foreign documents was limited, and international publications were rarely discussed.

In developing a progrm with balanced coverage of national, international, and foreign government publications, the following questions must be given proper consideration: How are the courses structured? Are separate courses necessary to cover all three types of publications? If so, can the courses be structured on similar patterns? What topics should be included in each course? What are the major difficulties in conducting one or more courses in three areas? What qualifications are needed to teach these courses?

COURSE STRUCTURE

The course program requires a carefully made design to acquaint students with (1) government organization and functions, (2) major publications and types of information sources, (3) selection and acquisition of government publications, (4) publication management, and (5) effective use. Effective use of government publications calls for a large percentage of time devoted to government structure and functions and to information and bibliographic sources.

A serious problem in government publication courses in many countries is inadequate bibliographic control of the sources. This is particularly felt in a course covering foreign publications. A review of government publication publishing in twenty countries and areas stated that fourteen provided some sort of current bibliography, and of the fourteen, nine had no extensive bibliography. The best bibliographical control of foreign government sources has been done in English. A bibliography of bibliographies of foreign government documents and a bibliography of government organization manuals are available.[3] Other titles cover other non-U.S. government publications.[4]

On current sources, the following periodicals are worth noting: *Government Publications Review, International Journal of Legal Information*, and *Government Information Quarterly*, all in English. The lack of adequate bibliographic control of sources in other languages is a major drawback to developing a foreign government publication course for most non-English-speaking countries.

Because the course in national government publications is well developed in American library schools, the course structure for national government publications can serve as a model for developing courses in national, international, and foreign publications. In general, the national government publication course studies the depository system, the official classification scheme, selection and acquisition, bibliographic control, and selected publications with stress on use. Four features of U.S. government publications are particularly important for comparative study.

First, the bibliographic control of U.S. government publications forms an unbroken chain from Poore, Ames, and the *Document Catalog* to the current *Monthy Catalog* and supplements. The *Monthly Catalog*, published since 1895, is the most important single tool for finding government publications during any specific month. In 1975 the *Monthly Catalog* began to use the *Anglo-American Cataloging Rules* and Library of Congress main entries, a welcome enhancement. Added access to many government publications is provided by *Monthly Catalog* supplements.

Second, U.S. government publication arrangement features the U.S. Superintendent of Documents classification scheme which consists of two categories separated by a colon: (1) class stem, a number assigned to an agency or author followed by a series number, and (2) an alphanumerical book number. The main SuDoc scheme problem is that government publications are not classified by subject; publications belonging to the same subject are scattered. Since arrangement is by issuing agency, because of change of subordination and names, the publications of certain agencies could be listed in more than one place. The *Monthly Catalog* must be used for subject access to government publications.

In the third place, many American libraries are designated by law as depositories. They receive government publications free of charge but are obligated to make them available for free use by the general public and not to dispose of them without authorization. All depository libraries now receive publications on a selective basis. They are permitted to receive one copy of any publication except as otherwise stipulated. Selection of at least 25 percent of the available item numbers on the *Classified List* is suggested as the minimum number necessary to undertake a depository library's role. The depository system is an effective means to encourage government information and publication dissemination.

Fourth, many U.S. government documents are also available as commercial publications. One such publisher is Congressional Information Service, Inc., which has published government publications in microfiche form. In law, most documents are published in different formats by commercial firms. The West Publishing Company, the Lawyers Cooperative, and Prentice-Hall, Inc., are among the larger law publishers. Their publications are better arranged than government documents and have other enhancements.

To study government publications as information sources, there are three common approaches: by agency, subject, or form. Study by agency is generally preferred. Publications are divided according to legislative, executive, and judicial branches of the government and under the executive, further divided by department and section or office in the United States.[5,6] Grouping publications by government functions into three branches is the most common course structure, with independent agencies often forming an additional unit. Publication study by form and by subject may be added, but the course is rarely taught by subject.

Government publication study by form is common because certain publications require special handling and training for use. Examples are maps, looseleaf services, law citations, and data bases. Data base use, also called online searching or computer-assisted reference service, has grown rapidly since its introduction in the early 1970s.

Many reference tools are available online, such as *Public Affairs Information Service Bulletin*, *Current Index to Journals in Education*, and *Resources in Education*. In law, LEXIS is the first data base with full-text information, and WESTLAW is produced by the West Publishing Company. Recently, the *Monthly Catalog* has become available online. Data base use must be considered an important part of any government publication course.

COURSE COVERAGE

National Government Publications

Effective government publication use requires that students familiarize themselves with government structure and functions and the legislative process. Adelaide E. Hasse considered government documents study to be the study of modern government as exposed in its publications.[7] However, in American courses government organization and functions are as a rule only slightly touched on or remain untouched.

Foreign Government Publications

As indicated by comparative and international librarianship course description, the scope of study is too broad for analysis in only one or two semesters. Simsova and Jackson are too extensive for single course coverage.[8] In comparative and international librarianship, study by region is a common approach. Yet, these approaches are far from manageable in terms of resources and bibliographic coverage.

In political science, the discipline of foreign or comparative government deals, as a matter of general practice, with major powers. Study is confined to different major political systems, such as the parliamentary, presidential, and communist systems as represented by Great Britain, the United States, and the Soviet Union, respectively, simply because their influence has been substantial.

The study of foreign law generally refers to the study of major legal systems, such as the civil law systems in France and Germany and the common law system in Great Britain and the United States. The influence of major legal systems has transcended national boundaries. The course in comparative government or law may provide guidelines for developing a foreign government publications course. The course should be limited to publications of major powers or countries by political and economic ideologies, such as nonaligned and socialist countries.

International Government Publications

A course in international government publications should cover three main areas: (1) the organization and functions of the UN system, the specialized agencies, and other intergovernmental organizations, (2) the UN depository system and the classification scheme of symbol series, and (3) effective publication use. Effective use requires thorough understanding of intergovernmental organizations. As the first advanced course in international documentation held in Geneva in 1972, one of the course objectives was to teach the essential functions of the UN family within the international political system.

There is no shortage of bibliographies on intergovernmental publications, so UN publications have been covered since 1946 in the *Check List, United Nations Documents Index* (UNDI), *UNDEX, International Bibliography, Information, Documentation*, and publication catalogs, including the *UNIPUB Bulletin*.[9] Published guides on how to use international government publications include Brenda Brimmer, a modern classic that is dated but still useful.[10]

For the international government publication course, the organization and function of the UN, the specialized agencies, and regional organizations, such as the North Atlantic Treaty Organization, the Organization of American States, and the European Community could be studied. Publications can be arranged for study by agency. For instance, UN publications may be structured by the General Assembly, the Security Council, the Economic and Social Council, the Trusteeship Council, the International Court of Justice, the Secretariat, and other subsidiary organs.

The Faculty

Ideally, a government publication instructor must not only be well versed in the publications but also have good knowledge of governmental structure, knowledge acquired by completing at least three government courses, including National and Comparative Governments and International Organizations.

A clear understanding of government structure and functions is helpful to answer questions such as: How does a bill become a law? What is UNESCO's relationship with the UN? Do differences exist between government and nongovernment publications in the socialist countries? Does an executive agreement have the same legal effect as a treaty? Why is the compilation of treaties by the UN extensive and in some cases exhaustive? Some knowledge of the legal system will be helpful in using court reports, in tracing the history of a law, and in finding citations to law and court reports.

In teaching foreign government publications, some knowledge of each national language is essential. Nearly all national government publications are published in the country's official language. As described by the American course listings, most courses with foreign coverage are limited to British, Canadian, and Australian government publications. Obviously, such an approach is the result of a severe language limitation.

The area-study field faces the same problem. Lack of language competence is one of the factors limiting the number of area subject specialist preparation programs offered by library schools. Effective use of foreign government publication requires understanding of the country's government organization, political ideology, and legal system. Unfortunately, in the United States an instructor who is well versed in the publications and the political and legal systems and is fluent in several languages is rare. The number of U.S. students who can read several languages is even smaller.

COURSE OUTLINES

An effective program with fair coverage of national, international, and foreign government publications requires three separate courses, one for each area. Below are suggested outlines of the three courses, each for one semester. Emphasis is placed on effective government publications use. Publications are arranged by agencies, and, when suitable, by form and subject as well. The foreign government publication course is limited to Great Britain, France, the Soviet Union, Japan, and China. Their role in the international arena suggests the importance of studying their publications. Publications emphasize the federal or central government level. U.S. documents are used as an example of national publications.

U.S. Goverment Publications

Part One. Introduction

Government Organization and Federalism

Legal System and the Judiciary

The Depository System, Selection, Acquisition, and Organization of Publications

Part Two. Federal Government Publications

Guides, Bibliographies, and Other Reference Sources

Congressional Publications

Executive Publications

Judiciary Publications

Constitution, Law, Treaties, and Regulations

Universal Postal Union (UPU)

International Telecommunication Union (ITU)

World Meteorological Organization (WMO)

Inter-Governmental Maritime Consultative Organization (IMCO)

General Agreement on Tariffs and Trade (GATT)

International and United Nations Laws

Part Three. Other Intergovernmental Organizations

Guides, Bibliographies, and Other Reference Sources

North Atlantic Treaty Organization, the European Communities, Organization of American States, Southeast Asia Treaty Organization, the League of Arab States, Union of African States and Malagasy, Organization of Petroleum Exporting Countries

Foreign Government Publications

Part One. General Introduction

Guides, Bibliographies, and Other Reference Sources

Selection, Acquisition, and Organization of Foreign Publications

Part Two. Great Britain

Parliamentary Government and the British Constitution

Government Publications

Crown

Cabinet

Parliament

Other Agencies

Part Three. France

The Fifth Republic and the Constitution

Government Publications

President and Premier

Parliament

Courts

Other Agencies

Part Four. Soviet Union

Political Ideology and the Communist Party

Government Publications

Communist Party

Supreme Soviet

Council of Ministers

Judiciary

CONCLUSION

In traditional library education, stress is placed on information collection, organization, and dissemination. Students are taught the concept and theory of handling information and service, but not the contents of subject discipline. Even in literature courses, the methodological differences between scientists and humanists may be discussed to better understand users' needs, yet subject discipline contents are hardly touched. In certain courses, simply dealing with material without knowing subject matter will prove to be inadequate. Knowledge of the government system is indispensable to grouping publications.

In socialist countries, there is no separation of powers, only separation of functions. Grouping publications by three government branches is not applicable. In the Republic of China, a five-power, instead of three-power, constitutional system has been adopted. Grouping of publications by agency will be different from that of the United States. In the United States, international treaties are considered part of laws, but not so in Great Britain. In common law countries, once a rule has been established by court it will be followed in all similar cases; this is known as the doctrine of *stare decisis*. The doctrine does not, however, apply in socialist and non-common law countries. Subject knowledge of a country's political, economic, and cultural aspects is a *sine qua non* of full understanding and effective use of government publications.

Requirement of subject competence is not unusual in library service. Reference librarians in American law schools are generally required to have adequate legal training, preferably a J.D. degree. In many academic libraries, librarians are sought who have an advanced subject field degree. An area bibliographer should have first-hand knowledge of the area.

Knowledge of government functions, structure, and legal system can have a far-reaching effect. It enables students to understand and interpret correctly the government's policies, political process, and foreign relations. A fundamental aspect of studying international government publications is that documents are produced to facilitate the participation of states in the UN.

Any government publications course consists of two main themes: acquaintance with publications and knowledge of the government. Knowledge of the government requires study beyond library education. The course is interdisciplinary in nature. As such, joint teaching that draws in several skills is desirable, particularly when dealing with foreign language material. In foreign and international government publication courses, adequate collections of material are necessary from library resources as well.

NOTES

1. 44 U.S.C. 1901.
2. Beverly J. Brewster, "Area Bibliography Programs in U.S. Library Schools," *International Library Review* 9 (January 1977), pp. 3, 11.
3. Vladimir M. Palio, *Government Publications: A Guide to Bibliographic Tools.* (Washington, D.C.: Library of Congress, 1975); and *The Government Organization Manuals: A Bibliography* (Washington, D.C.: Library of Congress, 1975).
4. Winifred Gregory, *List of the Serial Publications of Foreign Governments, 1815–1931* (New York: Wilson, 1932); Joyce Ball, *Foreign Statistical Documents* (Stanford, Calif.: Hoover Institution, 1967); and Barnard M. Fry, *Government Publications: Key Papers* (Oxford: Pergamon, 1981).
5. Peter J. Hartford, "The Government Publications Course: a Survey," *Journal of Education for Librarianship* 11 (Winter 1971), p. 255.
6. Joe Morehead, *Introduction to United States Public Documents* (Littleton, Colo.: Libraries Unlimited, 1983).
7. Adelaide R. Hasse, "How May Government Documents Be Made More Useful to the Public," *Library Journal* 26 (January 1901), p. 10.
8. S. Simsova and M. MacKee, *A Handbook of Comparative Librarianship* (Hamden, Conn.: Shoe String Press, 1975) and Miles M. Jackson, Jr., ed., *Comparative and International Librarianship* (Westport, Conn.: Greenwood Press, 1970).

9. See Mary K. Fetzer, *United Nations Documents and Publications: A Research Guide* (New Brunswick, N.J.: Graduate School of Library Service, Rutgers University, 1978).

See also Theodore D. Dimitrov, *Documents of International Organizations: A Bibliographic Handbook* (London: International University Publications, 1973) and Harry N.M. Winton, ed., *Publications of the United Nations System: A Reference Guide* (New York: R.R. Bowker, 1972).

10. Brenda Brimmer, *A Guide to the Use of United Nations Documents* (Dobbs Ferry, N.Y.: Oceana Publications, 1962).

BIBLIOGRAPHY

Guilfoyle, Marvin C., and Irma Tomberlin. "Government Documents Practicum: Completing the Basic Education." *Government Publications Review* 5 (1978), pp. 57–60.

Hernon, Peter. "An Approach to Teaching Documents Courses." *Government Publications Review* 6 (1979), pp. 275–282.

Hernon, Peter, and Sara Lou Williams. "University Faculty and Federal Document Use Patterns." *Government Publications Review* 3 (1976), pp. 93–108.

Parke, Carol. "The Advanced Training Course on International Documentations, Geneva, Switzerland, Feb. 18-Mar. 15, 1974." *Government Publications Review* 2 (1975), pp. 133–236.

22
CHILDREN'S LITERATURE COURSES

Hollis Lowery-Moore and Lesta Burt

The value of the international exchange of children's books has been recognized for many years. In 1925 the International Board of Education (IBE) was initiated, and Mrs. Leopold Stokowsky, with financial help from the H. Payne Fund, laid the foundation for IBE's international children's book collection. Jella Lepman organized the first international traveling exhibition of children's books in 1946 and was instrumental in founding the International Youth Library (IYL), Munich, in 1948.

In 1953 the International Board on Books for Young People (IBBY) was created. IBBY's objectives were to (1) promote international understanding through children's books, (2) encourage high literacy and artistic standards, (3) seek wide distribution of literature to children, (4) encourage establishment of national and international libraries, (5) encourage continuing education for those involved with children's literature, and (6) encourage publication of imaginative and challenging young people's books.

Organizations such as the International Federation of Library Associations and Institutions (IFLA) and the United Nations Educational, Scientific, and Cultural Organization (UNESCO) have been active in promoting international understanding and goodwill through children's books.[1]

According to Anne Pellowski, in preschool years and the early grades children have not yet formed definite concepts of nationality. They are, however, conscious of racial, religious, social, and cultural differences, especially if these differences are visible. Most research indicates that self-image improves as children experience the differences and sameness of things. Older children are ready for material that recognizes the concepts of nationality and country, region and continent, as well as social and cultural values, but they still prefer to view these issues as related to individual children.

The children's literature of all nations and cultures can be used to promote understanding and cooperation. Exposure to this literature, especially stories that focus on an individual child, will increase children's knowledge of other cultures, their sensitivity to and appreciation of other cultures, and their willingness to tolerate cultural differences.[2]

Teachers and librarians who are acquainted with world literature can provide books that enable youth to realize that many human hopes, fears, and joys are universal. By sharing books of international interest, teachers and librarians can help children to regard cultural and religious differences as interesting and stimulating instead of fearful or ridiculous. Are international interests reflected in the books and media studied in world children's literature courses? Internationalizing children's literature study is one way to ensure that each child forms an emotional link to children around the world.

A SURVEY OF CHILDREN'S LITERATURE COURSES

A sampling of course descriptions has been examined in order to determine the international aspects of present curricula. A committee of the Children's Literature Association (CLS) of the U.S. National Council of Teachers of English recently published 1983 survey findings on college and university children's literature courses.[3] An earlier survey revealed that these courses were most often offered in three departments: Elementary Education, English, and Library Science. The survey attempted to compare basic course emphases for the three separate departments. A randomly chosen survey was made of 251 U.S. departments teaching children's literature and listed by the American Library Association (ALA), the National Council for Accreditation of Teacher Education, and the Modern Language Association. Over sixty-five percent of the departments surveyed responded.

In Education departments, 40 percent of the respondents used a literature text with intensive study of each genre. In English departments, 57 percent emphasized intensive literature study, particularly of literary elements. In Library Science, 46 percent preferred extensive children's literature reading emphasizing children's interests.

Library Science utilized bibliographies more often than did English and Education. Only one children's book title was required for all students, *Charlotte's Web* by E. B. White. In Library Science and English courses, *Wind in the Willows* and *Alice in Wonderland* were extensively required. Titles listed in both Library Science and Education included many American Newbery and Caldecott award winners. More older classics and anthologies were listed when the course was taught in the

English Department. All three disciplines emphasized traditional literature, modern fantasy, animal stories, science fiction, and drama/short stories.

Library Science and Education departments placed more emphasis than did English departments on picture books, illustrations, realistic fiction, historical fiction, biography, and nonfiction. Poetry was mentioned most often as a focus in Education. Education and Library Science included learning theory and child development as related to literature, guidelines for selecting books and media, and material for classroom reading aloud. Education was more concerned about integrating literature with other subjects than were the other two disciplines. English departments placed a much greater emphasis on children's literature history than did Education or Library Science.

The teaching techniques regularly applied by more than half of the respondents were individual reports, text assignments, and reading specific books. All disciplines used lectures, class discussion based on critiques and texts read, small group discussion, student storytelling, and book media demonstrations by the instructor. Additional course offerings included one course in multi-ethnic literature. The survey reported minimal attention to international literature in basic children's literature courses, although certain institutions mentioned translations.

Five universities and fifty colleges were found to teach children's literature in Australia, although there was only one autonomous Department of Children's Literature.[4] The course was normally offered by the departments of English literature, teacher education, or school librarianship. In spite of a wide range of emphasis, most courses blended the literary approach with the practical application to children. Specific, thematic, literary courses based on close textual study existed, as well as courses concerned with comics, television shows, or writing and illustrating picture-story books.

Teaching strategies included written assignments and tutorial presentations throughout the term. Other activities included writing and illustrating picture books, making bibliographies of books read, learning stories to be told, writing book reviews, and short-answer questioning of familiarity with set texts.

John Foster has described a postgraduate correspondence course offered by the University of New England at Armidale which led to a Bachelor of Letters degree in children's literature.[5] The degree consisted of one year of course work on twentieth-century adolescent literature and a general historical course of classics and popular literature. A second year of thesis work was also required.

A course more oriented to sharing course's literature was offered at the University of Sydney at both undergraduate and graduate levels. The major emphasis was on the relationship between reading and children's literature and the importance to the child of simultaneously developing reading skills and gaining knowledge and experience through literature. Activities included building units based on the novels or picture books in the syllabus. Sometimes study of a particular book was a purely literary examination with no practical application.

A blend course was offered in certain universities, one in which the literary aspect was the primary focus but practical applications were also considered. At the Kuring-gae College of Advanced Education, Sydney, courses taken for the Graduate Diploma in Children's Literature gave students a knowledge of literature for all age groups. Students made tapes of children's playground rhymes, practiced storytelling, reading, and literature-inspired dramatic activities. Emphasis was placed on child development.

Undergraduate courses were offered by the Salisbury campus Department of Children's Literature of the South Australian College of Advanced Education, Adelaide, which allowed a full mini-term major with such units as traditional literature, fantasy, realism, history of both children's literature and illustration, and author and genre studies. Students presented puppet shows, dramatizations, and music.

Other Australian children's literature courses included an issue-based, interdisciplinary undergraduate course, a postgraduate unit on linguistic perceptions of children's literature, popular and humorous literature, the history of the adventure story, and fear and evil in children's books. There were also the more commonly listed courses on adolescent literature, mass media, picture books, nonfiction, literary criticism, and Australian Children's Literature.

Responses to a request from the editor of *Children's Literature in Education*, for either (1) a general description of college and university or (2) a more anecdotal account of some particularly interesting facet of children's literature education brought primarily an emphasis on the need for students to acquire a wide knowledge of children's stories.[6]

Hazel Davis (United Kingdom) encouraged students to gather story material resources both to read and to tell children. Often the basic children's literature course included an outline of children's literature development and an introduction to content, style, and format evaluation. Through student reports, classes may have a rapid introduction to as many as 120 books. She indicated plans for a course with time for students to attempt writing their own stories.

Certain courses have been designed to enable students to share knowledge of children's books and inspire their enjoyment. They dealt with a wide range of books and activities including opportunities for conversations with children. Students were asked to read fifteen to twenty books and to write brief, personal reviews. A short critical essay on a topic of personal choice was required. Many topics were discussed in lectures.

An alternative was to write an original story. Additional instructors submitted descriptions with many commonalities.

INTERNATIONALIZATION SUGGESTIONS

From the above sampling of course descriptions, interest in children's book internationalism does not seem to have influenced academic children's literature around the world. How might an instructor infuse the children's literature curriculum with a sense of the international?

Each type of literature has a different potential for world understanding. Traditional literature is the genre into which most courses infuse internationalism now. Certain folktales (such as *Cinderella*) can be found in several hundred versions throughout the world, and they suggest the universality of human needs and endeavor. Traditional literature can be shown vicariously to satisfy basic human needs for food, clothing, shelter, love, friendship, achievement, aesthetic, and spiritual fulfillment.

The contrast of values in cultures is also evident in traditional literature. Students learn that Far Eastern folktales often reward the quest of the hero or heroine with something of aesthetic value whereas many Western folktales reward for valor. The sameness and differences between people around the world are evident in all areas of traditional literature—myths, folktales, legends, fairytales, and fables as well as the modern tall tale. Humor demonstrates the universality of the human conditions; all cultures have their Simple Simon or husbands who brag that they can easily do a woman's work.

Like music, poetry can be a world language. The essence of other people can be understood by reading their poetry. Fantasy is an area akin to poetry in revealing people's dreams. Significant themes running through a nation's fantasy can reveal both a people's uniqueness and their oneness with others.

Science fiction, in addition to revealing dreams, a fresh viewpoint, and innovation, reveals a nation's conscience as no other genre being produced today. What a nation fears might happen will be depicted in current science fiction. From Jules Verne's era to 1945, the products of science were deemed to be only beneficial. However, with the advent of the atom bomb, it became apparent that these products could be both helpful and devastating.

Biography can introduce people from many countries. Through the actual lives of people, students gain understanding of political events, social pressures, and daily life. People's contributions can be studied, and students can gain a broadened appreciation of other lands. Historical fiction has many of the same internationalizing values and has the added advantage of examining a greater time span. Often several family generations are depicted to expose life's continuity and how the past influences the present.

Current realistic fiction concerning children in other countries can make them seem more real. The study of global nonfiction adds to intellectual understanding. Once emotional empathy has been gained through reading fiction, it must be substantiated with facts. Fiction has the capacity to catch and hold the readers' imagination as they gain in reading experience, but readers need to know that people and places in books do exist.

Two possible approaches to internationalizing the children's literature curriculum are the addition of books from foreign nations and other cultures to the existing course framework and the creation of a separate course titled International Children's Literature. Creating a new course can be difficult without dropping another one. In addition, unless students have a strong incentive to choose a new course over one already in place, it may have a small enrollment. Therefore, including an international component in an existing course is the more feasible choice.

Most courses seem to focus on extending students' experience with children's literature. An instructor may use the books of other nations throughout the course to illustrate specific genre, literary elements, or children's preferences. Another approach would devote several lectures to books by foreign authors and illustrators and provide an introduction to bibliographies with international interest.

Regardless of the approach chosen, both translations of books originally published in a foreign country and the original editions must be available. Providing both the original and the translation permits comparison and additional insight into a particular group of people.

An important trend is the interchange of children's books across national boundaries by means of translation. Many European countries have begun to translate foreign language books in order to increase the quantity of literature available. Certain countries have also increased the quantity and range of their own publications, and some of them have been translated into other languages.

International picture book co-printing is becoming widespread. When picture books are co-published and co-edited, the illustrations are printed in one country, distributed to publishers in other countries, and then in each country the translated text is inserted. Co-production is easy to implement, and books by authors from English-speaking nations are sometimes published simultaneously in these countries. Certain translations show modifications in the text or illustrations. A second problem is the difficulty in obtaining translated material from countries other than those in Europe, North America, or Japan, countries that dominate children's book production.

Pellowski, using the collection of the Information Center on Children's Cultures, New York, has identified only nine direct translations or adaptations of children's books from developing countries into American English during an eleven-year period. Only the largest publishing companies share children's books through translation.

The number of national awards given to children's book authors and illustrators is increasing. Books that win significant awards in the country where they are originally published may be chosen by a publisher from another country for translation. The Hans Christian Andersen Award sponsored by IBBY is given to an author and an illustrator who have made a significant international contribution to children's literature. Often the winning books have been translated into several languages before the award is announced.

The International Reading Association has established an annual award to be given to an author showing unusual promise in children's book writing. Candidates for this award are evaluated in their original languages.

The International Jane Addams Children's Book Award is given by the Women's International League for Peace and Freedom and the Jane Addams Peace Foundation. The Bologna Fair brings together 800 children's book publishers from fifty countries which display their publications, authors, and illustrators. Two awards are given there, the Critici in Erba Prize for the best illustrated book selected by a jury of children, and the Graphi Prize for the children's and young people's book considered best from a technical and graphic viewpoint by a jury of experts.

The Mildred Batchelor Award sponsored by the ALA Children's Service Division is given to a publisher for the best translation of a book originally published in a language other than English and in a country other than the United States.

The instructor who wishes to internationalize the children's literature curriculum must emphasize national and international award books and participate actively in organizations that promote cross-cultural understanding. IFLA promotes publication and distribution of good books internationally. IBBY, with national sections in many countries, is an organizing center for world children's literature activities and sponsors an annual international children's book conference. The International Association for Research in Children's and Youth Literature promotes research and meets for member discussions.

Building a material collection to support the children's literature course will be costly, and many titles will be difficult to obtain. Sharing among libraries with significant collections will be necessary. IYL collects, preserves, and promotes knowledge of world literature and serves several user groups. Children constitute an important group served by the multilingual leading section combined with workshops and other activities. A literary exchange clearinghouse provides editors and publishers with information on what should and can be translated.

A research and study center services mainly lecturers and student researchers concerned with literature in languages other than their own. Lastly, the research and publication office produces several kinds of book lists for librarians, preschool educators, and social workers who deal with the children of minorities and of immigrant or guest workers. Through its workshops, correspondence, and programs "Getting to Know One's Own and Other Cultures" and "Books Designed Specifically for Minorities," IYL attempts to enlarge reading horizons.

In addition to interlibrary loan, electronic transfer of information and computer-assisted instantaneous translation may become avenues for securing foreign material. The possibility exists that a user may, in the future, walk into a library and have the book requested printed out at once.

A national children's literature center in each nation and widespread acceptance of interlibrary loan programs would be useful in sharing this material throughout the world. Present examples include the Swedish Children's Book Institute and the U.S. Library of Congress Children's Book Center.

In addition to bibliographic aids, the instructor will want to read the international periodical on literature for children and young people, the quarterly *Book Bird*. Issued and edited by IBBY and International Institute for Children's Literature and Reading Research, *Book Bird* introduces books of international interest from various countries and publishers, as well as theoretical and critical articles, and reports on professional work and research. The quarterly also informs readers regularly on international writing and illustrating development.

Once an international collection has been started, the instructor can guide students in using books. Multilingual students can also share books in their languages. Early in the course, the instructor should identify the foreign language and cultural backgrounds of students and utilize that knowledge in planning classroom activities. Student reports as well as class visits with foreign authors and illustrators can broaden international interests. Foreign community members may share the literature of their childhood with students.

Pellowski has suggested making a specific course assignment in which students search out a country or even a small part of a country and language about which they have no preconceived notions. After choosing books about that country, students should try to identify the authors' objectives.

Another class assignment can require compiling a bibliography of material related to a small country or area little known to the student.

A short critical analysis of the material and how it could be used might be included. A study of material from a large country about which much has been written might also be undertaken. Students could describe what they think children can perceive about family and school life and about political and cultural values from that material.

Interviews with immigrants about the printed, filmed, or oral literature to which they were exposed as children can also provide insight into foreign children's literature. Comparing books from several nations with the same basic theme or subject matter can give students an insight into whether a particular subject is best approached from a local, national, or global view.

Requiring students to create displays and deliver oral reports on the literature of particular countries will provide brief overviews of many nations. Instructors should encourage students to develop units that expand concepts internationally, for example, using picture-story book presentations that include indigenous material, translations, and original language material.

The many similarities in children's literature teaching should facilitate integration of international material into existing curricula. The major problems include the sparseness of the literature from many countries and the difficulty in obtaining original and translated titles. Ultimately, the internationalization of children's literature will depend on instructor willingness to become knowledgeable about titles and issues, to acquire international material locally, and to include it in class presentations and required reading lists.

NOTES

1. Anne Pellowski, *The World of Children's Literature* (New York: R. R. Bowker, 1968), p. 1.

2. Anne Pellowski, "Internationalism in Children's Literature," in Zena Sutherland, ed., *Children and Books* (Glenview, Ill.: Scott Foresman and Co., 1981), p. 599.

3. Lynda Adamson, "Results of CLA's Survey of the Teaching of Children's Literature in Colleges and Universities," *The Bulletin* 11 (Spring 1985), pp. 9–11.

4. John Foster, "The Teaching of Children's Literature in Australia," *Book Bird*, 1 & 2 (1983), pp. 3–7.

5. Ibid.

6. Hazel Grubb Davis, "Education of Teachers," *Children's Literature in Education* 14 (May 1974), pp. 52–67.

SELECTED BIBLIOGRAPHY

Chase, Judith Wragg. *Books to Build World Friendship*. Dobbs Ferry, N.Y.: Oceana Publications, 1964.

Children's Books International I-IV Proceedings. Boston: Boston Public Library, 1976–1979.

Elleman, Barbara, ed. *Children's Books of International Interest.* Chicago: American Library Association, 1984.

Gardner, Frank, ed. *Reading Round the World.* London: Clive Bingley, 1969.

Haviland, Virginia, ed. *Children's Books of International Interest.* Chicago: American Library Association, 1978.

Kellman, Amy. *Guide to Children's Libraries and Literature Outside the United States.* Chicago: American Library Association, 1982.

Wertheimer, Leonard. *Books in Other Languages.* Ottawa: Canadian Library Association, 1976.

23

SCHOOL MEDIA CENTER COURSES

Sigrún Klara Hannesdóttir

School libraries, school library media centers, and school library resource centers are a late twentieth-century phenomenon that has gotten a new emphasis through changed teaching methods as well as modern concepts of students' need for lifetime information skills in the information society. A new integration into the school's curriculum as well as inclusion of varied nonbook material in the library has led to an effort to change its name to that of media or resource center.

In 1976 a School Library Section was added to the International Federation of Library Associations and Institutions (IFLA) Division Serving the General Public. And through its National Information System (NATIS) program, UNESCO has included school libraries within the scope of national library systems and thereby recognized that their bookstock can contribute to collective national information sources and services.

International acceptance of school librarianship as a field with a determined body of knowledge and skills has many benefits. The most obvious are the librarian's increased job commitment and the advancement of educational information use. School librarians can also obtain increased mobility. This mobility may occur both internally from one type of library to another within the country or from school libraries in one country to another. This step has the potential of ending the school library's isolation from the majority of libraries and to include it in the collective national library system. Such a change would inevitably extend or redefine general objectives. NATIS' conceptual basis is to analyze the performance and objectives of all types of libraries, documentation activities, and archives to increase coordination and efficiency. School libraries are accepted as a cornerstone for reading and cultural participation. This is a new development, and few countries have yet included school libraries fully in the national network.[1]

In certain countries there is little difference between the library's role in school and in public library children's services. In West Germany the public library is expected to assist the school in strengthening the desire and intensifying the ability to read. Yet in Denmark the school library is strictly a teaching tool with no relationship to the rest of the library community.

Many factors influence the school library's roles: teaching methodology, the availability of learning material, school financing, legislation, and teachers' ability to utilize multiple subject approaches. A school librarian's course is seldom a predetermined knowledge and skill package, but we can reach a certain consensus about which competencies are essential, independently of the type of library served and the level of media and facilities available.

We must assume that the course to be internationalized (a) is fairly extensive; (b) is offered to persons who will work in schools with facilities and conditions reaching the developed world's average; and (c) addresses school librarianship's total competency requirements and is not restricted to management. The librarian's commitment to the school's educational goals should be stressed. His or her school role is threefold—educational, professional, and managerial—so all must be addressed. We may conclude that improving educational program internationalization in the school library should lead to greater professionalism.

COURSE INTERNATIONALIZATION

The school library involves more than the classroom use of written sources to supplement the textbook. However, daily operations are often the responsibility of teachers with no library education or of clerks with neither a teaching nor a library qualification. In other cases, the public library operates a branch within the school which serves student information needs. The discussion on school library professionalization has focused on combining the educational and professional aspects, assuming that the ideal school librarian should be *both* a librarian and a teacher.[2]

Consequently, in many countries educational requirements have assumed either qualification as a base and have then added certain aspects of the other. The range varies from full qualification in both fields, which has been the case in much of the United States for many years, to short school librarianship courses added to teacher certification, which has been common in many other countries. Occasional library schools have a school library subcurriculum; Swedish and Norwegian library schools, for example, offer school and public librarianship subcurricula.

The question becomes what to change to make school library courses more international. Certainly awareness and knowledge of foreign developments can be beneficial. School librarians must keep abreast of new developments in order to offer good service. This idea applies to large as well as small countries. Constant international feedback and exchange should be beneficial.

Small countries tend to be strongly internationally oriented because they are aware of their small share of the world. They are accustomed to looking at foreign developments and to thinking through possible means of adapting them. Changing from local to international emphasis does not mean that the librarians should automatically adopt a foreign system. Increased awareness of international developments can help librarians gain broader views and see alternative problem solutions.

Information from other countries should be included in an introductory school librarianship course rather than creating a new comparative and international school librarianship course. Integration of foreign approaches should make librarians more flexible in searching for improvements and more aware of the need for full preparation before facing problems.

INTERNATIONAL ACTIVITIES

Two international organizations will be discussed here: the International Association for School Librarianship (IASL) and the IFLA Section for School Libraries. IASL was founded at a 1971 Conference of the World Confederation of Organizations of the Teaching Profession, and its objectives are to bring about closer collaboration among school libraries in all countries; to promote the professional development of school/teacher librarians; to encourage the development of school libraries and library programs throughout the world; to initiate and coordinate activities, conferences, and other projects; and to support the publication, loan, and exchange of pertinent literature.[3]

The Association's annual conference, which is its major forum for idea exchange, has been held in many different countries to draw attention to local school library development. IASL publishes the *IASL Newsletter*, annual conference proceedings based on a specific theme, as well as *Getting Started: A Bibliography of Ideas and Procedures; People to Contact for Visiting Libraries Media Centers*; and *Library Services to Isolated Schools and Communities*. Often the *Newsletter* provides the only available information on school library development in certain countries.

The IFLA Section started in 1973 and enabled school librarianship to link with the rest of the library field.[4] It has worked on a variety of problems funded by outside sources, including a 1978 Costa Rica Seminar.[5] Section agenda issues for the future include school library legislation and policy, the library resource center concept in schools, copyright, training teachers to use school libraries in teaching and learning, and school library education. Both IASL and the IFLA Section have important roles to play, and a course instructor should discuss their value and contribution. IASL conferences serve to establish personal contacts and to share the grass-roots experience. IFLA underlines librarianship as a field with a common core of knowledge and philosophy in which school librarians have a share.

HISTORY AND DEVELOPMENT

Tracing historical developments should show students the mode of thinking and the influences that led to establishment of school libraries, their initial organization and development. School librarianship must emphasize developmental patterns rather than historical perspective.

The developmental patterns have evolved from two main sources: (1) the public library, which initiated school service as a form of institutional extension and (2) individual educational authorities, which established library service in response to the need for changing educational methodology. This section lends itself to internationalization and comparison of developmental patterns, but the problem lies in the documentation shortage.

For example, documentation on Latin American school library development is poor in the English language, except for Venezuela and Jamaica.[6] For Africa, Nigerian, Ghanan, and Kenyan information is available. Most development literature comes from the United States, Canada, the United Kingdom, Australia, and the Nordic countries where school libraries have long been accepted and supported. Therefore, the first internationalization problem is the information scarcity.

The school library situation was studied by the University of Alberta at the request of the International Council for Educational Media and covered twenty-nine countries.[7] The percentage of primary schools with resource centers ranged from 100 percent in Switzerland and Denmark to 0.0 percent in Luxembourg, 2.5 percent in Belgium, and 3 percent in France. Among secondary schools, Denmark and Switzerland reported that 100 percent had resource centers, whereas Luxembourg reported no resource centers and Norway only 5 percent.

In 1977 Frances Laverne Carroll reported a machine search for school libraries in the ERIC and LIBCON data bases and a hand search in *Education Index* and *Library Literature*.[8] Forty-six nations were cited during 1970–1975. The countries that had publicized their school librarianship developments most during this period were Australia, Canada, Denmark, the USSR, the United Kingdom, the United States, and West Germany.

OBJECTIVES

The objectives of school libraries are usually defined in terms of the individual educational objectives of each country. This area is most informative for comparative purposes. The UNESCO Manifesto on School Libraries lists general objectives, and these objectives are reflected, with different emphases, in various national statements. The objectives from several countries should be compared, and an effort made to interpret the reasons behind local emphasis differences based perhaps on comparative education textbooks.

In discussing library objectives, it should be stressed that students become aware of the school library's potential role to a wider clientele, particularly in situations where alternative library service does not exist or is inadequate. Future school librarians should be encouraged to participate in discussions and plans for general library service involving knowledge and acceptance of cooperation and networking concepts.

TYPES OF SCHOOL LIBRARIES

Definitions of school population, educational level, and age are subject to national customs. In the United States, K–12, primary, middle, junior high, and senior high are some of the most prominent school grade-level breakdowns. In Australia, most systems consist of primary (K–6) and secondary schools (7–12). Iceland separates primary K–9 (age six to fifteen) and secondary school (age sixteen to twenty).

Other divisions exist. It may be necessary to study several countries as examples in which the educational system is used as a framework for school library operation. The view of educational authorities on the library role in various school levels can be studied because they are neither fixed nor homogeneous.

Many variations exist, but two trends can be outlined. First is the trend to use libraries as an integral part of instruction from the first school years through secondary school. Children come to the library initially for a story hour and start looking at it as an integral part of the educational program. Gradually, their use becomes more sophisticated, and by school leaving time they have acquired the necessary information skills. This trend is most common in countries following the Anglo-American-Scandinavian library tradition.

In the second trend the library is thought to be established for pupil use at the later compulsory education levels or even is restricted to the secondary level. The argument for this idea is that students need basic knowledge in subjects as well as good reading skills before being able to utilize libraries as information sources. Therefore, when certain European countries refer to school libraries they mean secondary level libraries. Both trends can be justified from the viewpoint of educational philosophy.

As an alternative, the combined school and public library has been set up where the local school and public library separately have not functioned adequately. This happens most frequently in thinly populated areas. Arguments exist for and against the combined library. The most common arguments in favor are that it allows more efficient use of budget for material and of premises and personnel. The most common problems involved in combination are administrative (whether the library is to be managed by the school or the local authority); and book selection policies and staffing, since public libraries frequently have different working hours and salary scales than school library personnel. Discussion of arguments for and against this type of library and the situations leading to such a combination will necessarily include some evaluation of the advances made in preschool educational service, countries that have made good progress, and its influence on school library development.

SYSTEMS AND NETWORKS

There are two methods of organizing school libraries. In one, each school finances the library from its own budget; and the other, the libraries are connected into a system based on a predetermined larger administrative division. The instructor should explain how the two systems differ and should use examples.

In the first system, the library is independent of networks and should be made as self-sufficient as possible. Cooperation in material sharing is optional. The libraries in a region may have formal or informal cooperative agreements in limited areas, but they are not connected administratively. This system is common in the United States and in other countries where local authorities are responsible for education with or without federal support. In the United States it is common for only one high school, one junior high school, and one elementary school to exist in a town; larger educational systems (with ten or more elementary schools) began to develop centralized services in the 1960s.

The second method is to connect the libraries into a network based on a predetermined region. It has been used primarily by countries that have had to build up library systems with limited funds. The centralized network operates a service center which provides book acquisition and technical processes as well as guidance and staff supervision for each library. Library material can be transferred from one library to another according to need.

Networks are essential in developing countries because the libraries are staffed by persons with no information-handling skills and the school allocates a minimum of time to library service. Where technical processing is centralized, the librarian can devote more time to public service. The Jamaica school library service can be used as a prototype for this kind of system, which also features cooperation between public and school libraries. It represents a *type* of centralized system adapted to local needs.

COLLECTION DEVELOPMENT

A collection development course unit should include selection, evaluation, and production of learning resources, and those factors that are prerequisite for systematic operation as an information storehouse. The librarian's main commitment is to broaden the student's knowledge base. Ingenuity and creativity should be shown. Collection development is hindered not merely by insufficient budget, but also by lack of adequate children's material written in the local language. It is useful to show students a variety of solutions used by persons lacking access to appropriate vernacular material.

As mobility has increased, few librarians have been without the problem of providing material for some minority group. For children speaking a minority language, collection development sometimes presents an almost unsolvable problem. A relatively small number of languages have active publication programs. The situation is particularly difficult in developing countries such as Angola, with several hundred tribal languages, many of which have not yet reached the script stage.

But it is not always a question of literacy. Small countries such as Iceland may have a high literacy rate in their own language, but with a population of 225,000 and only 4,500 Icelandic children born annually, the market is small. Iceland can provide only a limited number of new children's books each year, and prices rise as editions get smaller. These problems must be considered when discussing collection development in an international context and looking at the steps that attempt to alleviate the problems.

SELECTED TOOLS

The problem in countries with large publication programs, well-organized markets, and high competition is that of selecting the best quality. Selection and evaluation committees must guide librarians and teachers through the publication jungle. Basic lists of the most appropriate material are available in several countries but may be compiled from different viewpoints.

Countries with few appropriate publications must approach basic material lists differently. Where no appropriate local books are available, foreign and adult books may be included in subject areas. Well-illustrated books in geography, art, and crafts are usable even in another language.

Co-printing and international publishing cooperation can often increase the material available. Printing innovations facilitate co-printing books in many languages. The pictures are the same in all versions, but a translation into the local language replaces the original text. This is feasible, especially with fiction where illustrations have an international appeal.

Most publishers that offer their books for co-printing require a minimum number of copies; but it is usually beyond the capacity of the smaller language communities to buy them. Even 1,500 copies is too high a figure. Publishers must pay for the translations, typesetting, and film work, besides selling the whole edition in a short time.

Teachers and librarians everywhere want alternative sources of material. It is possible to type translations of foreign books or read the translation onto a tape cassette. In this way no copyright violation occurs since the book is used in its original form with additional help. British Jackdaw Publications provide an idea worth pursuing. They are selected journal articles, maps, and so forth, on a particular subject and can be prepared as a packet for local use. In this way librarians can use material located in pamphlet files or picture collections.

Use of audiovisual material is increasing. Criteria for selecting content are the same as those for books, but the presentation format must be considered. Nonbook media, especially those that require special electrical equipment, cannot always be used. In some parts of the world schools are without electricity. In developed countries, the selection problem lies in the lack of standardized media formats. One must either have varied equipment or use material in one format only.

Computers will have vast influence on future educational technology. In many developed countries, library computerization has already been accepted. Librarians should explore the computer's role and demonstrate through small, home-made data bases the importance of information skills. Enjoyable and educational information should be developed. The literature reports several interesting projects.[9] Educational software is creating some of the same problems as printed media. Children of small language communities lack access to appropriate material in understandable form. The equipment may be transferable internationally but the software programs are not.

The collection development unit must also cover evaluation criteria. This can be discussed from the standpoint of the alternative: what do you do when the only book available is not a quality source? Students could be encouraged to look at their usual tools and evaluate how many could be internationally useful. The availability of appropriate material to supplement the textbook must be discussed.

COLLECTION ORGANIZATION

An effort should be made to use the classifiction system and the cataloging rules that are employed in most of the country's other libraries. Students should have access to collections organized in a comparable manner to facilitate after-school use. Classification and cataloging are perhaps the most international aspect of library work because of extensive efforts to produce the *Anglo-American Cataloging Rules*.

The most commonly used classification scheme is the Dewey Decimal Classification. Its notations are simple and easily understood and can be used in a small library with a minimum of education anywhere. DDC system translations are available in a variety of languages, and the system is being made more useful by harmonization with other classification systems.

This unit should include procedures for ordering, receiving, and processing material. Classification theory and use as well as cataloging maintenance must be taught. Students should also receive instruction in basic indexing methods in order to make the collection quickly accessible.

SERVICE PROGRAMS

All properly functioning school libraries offer a variety of activities and programs; the list depends on the ingenuity of librarians and teachers, and should be prioritized according to the school library's objectives. Carol-Ann Haycock claims that school librarians[10] should serve as initiator and change agent. Teachers should be involved in creating library activities, and the librarian should be involved with curriculum development. Neither should be isolated from the other.

A Canadian report provides basic guidelines on how the principal, teacher, and librarian cooperate in resource-based programs. It also includes a chart that "lists the sequence of skills that students require to collect, organize and present information."[11]

The most important school library program areas are instruction in information-handling skills, reading guidance, development of information service, and development of bibliographies and pathfinders. *Library instruction* is an indispensable function and is best performed in connection with classroom assignments. Ann Irving has prepared an international bibliography on sources that offers ideas on creating instructional material.[12] Since cultural differences may influence children's interpretations of ideas, the production must be adapted to local needs.

Reading guidance has a different emphasis in each country. In developing countries, for instance, reading is often a major goal in itself, necessary to lower the illiteracy rate, whereas a Japanese librarian recommended transforming the school library into a recreation hall with a relaxed atmosphere.[13] Storytelling is usually the first service offered to the youngest students. This unit can be internationalized by selecting foreign stories, even stories in foreign languages, and retelling rather than reading them. Book talks are another type of reading guidance in which the librarian selects good quality books, reads excerpts from them, and hopes the students will borrow and read them.

Service must be offered to *handicapped students* and adapted to the kind of handicap involved, whether blindness, deafness, or mental deficiency. The trend to include them with healthy students in a school has come with recent ideas of democratization. This change has put pressure on the library to stock books in Braille or talking books for the blind. *Service* should also be provided for *ethnic children*. The right of children to preserve their ethnic culture is widely accepted, particularly for the guestworkers in many European countries. IFLA has established a Round Table on Library Service to Ethnic and Linguistic Minorities to produce service ideas. When we consider the importance of integrating children into society, along with the right to preserve their ethnic culture, the school librarian must be made aware of these ideas.

The school library is an ideal meeting-ground in which ethnic minority children can share their experiences, interact with other children, and contribute what is unique to them. Parents should also be involved with such programs.

JOURNALS

The journal literature on school librarianship is substantial, especially in English: *School Media Quarterly* and *School Library Journal* in the United States; *The School Librarian* in the United Kingdom; *Emergency Librarian* in Canada; *Australian School Librarian* in Australia; *Schulbibliothek Aktuell* in West Germany; and *Skolebiblioteket* in Denmark. Other journals carry school library information, such as *International Library Review*, which is useful for covering issues in a variety of countries. Librarians should also read journals that deal with media and educational technology and that discuss general library trends. Librarians must also use abstracting and indexing journals.

STANDARDS

Standards and guidelines are closely related to objectives that must be based on general goals. School library standards mean little because they can only count things, such as number of books per student, rather than public service activities.

Many national standards exist, such as the United States' *Standards for School Media Programs* (1969), the Australian *Standards and Objectives for School Libraries* (1968), and the United Kingdom's *School Library Resource Centres and Recommended Standards for Policy and Provision* (1970). It is also interesting to note the change in emphasis in standards. The newest U.S. standards, called *Media Programs: District and School* (1975), abandon the quantitative approach for the qualitative and so can be called guidelines.

International guidelines discuss all major issues in providing school library service. In teaching this unit, local standards should be compared to international guidelines. Students should review these guidelines from the standpoint of their own country, or of the foreign countries discussed in class.

School library legislation is not uniform. Provision for school libraries is compulsory in Iceland, for example, but in Denmark they have been included in public library legislation. A comprehensive international survey of school library legislation is still lacking. The school library has a potential role in serving a wider clientele than the school's population, particularly in situations where alternative service does not exist.[14]

MANAGEMENT

The need for effective school library management capabilities is only gradually being acknowledged. The library is one of the school's most complex posts, and librarians must have a clear view of budget allocation and stock and service cost.

A recent article lists twelve concepts that could be considered "core" in thirty-five American management textbooks. Evans concludes that, "Although the case is far from proven, I think there is sound reason to hope that we can define a core of management concepts that can be taught across cultural/national boundaries. My candidates for such a core are: Planning, Delegation/Organization, Staffing, Fiscal Management, Motivation, Innovation, Decision-making, Communication, Ethics/Law, Marketing, Leadership, Quantitative methods." Certainly thee concepts are applicable to school librarians.[15]

Personnel preparation is a controversial issue. The guidelines mention four types of staff members: professional, technical, clerical, and volunteer. The professional staff is in charge of designing and administering the library program; clerical staff members free the professional staff from time-consuming and repetitive activities that demand no professional preparation; and student volunteers can learn to perform specific tasks and also become more familiar with the library. In teaching this unit, it might be worthwhile to explore viewpoints on librarian preparation and competency requirements for certification. Staffing can be taught within general management.

PUBLIC LIBRARY SERVICE TO CHILDREN

Children's library service is part of public library service or school library service. They commonly share knowledge between them and their cooperation is vital, but their differences must also be shown. The main difference is the lack of a formal education setting and the absence of a need for teaching competency for children's librarians.

Children's service objectives are threefold: cultural, recreational, and educational. Educational objectives have been reduced from the first to the third priority as compared to the school library. In an international context, school-age children often have access to only one type of service or to public library branch service in the school. In certain countries, school and children's services are separated. This dichotomy is obvious in Denmark where there is little cooperation between them, and both serve all reading needs. Children's and school library selection policies differ, but a public library is needed to supplement school collections.

Children's librarians have had problems obtaining proper recognition. The stereotyped librarian is nowhere more obvious.[16] Children form no service pressure groups, and so are frequently the last to get an educated person in charge. This is unfortunate because the first library service children get strongly influences their opinions ever after. Children's librarianship has been represented within IFLA for a much longer time than has school librarianship. IFLA has had an active children's section which has planned good programs.

Children's service and literature are often dealt with simultaneously. School and children's librarianship have a common core of knowledge which is children's use and appreciation of library material. The International Board of Books for Young People is concerned mainly with the literary side, but its journal *Bookbird* occasionally publishes articles on children's service. Some countries have established children's literature research institutes, for example, Sweden's Svenska Barnboksinstitutet and the Internationales Jugendbibliothek in Blutenburg Castle, Munich.

Comparative research is needed on the field's conceptual basis in different countries, case studies of its influence in education, as well as each country's developmental history. Gradually, this body of knowledge should become better documented and available.

NOTES

1. Rosario Gassol de Horowitz, "The School Library and NATIS in Developing Countries: The Need for Integration" and Esther R. Dyer, "Including

School Libraries in National Bibliographic Systems," papers presented at the meeting of the IFLA Section for School Libraries, 1978.

2. Frances Laverne Carroll, *Recent Advances in School Librarianship* (Oxford: Pergamon Press, 1981), ch. 4.

3. Michael J. Cooke, "An International View of School Librarianship," *The School Librarian* 27 (October 1979), pp. 322–325.

4. Frances Laverne Carroll, "The Raison d'etre of IFLA's School Library Section," *Journal of Library History* 12 (Fall 1977), pp. 364–376; and *The History of the Section for School Libraries of the International Federation of Library Associations and Institutions* (Brussels: IFLA, 1977), 35 pp.

5. *Education of School Librarians—Some Alternatives*, edited and translated by Sigrún Klara Hannesdóttier (Munich: K. G. Saur, 1982), 115 p.; and Frances Laverne Carroll and Patricia F. Beilke, *Guidelines for the Planning and Organization of School Library Media Centers*. Revised version (Paris: UNESCO, 1979).

6. See Jean E. Lowrie, *School Libraries: International Development* (Metuchen, N.J.: Scarecrow Press, 1972), pp. 206–227.

7. David Friesen, Hans Kratz, and Christiane Prokop, *Resource Centres in Public Schools* (Edmonton: University of Alberta, 1984), and Frances Laverne Carroll, "School Librarianship," in John F. Harvey, ed., *Comparative and International Library Science* (Metuchen, N.J.: Scarecrow Press, 1977).

8. Carroll, "School Librarianship," p. 120.

9. See Jacqueline C. Mancall, "Training Students to Search Online: Rationale, Process, and Implications," *Drexel Library Quarterly* 20 (Winter 1984), pp. 64–85; and Fatimata Sylla, "Le Senegal et la Micro-informatique, paper presented at IFLA General Conference, Munich, 1983.

10. Carol-Ann Haycock, "Developing the School Resource Centre Program—A Systematic Approach," *Emergency Librarian* 12 (September-October 1984), p. 9.

11. *Partners in Action: The Library Resource Centre in the School Currciulum* (London, Ontario: Ministry of Education, 1982).

12. Ann Irving, *Instructional Material for Developing Information Concepts and Information Handling Skills in School Children: An International Study* (UNESCO/IFLA Contract No. 340024).

13. Mieko Nagakura, "Library is a Placc of Relaxation—A Japanese Identity of School Libraries" (Paper given at the IASL conference, 1983).

14. Sigrún Klara Hannesdóttir, "The Potential Role of the School Library as Centre for Communication and Culture Among Scattered Populations," *IASL Conference Proceedings 1983* (Kalamazoo, Mich.: International Association of School Librarianship, 1984).

15. G. Edward Evans, "Management Education for Archivists, Information Managers, and Librarians: Is There a Global Core?" *Education for Information* 2 (1984), pp. 295–307.

16. S. E. Gibbs, "The Training of Children's Librarians," *International Library Review* 15 (April 1983), pp. 191–205.

BIBLIOGRAPHY

Aaron, L. Shirley. *A Study of Combined School-Public Libraries*. Chicago: American Library Association, 1980.

Adcock, C. Donald. "School Libraries and Networking in North America: Principles and Problems of Participation." Paper presented at IFLA General Conference, Montreal 1982. Unpublished.

Berkeley, A. Virginia. "National Planning for School Library Development: Some Considerations." In J. Stephan Parker, ed., *Aspects of Library Development Planning*. London: British Council, 1983), pp. 144–157.

Corrall, Sheila. "School Libraries" (Bibliography). 2d ed. London: Library Association Library, 1984. Mimeographed.

Craver, W. Kathleen. "The Future of School Media Centers." *School Library Media Quarterly* 12 (Summer 1984), pp. 266–284.

Dankert, Birgit. "Political Aspects of School Library Legislation." Paper presented at IFLA General Conference, Copenhagen, 1979. Unpublished.

Education for School Librarianship. Proceedings, Findings and Recommendations. Canberra: Australian Government Publishing Service, 1973.

Education for School Librarianship in Canada. Ed. by Ken Haycock. Ottawa: Canadian Library Association, 1983.

Hannigan, Jane Anne. "School Media Standards." *Library Trends* 31 (Summer 1982), pp. 49–63.

Heathen, Paulin. *A Study of the Use of Books and Libraries by Children in Primary Schools.* Sheffield: Centre for Research on User Studies, 1984; and *Teaching Methods and the Use of Books and Libraries in Primary Schools: A Review.* Sheffield: Centre for Research on User Studies, 1984.

Irving, Ann. *Educating Information Users in Schools.* London: British Library, 1983.

Jones, L. Milbrey. *Survey of School Media Standards.* Washington, D.C.: U.S. Department of Health, Education and Welfare, 1977.

Library Service to Children: An International Survey. New ed. Edited for the IFLA Section of Children's Libraries by Colin Ray. Munich: K. G. Saur, 1983.

Library Work for Children and Young Adults in the Developing Countries. Ed. by Genevieve Patte and Sigrún Klara Hannesdóttir. Munich: K. G. Saur, 1984.

Pfister, C. Fred. "Competencies Essential for School Media Specialists." *Journal of Education for Librarianship* 23 (Summer 1982), pp. 29–42.

Preparing Teacher-Librarians. The Mid '80s and Beyond. Proceedings of a Seminar Held at the University of Sydney, 1981. Ed. by Janet Hansen. Surrey Hills, N.S.W.: Library Association of Australia, 1982.

Scott, L. A. "School Library Resource Centres: A Comparison of the US, UK and France in 1980." *International Library Review* 14 (October 1982), pp. 447–454.

Wilson, Pauline. "Librarians as Teachers: The Study of an Organizational Fiction." *Library Quarterly* 49 (1979), pp. 146–162.

24

PUBLIC LIBRARIANSHIP COURSES

Larry N. Osborne

At first glance, the internationalization of education for public librarianship might seem to be too ambitious a project. In the United States, instructors have difficulty preparing students for just the domestic public library range. The skills and knowledge needed to survive in an American New England association library (which might charge user fees) differ widely from those needed to administer a Hawaiian state-run library system branch. Yet somehow students find valuable what we teach. Indeed, this difficulty in identifying a public library may have conditioned Americans to accept the breadth of worldwide definitions. Certainly, it has taught understanding for differences in approach and ambiguities in operation.

Rochell's definition, which requires that public libraries (1) be an agency of local government, (2) have material, a facility, and personnel, and (3) have free and open access for educational and social purposes, is too restrictive.[1] It excludes (1) libraries that serve the general public for a fee (a number bound to increase in this "fee versus free" period), (2) those with no relationship to the governing municipality (an unfortunately declining number), and (3) those devoted to promoting to the public a special view of "truth." Examples of all three may be found internationally, and such considerations are becoming ascendant as the implications of the International Commission for the Study of Communications Problems (better known as the McBride Report and the New World Information Order) are considered.[2]

Similarly, the UNESCO Public Library Manifesto is too narrow, since, being hortatory in nature, it emphasizes what should be rather than what is. We must prepare graduates to improve libraries, but they must seek employment in libraries as they are now. An operational definition will be used here: public libraries are those which the field expects graduates of the public library curriculum to be competent eventually to administer. Alternately, one could define a public library as one to which the general public is expected to have access upon application.

We may assume certain things about a public library. Probably it is perceived as being free or inexpensive to the user at the time of use and open to the entire public in its (often arbitrarily chosen) service area. Recognition of diversity contains the best approach to internationalization of public library education.

CURRICULUM PLANNING

The first step toward change must be recognized that improvement is possible. A library school in British Columbia must accept the fact that, even if its graduates dedicate their entire careers to service there, recognition of alternatives is necessary for national level interaction. In the same way, a French library school must accept the fact that its graduates may interact with and perhaps even learn something from their counterparts in Tonga and Norway. Without this acceptance, internationalization is at best sterile and at worst prejudicial.

Of course, the entire curriculum content must be examined to eliminate insularity. Two goals stand out: (1) to foster understanding of the public library's organic nature nationally, and (2) to prepare all students to work in international and foreign enviroments, especially those ambitious to do so.

Internationalization should be carefully planned. Determination of the extent to which the goals can be implemented will necessitate a thorough inventory of current course content. For example, public library curriculum graduates in Australia can be expected to have the competencies needed to function usefully in the United Kingdom, New Zealand, and Canada, but to understand only the basic perspectives of Soviet librarians. After decisions are made concerning specific program objectives, public library requirements in those countries must be investigated.[3] Most surveys, however, are descriptive and often stress service differences and specifics rather than common abilities. Of course, a certain amount of pragmatism must always be involved.

Library schools should encourage faculty as well as student representation from other countries; the active participation of both in international affairs can improve the curriculum. Incentives must be offered to interact with foreign counterparts at both personal and organizational levels. This process should result in an international curriculum.

It is difficult to add material to a curriculum in the form of either additional course units or new courses. An international public librarianship course is not the answer by itself. Instead, integration of both attitudes and particulars is needed. We must provide the appropriate material for them and assume that students can extrapolate from it.

A detailed statement of common local practice with regional variations and international implications is needed. Most faculty members present to students a series of generalities consisting mainly of attitudes. In an internationalized environment, these attitudes, heuristics, and policies can be applied to the circumstances encountered in international situations. Student selection is vital, and a special effort must be made to identify admission candidates who, through experience, language skills, or education, are particularly suited to appreciate the international perspective.

METHODS OF CHANGE

Most library schools are committed to produce graduates for national service. To expect a sizable reduction of national in favor of foreign information is unrealistic unless foreign students constitute a significant proportion of total enrollment. However, some modification may be made. Material may be added or exchanged. Where international examples or materials are applicable nationally, they may be substituted for national material with the added benefit of exposing the student to a different viewpoint. In other situations, supplementary information may enhance the student's perspectives of national practice while preparing them to function in a world where unanimity is rare.

Faculty members should present as diverse a selection of material as possible. While, in a few cases, an extended two-country comparison may be useful, most students are better served by examples from a wide variety of countries. This approach has the added benefit of encouraging faculty members to extend their knowledge of international affairs. Isolation becomes impossible when the world literature is searched and international trends can be observed. Librarianship in other countries also changes rapidly.

No international textbook has been identified. Consequently, reading is best guided by bibliographies and by allowing students to locate their own sources. The quality of student bibliographic effort may be monitored by insisting on international content in term papers and reports. If international considerations are a normal part of instruction, students will include that component in their efforts.

A pleasant way to increase the international content of public library courses is by taking advantage of foreign librarians' visits. A long-term visiting faculty member might teach parts of several courses or team-teach a course alongside the regular instructor.

Sending students and faculty members to other countries should also be considered. Grants to support visits abroad are available.[4] Pay-as-you-go study visits and study tours are organized periodically by the University of Hawaii and other universities. Such tours allow students to compare reality with reports and to interact with librarians abroad. In addition, the College of Librarianship, Wales, has placed students in both Eastern and Western Europe for work study experience.

SPECIFIC COURSE CHANGES

The opening course lecture on the history, purpose, sizes, and types of public libraries provides the opportunity to show the diversity nationally and abroad. The national situation can be used as a base and can then be expanded to cover the structure and policies of other countries.

Care must be taken to avoid parochialism, chauvinism, and blind envy. Library governance is related to the organization's societal milieu, and benefits (as in a national public library enabling act) must be contrasted with dangers. The dogma that only state-organized public libraries are useful is as pernicious as the assumption that state-organized libraries are necessarily propagandistic. In the same way, students must be exposed to the concepts of the library as a provider of "correct" information versus its role as the defender of differing views. The lecturer should show what needs are met in given situations.

While public libraries at every social level may have mission aspects in common, the specific goals existing at various levels (national, regional, local) must be differentiated, as well as those at the same level (a local library in an urban versus a rural setting, for example). The judicious instructor should select both national and international examples. Even hierarchical library structure, with national, regional, and local libraries, is not universal, and examples of cooperative networks serving as national libraries (Barbados) and countries functioning without true national libraries (United States) may be cited, for example.

The wealth of library governance models is both the pride and despair of educators, but it provides a springboard to discussion of international library enabling legislation.

Public Service

Internationalizing course units on public service is largely a matter of applying good pedagogical techniques. It is essential that students learn to anticipate difficulties, often cultural in nature, which limit reference service provision. An assumption that the library exists to serve educated and influential society members may be found anywhere and may result in poor service. The danger is not that foreign examples will be avoided but that foreign will be equated with negative examples. Excesses, errors, and poor policies are found in all countries.

Based on discussions with librarians from many countries, it appears that circulation policies and practices are much more diverse across national boundaries than are reference services. Since students will read about and perhaps work in other countries, circulation policies must be described and their foreign rationale explained. The fiscal responsibility of the librarian, logistic difficulties in restocking, and lack of funds often underlie what seem superficially to be strange practices. Students should be encouraged to delve beneath the surface before criticizing.

Constraints that reduce material circulation may also limit inhouse services such as library instruction and reader's advisory work. The case study method and classroom discussion are especially well suited to elucidating the trade-offs that occur in every library. When such services as recreational reading, information and referral, research, and direct education must be balanced, role-playing may be used to explain the relationships of cultural bias, political considerations, staff limitations (both from attitudinal and educational standpoints), and logistic impossibilities.

Service to different age levels must also be considered. Here is the area where visiting practitioners may make their largest contribution by introducing a modicum of reality into the course. Several titles could be used to point out the universality of service. Worldwide structural differences are largely contrasting responses to the same underlying situations.

Finally, educators of future public librarians must stress the need for a plan of service and material development. Planning benefits are overwhelming, and their techniques have been promoted by UNESCO until they are almost universally known.[5] National or international standards are often mistakenly proposed in lieu of local planning. Only by comparing standards and planning (best accomplished in an international setting) can we detail the benefits and dangers of each one.[6]

Technical Service

That part of technical service which varies most widely and must be covered if internationalization is to occur is acquisition of material. Certain problems are cross-national—lack of money, for example. Others, such as difficulties in exporting currency, are problems for certain countries and not for others. In approaching these problems, the technique emphasized for internationalizing other course units should be followed: first deal with common problems, using examples from both national and foreign libraries, and then deal with the area- or country-specific

problems. They should be dealt with sufficiently for students to understand attitudes that may influence any forms of cooperation envisaged.

At least cursory attention should be paid to the problem of acquiring
material through depository plans, purchasing material that is most
suited to community needs, purchasing UNESCO and other international organization documents, and form of payment problems. The
good and bad points of classification schemes for individual regions or
countries and the schemes' biases should be discussed, as well as the
problems of the cult of cataloging and classification.

Branch and Remote Service

The decision as to whether to provide a centralized or decentralized
service is complicated, but the mechanics of decision-making are much
the same in most countries. The constraints of less developed countries
which limit alternatives such as bookmobile or mail service must be
pointed out, and the nation-specific nature of the basic question must
be emphasized lest librarians assume that what is right for one country
is also right for another.

Nonetheless, we gain insight into our own situation by studying programs such as South Korea's Mini-Library experiment. One need only
compare the reading habits of rural Koreans with those of one's own
rural population to sense the underlying thread of the public library
imperative. Service provision to outlying areas in developing countries
can stimulate discussion of technology's potential. Use of international
sources can both provide psychological distance for discussion and introduce students to extranational thought.

Special Collections and Services

Internationalization demands that special collections and services be
discussed in a broad context, with services appropriate elsewhere. Thus,
ethnic minority service should assume a higher priority in a multicultural
than in a homogeneous society. The richness of the cultural and educational infrastructure must also be considered.

The question of appropriateness must be stressed in public librarianship where society's library use varies so widely. An extensive newspaper collection may serve a largely archival function in a major Western
European city where most adults have access to the press, but an entirely
different one in Africa where the library's newspaper provision is a
primary source of public news. Similar considerations are true for pamphlets, government publications, microforms, and nonprint material.

Certain services and collections serve an inherently international function, and students should be aware of their value. The collections of

local authors, imprints, history, and documents may be the world's only accessible sources for this material.

Library Cooperation and Networks

Several library cooperation aspects deserve special emphasis in an internationalized curriculum. Centralized processing and bibliographic data bases are especially important to small libraries with modest budgets. Multitype library cooperation must also be emphasized. The split between school, academic, and public may not be a proper model for all of the world's public libraries. Certainly this point must be discussed with the pros and cons of extensive cooperation between the various library types considered from the standpoint of utility.

A final consideration is interlibrary loan in its various national manifestations and as an international tool. Here students must be exposed to the real world: where librarians are often jealous of each other's libraries, reluctant to trust precious material to the postal system, and often undertake interlibrary loans with the expectation that it will be profitable to cooperate. The existence of such attitudes is essentially self-defeating. Library cooperation thrives where competition is over how many items can be provided rather than how many can be borrowed. Programs should seek to instill in the student occupational pride coupled with personal humility.

Management Science

The course's managerial aspect is exceptionally fertile ground, since management science has a strong international flavor. Management technique examples from Scandinavia, Japan, and Arab countries are often used. The comparative study of public library buildings is effective in stripping away that portion of library architecture based on preference rather than function. In a country such as Argentina which embraces several physiographic zones, appropriate building paradigms are often found in other countries.

Students should be taught to search for appropriate rather than politically expedient or socially acceptable models, and they should be given the management tools necessary to interpret them in national settings. Library policy and procedure models for rural library service in Iran might realistically be found in other countries with a widely dispersed population rather than in England with a concentrated population. A Hawaiian library service might be found in another island nation like Indonesia rather than in Iraq.

Standards should be viewed in the same light. Their value or lack thereof should be debated in both national and foreign situations. Even friends of the library groups can benefit from pro and con consideration in a foreign setting.

ANCILLARY COURSE CONSIDERATIONS

The recommendations for change made in this chapter imply a series of parallel changes in other library school courses. The most obvious example is in cataloging and classification where increased coverage of classification schemes that are not in common national use must occur so that public librarians can understand foreign library collection organization. Both school and academic library courses must be modified to reflect the possibility for differing relations with public libraries abroad, and public library age group (children, young adult) courses must consider the ways in which these services are performed abroad.

Library technology courses must recognize that not all technology levels are appropriate in all countries; emphasis should be placed on identifying the appropriate technology. Jingoistic assumptions of foreigners' inability to handle and benefit from technology must be avoided. Bibliography and reference courses must include both material about other countries and material likely to be found abroad. Since questions often arise in other countries, integrating this material into courses should be easy.

CONCLUSIONS

Internationalization of public library courses is both less imposing and more beneficial than might first be expected. It is a less imposing task because the changes necessary are those of extension and modification rather than of addition or restructuring. Essential in internationalization is acceptance of the commonplace tasks needed to bring it about.

These relatively minor content and emphasis changes should be highly beneficial to students by allowing them to relate their experiences to those of foreign librarians. The ability to see through cultural and linguistic differences even when words are shared are among the most useful tools we can give students.

In order to bring these benefits to them, we must understand the field's differences. We must support comparative public library research, visit libraries abroad, and talk to colleagues in international organizations. Our greatest expenditure of energy must lie in such studies, for once we understand each other, curricular internationalization will follow easily.

NOTES

1. Carlton Rochell, *Wheeler and Goldhor's Practical Administration of Public Libraries* (New York: Harper & Row, 1981).
2. International Commission for the Study of Communications Problems, *Many Voices One World. Report* (New York: Unipub, 1980).
3. Miles M. Jackson, ed., *International Handbook of Contemporary Developments in Librarianship* (Westport, Conn.: Greenwood Press, 1981).
4. M. Keresztesi, "UNESCO's Work in the Field of Library Education and Training," *International Library Review* 14 (October 1982), pp. 355–357.
5. Vernon K. Palmour, *A Planning Process for Public Libraries* (Chicago: American Library Association, 1980).
6. H. C. Campbell, "A Method of Evaluation for Metropolitan Public Library Systems," *International Library Review* 12 (April 1980), p. 20.

BIBLIOGRAPHY

Ballard, R. M. "Library Education and Library Problems in Developing Countries." *International Library Review* 12 (January 1980), pp. 65–70.

Campbell, H. C. *Developing Public Library Systems and Services*. Paris: UNESCO, 1983).

Deckert, Glenn D. "The Availability and Circulation of Reading Materials in an Iranian City." *International Library Review* 13 (January 1981), pp. 43–73.

Fang, Josephine Riss. "Contemporary Developments in Librarianship in the People's Republic of China." *International Library Review* 13 (July 1981), pp. 211–219.

Ganitskaya, I. I. "Children's and School Libraries in the USSR." *International Library Review* 14 (January 1982), pp. 47–58.

Jackson, Miles M. "Library and Information Services in the Pacific Islands." *International Library Review* 13 (January 1981), pp. 25–41.

Keren, Carl, and Larry Harmon. "Information Services Issues in Less Developed Countries." In *Annual Review of Information Science and Technology*. White Plains, N.Y.: American Society for Information Science, 1980), pp. 289–328.

"Seminar on Public Library Policy: Four Views." *IFLA Journal* 6, No. 2 (1980), pp. 96–105.

25
INTERNATIONALIZING ACADEMIC LIBRARIANSHIP COURSES

Fritz Veit

Internationalizing academic library education may have various meanings. It is assumed here that international librarianship is a broad concept that embraces all aspects of nonnational library patterns and activities as well as international library relations. It is also believed that in a teaching situation, the nonnational and international librarianship aspects can be understood if they are compared with the corresponding aspects of domestic librarianship and that such comparisons should be made whenever appropriate.

Let us assume that the course is taught in an American setting. With this assumption, this discussion can be based on an American background into which can be introduced comparable aspects from the foreign and international scene. Examples from a wide range of foreign library patterns will illuminate many situations just as well as examples from America. Of course, this approach can be used with any country as its national setting.

Many forces influence a country's library situation. All must be considered in any evaluation and comparison of various library patterns. There are many reasons for working toward the internationalization of academic librarianship courses. One of the most compelling is that students will comprehend the workings of their own country's academic libraries better if they can analyze the foreign library scene and discover differences and similarities with it.[1]

By internationalizing academic librarianship courses, we acknowledge that the study and teaching of international library matters can be infused into various curriculum units. In other words, we recognize that the internationalization of library education need not be limited to a single course called Comparative and International Librarianship. The topics selected for the following discussion lend themselves to pertinent comparisons between American and foreign library patterns and should yield a comprehensive picture in a one-term or semester course.

TYPES OF ACADEMIC INSTITUTIONS AND THEIR LIBRARIES

First, we must define the term *academic library*. Simply expressed, an academic library is one that serves a higher education institution, also called tertiary or post-secondary school level education institution. Higher education occurs on several levels but begins after secondary education is completed. There are research-oriented universities which embrace all levels from undergraduate through doctorate; four- and five-year colleges and universities offering mainly bachelor's and Master's degrees; and junior and community colleges which cover the first two years of post-secondary education. In the United States and abroad, as students reach advanced stages, their assignments become more intricate and individualized and they are expected to engage in independent research.

In the United States, higher education is the concern of the individual states, and private institutions may be established throughout the nation and coexist with public institutions.[2] Generally, public colleges and universities are maintained by the governments of the states in which they operate. Most public community colleges, however, are established and largely controlled by their communities, counties, or other subordinate political units. They derive usually a portion of their financial support from these subordinate political units, although most states also contribute to their maintenance. The primary function of the higher education library is to serve the objectives of the institution of which it forms an integral part, though many libraries also permit outsider use.

Abroad there are numerous examples of libraries designed to serve clienteles beyond the institution's own constituency. In West Germany, for instance, several university libraries are also municipal libraries, such as the Stadt- und Universitätsbibliothek Frankfurt and the Stadt- und Universitätsbibliothek Köln. All Swiss university libraries are also designated libraries of their municipalities and/or their cantons. An example is the Stadt- und Universitätsbibliothek Bern.

University libraries may also function as national libraries and vice versa. For example, the University of Copenhagen Library carries out the responsibilities of a national library in medicine and the natural sciences, and the Royal Danish Library fulfills university library functions in the humanities and social sciences. In several developing countries, the university library assumed certain national library functions until such a library was established. This has been the case, for instance, in Malaysia, Nigeria, and Papua New Guinea.

Obviously, it is more difficult to administer a library that must respond to the reading and information needs of several kinds of clientele than to those of a university constituency only, but various causes make it impossible to serve the university exclusively.

The coexistence of publicly and privately controlled institutions can be found in many countries. In certain countries, however, private control is incompatible with the political order. In this category belong the Soviet Union and the People's Republic of China, for instance. It should be noted, however, that even privately controlled institutions are often subject to regulation by the nations in which they operate.

Libraries of the newer types of institutions, such as the community colleges, are less hampered by tradition and vested interests and so can be more innovative than old-line institutions. In Great Britain, polytechnic libraries use the newer communication media more widely and intensively than do older universities. They also encourage individualized resource use. Similar conditions prevail in Canada and Australia.

COLLECTION

There is unanimity among American and foreign libraries that a material collection should serve the institution's objectives well. In forming the material collection, the varying requirements of the different clienteles must be accounted for. It may be necessary to establish priorities, and sometimes a persuasive librarian is required before the university clientele will be treated as the primary user group.

CENTRALIZATION VERSUS DECENTRALIZATION

As might be expected, the large universities in all nations have generally larger, more diversified material holdings than the small institutions. We may compare the new college and polytechnic libraries with those of the Universities of Cambridge and Oxford. A material collection may be housed in one location or distributed over several. If it is relatively small—say under 50,000 volumes—and if the institution's academic activities occur in only a few adjacent buildings, then the collection is usually maintained as one entity. However, if the collection is large and the teaching facilities widely dispersed, the problem of departmental, branch, school, and institute libraries surfaces.

An American trend has existed to create a strong central library and eliminate, or at least reduce the number of, departmental collections. Certain institutions have combined departmental collections in related areas to form broader units called divisional libraries. Efforts to coordinate all or most institutional library resources have usually been successful. Usually, all academic library units are controlled by a director (or dean) of Library Services. In certain institutions, the law and/or medical school libraries have retained a large degree of independence than the other departmental or professional school libraries.

The struggle between centralization and decentralization forces also occurs abroad. In the past, many countries, among them Germany, Great Britain, France, and Italy, have permitted or even encouraged the various faculties to form and control their own seminar, institute, or faculty libraries. A large university may have over 100 such units, with none taking into account the central library or other existing departmental libraries. In many cases, the combined institute and departmental library holdings are larger than those of the central library.

Economic pressures and the desire to make all university resources generally available made changes imperative, and changes were spearheaded by the newer universities everywhere. The West German Universities of Constance and Regensburg provide examples of new administrative and physical structures that coordinate all university library resources. A number of the older universities combined certain departmental libraries to create larger, more viable units, established union catalogs covering campus-wide holdings, and moved toward centralized acquisitions.

LIBRARY MATERIAL SELECTION

Most librarians believe the selection of material to be a joint library staff and faculty enterprise. Considerable differences exist among American institutions in the extent to which librarians and classroom instructors share this undertaking. Certain institutions have adopted formulas that allot to the various departments exact portions of the material fund, while others are more flexible and honor faculty requests whenever possible. Over the years, library staff participation has become more intensive.

Whatever the respective shares of faculty and staff in selection may be, the library director and his or her associates must pursue a policy that will result in a well-balanced collection. Selectors have been aided by various tools. On the community college and college levels, comprehensive lists have proven most helpful in selecting basic material.[3]

Librarians of other countries are also generally in favor of faculty and library staff sharing this task. In certain countries, however, like Japan, librarians are almost completely excluded from selection.[4] In other countries, the subject specialist librarian, called the "referent" in West Germany, selects most of the material within the specialization area.

In recent years various American libraries have adopted approval plans. The libraries bring all books that fit a predetermined subject profile to a library soon after publication. Such plans are indicated when library staff and faculty members have difficulty finding time for selection and where they can trust an outside source to identify the appropriate material. Approval plans might prove advantageous to libraries in developing countries if distances and shipping time between dealer and library are not a problem.

STAFF MEMBERS

In nearly all countries, academic library personnel may be classed into several categories. At least two exist, professional and clerical, and more recently semi-professional categories have been added. Most American libraries also employ student assistants. As may be expected, librarians are generally assigned to more complex tasks, including selection, classification, reference, policy establishment, and administration. Most countries require specialized education for their librarians. In the United States it is provided by university library schools. All schools offer a Master's degree, and several also offer a sixth-year certificate and a doctorate.

Most American universities do not require formal education for semi-professionals, who are often called technical assistants or technicians. Nevertheless, some prospective assistants attend community college library technician programs. The two-year curriculum contains general and library science courses. Today, in Great Britain as well, most prospective librarians attend a library school where they pursue a systematic course culminating in a library science degree.

West Germany has two distinct librarian levels with different academic backgrounds and curricula. The highest service level attests to scholarly pursuit and is called "Höherer Dienst." To reach this level, a student must have undertaken university study for at least seven semesters before admission to the librarianship program. Typically, but no longer necessarily, students have also received a doctorate in their specialization field before entering a library school that requires one year of theoretical and one year of practical work.

The second level is designated "Gehobener Dienst." Students who complete their studies and pass the examination are awarded the qualification of Diplombibliothekar an Wissenschaftlichen Bibliotheken (Diploma Librarian at Scholarly Libraries). The time of study may require two to three years after secondary school (Abitur). Certain states also offer course preparation for a middle service category.

In the German Democratic Republic, differentiated library education prepares the student for three staff categories: Wissenschaftlicher Bibliothekar (Scholarly Librarian), Bibliothekar (Librarian), and Bibliothekfacharbeiter (Library Assistant). After Abitur, the East German student who wishes to become a scholarly librarian pursues library studies for four years at the Humboldt University Institute for Library and Information Science. The student who is considered especially qualified may continue studying for an additional three years and, if successful, be awarded a doctorate.

Second category members (Bibliothekar) study for three years after the Abitur at a separate library school. Library assistants (Bibliothekfacharbeiter) are usually trained for two years in special schools after having previously attended at least ten years of elementary and secondary school. In East Germany, lower level staff members may reach the next higher level by examination even if they lack the number and kinds of courses prescribed for that level. With modifications, East Germans follow the Soviet pattern.

In the Soviet Union, preparation for higher academic librarianship levels is offered at institutes of culture, pedagogical institutes, and university library science departments. The curriculum combines library science with general subjects. After having completed the general graduate work, a selected number of promising research-minded students may pursue postgraduate study and be awarded the doctorate. Students who work toward middle and lower level careers attend special schools.

In certain countries, such as Japan, the common practice is to appoint a nonlibrarian faculty member or administrator to head the library. These occurrences should diminish as library education is upgraded and familiarity with the technical aspects of library work becomes increasingly important.

Special problems may occur for library staffs in developing countries. When these countries gained independence from colonial powers, they usually lacked sufficient educated nationals and national library schools and relied on expatriates. In certain instances the libraries' national staff members enrolled in library schools in developed countries. In perusing the writings of librarians in developing countries, especially those from African countries, we encounter the frequent complaint that expatriates are unfamiliar with their libraries' special needs. Likewise, study abroad usually does not deal with material which students from developing countries find useful—their own literature and culture.

Efforts have been made to remedy these deficiencies, however. In certain cases, students from developing countries enrolled in British and American schools have been encouraged to write papers dealing with national problems and in this way prepare themselves for postgraduation work situations.[5] The French École Nationale Superieure des Bibliothécaires located at Villeurbanne, Lyons, has offered a course in African publishing, bibligraphy, and library science designed for students from French-speaking countries.

The influence of the former colonial powers has remained strong, and library development has therefore differed from Francophone and Anglophone African countries. In recent years, several African countries have established library schools to educate professional librarians as well as workshops to teach clerical tasks. The need to rely on expatriates in developing countries, has caused concern. Recently, this need has lessened and in certain instances has been eliminated. When positions can be filled by nationals, the location process may, as an intermediate stage, require one expatriate to be replaced by two or three less experienced or less fully educated nationals.

CATALOGING AND CLASSIFICATION

Although no government authority imposes cataloging procedures and classification schemes, most U.S. academic libraries follow the *Anglo-American Catalog Code* and the Library of Congress (LC) classification schedules. Formerly, many libraries used the Dewey Decimal Classification, but the LC scheme has increasingly been preferred, even among smaller libraries. Certain libraries consider the LC scheme better suited to academic library work, while others have turned to LC mainly for economic reasons. By deciding to follow exactly—without local adaptations—cataloging and classification reflected on LC cards, they could proceed most economically.

In most other countries there is less uniformity than in the United States, but nearly everywhere efforts are being made to create uniform schemes that will be accepted throughout the country. In Great Britain and other English-speaking countries, certain libraries have adopted the LC classification, while others use Dewey.

In the Soviet Union and several other centrally planned collectivist societies, classification schemes have been created which mirror the political philosophy. Collectivist society authorities may require libraries to follow the scheme prescribed by the government.

Classification brings like material together. With open shelf access, material must be classified; otherwise open access is not practical. While in the United States all collections are classified, libraries can still be found abroad which arrange material on the shelves in the sequence in which it was received. This arrangement requires less shelf space than a classified collection since each shelf can be completely filled.

THE CLIENTELE

Most academic libraries take into account the differing needs of user groups. The faculty usually has extended loan privileges, and, especially in larger libraries, may be provided with individual study carrels. Certain university libraries give undergraduate students special consideration through undergraduate collections and reading rooms, because it is felt that they can study more profitably with a collection of manageable size tailored to their needs.

Differentiated user group treatment is also practiced in most non-American libraries, especially in the Soviet Union. There, special reading rooms exist for faculty members, and for graduate and undergraduate students. Differentiation may also occur by subject or form. For instance, there may be reading rooms for physics and chemistry, as well as general or specialized periodical reading rooms.

LIBRARY ORIENTATION AND INSTRUCTION

American academic study and teaching have become increasingly library-dependent. Most instructors now encourage and often require library use; therefore, students must learn the location and use of the library's facilities and resources. To attain this goal, many libraries now offer orientation service: tours, lectures, media devices, handbooks, and information sheets.

Beyond this, many institutions provide library use instruction. It may be offered by the library and not be related to a specific course, or it may be course-related. The subject field instructor, such as English Literature or History, can structure assignments in such a way that the student must consult library material. Frequently, the instructor plans assignments with a library staff member designated to perform this service.

The form and amount of library orientation involvement differ among institutions. To the extent that students have received library use instruction in primary and secondary school, their college-level instruction may be modified or advanced. On the other hand, for students lacking previous systematic instruction, orientation must begin at an elementary level, especially in developing countries where elementary and secondary school resources are very limited.

In most countries each institution can decide for itself whether or not to offer library instruction and, if offered, can determine content and procedures. In the German Democratic Republic, however, the Minister of Higher Educational Affairs has promulgated library orientation guidelines for all institutions. These guidelines on the skillful use of library and information resources and facilities specify the number of hours to be devoted to it, the teaching material to be used, and the extent of professorial participation.[6]

COOPERATION

All librarians recognize that no single institution can satisfy all of the clientele's demands for material. Interlibrary loan is the preferred device for obtaining access to material not held by one's own institution. While a library is customarily required as an intermediary in the borrowing process, newer arrangements such as consortia, especially among neighboring institutions, have brought about direct mutual borrowing privileges for faculty and students of the participating institutions. Interlibrary loans have been encouraged by union catalogs—national, regional, and local—and bibliographic data bases provided with location symbols. Outstanding among these cooperative enterprises are the Online Computer Library Center and the Research Libraries Information Network.

Increasingly, librarians have recognized that within a country or region duplication of infrequently used material must be avoided and that a country's total resources should cover its library needs as fully as feasible. Various methods have been employed to attain this objective. In the United States, the former Farmington Plan provided that several libraries already strong in certain areas would receive government funds for acquiring foreign material in these areas.

In West Germany, the Deutsche Forschungsgemeinschaft (German Research Council) has financially aided research libraries to increase their already outstanding holdings. The Scandinavian countries have combined efforts to acquire mutually needed research material. The original agreement, the Scandia Plan, relied on participating library contributions. The plan encountered difficulties, and now the joint acquisitions enterprise has been put on a firmer basis by the Nordic Council of Ministers, through NORDINFO.

As contrasted with American, West German, and Scandinavian methods, which have strengthened libraries in their strong areas, the British have created one strong lending library, the British Library Lending Division (BLLD). It aims at complete science and social science coverage. While BLLD arrives toward full coverage of British items, it also acquires foreign material that is likely to be requested. BLLD's collection policy makes it unnecessary for British academic libraries to stock rarely used items. This system has proven satisfactory not only because of the BLLD collection's completeness but also because of the speed with which requests are filled. This system might not be as appropriate to the needs of a large country where research institutions are widely spread and therefore cannot be serviced speedily from one location.

Cooperation is especially urgent among the university libraries of developing nations. Newly founded university libraries must avoid duplication wherever feasible. This situation has led to numerous cooperative measures. For instance, in 1975 the six Nigerian university libraries divided up the responsibility for acquiring publications issued by various African governments. Malaysia has cooperative agreements among the five university libraries on purchases and interlibrary loans.

STANDARDS

Standards are norms based on the aggregate experience and judgment of the profession as to adequacy in library resources, services, and facilities. Standards usually reflect the concerns of the library field when they are produced. Certain writers distinguish standards from guidelines, the guidelines not having the force of standards. Librarians have welcomed standards as criteria to which they can compare their own institutions. Standards may be formulated by a library organization or a governmental agency. Most American national standards have been prepared by library associations, such as the American Library Association.

Since the objectives and needs of various types of educational institutions differ from each other in many respects, it has not been practical to create a single set of standards applicable to all academic libraries. There are *The Guidelines for Two-Year College Learning Resources Programs*; *The Standards for College Libraries*; and, finally, *The University Library Standards*.[7]

There has been a continuing controversy as to whether or not standards should be both qualitative measures accompanying quantative evaluations. In response to practitioners' wishes, the 1972 *Two-Year College Guidelines*, which were qualitative only, were supplemented in 1982 by quantitative measures.

The Two-Year College Guidelines assume that activities involving learning resources occur throughout the campus. Therefore, they are not limited to activities that occur in the library-learning resource center, but cover programs undertaken in any college area. Since research-oriented university libraries are complex institutions, many with unique features, it is difficult to create standards that can be applied generally. The university standards are flexible and are not intended to introduce quantitative prescription for uniform application.

In Great Britain the groups responsible for establishing standards agreed on polytechnic and college standards but not on university standards due to institutional diversity. The suggestion was made that British librarians refer to the American standards for guidance.[8]

Anthony Vaughan has pointed out that, of Britain's forty-six university libraries, all but one received most of their funds from a government-appointed body. This body might therefore prescribe standards, and it has done so, especially for building size. One proposal that caused much controversy advocated the "self-renewing library." In accordance with this rule, a library, after having reached a specified limit, would be required to discard as many volumes as it received.[9]

In many European countries, most staff members are employed by public institutions and are governed by comparable service rules. These occupational groups often seek to influence public agencies to establish standards rather than attempt to issue their own. In socialist countries, standards are promulgated by national government agencies.

Questions arise about standards for developing countries. A procedure used for the evaluation of Papua New Guinea university libraries seems appropriate. Rather than use the standards of developed countries, standards were derived from pertinent data on thirty-two university libraries in sixteen developing countries. While the categories chosen for comparison were similar to those used for developed countries, the achievement expectations were often at variance.

LIBRARY PERIODICALS

Library journals may be addressed to a general audience or to specific groups such as academic librarians. Journals may be published by associations, state agencies, university presses, or commercial publishers. The United States has examples of all four. Academic librarians read both general and special periodicals. Among the regularly read general journals are *Library Journal* and the *Wilson Library Bulletin* and among general research-oriented journals are *Library Quarterly* and *Library Trends*. *College and Research Libraries* and *Journal of Academic Librarianship* are specifically directed to a college library readership. Articles of interest on international librarianship will be found in *The Journal of Library History, Philosophy, and Comparative Librarianship*.

Both general and specialized journals are issued in other countries. Examples of the specialized are *Australian Academic and Research Libraries* and *Zeitschrift für Bibliothekswesen und Bibliographie*. On the multinational scene, several journals cover all types of libraries but give due consideration to academic libraries: *IFLA Journal*, *International Library Review*, and *Libri*.

BUILDINGS

The principle, form follows function, has been observed by the architects of most of the newer American library buildings. Most buildings are flexible, and many feature modular construction with equally spaced columns to form uniformly sized floor space modules. All floors are sturdily built so that they can support book-filled stacks. Since most libraries must hold not only books but also other communication media and equipment, modern design has taken these requirements into account. Size is determined by the number and form of library materials to be accommodated, by the number and type of user, and by staff size. Attention must be paid to possible future growth and to building adaptability to new media. The building design should fit into the total campus plan.

Librarians in some developing countries have observed that foreign architects sometimes fail to take into account the special requirements of tropical areas. For example, the structure may require air conditioning for comfort at all times, although the country does not yet have the means to maintain the cooling system.[10]

TEACHING METHODOLOGY

The foregoing discussion has dealt with topics usually included in academic library courses. Although an effort has been made to cover the basic subjects, space limitations have necessitated selection among them. For instance, the course could be divided into two parts. The first and probably longer part could deal with the national (in this case, American) library scene in the same way as would a traditional local course. Various local language textbooks would be recommended for background reading and further references suggested.

After having achieved a foundation in national academic librarianship, the class would continue with the second part of the course. For each one of the major topics covered in the traditional part, corresponding examples from other countries would be introduced. Encyclopedias and handbooks on international and comparative librarianship could be useful to the student in acquiring an overview and then be supplemented by pertinent monograph and periodical literature.

Another method—preferred by this writer—would refer to the foreign aspects throughout the course, except for the few initial class meetings devoted exclusively to the national scene. Since an internationalized course is concerned with domestic, foreign, and international subjects, it may need to be lengthened to two semesters (or terms), or alternatively, the number of topics may need to be reduced.

Certain institutions offer seminars in addition to basic courses. Students enrolled in a seminar are expected to build on the basic knowledge of the foreign library scene acquired in the general course. Study and teaching are more individualized and each seminar participant investigates one or more specific topics in depth.

NOTES

1. Frances Laverne Carroll, "Internationalism in Education for Librarianship," *International Library Review* 4 (April 1972), pp. 102–126.

2. Louis R. Wilson and Maurice F. Tauber, *The University Library* (New York: Columbia University Press, 1956), p. 30.

3. Fritz Veit, *The Community College Library* (Westport, Conn.: Greenwood Press, 1975), pp. 80–86.

4. Yukihisa Suzuki, "Japan," in Miles M. Jackson, ed., *Contemporary Developments in Librarianship* (Westport, Conn.: Greenwood Press, 1981), pp. 204–205.

5. Martha Boaz, "The Comparative and International Library Science Course in American Library Schools," in John F. Harvey, ed., *Comparative and International Library Science*, (Metuchen, N.J.: Scarecrow Press, 1977), pp. 169–175.

6. Gisela Hülpüsch, "Zur Nutzerschulung von Studenten an Hochschulen and Universitäten," *Zentralblatt für Bibliothekswesen* 93 (February 1979), pp. 61–64.

7. See *Library Trends* 31 (Summer 1982), ed. by Terry L. Weech, and *Library Trends* 21 (October 1972), ed. by Felix Hirsch.

8. L. J. Taylor, *A Librarian's Handbook* (London: Library Association, 1980), Vol. 2, p. 29.

9. Anthony Vaughan, "Standards for British Libraries," *Library Trends* 31 (Summer 1982), pp. 155–164.

10. See Anthony J. Loveday, ed., *University Libraries in Developing Countries* (Munich: K. H. Saur, 1985).

BIBLIOGRAPHY

Avafia, Kwami E. "Subject Specialization in African University Libraries." *Journal of Librarianship* 15 (July 1983), pp. 183–205.

Bibliotheken in der Schweiz, Bibliotheques en Suisse. Bern: Vereinigung Schweizerischer Bibliothekare, 1976.

Busse, Gisela von. *Libraries in the Federal Republic of Germany*. 2d rev. edition. Transl. by John S. Andrews. Wiesbaden: Harrassowitz, 1983.

Chandler, George. *International and National Library Services: A Review of Some Recent Developments 1970–1980*. New York: Pergamon, 1982.

Encyclopedia of Library and Information Science. Ed. by Allen Kent and others, vols. 1–36. New York: Marcel Dekker, 1968–1983.

Kon, Madoki. "Present Status and Problems of Library Service Networks in Japan." Montreal, 48th IFLA General Conference, 1982 (Processed).

Lyle, Guy R. *The Administration of the College Library*. New York: Wilson, 1974.

Resource Sharing of Libraries in Developing Countries. Ed. by H.D.L. Vervliet. Munich: K. G. Saur, 1979.

Rogers, Rutherford D. *University Library Administration*. New York: Wilson, 1971.

Stirling, John F., ed. *University Librarianship*. London: Library Association, 1981.

Vig, Morton L. "Centralized Control and Co-ordination of Research Libraries—Similarities and Differences—in the Nordic Area." *Libri* 29 (June 1979), pp. 93–126.

INDEX

ABOUT THE CONTRIBUTORS

ROBERT BERK is Chairman, Department of Information and Communication Sciences; Director, Medical Library; and Professor, Southern Illinois University School of Medicine, in Springfield. He has a Ph.D. degree from the University of Illinois at Urbana. Berk was an HEA Title IIB Fellow during 1968–1971 and is a member of the Beta Phi Mu honor society.

EMILIA BERNAL, born in Puerto Rico, is active in the Asociación de Bibliotecas Universitarias de Investigación e Institucionales del Caribe. She has a Ph.D. degree in library science from the University of Illinois at Urbana. She is presently an external examiner, University of West Indies, Jamaica, and is Professor, Graduate School of Librarianship, University of Puerto Rico, in San Juan.

MARTHA BOAZ, Dean Emeritus, School of Library and Information Management, University of Southern California, is past president of the ALA Library Education Division and Association of American Library Schools. She served in Pakistan and Vietnam. She holds a Ph.D. degree from the University of Michigan.

HAROLD BORKO, Professor of Library and Information Science, University of California, Los Angeles, has been President, American Society for Information Science, and a member of the U.S. National Committee for FID. He has a Ph.D. in psychology, University of Southern California, and is a member of Phi Beta Kappa.

LESTA BURT, Ph.D., is Professor, School of Library Science, Sam Houston State University, in Huntsville, Texas. She teaches courses in children's and young people's literature and in school librarianship.

FRANCES LAVERNE CARROLL has a Ph.D. degree from the University of Oklahoma, and teaches in the School of Library Science, University of Oklahoma, in Norman. Previously, she was Head, Nedlands College of Advanced Education Department of Library Studies, Australia, and founder of the IFLA School Libraries Section. She has lectured in the United States, Australia, and Iran.

HARRY CLARK, Professor of Library Science Emeritus, University of Oklahoma, has a Ph.D. in Librarianship. He has had research fellowships for paleographic work from the Center for Reformation Research and the Folger Institute for Renaissance and Eighteenth Century Studies.

DONALD G. DAVIS, JR., an exchange lecturer, 1980–1981, Department of Librarianship, Birmingham Polytechnic, United Kingdom, is now Editor, *Journal of Library History, Philosophy and Comparative Librarianship*. He is also Professor and John P. Commons Fellow at the Graduate School of Library and Information Science, University of Texas, Austin.

ROSEMARY RUHIG DU MONT was an Illinois State Scholar and Northwestern University Scholar and holds a Ph.D. degree from the University of Pittsburgh. She was listed among the Outstanding Young Women of America in 1983. She is now Associate Professor of Library Science, University of Oklahoma in Norman.

DONALD P. ELY is Professor of Instructional Design, Development and Evaluation, and Director of the ERIC Clearinghouse on Information Resources, School of Education, at Syracuse University. He is Past President of the Association for Educational Communications and Technology and holds a Ph.D. degree from Syracuse University.

MAE L. FURBEYRE is Director, Stoops Library of Education and Information Studies, University of Southern California (USC) Los Angeles. She has a Ph.D. in librarianship from USC and taught at the University of the Philippines library school for eight years.

EDWIN S. GLEAVES is Chair, Department of Library and Information Science, George Peabody College for Teachers, Vanderbilt University, Nashville. He has been a visiting professor at the University of Guanajuata Master's Program in Library Science, Mexico, and, among other credentials, has a Certificate of Spanish Studies, Escuela Normal de Profesores, Saltillo, Coahuila, Mexico.

EILEEN GOLDSTEIN, a Ph.D. from the University of California, Los Angeles, was formerly Director, Library System, Instituto de Investigaciones Electricas, Mexico. She also served as visiting professor, University of Guanajuato Master's Program in Library Science.

ROBIN FREDERICK GUY is a graduate of the College of Librarianship, Wales, Diploma in Librarianship. He is editor of *Education for Information*, and is now Head, Library Liaison, SCOLCAP, National Library of Scotland, Edinburgh.

SIGRÚN KLARA HANNESDÓTTIR has a Certificate of Advanced Studies, University of Chicago, and has served as Chair, IFLA Working Group for the Education of School Librarians, and as President, Icelandic Library Association. She reorganized the University of Iceland library science program and is now a Docent (Associate Professor).

JOHN F. HARVEY is an international library and information science consultant and has prepared fifty-seven reports since 1960. He obtained his Ph.D. degree from the University of Chicago Graduate Library School and founded the *Drexel Library Quarterly*. He now lives in Nicosia, Cyprus.

PETER HAVARD-WILLIAMS, a library consultant in eighteen countries, has also been Vice-President of both IFLA and the Library Association. After an Oxford Diploma in Education, he obtained an Honorary Ph.D. from Sung Kyun Kwan in Seoul. He is Head, Department of Library and Information Studies, Loughborough University, Loughborough, Leicestershire, England.

RICHARD KRZYS is Director, International Library Information Center, and Professor, Graduate School of Library and Information Science, University of Pittsburgh. He received his Ph.D. degree from Case Western Reserve University. A Fulbright scholar, Instituto Cara y Cueruo and Universidad de Los Andes, Colombia, he has contributed to the *Encyclopedia of Library and Information Science*.

TZE-CHUNG LI, a former Republic of China National Librarian, was also Founding Chair, Graduate Institute of Library Science. Li received the Sang Award for Excellence in Teaching, Republic of China Ministry of Education Citation and Phi Tau Phi Service Award. He has a Ph.D.

degree and is Dean, Graduate School of Library and Information Science, Rosary College, River Forest, Illinois.

HOLLIS LOWERY-MOORE is Lecturer, School of Library Science, Sam Houston State University, in Huntsville, Texas. She teaches undergraduate courses in children's literature there. Her Ed.D. is in curriculum and instruction in reading, literature, and language.

LARRY N. OSBORNE, a Ph.D. recipient from the Graduate School of Library and Information Science, University of Pittsburgh, is Assistant Professor, Graduate School of Library Studies, University of Hawaii, Honolulu.

JASHU PATEL, University of Pittsburgh library and information science Ph.D. graduate, taught previously at the Northern and Eastern Illinois Universities, Rosary College, and Governors State University. He is now Associate Professor, Department of Library Science and Communication Media, Chicago State University, Chicago.

ANTONIO RODRIGUEZ-BUCKINGHAM is Professor, School of Library Service, University of Southern Mississippi, in Hattiesburg. His interests have revolved around anthropology and the history of books and printing in South America, in both Spanish and English. He has degrees in Romance languages, anthropology, and library science, and a Ph.D. from the University of Michigan.

FRANK L. SCHICK, a Ph.D. from the University of Michigan, was formerly Chief of Learning Resources, National Education Statistics Center, Associate Director, Teachers Corps, and Senior Research Associate, National Institute of Education. He was also a leader in UNESCO and IFLA statistical programs. He now heads Schick Information Services in Bethesda, Maryland.

C. WALTER STONE is Consultant/Senior Training Officer, Trans-Asia Engineering Associates, Inc., in Jakarta, Indonesia. His most recent activity has been in government department training program design, editing, proposal preparation, and contract negotiation. He received an Ed.D. degree from Columbia University.

FRITZ VEIT received the J.U.D. degree from the University of Freiburg and the Ph.D. degree from the Graduate Library School at the University of Chicago. He has taught in five library schools and is presently Director of Libraries Emeritus, Chicago State University.

JOHN WILKINSON, a Canadian, is Professor, Faculty of Library and Information Science, University of Toronto, and was previously Director, Center for Research in Librarianship there. He has his Ph.D. degree from the Graduate Library School, University of Chicago.

KIETH C. WRIGHT, Chairman, Department of Library Science and Education Technology, School of Education, University of North Carolina, has led workshops for librarians working with the handicapped. His book, *Library and Information Services for Handicapped Individuals*, is now in its third edition. Wright received his D.L.S. degree from Columbia University.